PATROL ADMINISTRATION

management by objectives

Donald T. Shanahan

UNIVERSITY OF LOUISVILLE

holbrook press, inc.
boston

PATROL

They may not be everywhere,
but they may be expected anywhere.

Sir Robert Peel

to my family

Copyright © 1975 by Holbrook Press, Inc.
470 Atlantic Avenue, Boston

All rights reserved. No part of the material protected by this copyright notice may be reproduced or utilized in any form or by any means, electronic or mechanical, including photocopying, recording, or by any informational storage and retrieval system, without written permission from the copyright owner.

Printed in the United States of America

Third printing . . . June 1977

Library of Congress Cataloging in Publication Data

Shanahan, Donald T   1932-
  Patrol administration.

  Includes bibliographical references.
  1. Police patrol. 2. Police administration.
3. Management by objectives. I. Title.
HV8080.P2S5   363.2   74-16449

CONTENTS

PREFACE

Although this book is entitled *Patrol Administration,* it should be of interest to those involved in all areas of police service. An understanding of the principles discussed is important to police managers in every capacity, criminal justice educators, and students of police administration and criminal justice. Regional criminal justice academies, state police, and county and municipal police academies will find the contents useful.

Patrol Administration focuses on the need for a management by objectives approach in this area of law enforcement. America's complex policing needs call for the development of individual leaders who are capable of facing problems by examining alternatives and making decisions that are innovative and effective.

The elementary objectives of today's patrol administrator are: 1) to protect life and property, 2) to prevent crime, 3) to apprehend criminals, 4) to preserve the peace, and 5) to maintain order. In addition, the patrol administrator must be sensitive to his community's problems in order to maintain its stability. Finally, in his role as a leader, the patrol administrator must be able to sustain among his subordinates the high degree of motivation necessary to achieve the objectives of law enforcement.

To be effective in accomplishing patrol goals, the patrol administrator must reach out to understand the workings of other parts of the police organization, since the operations of these other divisions affect patrol. The patrol administrator must reach out to the community as well. With an understanding of government organization and operations, he must know those persons in decision-making positions, and must deal with them effectively and diplomatically, maintaining a neutral political stance.

The police administrator should take time each day to review his objectives with regard to service, peace keeping, and crime related missions. In this way, he will be able to anticipate trends and the community's police needs. In reviewing objectives, the patrol administrator should examine alternative methods in his management of human and material resources and procedures. He must give emphasis to his most precious resource: the patrol officer. Because today's patrol officer has a questioning attitude toward illogical or irrational orders, the patrol leader must create an atmosphere that allows for free discussion of alternative procedures, and should encourage the innovative and creative ideas of his patrol officers. An atmosphere of openness is prerequisite to the professional-ization of a police organization.

The patrol leader must exhibit this same openness toward the com-munity, in attempting to understand the viewpoints of both extremists and moderates. His ability to reconcile conflict will be reflected in the stability of the community. The concerns of the community must be uppermost in the mind of the patrol officer. If citizens feel unsafe and fearful, innovative ways must be found to deal with these concerns. Through an understanding of the total system of government, the patrol administrator can gain the proper perspective of his role within that government, and can participate fully in providing leadership for a safe and secure community.

This book attempts to point out the several areas where job enrichment can be realistically innovated in the patrol function, so that talented officers will be motivated to develop within patrol, rather than transferring out of the unit or the police organization. With newly developed and innovative programs such as team policing, joint citizen police committees, and lateral entry into the operational field, the patrol administrator has an enormous spectrum available for creativity and innovativeness.

Management of human resources is the patrol administrator's most immediate and important function. Since most police departments through-out the country expend from 80 to 90 percent of their budget for per-sonnel and anywhere from 50 to 60 percent or more on patrol personnel, there can be no doubt as to where patrol should stand in order of priority. The blending of good management principles, leadership, and understand-ing of the total patrol function will lead to patrol's earning its position as the backbone of the police department.

The management by objectives approach encompasses the behavioral science concepts in leadership and the humanistic ideas reflected in par-ticipatory management. A good start toward the implementation of these objectives would be the adoption of Standard 8.1 of the National Advisory Commission on Criminal Justice Standards and Goals, "Report on Police," which follows. A good follow-up would be the adoption of Standard 8.2, "Enhancing the Role of the Patrol Officer."

STANDARD 8.1 ESTABLISHING THE ROLE OF THE PATROL OFFICER

Every police chief executive immediately should develop written policy that defines the role of the patrol officer, and should establish operational objectives and priorities that reflect the most effective use of the patrol officer in reducing crime.

1. Every police chief executive should acknowledge that the patrol officer is the agency's primary element for the deliver-ance of police services and prevention of criminal activity.

2. Every police chief executive should insure maximum efficiency in the deliverance of patrol services by setting out in written policy the objectives and priorities governing these services. This policy:
   a. Should insure that resources are concentrated on fundamental police duties;
   b. Should insure that patrol officers are engaged in tasks that are related to the police function;
   c. Should require immediate response to incidents where there is an immediate threat to the safety of an individual, a crime in progress, or a crime committed and the apprehension of the suspected offender is likely. Urban area response time—from the time a call is dispatched to the arrival at the scene—under normal conditions should not exceed 3 minutes for emergency calls, and 20 minutes for nonemergency calls;
   d. Should emphasize the need for preventive patrol to reduce the opportunity for criminal activity; and
   e. Should provide a procedure for accepting reports of criminal incidents not requiring a field investigation.
3. Every police chief executive should insure that all elements of the agency, especially the patrol and communications elements, know the priority placed upon each request for police service.
4. Every police chief executive should implement a public information program to inform the community of the agency's policies regarding the deliverance of police service. This program should include provisions to involve citizens in crime prevention activities.[1]

The revolution in patrol which integrates sound principles, contemporary leadership, intellectual assistance, technological innovation, and sincere concern will survive and succeed in our fast changing society. Hopefully, this book will help achieve the Revolution.

DTS

ACKNOWLEDGMENTS

I would like to thank William J. Bopp of Florida Atlantic University for his editorial criticisms and suggestions; Wilbur Rykert, Director of the National Crime Prevention Institute, for his major contribution to the chapter on crime prevention; Chief of Police Bert Hawkins, Oak Ridge,

[1] National Advisory Commission on Criminal Justice Standards and Goals, "Report on Police," Standard 8.1, Washington, D.C., 1973, p. 191.

Tennessee, for his contribution to the section PPBS of patrol planning; Chief of Police Carl Goodin of Cincinnati, Ohio, for his paper on Com-Sec team policing; and Lt. Col. Kenneth Duckworth, Wichita, Kansas, for all his assistance in the chapter "Command and Control" from the viewpoint of a Chief of Patrol utilizing the concept.

Grateful appreciation is given also to the many chiefs of police who gave permission to use material that allowed me to lend reality to theory. They include: Chief Clarence Kelly, Kansas City, Missouri (now Director FBI); Chief Winston Churchill, Indianapolis, Indiana; Chief Frank Dyson, Dallas, Texas (Ret.); Chief Ray Hoobler, San Diego, California; Col. Robert Chiaramonte, Superintendent Ohio Highway Patrol; Chief Eugene Camp, St. Louis, Missouri; Chief Jerry Wilson, Washington, D.C.; Col. E. Wilson Purdy, Metropolitan Dade County; Commissioner Donald F. Cawley, New York City Police Department; Chief Paul Calhoun, Greensboro, North Carolina; and Sheriff Peter Pitchess, Los Angeles County Sheriff's Department, California.

A very special thanks is due the clerical staff, my daughter, Robin-Anne. Without her efforts there would be no book.

**Consulting Editors for the
Holbrook Press Criminal Justice Series**

Vern L. Folley
*DIRECTOR
POLICE TRAINING INSTITUTE
UNIVERSITY OF ILLINOIS*

Donald T. Shanahan
*ASSOCIATE DIRECTOR
SOUTHERN POLICE INSTITUTE
AND UNIVERSITY OF LOUISVILLE*

William J. Bopp
*DIRECTOR, CRIMINAL JUSTICE PROGRAM
FLORIDA ATLANTIC UNIVERSITY*

police patrol in historical perspective

Police patrol is the first line of defense for sustaining domestic tranquillity. Recently, we have heard many voices from many areas telling police how to do their job. Some of these suggestions have been realistic and good; others have been unrealistic and poor.

If patrol is to be the backbone, utilizing more resources than any other unit in a police organization, then it should follow that maximum use and effectiveness of the patrol operation is necessary. Citizens should be able to go about their daily activities in a safe and secure manner, and it is to this end that the patrol administrator must work.

To best produce this patrol effort, many observers believe that law enforcement must select the best possible candidates, and then train and retrain, drill and drill again, until the patrol operation becomes as sharp as a finely honed blade. This takes good planning. The patrol administrator should take a lesson from Vince Lombardi, who drilled the Green Bay Packers football team until the execution of the play was so smooth it wouldn't be stopped even when the opposition knew it was coming. This team effort can work for patrol operations.

If the task concept and total-planning process is advanced in recruit school, roll-call training, in-service training, and by the supervisor in the field performing his leadership responsibilities in training, the patrol function will be enhanced sufficiently to earn the title "professional." If by doing, learning is improved, then the method prescribed above shall allow existing and future patrol administrators to concern themselves with innovation and creativity in managing by objectives.

To do an in-depth report on policing from the 1600s to the present day would be inappropriate for this book. And even though the oldest form of patrol is the foot beat, the present-day officers have not had the proper instructions on how to use this type of patrol to its maximum effectiveness. It seems that the rhetoric attached to mechanized patrol has caused misrepresentatation. Instead of all officers being foot-patrol officers with the added mobility of an automobile, citizens tend to believe the officer to be patrolling fully in a vehicle and walk his beat only when he responds to a call for service. Since an officer may walk without a radio any time he and the dispatcher agree he has the time and enough cars are available for calls for service, and an officer with a transceiver may walk any time so long as the radio frequencies are sufficient, I believe the best name to apply to our officers in the vehicles is "motorized foot patrolmen."

It would be appropriate, however, to highlight some of the leaders of law enforcement of the past, present, and future, and give a short account of the events that have had an impact on policing.[1]

The first city in the United States to have a permanent night watch was Boston, Massachusetts, in 1801. This was done by statutes and on March 10, 1807, the first police districts were established.[2]

In England, Sir Robert Peel submitted the Metropolitan Police Bill to Parliament in 1829, and the same year this important bill was passed. On September 29, 1829, formal policing began in London as 1,000 men in six divisions were assigned to patrol the city.

As America grew, so did its problems. Large-scale rioting erupted, which brought about the reform of the police system at that time. In 1833 a wealthy philanthropist bequeathed money to the City of Philadelphia to finance a competent police. Additionally in the same year, an ordinance was passed that provided for a day force of 24 policemen and 120 night watchmen. Later the force was centralized and a single head, captain, was appointed by the mayor. Even though the intent of the ordinance was good, it only lasted two years when it was repealed.

New York entered the urban police system in 1844, followed by Cincinnati in 1855. From this time until the early 1900s America saw its police go from a disorderly, politicized group to the introduction of the International Association of Chiefs of Police.

In 1867 the first call boxes were installed, and in 1878 Washington, D.C., was using telephones in precincts. Cincinnati became the first police department to use the telephone exclusively, and in 1886 replaced its foot patrolmen with mounted policemen in the outlying beats. This seems to be the first example of using specific methods of patrol for resolving problems of varying degrees and complexities.

The first bicycle patrol appears to have been initiated in 1897 by the Detroit Police Department. These officers were known as the Scorcher Cops. Their assignment was mostly to apprehend speeding bicycle riders. Detroit also had the first police car, a Model-T Ford with an antenna that was homemade.

VOLLMER PHILOSOPHY

August Vollmer was elected town marshal of Berkeley, California, in 1905. He later was appointed chief of police when that position replaced the old one of elected marshal. He held this position until 1932. Because of the significance of the philosophy of August Vollmer upon law enforcement, we state it here:

1. The public is entitled to police service as efficient as budget and manpower permits.
2. Courtesy is of paramount importance in all public and private contacts with citizens.
3. Police personnel with the highest intelligence, good education, unquestioned integrity, and with a personal history demonstrating an ability to work in harmony with others are necessary to effectively discharge the police responsibility.
4. Comprehensive, basic, advanced, and specialized training on a continuing basis is essential.
5. Broad responsibilities should be assigned to the beat officer.
   a. Crime prevention through effective patrol
   b. Investigation of all offenses
   c. Traffic law enforcement
   d. Juvenile duties
   e. Public relations expert
   f. Report-writer
   g. Thoroughly competent witness
   h. A generalist rather than a specialist
6. Superior supervision of personnel and effective leadership
7. Good public relations in the broadest sense
8. Cooperation with the press and news media
9. Exemplary official and personal conduct
10. Prompt investigation and disposition of personnel complaints
11. Adherence to the law-enforcement code of ethics
12. Protection of individual rights while providing for the security of persons and property.[3]

POLICE CODE OF ETHICS

It would be appropriate at this time to put forth a police code of ethics stated in terms of basic objectives and general rules of official conduct. This code of ethics was adopted by the International Association of Chiefs of Police in 1957. It goes without saying that before professionalism in police service can ever be reached, adherence to this code is sine qua non.

> As a law enforcement officer, my fundamental duty is to serve mankind; to safeguard lives and property; to protect the innocent against deception, the weak against oppression or intimidation, and the peaceful against violence or disorder; and to respect the Constitutional rights of all men to liberty, equality, and justice.
>
> I will keep my private life unsullied as an example to all; maintain courageous calm in the face of danger, scorn, or ridicule; develop self-restraint; and be constantly mindful of the welfare of others. Honest in thought and deed in both my personal and official life, I will be exemplary in obeying the laws of the land and the regulations of my department. Whatever I see or hear of a confidential nature or that is confided to me in my official capacity will be kept ever secret unless revelation is necessary in the performance of my duty.
>
> I will never act officiously or permit personal feelings, prejudices, animosities, or friendships to influence my decisions. With no compromise for crime and with relentless prosecution of criminals, I will enforce the law courteously and appropriately without fear or favor, malice, or ill will, never employing unnecessary force or violence and never accepting gratuities.
>
> I recognize the badge of my office as a symbol of public faith, and I accept it as a public trust to be held so long as I am true to the ethics of police service. I will constantly strive to achieve these objectives and ideals, dedicating myself before God to my chosen profession—law enforcement.

The next highlight of law enforcement was the appointment of J. Edgar Hoover as director of the Federal Bureau of Investigation. At the time of his appointment in 1924, the FBI was in trouble. Hoover reorganized the agency, taking it out of politics and toward professionalism. By 1935, Director Hoover had a clearinghouse for criminal fingerprint records, was able to aid other agencies in the technical aspects of investigation, and opened the National Academy, which was to contribute tremendously to the police profession. State, county, and local police agencies were then and are today receiving training from the Federal Bureau of Investigation. Any police agency would do honor to itself if modeled after the FBI.

In 1928 Orlando W. Wilson was appointed Chief of Police of Wichita, Kansas. Wilson later went on to be Superintendent of the Chicago, Illinois, Police Department where he reorganized and implemented his administrative and scholarly philosophies of integrity, dedication, and knowledgeable leadership. He championed college education for police, upgrading standards, police training, and expanded methods of patrol. He updated record keeping and the proper use of the principles of management. Law enforcement owes a great deal to this police administrator. Of all the accomplishments of Wilson, one of the most significant occurred in 1935 when he was chief of police in Wichita, Kansas. He introduced the first police cadet program when he agreed to hire annually fourteen University of Wichita upper-division students. The students worked part-time and went to the university continuing their education.

Next on the scene was Chief William H. Parker. He was appointed chief of police of the Los Angeles Police Department in 1950. Chief Parker possessed courage and an ability to achieve the objectives. He introduced the helicopter patrol, internal investigation, intelligence, community relations, research, and planning to the police world. It is easy to see today the impact this man had on law enforcement.

Now law enforcement has assistance from the federal government, foundation funds for research, and private concerns offering technical know-how for the police field. This is good; a mountain of talent is needed to help produce domestic tranquillity in our country. Additionally, enlightened leadership in the sixties and continuing on into the seventies has been with us by way of E. Wilson Purdy of Dade County, Florida; Edward Davis of Los Angeles, California; Peter Pitchess, Los Angeles County Sheriff; Clarence Kelly of the FBI; Jerry Wilson of Washington, D.C.; Carl Goodin, Cincinnati, Ohio; Patrick Murphy of the Police Foundation; and numerous other chiefs throughout the country. Last but not least would be the International Association of Chiefs of Police.

INTERNATIONAL ASSOCIATION OF CHIEFS OF POLICE

The contribution made to law enforcement by this association cannot be measured. Quinn Tamm, appointed the executive director in 1962, is almost a legend in his own time. Through his leadership the International Association of Chiefs of Police has made an impact on so many police agencies on a national scale that history may record that professionalism of policing was a figment of the imagination until this organization permeated the roots of state, county, and local police. Using talent from all fields of police work, both academically and empirically, is the core of its success. As long as Tamm and his tremendously qualified staff continue in the field, optimism should prevail regarding the possibility of professional policing becoming a reality.

At this point it is too early to judge the degree of impact on law enforcement that has been made by the Law Enforcement Assistance Administration. However, the educational aspect alone would suffice for qualifying the administration a success.

Law enforcement should view the Police Foundation and all other foundations that contribute to the many funds in the field with sincere gratitude. Law enforcement science and technology has exposed the police agency to new ways of doing things.

Patrol administration of the future will use the management by objective approach, complemented by creativity and innovation.

MANAGEMENT BY OBJECTIVE

The last section of Chapter 3, Patrol Planning, discusses the interrelationship between planning and budgeting in the context of goal achievement, since allocation of resources and the budgeting for these resources directly affect the ability to attain objectives.

Management by objective means defining objectives or goals, allocating resources concurrent with the defined objectives, allowing a complete understanding of the objectives by all members of the department, developing a parallel path between the organization and individuals toward achieving the defined objectives, providing subgoals for specific components of the organization, establishing short- and long-range goals, designing and implementing programs for achieving the goals, and self-renewal.

In order to define the objectives, it is necessary to define the role of the police agency. The objective of a police agency can't be defined as reducing crime if the number-one priority of the role of the police agency is to provide ambulance service, escorts to banks, or towing or wrecker service. The community, government, and police agency must first agree upon the objectives, the role of the police in attaining the objectives, and the amount of resources that should be allocated for the same. Additionally, if the community is willing to accept a given level of crime in order to have a two-minute response time to each call for police service, then this service should be provided. However, everyone should realize that the priority has been agreed upon by all parties. The police agency should then develop the manpower-workload analysis that provides this service. In most cases the elected officials of the community will communicate their feelings concerning the priorities of service. If the community is apathetic toward gambling and vice, there will be little pressure exerted by the elected officials relative to strict enforcement of this type of violation.

DEVELOPING GOALS

The police agency should be a partner in developing the goals of the community regarding the police service. They should also act as an extension of the community through the implementation of the policy of the community as communicated by the legislative and executive branches of local government. When these goals are put in final form, they become the focal point upon which all objectives and subgoals are based and should lead. One of the most important aspects of leadership within the management by objective approach is the ability to evaluate, on a continuing basis, all production to insure it leads to the total goal of the department. Many times patrol leaders get caught up in the immediacy of the situation and allow resources to be committed into areas that are not concurrent with the defined goals. Monitoring of operations that are off on a tangent will prevent misuse of resources.

If the goal and first priority of the police department is to reduce crime, then the patrol force must relate all actions to attaining that objective. Primarily, the prevention of crime will cause a reduction; therefore, all efforts of the patrol force should zero in on this task of the patrol function. These efforts would include omnipresence, apprehension of offenders, and citizen participation in crime-prevention programs. In essence, in the management by objective approach, the goals of the agency will determine the structure of that agency. Hopefully, police departments around the country will increase their efforts to integrate the traditional hierarchical structures with the management by objective approach, resulting in a balanced organization that fulfills the needs of both regimentation and self-actualization. This blend may possibly produce the standard of excellence in police service on a broad scale.

RESOURCE ALLOCATION

Goals cannot be simple rhetoric; they must be accompanied by outward signs that can be observed as a commitment to the achievement of stated goals. If the goal "reduce crime (index) by 5% this year" is not accompanied by movement of personnel into the critical area necessary to achieve that goal, then commitment is not present. These goals become in a sense unreal goals, obvious to enlightened personnel. Additionally, if support units are not provided with goals to help the operational forces achieve the total goal, there is no commitment. There can be no real goal unless all objectives and programs are designed to achieve the goal. To do this, the proper allocation of resources must be made to each unit so that the objectives and subgoals, which lead to the accomplishment of the total goals, are achievable.

UNDERSTANDING OBJECTIVES

In order to understand objectives, it is necessary to relate to them specifically. Therefore, it is essential that objectives be realistic. For example, a watch commander should not be expected to relate to "reduce crime generally." However, he can relate to reducing burglaries by 2% in a given section of his area of responsibility. Also, a sector sergeant and the officers working in the sector can relate to reducing burglaries by one or two in a given period of time. Together, all personnel can analyze the specific problem and coordinate efforts to attain the objectives by using several patrol techniques. This way, the action can be understood by all, implemented, and then coordinated with other units within the department. The reduction of burglary for a given watch, sector, or beat may necessitate the formation of a task force consisting of patrol, criminal investigation, juvenile, crime prevention, and tactical officers. Each member of the task force must understand his part in achieving the stated objective. This modular approach may become more and more necessary as the management by objective approach is used.

Whatever the objective may be, it should be compatible with fiscal input. The need to view each officer as a precious commodity cannot be forgotten. The objective of reducing burglaries by 2%, or whatever, should be viewed from a profit/loss posture. What amount of men and equipment will it take to accomplish the 2% reduction? What may happen if the commitment is not made? What approach or place of action if implemented will give the correct dividend for the investment made? How much impact will this operation have upon achievement of the total goal? The answers to these questions should be obtained and evaluated before implementation. Those persons involved in the operation should be consulted for input of alternative solutions. Participatory management becomes inherent in the management by objective approach. Through this approach, objectives are understood, organizational and individual goals are congruent, objectives are realistic and achievable, coordination between units is made easier, and because of subgoals, everyone is able to relate. For example, "Officer Smith, your objective for the next month is to reduce burglaries on your beat by 2; Officer Doe, because of the complexity of your beat, your objective is to reduce burglaries on your beat by 1; Sergeant, your objective for the next month is to reduce burglaries in your sector by 8; Lieutenant, your objective for the next month is to reduce burglaries on your watch by 12"; etc. These specific objectives are also made for criminal investigation, juvenile, and special force officers. Programs are those developed on a real-time basis as they relate to the objectives. Long-range goals (reduce crime) have been formulated as a matter of policy, while short-range goals are developed in accordance with priorities, progress of implemented operations, and self-renewal.

SELF-RENEWAL

An integral part of the management by objective approach is self-renewal. It is necessary to maintain flexibility so that a change of direction can be implemented when measurements indicate the change will enhance the success factor. All personnel should know where they are going, how they are going to get there, and then be able to determine if, in fact, they are going in the right direction. The importance of being able to relate to specific goals is the prelude to self-renewal. The fact that the sector sergeant knows that after three weeks of the month his sector will not achieve the objective, if the same method of operation is continued or if assistance is not obtained, is imperative to self-renewal. It may be necessary, after the evaluation, to modify the short-range goals. The modification should not be made, however, unless an in-depth analysis is completed, to include a comparison of similar sectors using criteria compatible to both. It should be expected that sectors experiencing a large amount of burglaries will be accompanied by arrests. Reasons why one sector is successful while another sector fails should be reviewed very carefully. Tellers in a bank need inspection if they are short money and also if they are over money, since both cases indicate need for adjustment.

It is very important to communicate to all officers that information upon which evaluations will be based, how the information is to be used, and over what time period the evelution will extend. The experiment conducted by the Kansas City, Missouri, Police Department on the effectiveness of preventive patrol (see Chapter 8) is a good example. The experiment was conducted in an area of 35 square miles in Kansas City from October 1, 1972, until September 30, 1973. Monitoring of experiments is very necessary so that renewal of objectives can take place.

The management by objective approach is similar to submitting a proposal. The proposal indicates where the individual units want to be in a given period of time. For example, the patrol force would like to reduce burglaries and robberies by 5% in six months. Next the individual units tell how they intend to arrive at that point. Resources are then provided according to the priorities of each unit. If patrol receives highest priority because the objective is realistic and feasible, then appropriate resources are committed to achieve the stated objective. Personnel must participate and be motivated to implement the plan for achieving the objective.

Patrol administrators should solicit participation and stimulate motivation of all patrol personnel to implement plans that will achieve the objective. The approach should be viewed in the context of investment and dividend. Careful analyses of the plans are necessary to insure minimum disruption of the organization's ability to perform the necessary community services. There is some risk in the management by objective approach, but if patrol and patrol administrators are going to lead law enforcement into the future, reciprocal confidence on the part of all members of patrol is necessary. It is realistic to expect that patrol officers, possessing an enormous amount of talent ready to be tapped, can contribute creative programs designed to fulfill themselves and increase the effectiveness of police service in their respective communities. If these patrol officers can show true concern for their communities, it is reasonable to expect the communities to return that concern with respect, support and participation in the achievement of objectives (reduce crime). Effective patrol leadership can produce this two-pronged thrust, so necessary to the success of police patrol, and a safe, secure community.

Police management must not be contained in a responsive mode. Innovation, creativity, willingness to change, and anticipation of future events should prevail in modern patrol administration. There should be no submission to negative thought or pessimism about the future of policing. A goal-oriented philosophy should be emphasized through management by objective. Results rather than methods should be primary. There should be a blend of excellence in performance of tasks and a mutual understanding of the organizational direction and goals. There should also be an accompanying ability to measure and evaluate the performance of the organizations and individuals. Participatory management; coordination; cooperation; integration of mutual respect; open, up, down, and lateral communication; responsibility-authority-accountability; information retrieval; feedback and follow-up; internal and external influences; are all factors that should be considered when a management by objective approach is used.

IMPLEMENTING MANAGEMENT BY OBJECTIVES

No management by objectives system will work unless the chief and the command personnel support the effort. The amount of interest shown by the top echelon of the department will filter down through the ranks, and response by each level will be greatly affected by the extent of interest. As police management becomes more conscious of the need for flexibility in management structure and style, the importance of the management by objective approach will be seen. This importance has been recognized by the National Advisory Commission on Criminal Justice Standards and Goals. Its *Report on Corrections* (1973) states:

> As human resources, corrections must make a special effort to integrate various functional specialties into an organization team that holds mutual objectives vis-à-vis the client, not only among its members but also between members and the organization. Accomplishing this organizational climate will require a participatory and nonthreatening leadership style in which employee, offender, and the organization needs are met in a compatible way.[4]

The application to police is obvious. Additionally, the same report describes sequential steps necessary to achieve the design and implementation of management by objectives:

1. An ongoing system capable of accurately identifying and predicting changes in the environment in which the organization functions.
2. Administrative capability through a management information system to provide data quickly to appropriate organizational members, work groups, or organizational units for their consideration and possible utilization.
3. Clearly established and articulated organizational and individual goals, mutually accepted through a process of continuous interaction between management and workers and between various levels of management. Unilateral imposition of organizational goals on lower echelon participants will not result in an MBO system but another bureaucracy.
4. An ongoing evaluation of the organizational and individual goals in the light of feedback from the system. Such feedback and evaluation may result in the resetting of goals.
5. A properly designed and functioning organizational system for effective and efficient service delivery. In such a system, goal-oriented collaboration and cooperation are organizationally facilitated, and administrative services fully support efforts at goal accomplishment.
6. A managerial and work climate highly conducive to employee motivation and self-actualization toward organizational goal accomplishments. Such a climate should be developed and nurtured through the application of a participative style of management.
7. A properly functioning system for appraising organizational, work group, and individual progress toward goal attainment.[5]

In summary, for law enforcement generally, and police/patrol work specifically, the long-range, anticipatory style of management can be accomplished. Crisis-oriented, short-range/short-sighted management can be removed from policing. The management by objective approach to patrol administration will assist.

NOTES

1. William J. Bopp, Donald O. Shultz, *A Short History of American Law Enforcement* (Springfield, Ill.: Charles C Thomas, 1972). Used as the major source for this discussion.

2. Roger Lane, *Policing the City, Boston 1822–1825* (Cambridge: Harvard University Press, 1967), p. 11.
3. Bopp and Schultz, op. cit., p. 88. Reprinted by permission from the publisher, Charles C Thomas.
4. National Advisory Commission on Standards and Goals, "Report on Corrections" (Washington, D.C., 1973), p. 449.
5. Ibid., p. 446.

patrol techniques

The choice of patrol techniques that will be used by the patrol officer is basic in most cases, but the importance attached to that choice has been underestimated. The achievement of the total objective of the patrol force depends upon selecting the proper technique for the specific situation. Foot patrol for community relations, motorized for mobility, and canine for special events and suspect search are just a few. When officers at the level of execution are able to select one of several patrol techniques based on existing conditions, objectives are more readily attained. This chapter discusses the several techniques available.

FOOT PATROL

It has been said that foot patrol is the most expensive method or type of patrol. However, a more realistic approach is that the application of foot patrol should be measured by the net income, so to speak, that this type produces for a given location and clientele. A recent discussion with a chief of police of a large city revealed that many police officers today do not even know how to patrol on foot. This police chief stated that he was going to institute an in-depth study to determine the training needed for instruction on foot patrol within his department. Therefore, the patrol administrator who attempts to achieve the objective should not limit himself to an analysis of the expense of each type of patrol alone but include an analysis of the expense as related to the accomplishments made by a given selection or method of patrol. If one had gone through a police academy years ago when foot patrol was the predominant method used by the police department, instructions would probably have been given as follows:

> Know the people on your beat; their occupations, and their habits; know personally night watchmen, janitors, and all other persons who may be working at unusual hours of the day and night; acquaint yourself with operators of taverns, pool rooms, and clubs and all laws relating to the proper conduct of such establishments; know the opening and closing hours of all business establishments on your beat; know where your call boxes are located and your firealarm boxes. Additionally, officers should know the same information about the adjoining beats. Be so intimately involved with the residents of your beat that knowledge of when they are away on vacation and advice about the safeguards they should take to insure the protection of their property can be given freely, and accepted sincerely. Officers should not only know those proven law-abiding residents, but those of questionable character. Also, be alert for any vice activities being conducted on your beat or post; first-aid training is necessary to save lives and decrease the possibility of serious injury—and you just may have to deliver babies. The officer should make himself familiar with all locations of important buildings, city, state and federal within his area. He should exercise great vigilance in his inspection process of police hazards. (Note: a *police hazard* is defined as any event which requires police action or better yet any situation that may induce an incident calling for some police action.)
>
> An officer should note all removal of residents and all new additions to his beat. He should be vigilant to prevent fires, make every effort to curb juvenile delinquency, and carry out any plan necessary or that he is capable of with regard to crime prevention (see Chapter 8). Officers should maintain a night reference book containing records of the name, address, and telephone number of the owners of all business establishments on his beat. He should know the location of all safes on his beat and encourage the owner in the area of crime prevention to keep the inside of the building well lighted and especially have a light burning over the safe. He should be aware of any pawnshops or secondhand dealers or junk dealers where the possibility of disposal of the stolen goods could take place. He should be suspicious by nature and inquisitive at all times with regard to persons who do not look right, and vehicles whose occupants may appear to be out of place. He should build up his sources of information and note any person whom he could call upon to help him in case of emergency. The officer should patrol constantly and intelligently. He should keep a case book where all arrests are noted for information which he may need at a later date. His original notes should be kept meticulously so that he would be able to testify in court in a very knowledgeable and

intelligent manner. In summary, the officer must attain the objectives by winning the confidence and respect of the public. He can do this by performing his duties in an efficient, honest, and business-like manner by projecting himself as an exemplary member of the community and setting an example both on and off duty.

While this last task still remains a very important part of the duties of the patrol officer, we have seen changes made in patrol. Task forces, tactical, team policing, have all involved the patrol function. It has been estimated that 70 to 80 percent of the officer's time today is spent on noncriminal activity. This increases the need for closer contact with people living in the area of an officer's beat. In most departments today there are enough transceivers for each officer to have one provided for his particular beat, especially if he is working a one-man car. This constant communication increases the types of patrol available for the patrol administrator and for assignment to a given area or situation. In areas of high concentration, such as downtown areas where policing today has a tremendous investment, a foot officer is most appropriate, especially if he has a walkie-talkie. Most cities have, or are in the process of developing, their inner city areas to the point where the tax base will be increased. Proper patrol techniques are an integral part of the total process of rejuvenation of these business districts. The foot officer has not become obsolete, and foot patrol is a very effective type of patrol for progressive law enforcement agencies.

CONSTANT AND INTELLIGENT FOOT PATROL

Generally, the only regularity of patrol is its irregularity. Specifically, the officer must know his beat intimately. Since the foot beat is not as large as a motorized foot beat, he must develop constant patrol, yet be able to give the impression that it will be difficult for anyone to know exactly where he is at any given time. The intelligent patrol officer knows the patrol hazards,[1] (persons, property, places, and situations) and anticipates the consequence of his actions with regard to these hazards.

WALKING THE BEAT

The foot patrol officer knows the "how" of walking his beat. He has had explained to him and understands how to set priorities when determining which hazards need more attention than others. This is done by shift. The day shift emphasizes omnipresence, while the night shift has the advantage of darkness. The officer should use darkness as a tool; e.g., on day shift you walk by the curb, on night shift you walk next to the buildings. Remember, at night whenever you get to the corner of a building, stop, and look around the corner before you proceed. The officer does a survey of his beat in which he determines which business establishments have silent alarms, which have audible alarms, and which have no alarm at all. It is important for him to know by what means these different alarms will be set off. By doing this he enhances his ability to decide correctly how he will approach the establishment when he believes a burglar to be inside. He will also be able to advise assisting officers of any pitfall in their approach to the building. By doing a survey of the building and studying the alarm systems, he will know the possible escape routes from the building, and this will improve the search technique used.

To repeat, the only regularity of patrol is its irregularity, and we must expand this concept to the actual technique used when inspecting premises. Do not try up each door the same as the one before. This causes routinizing, which is the greatest evil to patrol. Whenever checking a door for entry, use the flashlight to look for pry marks that may be fresh around the complete door, but most importantly, around the hinges, doorknob, and locks. Pry marks include those that might also be made by a saw. In such a case burglars may be attempting to force their way into the building by sawing the bolts or locks holding the door. One important fact is that you do not enter the building yourself. You call for assistance and use proper building-search techniques. However, by using the described survey method and attaining an intimate knowledge of the respective premises on your beat, the building-search technique will be improved.

VICARIOUS FOOT PATROL

When walking a beat, an officer can place himself in hypothetical situations to determine the best way of handling each given situation. This vicarious approach in evaluation will help develop alternate solutions to problems. You can do this on each shift using holdups on the day shift and 4–12 shift, burglaries on the 12–8, and auto theft on the 4–12 and 12–8 shifts. This preparation of response to the given situations develops the thought process so that reaction is speedy yet intelligent, without jumping to conclusions. This will increase the patrol officer's confidence in knowing what to do in a given situation.

USE OF TELLTALES

The word "telltale" is familiar in the eastern United States. The procedure is used in many police departments around the country even though a different name is used. In effect, it means that in the process of inspecting premises, after each inspection a piece of tape or string of cotton is placed across entrances and exits to buildings and doorways, which will allow for a more efficient inspection the second time around. You may use matchbook covers, match sticks, toothpicks, and such item that can be placed on a window sill from the pane to the side of the window, or anywhere that would indicate to you that the particular item you are inspecting has been disturbed. Some supervisors have used this technique in order to inspect officers and it has been overt inspection. Sergeants have told officers that they will place telltales to indicate whether officers have inspected certain premises and have inspected them properly. It is a valid method so long as it is used overtly. There are other ways to handle officers who do not perform; the advantage gained in resolving a problem with one officer is not worth the effect a covert operation may have on the other officers within a supervisor's area of responsibility.

PRIORITIES

When a determination is made regarding which premises do have alarms and which do not, then set priorities to inspect premises according to needs. If a building has an alarm system, have procedures available on how to inspect the building to determine whether or not anyone may be inside. This would indicate that premises not having alarm systems are a greater potential hazard than those that do. In developing a plan of action on how to patrol a beat, it is necessary to set priorities so that the places more in need of inspection are inspected more than those which are not. This does not mean that all premises will not be inspected; however, it will allow for effective patrol. This priority system is just part of the total thought process necessary for a foot officer to possess, so that he obtains an intimate knowledge of his beat. This can be related to the day-shift officer who knows that when walking by business establishments he will observe certain things; if these things are out of place he will become suspicious and inspect further. An officer can develop a nonverbal communication system between the business community and himself. For instance, while walking his beat the officer passes a grocery store, knowing that at a given time of the day he should see a certain person operating the business. This person usually gives a routine signal, which means everything is in order. If the officer sees or notices anything different or unusual, this indicates that things are not running normally and should cause him to inquire further.

OBSERVATION

Observation is one of the advantages of foot patrol. It is necessary that the foot-patrol officer enhance any tools available to him. This includes the tool of observation. In improving this ability, he should first know what to look for in any given area. For example, travel depots have baggage stolen by con artists. The officer, therefore, should look for the type of people and the type of crime. Hospitals have rapists and purse snatchers; therefore, he should look for persons who have the potential to commit those crimes. Business areas have commercial burglars; residential areas have dwelling burglaries, purse snatchers, etc. The officer must become instinctively familiar with placing certain extensions to use as powers of observation. The basic rule in using observation is to look for differences. The officer should note any unusual acts regarding dress, (a person just does not belong), or unusual mannerisms, or ways of doing things that do not appear to be normal. The officer should give special attention to those who pay too much attention to him or those who try to avoid his glances or who are loitering in a place where usually no one has a reason to be. He should make special note of those who have no apparent destination, since this possibly indicates a potential hazard to him. The officer should be aware that it is necessary for him to look up and down, not only horizontally, while patrolling, since he must be aware that there are lookouts, who may not be in familiar places, observing the officer's actions while a partner is committing a crime.

Total observation is the use of all senses while patrolling your beat. For a crime to be committed in your presence, it does not necessarily mean that you have to see it. If you are standing on a corner looking in one direction and glass breaks behind you and you turn and see someone running from the location with some type of apparel or item, you have used the sense of hearing in order to provide you with the criteria necessary to have a crime committed in your presence.

In developing observation, improve upon objectivity so that when viewing something, view the whole something, not just what you would like to view or part of that something. Since each of us observe as individuals it is necessary to understand that we view things from individual perception.

Usually, in police academies there is a very simple demonstration of observation. The instructor, while teaching the class, has one of his secretaries or associates come into the room and hand him a piece of paper. They discuss the paper for a minute or so while the class is viewing both of them. After the assistant leaves the classroom, the instructor then asks each member of the class to describe the person as he saw him (or her). There will be many different descriptions. When actively participating in patrol, this same situation occurs whenever an attempt is made to get descriptions from different people who observe the same incident. For instance, in a bank robbery you will have different descriptions from the teller, the manager, and from the person outside who may have seen the subjects running away.

FACTORS OF ATTENTION

There are several factors which should be considered in the observation process. For instance, the factor of size: when someone is unusually tall or unusually short, attention is drawn to him. A person is walking normally, but as soon as the officer is seen, the person begins to run. At this point, the officer should be ready to observe. Other factors involved are those of shape, repetition, interest involved, sound or noise, or the striking quality, organic condition, of an individual. Additionally, the ability to understand what we have observed in analyzing and viewing these factors is most important.

The ability to observe properly includes mental capacity, the clearness and quickness of mind, the amount of observation the mind can absorb, educational background, the experience previously acquired, and occupational background. Other factors affecting information received from citizens, when obtaining descriptions of persons who have committed crime and where citizens have been the victim of crime, include the citizen's vocabulary and ability to relate an actual observation to the police. Also, the amount of time that has taken place between the incident and the time it is being reported, and if people have had similar incidents happen to them in the past, so that they would be informed and better able to give more accurate descriptions. Included in this would be the emotional state of the person who made the observation, and the age of the person who made the observation. Usually younger people, especially young males around the age of thirteen, give the best descriptions.

PROSECUTION

In any discussion on observation, it is necessary for the patrol officer to realize that in policing, whatever observations are made and descriptions given at the time of the occurrence will have to be available at a later date when and if prosecution takes place. Inaccuracy of fact will bear heavily on the credibility of testimony given in court. Poor use of words, poor expressions, and exaggerations all tend to discredit the witness. Experience has shown that most police officers have control of all their senses, have the power and ability to concentrate and not allow their mind to wander when their duty is at hand, are able to form a clear and accurate picture of what they see before them, and are able to look beyond the initial observation to what else will be affected by their ability to observe properly and accurately. However, training repetition is necessary if proficiency is to continue.

In summary, observation consists of really seeing what was viewed, developing the ability to tell what was seen, and training ourselves to insure accuracy. Show interest in work and use all the empirical knowledge developed during our training and work.

DESCRIPTION

Describing another person or event is very difficult. All one needs is to have an incident occur and question a few people about the same incident and you will see the difficulties involved in describing an event accurately. Common mistakes in describing events are similarity in events, bad lighting, emotional conditions, suggestions from others, and time lapses. Officers should use and explain to people, when they are attempting to obtain descriptions, "portrait parle" and what importance physical features play in giving the descriptions of individuals. Officers should realize that the head is divided into three parts:

the hairline to eyebrows, the eyebrows to the bottom of the nose, and the bottom of the nose to the chin. These are basic in describing individuals from the top of their head to the chin and should always be considered when obtaining descriptions to transmit to other officers for possible apprehension.

POINTERS ON OBSERVATION

1. Observation is a complete and accurate awareness of surroundings.
2. Officers should make notes of observations; specifically, should answer who, what, where, how, and why.
3. Factors significant in causing errors concerning an observed event are:
   a. false perception
   b. false interpretation
   c. memory
   d. time lapse between perception and recall
4. The most important element of any personal description is any outstanding or distinguishing peculiarity or characteristic.
5. The eye-level method is the best method for estimating a person's height. (International chart: 5'6" and under = *small*; 5'6" to 5'10" = *medium*; and 5'10" and over = *tall*.)
6. Visible scars or marks are those visible when the individual is fully dressed. TATO's
7. Where the time for observation is short and there is an absence of outstanding features, concentrate on the ear and nose.
8. The form of the nose is observed in profile.
   a. depth of the root
   b. general form of the line of the nose
   c. the slope of base
9. Since the ear is that part of the body having a minimum amount of variation of form, it is acknowledged to be the most important factor of the identification on the whole face.
10. The ear is composed of a series of ridges and hollows of which it is proposed to describe only the ridges. (Terms: *helix, lobe, tragus, antitragus,* and *folds.*)

HAZARD FACTORS

Most important to the foot officer is the ability to recognize those factors that create hazards. His doing so would be a definite asset in preventing crime or the possibility of crime. This prevention, meaning eliminating the opportunity for successful completion of a crime that is the second part of desire and opportunity, becomes a direct challenge to the foot patrol officer (see Chapter 8).

PATROLLING CONSPICUOUSLY

Patrol comes from the French word "patroluiler," which means going through mud puddles. As a good patrol or selected foot-patrol officer, you have a choice to patrol conspicuously or inconspicuously. In the conspicuous patrol you are attempting to prevent crime or attempting to prevent the opportunity for the successful completion of that particular crime which is the primary mission of the patrol officer. This patrol allows the public and the criminal to know you are on the job, in the belief that omnipresence discourages any thief, whether amateur or professional, from committing a crime by increasing the risk. Conspicuous patrol promotes good public relations, even though it obligates the officer to the public in that they will see you and more likely seek your help. By patrolling conspicuously you must be very alert to avoid any routine patrol.

Good patrolling means going through all areas regardless of conditions, in all kinds of weather, day or night. Remember that criminals choose the time to work and they choose their time when they think you are not doing your job.

INCONSPICUOUS PATROLLING

Inconspicuous patrolling means that patrol activity which attracts little attention: walking close to buildings, dropping in alcoves, walking up and down alleys, walking through parking lots and out of the way places. This is part of the apprehension-prevention concept, which means a professional may be working on a beat and no amount of prevention is going to deter this professional from committing the crime or his successful completion of the particular crime. In this case, an officer must develop a type of inconspicuous patrol that allows apprehending the offender, thereby preventing any future crimes.

The best possible patrol would be a combination of timely conspicuous and inconspicuous patrol. For successful patrolling, one of the main feaures is to avoid developing any habits whatsoever. Do not eat at the same place each day; do not talk to residents at the same time each day; if coffee is needed when beginning a shift, drink the coffee at a different place and purchase your coffee from a different location each tour of duty. The foot-patrol officer is still the most important segment of policing, when considering the development of information and who shall be the eyes and ears of the department.

DISADVANTAGES OF FOOT PATROL

One disadvantage of the past has been alleviated with the availability of the walkie-talkie. Foot officers are available for calls for service, even though on a limited basis in the areas where they are patrolling on foot.

Another disadvantage is the limited response to calls for service and lack of mobility, in that officers are not able to get from one point to another without developing fatigue and within a reasonable amount of time. Because of these disadvantages, it is most important that a foot officer or a selected foot officer plan his patrol strategy wisely and physical-fitness programs be an integral part of the patrol program.

MOTORIZED FOOT PATROL

Motorized foot patrol is in most cases, and should be, the most prevalent form of patrol in America today. Motorized foot patrol combines the advantages of foot patrol (observation, sources of information, eyes and ears of the department, citizen contact, community relations) with the mobility necessary to alleviate the disadvantages of foot patrol. Motorized foot patrol also calls for the complete team effort between the dispatcher and the motorized foot-patrol officer. Each motorized foot-patrol officer is furnished with a portable radio so that he maintains constant communications with the dispatcher.

Several procedures are available today in the use of the walkie-talkie: e.g., changing batteries after each tour of duty or having portable rechargers in the vehicles themselves. Officers working the motorized foot-patrol method must be made aware of the proper manner of carrying these walkie-talkies. Considerations are: On what side shall it be carried, opposite the revolver or the same side? Will the safety lanyard be carried parallel to the body or across the body? How shall it be worn during periods of inclement weather? Different seasons? And last but not least, inspection as to the condition and procedure for care and use of this equipment.

While patrolling on foot, the officer should be keenly aware of where he parks his vehicle. He must be sure to lock the car and close the windows to prevent anyone from fire-bombing, stealing, or damaging the vehicle when it is not being driven.

The motorized foot-patrol officer must answer two basic questions relative to the location he parks the police vehicle: (1) At what location will the vehicle pay most dividends in omnipresence and prevention? (2) What is my plan for walking so as not to be too far away from the vehicle in case of needed mobility? The second aspect would defeat the advantage gained for motorized foot officer if the car was not available to be used effectively for apprehension of an offender.

In our attempt to have an efficient motorized foot patrolman, it is necessary to understand that a manpower allocation and distribution study should precede the assignment of motorized foot-patrol beats (see Chapter 9). Beat layouts must be compatible to the motorized foot-patrol concept to calls for service so that he can perform the foot-patrol facet of his total patrol responsibility.

The combining of motorized foot patrol should in no way presuppose any fault-finding with the type of motorized patrol that has been prevalent in law enforcement for the past few years. Instead, it is a meaningful advancement of both systems of patrol brought about through the development and general use of the personal radio. Consider the equation in Figure 2.1.

$$
\text{A.} \quad \begin{array}{c} 1 - 2 \text{ man} \\ \text{beat car} \end{array} \quad \left(- \left(\begin{array}{c} \text{car} \\ \text{radio} \end{array} \right) + \left(\begin{array}{c} \text{personal} \\ \text{radio} \end{array} \right) \right) \quad \begin{array}{c} 1 - 2 \text{ man} \\ \text{foot motorized} \\ \text{unit} \end{array}
$$

$$
\text{B.} \quad \begin{array}{c} 1 - 1 \text{ man} \\ \text{beat car} \end{array} \quad \left(- \left(\begin{array}{c} \text{car} \\ \text{radio} \end{array} \right) + \left(\begin{array}{c} \text{personal} \\ \text{radio} \end{array} \right) \right) \quad \begin{array}{c} 1 - 1 \text{ man} \\ \text{foot motorized} \\ \text{unit} \end{array}
$$

FIGURE 2.1   Beat Car to Foot-Motorized Unit.

This equation conveys the fact that originally we had a beat car, either one- or two-man, with a radio. Now the radio has been removed from the vehicle, but in its place the officers are given personal radios (portable) that they can take with them wherever they go. They still have the old capabilities of patrolling their assigned beat in an un-ridged pattern while in their vehicle, but now they can park and lock vehicle, notify the communications center, and continue their patrol on foot. After completing their objectives and walking the beat, they return to the vehicle, notify the communications center, and once again become motorized unit. At any time while they walk they can be ordered back into their vehicle by the communication center. A communication channel for this motorized foot patrol has not been altered (see Figure 2.2).

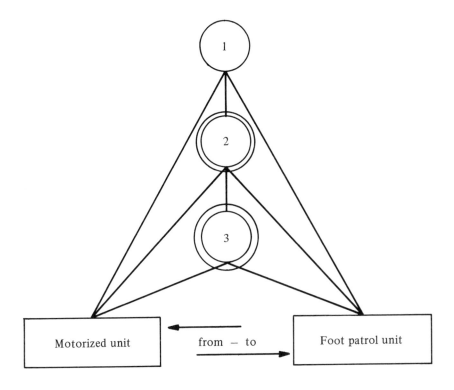

1.	Communications center
2.	Field lieutenant
3.	Patrol/Tactical sergeant

FIGURE 2.2 Foot/Motorized-Patrol Communications Channel.

Selective patrol operations are indispensible and will continue to be the backbone of the police service. Patrol officers are responsible for the performance of all primary police tasks. To be efficient in his duties a patrol officer must use all the tools available. The squad car created increased mobility and contained the communications equipment vital in maintaining the lifeline of the officer on the street. Now the squad car serves as transportation to get around his beat and expedite him to the scene of a crime, disturbance, etc. when needed. While on foot through individual contacts with citizens, the officer can fulfill his patrol objectives and gain the positive community support necessary to achieve the total goals of the department.[2]

SELECTIVE FOOT PATROL

Selective foot patrol combines the old with the new. The criteria necessary for the complete foot-patrol officer twenty-four hours a day is based upon many ingredients that can be elicited from the computer printouts regarding manpower allocation and distribution and the appropriate method of patrol. Selective foot patrol uses all the quality know-how, judgments, duties, and responsibilities of the regular foot patrol and in recent times includes the area of community stability.

We have often seen an officer lose contact with persons or residents of the area within which he is working because of mechanized patrol and an alienation and a hostility develop to the point where in some cases he is even considered an occupation force. Clearly written procedures and professional police training can decrease this type of confrontation and conflict between the patrol officer and the community. However, the increase in mechanized patrol was accompanied by confrontation, especially in the urban area. The use of innovation in patrol should help to solve this particular problem.

There are two areas where selective foot patrol will apply: the area of crime (whether it be burglary, auto theft, larceny) and the community stability problem.

CRIME PROBLEM

Historical crime data must indicate that the given area is not too large for effective foot patrol and is temporally distributed so that an 8-hour shift of foot patrol officers can be effectively implemented. In some cases a 16-hour broken shift may be necessary to solve the several categories of crime related to a given area by location and time. For example, a certain area (outline of that area could be in the shape of a straight-away, cross, T-shape, X) to be covered by the foot-patrol officer must be designed in a way that it is within his means to do the job for which he has been assigned. Second, isolate and analyze each particular situation and apply the best method of patrol to decrease the particular crime prevailing on the beat. Naturally, the patrol administrator must analyze, evaluate, and "act before the fact." Third, establish the best method of patrol, and then select the appropriate officer to perform that method of patrol for a given category of crime. For example, in the category of robbery, purse snatch, we would look to our younger officers who have the running ability to apprehend any subject perpetrating such a crime and possess the alertness and aggressiveness to maintain constant vigilance on a given area. Advise the officer of the total situation and then evaluate, document, and inform the officer of the effect his patrol has had on that given area and that given category of crime.

In effect, the area of selective foot patrol for crime problems contains within it the total application of patrol administration. We see planning, selection, training, informing, leadership, documentation, analysis, evaluation, and flexibility. Allowing the officer to be part of the initial planning of the selective foot beat will enhance the possibility of success. The selection of the area by using the historical data for a given 8-hour period must be done on a need basis and all the principles of organization must be taken into consideration; e.g., span of control and unity of command.

COMMUNITY STABILITY

The other main purpose for a selected foot-patrol beat is to maintain community stability within a given area. Experience tells us that in certain cases police officers can be catalyst to riots and explosive situations. This can develop from mishandling a family problem or a fight or a disorderly person who has been drunk on the street and can occur anytime from the evening hours to the morning hours when most bars close.

An indication that the leader in patrol must take special interest in a given area comes from the crime and the realization that community stability may be at best poor in a given area where police officers are being assaulted, beaten, and having to call for officer assistance each time they make an arrest. In acting before the fact, selective foot patrol is one of the methods to combat this type of activity against your officers in urban areas. The police leader must continually be aware of these types of activities and maintain a feeling on the pulse of the respective communities within his area of responsibility so that he may determine the degree to which this hostility has extended and know when selected foot patrol would be the best method to alleviate the condition as it exists.

Community relations units may render assistance to patrol in given areas, by identifying potential problems (poor police attitude, no recreation facilities, etc.) However, it is the immediate supervisor and the police leaders of the command structure who are responsible for maintaining the community's stability, not the community relations units. These units within a police organization should be used to provide supplements to the initial community relations person, the beat officer, for solving community problems. Selecting the proper officer to walk a foot beat using all resources that have a bearing on the solution to the community problem is one of the most effective means available for solving that type of activity.

An example is a street intersection where the four corners were occupied by a bar, grocery store, a cleaning establishment, and a laundromat. This intersection had problems throughout the evening hours and into the early morning hours. Arrests had been made in the area and each time officers made arrests, rocks and bottles were thrown, police vehicles were damaged, officers were injured, and the community in general was shaken into a pathetic position. The identification of the obvious problems and the analysis of the in-depth problems indicated a need for a concentrated effort on the part of a selected police officer who had the ability to deal with this type of a situation. In effect, this officer was given a staff study to do while working his beat. After months of working this selected foot beat, the officer realized that the majority of the community was in support of the police officers working in that area. However, a very few of the younger males were attempting to exercise leadership over a larger group of young people in the area and found that by showing this type of contempt for the law-enforcement officers, leadership would come their way. The institution of the selected foot beats were for 8-hour periods. This particular one was from 6:00 P.M until 2:00 A.M. The results were almost instantaneous: a reduction in criminal activity. While this particular officer was working, no other incidents such as had been experienced in the past with relation to community stability and assaults on officers or explosive incidents occurred.

Selective foot patrol, especially with constant communications available, has a definite place in law enforcement today. It is difficult to envision any period in the future when selected foot patrol would not be one of the best possible solutions to a given problem. Technically, the officer needs to know how to patrol on foot, relate to crime problems, know the importance of community relations, and have a feeling of belonging both to the police organization and to the community that he is serving. If these five qualities exist, the selective foot-patrol beat will be a success. Beneficial results should prevail in police agencies where patrol leaders have developed the expertise to use selective foot patrol properly.

MOTORIZED PATROL

The effectiveness of motorized patrol cannot be denied. To accomplish the three basic missions of a patrolman: (1) prevent crime and disorder, (2) enforce laws, and (3) provide a superior product of service to the community, in today's society, the auto is sine qua non.

Prevention of Crime and Disorder

The auto allows an officer to respond rapidly to any incident, and, since apprehension is directly related to response time, the auto increases the opportunity for apprehending the criminal. Less fatigue on the part of the officer in driving as opposed to other types of patrol allows him to be more alert, especially at the end of his tour of duty. The auto easily handles the prevention aspect of patrol, since the irregular driving pattern of an auto allows different approaches. Double-back, concentric, stationary, and zig-zag patterns are all part of the unpredictable patrolling of a beat. Omnipresence, conspicuous patrolling, and reducing opportunity for successful completion of crime are all important parts of crime prevention. The auto is instantly involved. The officer on patrol must remember that crime prevention is the responsibility of everyone. Thinking about crime prevention in its totality will assist the officer in understanding the awesome challenge confronting the intelligent police officer.

The quadrant style of cutting off escape routes is available only to auto patrol. There is no way to do an effective manpower-workload analysis and implementation if auto patrol is not one of the choices of patrol methods. In the outlying section of urban areas, the beat sizes are legitimately large enough so that the only way each citizen is provided his fair share of police protection and service is by the use of auto patrol.

Disorders, whether large or small, can be controlled most effectively if the ability to respond with sufficient force (people) is available at all times to the patrol commander. If it's an athletic event that erupts; a rock-and-roll dance that ends in a highly emotional state, sending thousands of youths into the streets at the same time in a frenzied condition; or a spontaneous incident, such as an arrest on the street of a drunken couple at the time the bars are closing, the auto patrol provides the tool to meet the time and force factor. Additionally, where an officer needs assistance, just the fact that vehicles are on the way with sirens, lights, or both activated may reduce the probability of serious injury to an officer.

Two factors are significant when dealing with auto patrol. One is the need to control response to the many different situations in number of cars and approach of cars. Second is the need to emphasize proper driving techniques, especially when patrolling routinely (most police accidents occur on routine patrol) to insure an adequate fleet safety record. The importance of supervision in patrol is highlighted when attempting to resolve these two problems. It seems that when officers have certain calls (robbery in progress, assist an officer), all hell breaks loose inside them. The adrenalin begins to work and they become the only persons on the road. The need for good supervision is tantamount to a good fleet safety record.

If the officer is provided with proper information, he will be able to place himself in a position to prevent a recurrence of the same crime by developing a strategy for patrol. If an officer recognizes police hazards, he will realize the hazard of a bus-transfer corner, for instance. Intersections where people must transfer from one public conveyance to another are locations where purse-snatching can be prevented. An officer who is aware will position himself at that location at critical times in order to prevent any incident. From this point he can proceed to the next location on his beat where his presence gives him the opportunity to receive maximum dividends for his investment of time as a preventive action. In combining instinct, knowledge, awareness, planning, and information, with the officer, auto, and communication, a real tool for prevention is completed.

Let's add to this the International Association of Chiefs of Police three types of crime prevention. First is through mechanical devices: use of safes, locks, burglar alarms, bullet-proof glass, light, leaded or barred windows; second is by controlling conditions through athletic clubs, recreation centers, dispersing gangs, and returning juveniles to their homes; and third, through juvenile counseling. When the thought process is put to use by each officer in the crime prevention area, and resources are provided, and the proper training is available, there can be an all-purpose officer with enough challenge for an immersion into the patrol function and the potential for improvement in innovation and creativity in the patrol force.

Enforcing Law

The mobility given an officer by the auto will also enhance the inspection of persons, places, and things that might be termed violations and thus lead to an improved ability to enforce the laws of the community. Weather is not a deterrent to the use of the auto, and the auto permits the patrol function to be accomplished constantly. In performing the law-enforcement tasks of arrest, search and seizure, field interview and investigation, the auto can carry that equipment necessary for performing these tasks.

Service

Any incident that occurs to any one of our citizens at the time of occurrence becomes an all-encompassing situation when related to the interaction between the citizen involved and the police department. Providing service to the community in some areas has become the primary function of the police departments. Statistically speaking, more than two-thirds of the police calls for service are of the non-criminal nature. In effect, policing has become primarily a service agency. There is really nothing to equal the feeling a citizen gets when a call for police service is made and in a matter of minutes an officer arrives and intelligent service is provided. The prompt service and the knowledge of what to do after arriving are equal partners in response to calls for service. We may reduce response time by adjusting the formula in manpower-distribution studies, but it will be to no avail if after the officer arrives he does not complete the request knowledgeably and sincerely.

For any department to give service to the best of its ability, a distribution of the patrol force according to need, by time and place, should be the policy followed. The use of all types of patrol and reduction of response time to call for service are basic ingredients for consideration when reaching a decision on proper beat layout. The proper layout has a large impact on a department's ability to respond to calls for service effectively.

ONE-MAN CAR

Very few police departments can afford the assignment of two men to every beat car. Even in the past, when most of the officers in a police department were walking beats, the patrol leader had to decide where and when the officer would walk alone or in pairs. A foot officer walking alone must know where the closest call-box is located and possess the equipment to signal a side-partner for assistance (whistle, flashlight, baton). Each officer should develop for himself the best method to obtain assistance by the quickest means available. Developing rapport with the citizens on the beat is of primary importance, since many times it is a matter of self-preservation.

In deciding upon the use of the one-man car, patrol administrators should consider police hazards, calls for service, seriousness of crime, amount of activity by time and place, arrests, access to the individual officers by other officers (this factor considers the routes that would have to be taken by assisting officers in case of emergency and is more relevant in outlying areas), assaults on police officers, and incidents where weapons have been used. These same factors apply also in determining the beats where two-man cars should operate.

Advantages of One-man Car

First, the cost of providing two-man cars to every beat is not feasible. Therefore, the use of one-man patrol would reduce costs. Second, the areas covered by patrol would be doubled. Third, the ability to respond to a citizen's call for service would be insured since many calls can be handled by one man. Instead of having two men out of service as would be the case in a two-man car, one of the men would be available for additional calls. Fourth, the one-man car operation enhances the team concept. Each of the officers assigned a one-man car beat within a sector of patrol is like a player on a team. If one officer makes an error, he might not be available to assist his fellow officers, so he automatically becomes more aware of the position he plays on the team. This makes for an improved total operation. Fifth, one officer alone knows he must perform using his own ability primarily. This makes him more observant, more aware and alert regarding his surroundings. He is not distracted by the conversation of a partner. He operates more intelligently and objectively since he does not have to prove himself to anyone. The officer operating a one-man car is more easily evaluated, and responsibility, authority, and accountability is more easily placed. This placing of responsibility, authority, and accountability is a motivating factor for individual performance.

Objections to the One-man Car

Officers in Britain, some observers have said, must be more courteous because they do not have the assortment of weapons that American officers have. This may not be totally true, but one point is very significant. The British police must develop courtesy and the ability to go that extra step because of the lack of weapons, and also the British culture is affected by gentlemanliness. This does not mean less masculine, but the British police officer does not resort to authority quite so fast as his American counterpart. On the other hand, the American police officer has developed from the concept of self-reliance and masculinity and has consequently resorted to his authority quicker. The one-man car is compatible to an increased use of courtesy. Finally, the use of more cars on the street via the one-man car system certainly gives the impression of police being everywhere and will decrease the sense of fear in the community.

The first objection to the one-man car is that there is more safety for officers when they work in pairs. However, the chart taken from the Uniform Crime Reports of the Federal Bureau of Investigation 1972 (page 46) shows that in ten years from 1962 to 1971 more officers were killed while operating the two-man car than the one-man car. Additionally, with the use of one-man cars officers are more likely to "not take chances" or "perform carelessly." The two-man vehicle operation does lead to the officers being slightly more reckless. There is a theory that the one-man car will not perform aggressive patrol. The theory is rejected based on many years of experience walking a beat alone without any communication. The independent officer and his intelligent use of procedures and cunning will prevail in the art of aggressive patrol. Two officers in a car will not necessarily insure aggressive patrol; it might, in fact, insure more recklessness and unproductiveness.

Another objection to the one-man car is that the officer cannot possibly drive a car and observe at the same time. On the contrary, no studies have shown that when there are two men in the car observation is increased or improved. The one-man car operation demands that the officer be more observant rather than less.

In the final analysis, the selection of the one-man or the two-man car is one needing study and review. The patrol administrator must necessarily take into consideration the safety of the officer.

Success of the One-man Car

For the one-man operation to be successful, standard operating procedures should be written and published. Procedures should be applied locally, but certain principles can be applied to all one-man car operations, such as: (1) team effort between dispatcher and officer; in the car, the officer must let the dispatcher know what he is doing (e.g., when stopping a vehicle, inform the dispatcher of the tag number and the location of the stop). The dispatcher should attempt to give the one-man car officer as much information as possible about an assignment. (2) The one-man patrol car officer should know the beat and for the most part stay within the boundaries, understand the part played by the dispatcher regarding his own safety, and respond only in the direction "of" rather than "to" a call given to the officer on an adjoining beat. He should stay within his own beat, ready to strike, always alert, and at the most appropriate location.

Finally, the administrator must consider the supporting services necessary to sustain the increase of vehicles to provide one-man car service. Only after conducting a manpower-workload analysis and considering resources can the final decision be made. If done on a need basis, the administrator can feel confident of a proper decision.

TWO-MAN CAR

There is justification for two-man vehicles. Factors to consider have been stated previously under the one-man car operation. The patrol administrator should not be limited to the use of two-man cars when the situation indicates a need for more officers. Intelligence gathering becomes a significant factor under certain conditions relative to assignment of manpower to a particular beat.

For example, information received by a patrol commander that after a demonstration, one of his officers would be surprised and attacked; also, if he resisted too much, he might even be killed. Assessment of the information is so very important because from the intelligence, a decision must be made on manpower assignment. If the intelligence is accurate and the time can be pinpointed, it's not too difficult to make effective decisions. If the approximate time of the alleged attack is not available, then your decision becomes more difficult. Factors to be considered in this situation are: manpower available, manpower flexibility: Should you supply two men to the beat involved? Should you supply two men to each adjacent beat? Should a supervisor ride with the beat officer involved? What additional equipment should they carry, if any? If a shotgun is selected, should it be carried openly? Questions such as these must be answered by the patrol administrator. The best answer is a decision based upon need, conditions, and most important, the safety of all officers concerned. The ability to be flexible, being an asset developed by the patrol administrator, would provide any resource necessary to resolve the problem. The solution may be a three-man car for a given period of time; if so, the administrator should be willing to make this decision.

Officer Safety

No discussion of patrol and the use of one-man vs. two-man patrol can be concluded without reviewing what has happened in the past relative to the safety of police officers. The patrol administrator must never forget the time when he was a patrolman. He must always be aware of what was most important to him then. Knowledge by the patrol officer that his leaders have painstakingly researched the criteria involved in deciding on the selection of the type of patrol cannot be relegated to a low position on the rung of priorities. The impression that the officer's safety has been considered rings loud and clear in the minds of patrol officers.

A review of the history of officers killed in the police field reveals significant facts that the administrator should be aware of. These facts indicate areas of concern for the patrol administrator, especially where the need for increased training is shown. If by emphasizing a particular police technique an officer's life may be saved, the emphasis placed is well worth the review of statistics and the appropriate follow-up to attain the objective of less fatalities. If more officers are killed when attempting to take a person into custody, then the inspection process by line commanders of proper arrest techniques should be first priority. Nothing is more important to the patrol officer than his life.

Officer Deaths

A total of 126 law-enforcement officers were killed in the United States due to felonious criminal action in 1971. This is an increase over 1970 when 100 law-enforcement officers were slain. During the ten-year period 1962–71, 722 officers were killed. The average number of law-enforcement officers slain was 72 a year during the period 1962–71. Specifically, there were 48 officers killed in 1962; 55 in 1963; 57 in 1964; 53 in 1965; 57 in 1966; 76 in 1967; 64 in 1968; 86 in 1969; 100 in 1970; 126 in 1971; and 112 in 1972.[3]

Circumstances Surrounding Deaths

Examination of circumstances under which police officers were murdered in 1971 continues to disclose a most urgent need for officers to be more alert in connection with all their duties, regardless of how routine these duties may have been in the past. It is essential that officers be extremely alert with all individuals whom they contact. No arrest situation can be considered as routine as evidenced by the fact that during the period 1962–71 more officers were killed attempting arrests than in any other matter. During 1971, 22 officers were killed attempting arrests for crimes other than robbery or burglary. Twenty-five officers were slain by persons they encountered during the commission of a robbery, whom they were pursuing as robbery suspects. In connection with the crime of burglary 7 officers were killed at the scene of the burglary or while pursuing burglary suspects.[4]

What is most important to the patrol administrator is indicated by Chart I of the FBI Uniform Crime Report, 1972, page 43. This indicates that most officers are killed while attempting other arrests. An analysis of reports within each department indicates the number of arrests that fall in this category. These arrest reports provide information pertaining to the number of officers injured or those who may have been killed due to improper techniques of arrest. In effect, the patrol commander would perform a similar analysis of his patrol command as that done by the FBI to indicate its position relative to the national trend. Additionally, whatever conclusions were drawn from the analysis of the facts could be disseminated throughout the field listing areas of special concern for each situation and officer. An awareness of the potential for injury or death by activity would be most beneficial to the officer.

It was suggested in Chapter 1 that policing would become more professional by following the methods used by Vince Lombardi of the Green Bay Packers. This point is exemplified in reviewing these statistics on the arrest techniques and situations with regard to law-enforcement officers being killed. Refining the officer's task and the procedures used in attempting to accomplish his mission is most important. Expertise in methods of patrol and arrest techniques can contribute to a decrease in the number of officers killed. In an ambush situation, officers' lives will be taken because of an inability to prevent this type of an operation. However, detailed analysis and review of actual incidents could make them aware of the atmosphere conducive to possible ambush and would provide some training. Better preparation should result in a decrease in the number of officers killed in the line of duty.

Hour of Day

Chart 2 of the FBI Uniform Crime Reports 1972, (page 47) gives the hours of the day law-enforcement officers were killed. An analysis of this chart indicates information that could be disseminated to officers in the field. It shows that of a total of 615 officers killed nationally, 388 were killed between the hours of 7:00 P.M. and 3:00 A.M. This means that almost two-thirds of the officers killed in the nation were killed during that eight-hour span. An analysis of this information in conjunction with the analysis of information pertaining to the activity would then become more significant to the officers in the field. It would reveal that they should be more careful between these hours and when performing those tasks that have a greater degree of possibility for their injury or death.

Chart 3 (ibid., p. 48) indicates the number of law-enforcement officers killed by type of assignment between the years 1962 and 1971. It is rather obvious that the number of officers killed in two-man vehicles between the hours of 4:00 P.M. and 8:00 A.M. is greatest. The relationship of this chart and similar statistics from the individual departments would indicate an explanation to the officers involved when the selection of one-man versus two-man vehicles is being considered.

FOOT AND AUTO COMBINATION

There are two combinations of patrol games that can be played: one by the two-man car; the other, by a one-man car with a foot beat included. In the former, the manpower-workload study has indicated a beat should be a two-man car operation. Statistics indicate a need for increased preventive patrol of a given location within this two-man beat. One way to accomplish this preventive patrol would be to make two one-man cars out of this one two-man car, yet maintain the essential feature of the two-man car concept.

Intelligent and informed officers would resist the change of a two-man car to a one-man car or even two one-man cars if done arbitrarily and without explanation. Patrol administrators should handle this patrol responsibility using participatory management. Benefits may accrue that might not be possible ordinarily. Including personnel in the decision-making process is most important when attempting to implement change. In this case, the officers involved were consulted and the procedure was explained, ample time was provided to offer suggestions and, finally, agreement was reached to give it a try. The commander must emphasize the fact that, whatever the outcome, he will be responsible for any negative accusations that might be made by the citizens. (A potential exists for reduced response by both cars.) The procedure consists of:

1. Defining the area (concentrated) needing more preventive patrol located within a two-man beat.
2. Stating the objective of the procedure to the officers and supervisors involved.
3. Determining the call numbers of the now two one-man cars; e.g. 911 and 911A (This procedure is the only one involving this type of call number which distinguishes the method being used.)
4. Reviewing together the areas and category of crime (*robbery* [purse snatching, etc.]), *burglary* [commercial-dwelling]) by time of day—day of week and location.
5. Determining ahead of time the way the area will be patrolled (random saturation) or whether each officer shall allot a given time for coverage of the area; e.g., one-car—hour to half-hour, two car—half-hour to hour.
6. In no case will either officer respond to a call for service without the other.
7. If for any reason (lunch, personal) one officer is out of service, so is the other.
8. If an on-view situation occurs, the officer observing will call the other before taking action. (The second car will not have anything delaying response and in most cases will not be more than a few streets away.)
9. Set up a procedure for a careful analysis of crime prior to, during, and after the use of the combination-team effort.
10. Insure the officers that the deployment is temporary and is being attempted to resolve a problem. After the problem has been resolved, the traditional two-man car will be reinstated. This is necessary and

will be accepted. Officers realize the reasons why cars are two-man. They will accept this procedure knowing it is being done for a reason and on a need basis. If trust and credibility are not included, the innovation will fail.

11. Advise the communications personnel of the procedure and describe to the dispatcher his important role in accomplishing the objective.
12. Document and commend as appropriate all concerned after the goal has been reached.

A similar team effort is employed between the one-man car operation and the foot officer. Coverage of a given area where high incidents of crime occur can be done by time and location. When prevention has not worked, a game of apprehension can be implemented. An officer working a foot beat can make himself obvious at the other end of the beat. The perpetrator, thinking he is clear to commit his crime, does not realize the one-man car officer has taken a position of surveillance and possibly has received help from his supervisor who would cover an escape route. As a result, the perpetrator is caught in the act of committing the crime.

A game of inspection of police hazards between the foot officer and the one-man car officer can be played by breaking up the hour into time segments and having each responsible for a part of the hour. For example, the car officer will be responsible from the hour to quarter past and from the half-hour to quarter of the hour. The foot officer would be responsible for a given location from quarter past to the half-hour and from quarter of the hour to the hour. This rotation can be changed anytime they agree, by the day or during the watch. In this example, whatever time an offense occurred, the officer responsible would have to justify why it occurred and why he didn't make the arrest.

CANINE

The use of dogs as a method of supporting the patrol officer and becoming part of a canine team has been accepted by enlightened police administrators. Some police departments have canine units with their special operations or tactical divisions, and some departments use the service of canines on a need basis.

The use of canine teams on patrol depends on the need and evaluation by the patrol administrator as to the dividends received from applying such patrol to a given area or situation. Police dogs are used in preventive patrol, crowd control, security of buildings, building searches, trailing escaped convicts, detecting crimes, locating marijuana, explosives, and missing persons. Several types of dogs are used in police work around the world: German shepherds, bloodhounds, Labradors, and Doberman pinschers. Of these, more departments use the German shepherd than any other type of police dog. The State of Georgia has used bloodhounds for years, for the sole purpose of apprehending escaped convicts. Many police departments in the United States use canine teams. Some of these are Baltimore, Maryland; Washington, D.C.; St. Louis, Missouri; Jefferson County, Kentucky; Philadelphia, Pennsylvania; Atlanta, Georgia; Miami, Florida; and Chicago, Illinois. However, the canine unit in Atlanta has been discontinued as of January 1, 1973.

Some departments, such as Los Angeles, California, lease dogs to provide security for selected facilities. Additionally, some departments have assigned a limited number of canine teams on a permanent basis to special units, such as the Scientific Investigation Unit, for the purpose of detecting marijuana and explosives.

The St. Louis, Missouri, Police Department began using police dogs in October 1958. Officers of the department were sent to London, England, for training and handling of dogs for police service. After review and analysis, the German shepherd was selected as the most practical for all-around police work. Police dogs are either purchased or received as a gift from citizens. Training is accomplished by the in-house training school, and any other location deemed appropriate for the team, and locate for fourteen weeks initially. In-service training is given in the amount of one training day for each twenty-one day period. The recommended number of teams to be trained at one time is five, and no more than six (see Figure 2.3).

Applicant requesting to become canine officer should possess the following qualifications:

1. Below the age of forty
2. Three years experience as a police officer
3. Agreement of wife that he join that branch of police service
4. Agreement of wife to house the dog at home
5. Own or be buying a home (or rent from relative, with assurance that he will not have to move)
6. Permission of neighbors living adjacent to applicant's home

After selection, the officer is given a dog, preferably his own choice. Instruction is usually divided into three parts: (1) obedience,

FIGURE 2.3   St. Louis, Missouri, Police Canine Training Service. Photo courtesy of Jefferson County Police Department, Jefferson County, Kentucky.

(2) development of scenting powers, and (3) criminal training. The dog selected should have a good sense of hearing, a good sense of smell, be mobile in that he can traverse complex terrain, possess intelligence, and most important of all, be persistent. Course teams are assigned to the Tactical Deployment Division and are used for tracking problems, locating missing persons, building search, chase of fleeing criminals, crowd control, scent for evidence at scenes of crimes, scent for marijuana and explosives, and regular motorized and foot patrol.

Consideration is also given to the duties of the handlers, duties of handlers while the dog is ill or unfit for duty, responsibilities of handlers regarding sickness, and vacation.

Officers are issued the following equipment: kennel or doghouse at handler's home, ordinary leather lead (quick release type), choke collar (chain), choke collar (leather), tracking line (twenty feet long), and harness or collar, currycomb, water bucket, feed bowl, scrub brush and handle. Veterinary services and food are provided by the department.

As of 1972, the Baltimore City Police Department had more than forty canine teams. The canine unit is assigned to the tactical section of the patrol division. The unit is supervised by a lieutenant and provides service to the department on a twenty-four-hour basis. Officers are assigned to foot beats around the clock (Shift 1—2400 to 0800, Shift 2—0800 to 1600, Shift 3—1600 to 2400). These foot beats are usually in the business areas of the city. Other selected foot and motorized canine beats are assigned on a measured proportional need basis where maximum use of their special capabilities occur. One additional duty for the canine teams is the assignment of canine teams to the business area of any city for protection against glass breaking and looting during riots, large demonstrations, or when large numbers of youths attend rock concerts in the downtown district. An additional consideration for the latter situation is the removal ahead of time of all articles (such as trash cans, rocks, debris) that could be used to break windows.

Most of the selection, training, and assignments included in the St. Louis Police Department are also considered in the Baltimore Department. The Baltimore Department also uses psychological testing for the officers and the animal. The psychological test for the dog attempts to determine if it is gun shy and if it is aggressive with built-in protection. Psychological testing for the handler determines if the handler has a primary love for animals, an even temperament, is amiable to the smell and other small annoyances of working with an animal for a tour of duty. Any deficiency in these areas is cause for refusal to enter the canine unit.

LONDON METROPOLITAN POLICE DEPARTMENT: DOG SECTION

As long ago as the fifteenth century, parish constables patrolled with dogs, but the dogs were probably used more for companionship than for police work. Between the two World Wars, police forces in Britain experimented with various breeds of dogs; some trained for tracking and some for patrol and criminal work. It was thought that dogs must be specialists, but experience has since shown that the right type of dog can be trained as an all-rounder. The only specialized dogs at present are the narcotic-detection dogs.

In 1938 the London Metropolitan Police experimented with two Labrador retrievers, but in the absence of organized training the experiment proved of little value and had to be abandoned. In 1946 the worth of dogs as an aid to the Metropolitan Police was again explored, and towards the end of that year six dogs were purchased, Labradors again. This time the dogs and handlers were given a thorough training course before being posted to patrol duty.

A number served in Central London and achieved spectacular success in Hyde Park, where the crime of handbag-stealing was practically eliminated. Successes like this and a number of arrests in divisions as a result of tracking, searching for, and pursuing criminals, encouraged the increased use of dogs throughout the whole of the Metropolitan Police District.

The 7.90 square miles covered by the Metropolitan Police District varies in character from open country to the closely built-up streets of Central London and includes housing estates, commercial areas, warehouses, docks, public gardens, and parks. The use of dogs has been developed to meet the varying police problems in such areas.

The number of successes achieved by police dogs has risen each year, and more and more cases have been brought to a successful conclusion through the work of the dog itself, particularly in the area of tracking and searching buildings and open spaces.

Breeds

The German shepherd is accepted by police trainers throughout the world as the best all-purpose dog at present available for training. Experiments at the larger training establishments during the last twenty years have shown that no other breed surpasses, and rarely equals, the German shepherd for police-dog duties.

The preference of police trainers for these dogs does not by any means exclude the use of other breeds. An individual dog of a breed not favored as a whole is frequently trained up to the working standard required of a police dog. Among these are the Doberman, Rottweiler, boxer, Airedale, and the Labrador retriever. The latter are used both as normal patrol dogs and also for security at the royal residences. Since 1965 four Labradors have been trained to detect concealed drugs and have been most successful in finding drugs hidden in sealed tins, plastic containers and bags, drawers, and cupboards, and in other places. It is the dog most widely used by this force after the German shepherd.

The problems of finding enough suitable dogs to meet a growing demand led in 1960 to the introduction of selective breeding from proved working stock. Seven bitches and three dogs were purchased by the Metropolitan Police and from their blood lines, by selective breeding, a number of dogs of fine physique and firm temperament have been bred. During whelping the bitches and their puppies are cared for in a modern breeding block situated at the Dog Training Establishment at Keston in Kent. From the age of three months the puppies live at the homes of their handlers getting used to rural and urban surroundings. This "home" life is important as a dog conditioned only to the kennel and the show ring will generally fall short of police requirements.

Many dogs come from the public, either as a gift or by purchase. These dogs, which are preferably between the ages of ten and eighteen months, are kept at the Training Establishment for approximately one to three weeks in order to assess their health and working capabilities. If found satisfactory, they are allocated to a handler who, after a short course of instruction, takes the dog to his home to begin a period of familiarization. This period is essential in creating a feeling of trust and understanding between dog and handler before serious training is undertaken. Bitches are not generally accepted unless they are of exceptionally good stock and their blood lines show that they will help with selective breeding program.

Perhaps the most important quality in a dog for police purposes is its acute sense of smell, which is used equally well by day or night, for tracking on ground scent or scenting by air scent. Important, too, is a dog's acute hearing, which is attuned to sounds the human ear is incapable of receiving. These qualities are of great value in revealing the presence of individuals who would not otherwise be discovered.

Training

Metropolitan Police dogs and handlers, as well as those from some provincial and overseas forces, are trained at the Dog Training Establishment. Continuation training is carried out at five other centers situated within the Metropolitan Police District.

At three months of age, puppies bred at the Training Establishment are allocated to handlers to be "walked" in the Division where their handlers are stationed; at the age of nine months they receive a week's course in elementary obedience and nosework; and when they are a year old, they attend a basic fourteen-week training course. Dogs and their handlers are trained in small classes consisting of not more than six dogs with the emphasis on individual tuition.

Obedience is essential in any police dog and more advanced exercises are not introduced into training until the dog is fully obedient in the general sense. Elementary agility and manwork, which are stimulating to the dog, are introduced at an early stage of training, as it has been found that a judicious mixture of working exercises keeps the dog active and alert and prevents boredom.

When obedience is established, the dogs are introduced to tracking by following a ground scent, the distance and age of which is progressively increased. They are then taught to search by day and night, in open country, wooded areas, and various types of buildings, for hidden criminals or property and to give tongue when they find what they are seeking—this is especially important if the handler is some distance away—and are also taught to chase and stop a running criminal firmly but without aggressiveness.

It is vital that the benefits gained during the basic-training course should be developed and extended so dogs and handlers attend continuation training at frequent intervals at the training centers previously mentioned.

Much of the success in training dogs for police purposes depends on the handler. He must be a dog lover, be able to show extreme tolerance toward the dog, have infinite patience .and understanding, and be able to appreciate the known instincts of the dog. He must know the characteristics of his dog and how to apply these to police tasks. He is also expected to show a degree of initiative and be able to work with the minimum of supervision.

Dog-training and operational duties are physically arduous. The handlers, therefore, must be fit and active, especially when called upon to follow the dog who is tracking or chasing over difficult terrain. The dog's agility and special qualities would be wasted if the handler were unable to take advantage of his dog's efforts.

Duties

Dogs normally patrol for at least seven hours a day, working early, late, or night shifts. Another hour a day is allowed for feeding, grooming and exercising. A dog's real value is as a deterrent and to detect crime, but this is only achieved when on patrol and not held in reserve awaiting emergencies. The way dogs are used necessarily depends on the area to be policed: whether it is urban or rural. In the former, dogs patrol near vulnerable premises; while in rural areas, they patrol near a strategic point where they can be quickly contacted. In recent years this system has been extended and greater use is now made of groups of dogs and handlers on special patrols to combat a particular policing problem. Where "unit" policing schemes are in operation (where a group of police officers is responsible for policing an area instead of individual officers patrolling fixed beats), the dog and handler teams have been superimposed on these units and are available to work with the unit wherever they will be of most use. The issue of personal radios to officers has meant a more efficient use of police dogs, and the increased use of wireless-equipped vans to patrol and transport dogs and handlers has added to their operational efficiency. Dogs can be conveyed quickly to the scenes of crimes, to places where rowdyism is likely, or to any place where there is a need for their services.

> In addition to patrolling, searching, chasing, and tracking criminals, dogs are used for recovering stolen property which has been abandoned and for finding missing persons. The scope of properly trained and handled police dogs is likely to be extended with further experience based on continuing experiments in new methods of deployment.[5]

In conclusion, the use of the canine team should depend upon the need of the protected locality. Positive and negative aspects should be considered, and the decision based on the best method of patrol for the solution of the problem and the attainment of the objective.

HELICOPTER PATROL

In 1967 the first symposium on Law Enforcement, Science, and Technology was held at the Illinois Institute of Technology. The objective of this symposium was to get the three areas to work together in order to have the scientific community inject innovation and thought, and the technological community produce end products for law enforcement. The helicopter and its application to police patrol has reached the point where evaluation of its use is possible and practicable and holds forth great expectations. The helicopter is a development of science and technology; the third area, law enforcement, is now making use of this tool.

A history of the use of aircraft in police service is not necessary here since it deals in generalities. Our objectives can be met by dealing specifically with the helicopter as a patrol resource. The Los Angeles County Sheriff's Office in 1955 joined the New York City Police Department in using helicopters directed primarily at water patrol and rural inaccessible areas. The border patrol, state highway patrols, and state police use aircraft helicopters for traffic enforcement, athletic events, parades, and disturbances.

Project "Sky-Knight" was the code name for a project that was to determine if the concept of using helicopters for routine police patrol was feasible. This was a joint venture between the Los Angeles County Sheriff's Department, the Aircraft Division, Hughes Tool Company, and the Law Enforcement Assistance Administration. The location of the project was Lakewood, California, which had experienced a crime increase between 1961 and 1965 of 42%.[6]

Helicopter patrol was applied to a mesh effect combining alternately East to West, then North to South, patterns with particular attention given to high-hazards major offense areas. The time of the patrol utilized was 10:00 A.M. to 6:00 P.M. and 6:00 P.M to 2:00 A.M. The first year's results showed a decrease of major crimes by 8%.[7]

To further evaluate the concept, Sheriff Pitchess removed two patrol cars from each of two shifts, day and evening, for a four-month period. The audited cost of helicopter patrol was $65,333. Savings through deletion of two ground units was $42,265. The quantity of work did not decrease, arrests were 63% higher in the test months and total cases handled were 32% higher.[8]

The Lakewood officials conducted a public survey. The public gave overwhelming approval to the project, 94% wanted the project continued, and they were willing to support the continuance with a tax increase.[9] At this time the Los Angeles County Sheriff's Department has extended their helicopter fleet to almost thirty helicopters.

Many other police agencies throughout the country are now utilizing helicopters for routine patrol. It is, in fact, one of the methods of patrol that many police administrators and patrol administrators have in dealing with specific problems and situations. The selection of this type of patrol for a given type of situation necessarily means planning and analyzing to insure maximum return on your investment.

The Kansas City, Missouri, Police Department and the Baltimore, Maryland, Police Department are two of many who are applying helicopter patrol to specific crime areas, responding to calls for service in minimum time and, all in all, gaining the many by-products of service for their communities through helicopter patrol. There are many similarities between departments that use helicopter patrol in the areas of selection, training, patrol assignments, and use of accessories.

Selection and Training

Officers applying to be a helicopter pilot in the Kansas City Police Department must have fifteen years of service remaining with the department, have at least five years of experience, excellent general physical conditions, and vision of 20/100 correctable to at least 20/20, and have the ability to distinguish color signals red, green, and white. The Baltimore Department selects an individual who has already shown an ability to fly helicopters and usually has hundreds of hours of flight time. (For example, one of the first helicopter pilots had approximately 2,700 hours flight time, mostly in combat.) In this case, the individual hired will then proceed on through the police training academy and after graduation is assigned to the helicopter unit. During the academy training, experience on patrol is gained by the future pilot in order to help him relate to the ground forces in a more knowledgeable way when he begins piloting a helicopter on his regular assignments.

Officers are required to submit information concerning their background and interest in flying, application and utilization of the helicopter in police patrol, and their ideas and goals for the future of helicopter patrol.

The next step is the convening of an oral board. The oral board conducts examinations and interviews to select the individuals. Officers selected must pass the Federal Aviation Administration physical examination given by a Federal Aviation Administration approved flight surgeon. Selected personnel are then placed in temporary trainee status until a private pilot's license is obtained.

Observation officers are selected from within the patrol unit in a fair and equitable procedure. Assignment is for sixty days, during which time an officer must demonstrate the ability to complete the observation officers' training course. Initial training includes (1) flight orientation of one hour; (2) visual acuity testing and training for three hours; (3) geography, high-rise obstacles, contact points, safety corridors, etc. for one hour; (4) preventive helicopter maintenance for one hour; (5) accessories-equipment training for one hour; (6) communications training for thirty minutes; and (7) specialized report-writing for thirty minutes. Training for the pilots comes under the Federal Aviation Agency Requirements.

Preacquisition Planning and Justification

As in any other major purchase for a police department, planning is most important in order to effect a smooth operation. The Kansas City Police Department identified their work, prior to the purchase of helicopter, as Project 67 after the operational demonstration during the International Association of Chiefs of Police convention in 1969 at Kansas City, Missouri. The pilots, helicopters, and logistics were provided by the Aircraft Division of Hughes Tool Company. The project lasted ten days and some of the results were: (1) Response to calls for service was the number one priority. Final project report contains reference to innumerable incidents where the provided service was of great value. (2) Crime prevention. The crime category of the robbery and burglary were the specific targets. The time of day and area of city where these crimes were prevalent were established. A comparison of five days October 19–23 without the helicopter to the five days of October 26–30 with the use of the helicopter was made. There was a 21% decrease in these crime categories. Project 67 did not encompass the totality of acquisition planning and justification. For example, the city's 316.8 square miles can be patrolled by helicopter crew three times while the automobile accomplishes the same feat once. The airborne crews' observation capabilities are ten to one over ground patrol.[10]

In conclusion, all parts of the planning process must be developed into a helicopter program.

Helicopter Patrol Procedures

Analysis of crime by time of day and day of week and location as is done in manpower distribution must also be done for effective helicopter patrol. The primary and secondary functions need to be identified, i.e., response to calls for service, crime deterrent, preventive patrol, and apprehension. The evaluation criteria and the procedure to be used for evaluation must be stated. Additionally, how to obtain maximum use of helicopter patrol as it relates to each goal, how to use the natural advantages of the helicopter effectively, and the best way to coordinate the ground forces with the helicopter should be considered.

Response Calls

The following list of calls is not all-inclusive but it does include most situations where the helicopter will become involved. In most cases the helicopter will give assistance to the patrol forces in: arrests, car checks, pedestrian checks, building checks, area illumination, business-building roof inspection, stolen cars recovered, prowler calls, robbery calls, car chases, detection of fires, aerial surveillances, and traffic control.

If a patrol pattern is decided upon, a decision must be made as to when and under what conditions the helicopter patrol will leave the control zone and respond to one of the calls for service. In most cases, this decision is made by command, generally with allowance for emergency conditions. In this case, usually the observer would make the decision.

City X

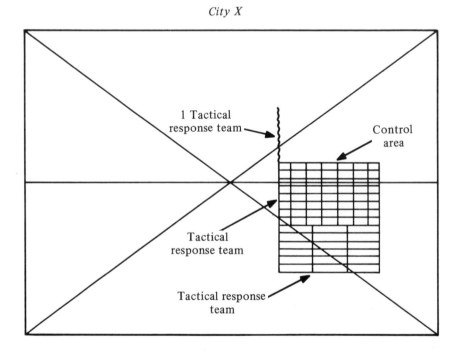

FIGURE 2.4 Helicopter patrol in control areas with tactical ground support.

Air-Ground Coordination

If a type of helicopter patrol is used that necessitates the coordination between the helicopter and tactical ground units (Figure 2.4), several considerations should be resolved: (1) Will the helicopter and the tactical response team work in the same area? (2) If the helicopter and the tactical response team(s) do work in the same area, will they both give coverage in the same subarea at the same time or at different times? If they do not work the same area at the same time, will it be necessary to cover that area with a tactical team, or would it go uncovered during the time the helicopter is away from the control areas? All personnel involved must be briefed so that the decisions can be understood by everyone, and a maximum utilization of each unit will take place.

Where helicopter patrol is used without tactical and ground support (Figure 2.5), then the officers working the control areas as a matter of daily routine must be notified. Middle management, research and development (Crime Analysis Units), and helicopter command

City X

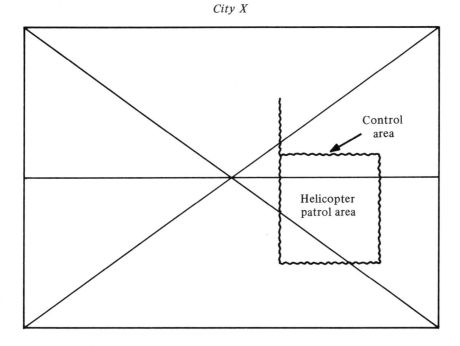

FIGURE 2.5   Helicopter patrol in control areas without tactical
ground support.

should meet to determine time of day, day of week, location of crime, and potential patterns of helicopter patrol. If prevention is primary, then the helicopter must patrol, by order of priority and crime hazard, the area where crime has been prevalent. For example, if robbery and burglary are primary concerns, then the location and time of the crimes must be recorded and the patrol patterns of the helicopter must be such that it patrols that area at the times indicated. The ground officers must know of the pattern in order to coordinate the efforts as a total team.

In many police departments, the call numbers of the beat cars are placed on the vehicles in a way so that the helicopter observer could advise car 10A to go North one block and West two blocks to intercept suspects who may have just committed a crime. Without this identification and communication, the effort will be less than sufficient.

Patterns of Patrol

The first pattern of patrol, mentioned earlier, was the mesh pattern where the helicopter patrol was North and South and then East and West. The mesh pattern can be used for a specific type of patrol as well as a specific type of search. The second type of search would be similar to the concentric circle search where the pilot would fly to the place of occurrence of the crime and then make a 360° turn. From there he would enlarge the perimeter in a systematic search pattern. The limits of the circle searched will be judged by the information available concerning the suspects and potential route and method of escape. Every conceivable type of search is available from the helicopter and, in some instances, information from the ground forces will guide the movement of the helicopter and the method to be used for the particular search. Two points should be made: (1) safety first, and (2) the slower the pilot makes the flight, the better the search. Additionally, if two helicopters are used for the search, coordination is imperative.

Assistance from Personnel Manning the Helicopter

There may come a time when it will be necessary for the observer of the helicopter to become the assisting officer, as in the case of a one-man car operation and where the observer acts as the back-up car. If this occurs, the pilot, because of safety factors, shall have the discretion concerning the decision to land. If the decision is made to land and assist, the pilot must insure that the aircraft is secure. Only in the case of imminent physical danger to one of the other officers should the pilot leave the aircraft. This is not likely since the helicopter will usually be working in conjunction with several ground units, especially in municipal law-enforcement agencies. If the situation occurs in rural areas, then the procedure stated above should be followed. Operation of the helicopter when responding to all types of calls and the procedure to be used should be in writing.

Riot, Rescue, and Flood Operation. If the helicopter is assigned to civil disorder, flood, or rescue operations, two pilots should be assigned. The helicopter should have dual controls as a precaution against crash if one pilot is injured or incapacitated.

Landing Sites. Landing sites should be preselected and approved. Dissemination of these sites to the appropriate personnel would improve the total operation.

The Helicopter

There are several companies that produce a variety of models that can be used for patrol service. Among these are the Bell 47 G4A, Hughes 300, Bell 47G2, and supercharged Bell Model 47s. The department should base its decision regarding the purchase of any helicopter upon "operational requirements." The following are some of the points to be reviewed.

1. What are the budget restrictions?
2. Is there a requirement for small, medium, and large helicopters?
3. Is there a helicopter that could be all-purpose? In other words, is there a helicopter made to handle all tasks?
4. What is the weight limitation?
5. What is the fuel load?
6. How much flight time will be received from the particular helicopter?
7. What is the refueling time?
8. Will size affect the uses? (You may have a need to fly into small areas.)
9. What type of powered helicopter gives best service at the best cost?
10. What is the rate ratio between speed, cost, and service?
11. What are the maintenance costs?
12. What is the initial cost and the amount of depreciation by year?

These considerations are not all-inclusive but they give some idea of the amount of planning necessary before purchasing a helicopter.

Communication

The helicopter patrol is usually equipped with two radios. One is the regular police communications-system radio that has the ability to communicate with all patrol areas and a city-wide band. This allows the helicopter patrol to communicate to a ground unit no matter where the helicopter is assigned just by switching to their respective patrol area. The city-wide frequency usually entails operations during emergency conditions and automatically makes the helicopter available for riots, demonstrations, etc. The second radio affords the helicopter communication between itself and the airport and other aircraft. The helicopter should also have a loud-speaker system, a siren, and illumination capability. Depending on operational requirements, armor and stretcher-bearing equipment (hoist) should be considered. (There may be a fire in a hotel with people trapped on high floors. The helicopter would rescue many individuals with the hoist and stretcher-bearing capability.)

Advantage of the Helicopter Patrol

The major advantage of the helicopter patrol is being able to observe incidents and situations from the air much more quickly and therefore being able to respond in minimum time. Officers in the air have a much broader view of an area than ground units. Because of this view, they are able to direct ground units and increase the possibility of successfully completing the mission. In unusual conditions, the helicopter patrol is able to see possible attackers that the ground officers may not see and thus increase the safety factor for the ground units.

Business/Community Relationships

Although it may be difficult for the observer to know the exact number of persons in a vehicle and to give license numbers, individual identification can be made by the type and color of clothing, sex and age group, and race. Usually individual house numbers are almost impossible to identify, but general areas and locations can be determined. Several police departments around the country have set up code numbers for moving vehicles to be identified. For example, in one department, the trucks belonging to a certain wholesale liquor business, which is subject to hijacking, have letter and number combination so that they are easy to spot from the air. Additionally, the color of the truck is added to the code combination to improve identification. Any business having trucks that have a high probability of being hijacked are invited to join the program.

Kansas City, Missouri; Washington, D.C.; Seattle, Washington; Los Angeles County and Los Angeles, California, and many other state and local police agencies are doing this quite successfully.

Marking house numbers on the roofs of buildings has also increased the potential for the helicopter to respond faster to a call for service. One suggestion is to paint bricks with white luminous paint so they can be seen by day and night. Another suggestion is to have the numbers spelled out on a slant (45° angle), which makes for easier reading. Another reason for using painted bricks is to decrease the possibility of heavy winds blowing the numbers from the roof. These numbers on rooftops can be identified from as far away as one and one-quarter miles if they are 4' × 6'. Other recommendations are numbers 5" × 30" with a 6" separation.

Studies should be conducted in using sirens or some other electronic device placed on the roofs of buildings at strategic locations that could guide helicopters to their points and could be used for locating more specific action. This would enhance the night potential of the helicopter. Presently, the helicopter must look for the radio car at a specific location in order to determine where the incident is taking place. Since the use of personal radios is on the increase around the country, there is a need for increasing training in the area of communication by the officers. In this case, officers will not find it necessary to return to their vehicles in order to talk to the helicopter patrol; therefore, it will be necessary to know how to direct the helicopter in terms they both understand (e.g., "go one-half block West from radio car #505, turn North and you will observe," etc.). An officer from Memphis, Tennessee, Police Department reported the helicopter spotted a suspect hiding under a bush during the 1968 disturbances, indicating the great potential for surveillance. This leads one to believe that the best escape from the helicopter would be to remain still, if that is possible.

The helicopter is a tremendous asset in times of surveillance of professional criminals who may be nervous or difficult to follow and spot. Preplanning with the ground units is essential, since the ground units wish to be unobserved and the need for coordination is rather obvious.

Snipers, Ambush, Barricaded Persons

With the advent of snipers, ambush, and barricaded persons, and the increase of such incidents over the last few years, the helicopter has proved to be a tremendous and valuable tool. The situation that occurred in a southern city where person(s) had gone to the roof and were sniping, has shown the value of the helicopter patrol. This incident, I am sure, has shown other departments throughout the country the need for aerial photographs that can be taken by the helicopter patrol. This act of planning may save the lives of many persons in the future.

Missing Persons

Missing persons, especially children, have been located sooner than ordinarily possible by using the helicopter. This is because of the noise made by the engines and loud-speaker system of helicopters used for this procedure. Most parents should identify the police helicopter as an extension of the officer on the beat so they will have the proper relationships between children, the police, and the police helicopter.

Crowd Control

Experience has shown the use of the helicopter for crowd control to be of great value. Being able to direct ground units, having a total picture of athletic events, parades, demonstrations, or mini-riots provides assistance in the following areas: (1) saves manpower; (2) utilizes each squad and patrolman to the maximum; (3) improves traffic flow; (4) increases accuracy of crowd estimates; (5) improves decision-making; (6) allows for immediate intelligent planning; (7) allows observation of splinter groups who may break off from the main group of disruptors and cause trouble (which means you are able to relay this information to ground forces who are then able to move in immediately and prevent disruptions and personal and property damage); (8) lets you maintain constant surveillance of previously identified leaders who disrupted groups who may have slipped ground surveillance; (9) gives the chief of the department immediate, accurate coverage of the situation at the command and control center within the headquarters buildings not only for his information, but for the other selected and appointed officials of government as appropriate.

Operational Examples

The following are examples of actual helicopter operations in different departments throughout the country. The department will not be named because each incident could have occurred in most of the departments mentioned. In one agency the helicopter received a radio lookout message identifying purse-snatchers who were riding in an automobile. In searching the area the helicopter located the wanted vehicle. Its location and direction of travel were relayed to ground units and intercepting ground units were placed in the proper position and cut-off points. The occupants of the vehicle then discarded the vehicle and attempted to escape on foot. The direction and travel of these suspects was relayed to ground units. Locations where several of the suspects were hidden was also relayed and the total observation and cooperation/coordination process was successful, resulting in arrest of the suspects.

In another document, reports were given to the helicopter and patrol when a holdup had taken place. A broadcast was put out indicating the suspect to be driving a particular car. In their concentric-circle search the vehicle was observed. A position was given to ground units and the arrest was made. This arrest would not have been made because of the distance from the scene if only ground units had been looking for the vehicle. Another department reports the holdup of a jewelry store: the suspect fled in a vehicle, abandoned the vehicle, and then fled on foot. The helicopter was able to keep the suspect under observation even though he went under bridges, across streams, and through fields where ground units were not able to follow immediately. The suspect hid under a clump of bushes and not only was he arrested, but the observer in the helicopter was able to state where the suspect had dropped his hat, his coat, and some of the articles taken from the jewelry store.

Evaluation of Helicopter Patrol

As stated earlier, comparisons were made in crime rates in the Lakewood and Kansas City Projects that indicated there was a decrease in crime. It necessarily follows that an additional study must be done to include an evaluation of the crime rates of adjacent communities to see if the crime was displaced to other areas or if it was in fact reduced. This is the case in most studies done in police departments, and the in-depth analysis of such studies is very difficult in terms of the many variables involved. The adjacent areas, when analyzing an increase or decrease in crime, should be compared with areas where a new type of patrol has been implemented. An analysis of the two projects was done by Dr. Michael D. Maltz, program manager of mobility systems, the Center of Criminal Justice Operations and Management of the National Institute of Law Enforcement and Criminal Justice, LEAA, Washington, D.C., and reported in the April 1971 issue of the *Police Chief*. Dr. Maltz's report follows. The accompanying two examples (Figure 2.6) show how the helicopters are presently evaluated and how it is believed they should be evaluated. The first example is typical of the accounting found in most police departments' annual report. It gives the reader an idea of the effectiveness of a helicopter in countering robberies, but only a vague idea. It does not show how the effectiveness is related to the actions of a helicopter or the rest of the department. A second example is a more thorough evaluation of the role of the helicopter. First, the evaluation is based on the total number of calls for service which indicated robbery in progress, not on the number of cases in which the final classification of the incident was robbery.

> Most police resource allocation studies are based on the statistics of final classification of calls for service. To show why this is misleading, consider the following hypothetical example: A robbery alarm goes off in a liquor store and a police car rushes to the scene. The owner of the store comes out and apologizes to the policeman saying it must have been a false alarm, or it must have been tripped by accident. "But while you are here, could you take care of this drunk that's setting on my door step and bothering my customers?" Such a call is logged as drunk and disorderly in terms of final classification, yet the resource one police-patrol unit was allocated on the basis of robbery call.

Additionally, Dr. Maltz said, with all the present emphasis on reducing police-response time, it is difficult to find any police department that collects statistics with a view to determining usefulness of reduced response time. It would seem to be a fairly simple matter to assign a special code to the in-progress or other emergency calls and calculate the response time and other measures for those calls separately from the nonemergency calls. This type of data is crucial in assessing the value of air-mobility projects.

Dr. Maltz also points out that a comprehensive evaluation of a police air-mobility program has recently been prepared by the Los Angeles Police Department for the 1970 annual report of the heli-

1. _Present_ (As it might appear in a police department's annual report):
   In 1970, the police helicopters were instrumental in effecting three arrests of robbery suspects. This is a 50 percent increase over 1969.

2. _Proposed:_

Dispositions of 146 "Robbery in Progress" Calls

	Success, e.g., arrest	No success	False calls	
Helicopter used	3	17	24	Success rate using helicopter: $\frac{3}{20}$ = 15%
Helicopter not used	6	44	51	Success rate not using helicopter: $\frac{6}{50}$ = 12%

Helicopter not used because:
Not scheduled to fly at that time 21
Unscheduled maintenance 10
On another assignment 8
Pilot not available 4
Other 7
$\overline{50}$

Helicopter used unsuccessfully because:
Unable to locate suspects 8
Long time delay in getting to site 5
Other 4
$\overline{17}$

FIGURE 2.6 Two examples of helicopter evaluations.

copter section. Although Dr. Maltz's report and the annual report were prepared independently, many of the evaluations reported by Dr. Maltz are also incorporated in the Los Angeles Police Department report. They conclude that not only is such an evaluation useful, but it can be implemented practically by a police department. The point is that evaluations of any program are an important part of a total process. It points out the need for continued evaluations and innovations in the law-enforcement areas relating to helicopter patrol. The use of the helicopter patrol as a positive tool cannot be questioned. However, the effective use of it is something that needs time and study and experimentation—something that law enforcement needs more of. The inclusion of the scientific, technological, and academic communities in the total process of police work is good. If all areas become open and allow each to contribute to its fullest, the goal of having a better place to live in our country will be closer to attainment.

BICYCLE PATROL

Bicycle patrol has been and will continue to be a selected method of patrol. In managing by objectives, the goal should always be manifested as the end, and the means should always be a game of "anything goes" when applying specific patrol methods to crime problems. Whatever works best for preventing crime by category and area shall be the selected method. The patrol administrator need only have a willingness to innovate and participate intimately in solving problems by other than traditional ways.

European countries have used bicycles as a method of patrolling for years. Baltimore, Maryland, used bicycles as far back as 1915 when sixteen officers patrolled the northern areas of the city. As late as 1919 the bicycle patrol was increased to twenty-one patrolmen. Bicycles were used during World War II by the British.

In some ocean-front resorts, bicycles are used for patrolling the boardwalks in the late evening and early morning hours when fewer people are walking.

Recently an experiment was implemented in the Baltimore, Maryland, Police Department with bicycles. The philosophy of using what works best in selecting the proper patrol for a given problem was applied. One of the police districts was experiencing an increase in residential burglaries. Preventive and apprehensive patrol had not been successful using the conventional auto patrol, and foot patrol would not give the officer enough mobility to respond in time to increase the possibility of apprehension. Additionally, the alleys in the rear of the homes were too narrow for the patrol car to maneuver. Since the suggested solution contained ingredients of all the advantages of foot patrol plus mobility, bicycle patrol was selected as the method of patrol for decreasing the crime.

Several aspects of the selection process came into focus: the officer, bicycle, size of beat, number of hours, storage of bicycle, training, additional equipment, maintenance, and changing shifts.

Officer

After reviewing many types of bicycles, the Schwinn 5-speed English racer was selected. The 5-speed type gave the officer enough speed without fatigue for patrol. Also, it had the necessary attachments for placing needed equipment.

Beat Size

The size of the beat had to be determined so as to obtain maximum effectiveness. Analyzing the crime by time of day, day of week, etc., it was decided that a six-block straight-away beat would produce the desired results. The area selected had experienced such a high incidence of burglaries and robberies it warranted a specific resolution. The officers were to work the front and rear of both sides of the street. The size was small enough for concentrated patrol and large enough for diversion to reduce boredom.

Number of Hours

Analysis of the time of occurrence of the index crimes indicated a need for patrol from approximately 0900 A.M. until midnight. It was therefore decided to have two shifts, one officer to work from 0800 to 1600, and his relief officer to work from 1600 to 2400. The days selected were Monday to Friday, since very few burglaries were occurring on Saturday and Sunday when most people were home from work, and burglaries made up the major portion of the index crimes.

Storage of Bicycles

It was thought that a problem might exist relative to where the officer could store his bicycle when he decided to go on foot patrol. Experience shows that both the business establishment and residents of the area are most happy to have the officer leave his locked bicycle in their stores or homes. This was not a problem during the experiment.

Training

After discussing the training aspect of learning how to ride the particular bicycle with the experts, it was decided that approximately two and one-half to three days would be needed for the first two officers. This was necessary so that the original officers could then train any additional officers who might be selected at a later date. Learning the use of the hand brakes can be quite difficult. One officer on his first day out on patrol was adjusting his walkie-talkie and while doing so, grabbed hold of the hand brake too hard and went tumbling over the handlebars headfirst. Questions such as how do you patrol when being chased by dogs and how far is the nearest gas station are important. Training in the beginning will alleviate many problems later on.

Additional Equipment

The regular equipment of a foot officer must also be carried during patrol on bicycles. The baton, citation book, flashlight, and whistle are basic. But in addition to the regular equipment, you must have the warning bell, chain and lock, tire repair kit for minor repairs, clips to hold the baton and flashlight, basket, and leather folder to hold reports, and any other material that might be necessary for a particular locale.

Maintenance

In writing the specification for the purchase of the bicycles, the maintenance aspect should be included. As in the auto patrol, some of the minor repairs, such as fixing flats, adjusting a bolt or nut, may be taken care of with a small repair kit. The major repairs should be done by an expert and this should be so stated in the contract.

Changing Shifts

How the officers will attend roll call and proceed to their beats should be considered. If the distance is acceptable, the officer can ride the bicycle to and from the beat. If the distance is too far, the bicycle can be transported to and from the beat by car, station wagon, or cruising patrol wagon. This is not a serious problem and can be overcome easily.

Total evaluation is not yet complete, but continuance of selected bicycle patrol in Baltimore suggests at least a measure of success. A decline in burglaries and an overwhelming enthusiasm on the part of the residents in the area indicates a need to consider other areas that might be amenable to such patrol.

A byproduct of the experiment was its tremendous value regarding community relations. Youth in the neighborhood are recognized by the officers and the bicycles viewed with extreme curiosity. One officer has the kids waiting for him at school break. Another officer stated, "I've got one group of youngsters who follow me around on my rounds; I call them my posse." Another officer was heard to say, "I've been told that this is the first time in years that residents have invited officers into their homes for food and drink."

The bicycle patrol, with communications from the walkie-talkie available, has many assets when used properly. It appears to be part of the method of policing and is here to stay, especially on a selected basis. This method of patrol, as indicated, is as applicable to urban policing as it is to rural or resort areas. It all depends on the imagination of the patrol administrator.

SCOOTERS

Scooters have been and are being used in various ways throughout the country. Cities such as Detroit and Washington have utilized the scooter as a replacement for the foot-patrol officer. The use of scooters in an area amenable to this type of patrol has several advantages. Naturally, the scooter increases the officer's ability to move around his beat more frequently. The loss of observation from scooter patrol is minimal, and the mobility provided for apprehension far outweighs any loss. One department revealed that an officer, assigned to a Vespa scooter in a business area surrounded by high-rise public housing,

FIGURE 2.7 Scooter Patrol for Supervisors.
Courtesy *Spring 3100,* New York City Police Department.

chased a young purse-snatcher up and down curbs, sidewalks, in alleys, and areaways until he caught the culprit. The apprehension was made possible by the use of the Vespa.

Cushman scooters, having roofs on them, are excellent for patrolling the high-density area of the business districts. They protect the officers during inclement weather, which allows continuous service of parking citations (until police officers can be relieved of this task).

The several types of scooters, depending on the objective, are very useful in patrolling park and recreation areas, where the shortest distance from the present position of the officer to the location where he may be needed is across the grass and field of the park. This added dimension may be quite advantageous during periods of high use of the park facilities.

An area of concern would be the speed with which scooters should be operated. The primary purpose for police would be mobility at safe speed. Officers should be carefully trained in this aspect of scooter patrol.

Urban Setting

The selection of the method of patrol should be made very carefully. An analysis of the total situation of the area where scooters are assigned is necessary. You should consider size of beat, crime, citizen relation, mobility, flexibility, price, and upkeep. If the desired results are seen as a plus in selecting a scooter as a method of patrol, then choose it. If the application is made in an urban setting, efforts must be made to minimize the possibility of theft of the scooter. Some scooters are small enough so they can be picked up easily by two men and carried away. In selecting an area for use, this disadvantage should be considered.

Crowd Control

One of the less-publicized features of the scooter patrol is its use in crowd control. One officer, trained properly, can control and influence many people. With techniques similar to those used by horse-patrol officers, people can be made to move in the direction desired by approaching from the front and directly at a group, or approaching from the side in a sort of layer effect to move people back from a given point. Additionally, when using officers on scooter in a squad or team concept, there is a forceful result with maximum safety for the officer. This method is very successful in dispersing crowds with minimum contact between the officer and persons in the crowd.

24-HOUR PATROL

Patrol administration would not be complete if some consideration were not given to 24-hour patrol. The leader in this new program was the Indianapolis, Indiana, Police Department which began using it in September 1969. Since then, many police departments across the country have developed the 24-hour patrol operation. The success or failure of their plans will depend on several categories that are common to all of the program but must be evaluated by each department on an individual basis. If omnipresence is believed to be the leading factor to decreasing crime, one would believe presumably that 24-hour patrol has to be a good procedure. However, other considerations, such as cost, risk, accidents, crime and its actual relationship to the omnipresence approach must be reviewed before a conclusion can be drawn.

The initial planning for 24-hour patrol would encompass budgeting, specification, and maintenance. Local government would have to be willing to expend, in some cases, a sizeable amount of money to initiate a 24-hour patrol plan. The Indianapolis program necessitated an increase of more than $400,000 which moved the fleet from 110 vehicles to 455 vehicles. Also, average annual increases in vehicle replacement, prevention maintenance, repair costs, and insurance premiums must be considered. As in all programs, the effectiveness of such a plan must be able to be measured. Therefore, standard criteria and measuring devices must be set up prior to implementation to insure proper and accurate evaluation. The administrator should be able to state honestly the amount of success or failure of a program and recommend either continuing because of the amount of success or discontinuing because of failure. If the plan has not failed completely, but has not paid off in a worthwhile amount, the department should state so frankly, and take the appropriate action.

Internal Orders

Prior to implementing such a plan, it is necessary to put in writing orders covering the "who," "when," and "where" concerning the use of police-department vehicles. Will all personnel be issued a marked vehicle? If not, who, and what rank? Those personnel who are issued a marked patrol vehicle for full-time use must have clear and concise responsibilities spelled out. The Indianapolis, Indiana, Police Department states the following responsibilities:

> The department purchases the vehicle, provides: all preventive maintenance, gasoline, repairs (mechanical and body) and pays for insurance coverage. Field lieutenants, sergeants, and patrolmen are usually the first to be issued personal marked patrol vehicles. They are solicited to use their patrol vehicle while off-duty, but when doing so, must maintain radio contact at all times so as to be available for emergencies which may occur in their immediate vicinity. Individual officers are responsible for cleanliness of their vehicle, inside and outside, must change their own flat tires when off-duty, and are responsible for washing their own car.

Areas of Analysis for Evaluation

If the goal of the plan is to reduce crime, it is necessary to determine which crimes are related to the types of patrol. Preventive patrol is usually best used when affecting those crimes which are potentially suppressible; specifically, burglary, robbery, auto theft, and larceny. Therefore, an evaluation relative to these specific crimes would be most meaningful.

In addition to achieving the goal of reducing crime, the amount of omnipresence patroling would have byproducts. Added man-hours on patrol, increased patrolling, availability of officers for mobilization under emergency conditions, and response to calls for service while in off-duty status. These byproducts are very difficult to evaluate. Other areas regarding extra patrol that can be measured are: (1) travel for preventive maintenance, repairs, etc. while off-duty; (2) patrol time picked up at change of shift; and (3) additional patrol time for each officer reporting for work and returning home.

Accidents and Citations

These categories of increased or decreased fleet accidents, citizen accidents, and increased issuance of citations are important to any program involving the increased use of marked patrol vehicles. Very few patrol administrators are satisfied with the number of accidents involving their police vehicles. Most would agree that more accidents occur while on routine patrol as opposed to emergency response. The 24-hour patrol plan would increase the use of police vehicles in a manner similar to routine patrol or nonemergency conditions. Therefore, a very important consideration for the administrator would be fleet accidents. Second, when relating the total picture to the 24-hour patrol program, if citizen accidents can be decreased, the program would be able to show a saving for the citizen in terms of loss of money, loss of time from work, repair bills, hospital costs, insurance premiums, and most of all, possible saving of lives. The category of citations is relative, and must be equated to enforcement index and decrease of accidents.

Prince George's County, Maryland, policemen using their patrol cars during off-duty hours made 1,438 arrests in the first year of the experimental project, according to a report released recently. The report, considered the most complete ever attempted by any police jurisdiction on an off-duty patrol-car-use program, said 139 of the arrests were for serious crimes, 354 for misdemeanors, and 900 for traffic.

The county instituted the project in the hope of reducing crime by having more cars on the streets at all hours of the day and night. The

365 policemen—about two-thirds of the force—who participated in the program were permitted to take their patrol cars home and use them off-duty hours for shopping, running errands, and even dates. All told, they investigated 12,799 incidents, 7,355 of them responses to situations observed by the off-duty policemen themselves.

Other advantages resulting from the program included increased contact between policemen and citizens, quicker response to calls and to off-duty personnel returning to duty for emergencies, and increased morale.

The use of 24-hour patrol is a decision to be made after considering many factors. Comparisons of similar advantages and restrictions between departments are most helpful, but in the final analysis, each department must be its own judge regarding implementation of the 24-hour patrol program. Experimentation in one area or one shift or one district or one division may help decide on the proper course of action.

Chief Winston Churchill of the Indianapolis Police Department, the members of the department, the city, and the government officials should feel great satisfaction in their attempt to produce better methods of police service.

The following is a conclusion drawn from the study of the 24-hour patrol plan of the Indianapolis Police Department by Raymond A. Walton, Jr. It is reprinted here by permission of Chief Winston Churchill. This section could not have been written without the cooperation of the Indianapolis Police Department.

Conclusion

This study has attempted to analyze the Indianapolis Police Department's Fleet Plan. To arrive at a conclusion on a cost vs. savings basis, as many areas as possible have been translated into dollar values. The table on page 71 gives the findings.

Therefore, the result of this study is that the citizens of Indianapolis have thus far saved about $1.3 million on the Indianapolis Police Department Fleet Plan.

Further, it is recommended that any police department considering conversion to a Fleet Plan should include in this conversion a pre-established method of collecting data for periodic analysis of the plan's effectiveness. In this way a department can either justify the continuation of a Fleet Plan or make necessary changes in the plan which keep it an on-going and effective program.[11]

Costs

Initial cost		$ 650,000
Minus the 255 cars which would have been purchased under the old Plan in 1969, 1970, 1971		— $ 510,000
	Net Cost	$ 140,000
Increase in Preventive Maintenance/Repairs		$ 317,000
Increase in cost of insurance coverage		$ 52,000

Savings

Car Washes		$ 7,000
Decrease in Visible Crimes		$ 500,000
Decrease in Citizens' Accidents		$ 700,000
Increased Man-hours of Patrol Time		$ 635,000
Total Costs		$ 509,000
Total Savings		$1,842,000
	Difference	$1,333,000

MARINE PATROL

The need for marine patrol units will naturally be determined by the amount of water area requiring police services. Most ports in the United States have some type of marine unit. New York, Baltimore, New Orleans, and San Francisco are just a few. There are also inland police departments that provide water patrol; for example, Jefferson County, Kentucky, patrols areas of the Ohio River.

The type of boat for marine patrol depends upon the duties and responsibilities of the particular police department. The New York Police Department uses a launch; the Dade County, Florida, Department of Public Safety uses a speedboat. The size of the patrol boat will also determine the equipment carried, from the minimum amount to various weapons and rescue material. This may include deep-sea diving or scuba-diving equipment as some departments have divers assigned to the marine unit.

The Dade County, Florida, Department of Public Safety lists the following responsibilities for their marine patrol unit:

1. Enforce state laws and county ordinances.
2. Promote water safety and conduct safety inspections.
3. Perform routine patrol.
4. Assist United States Coast Guard and other law-enforcement agencies.
5. Remove navigational hazards.
6. Tow disabled craft as practicable.

FIGURE 2.8 Dade County, Florida, Department of Public Safety removing hazard to navigation. Photo courtesy Dade County, Florida Department of Public Safety.

FIGURE 2.9 Dade County, Florida, Department of Public Safety towing a disabled fishing boat. Photo courtesy Dade County, Florida, Department of Public Safety.

Marine patrol units perform routine patrol as needed. During inclement weather the patrol craft remains berthed but is available for any emergency that might arise. The United States Coast Guard is responsible for enforcing federal law as it pertains to vessels, harbors, and waterfront facilities. Where state or local laws have been violated, it becomes the responsibility of the local police department. Such a situation occurred in the Baltimore, Maryland, harbor in 1972 when the captain of a ship anchored in the harbor was assaulted by a member of the crew, and there was a potential for other violence erupting. The Baltimore City Police Department was required to take the necessary action. In March 1972 the United States Coast Guard called on the Dade County, Florida, marine patrol unit to take action in a case of destruction of private property. Even though jurisdiction responsibilities are separate, experience has revealed that cooperative efforts and assistance between the United States Coast Guard and local police department marine units always exist.

HORSE PATROL

Ask any patrol commander who had a potential riot evolving and has exhausted his manpower to numerous assignments, if horse patrol has any value in police work, the answer would be a resounding yes. Many veteran officers will argue that the value of horse patrol for crowd and traffic control alone will compensate for the investment allocated to the mounted unit. However, patrol administrators cannot make decisions without considering all the facts as they relate to horse patrol.

Usually, the officers assigned to horse patrol in a police agency (federal, state, or local) have a high degree of camaraderie. Their personal appearance and the appearance of the animals are well above the standards set for the department as a whole. The men assigned to the horse-patrol unit are required to work more hours since they must arrive early to prepare the horse and equipment. This effort is repeated when the officers go off duty.

Horse patrol is in limited use throughout the country. Areas having difficult access routes are conducive to horse patrol. However, helicopters and other air patrol are quickly replacing the horse. Where horse patrol exists, so does their inclusion in parades, because of their impressive appearance.

Advantages

Because of the size of a horse (the average horse used in patrol weighs approximately 1,100 pounds and stands 15 to 16 hands high or 63 inches at the intersection of the neck and shoulders), people are inclined to respect them. This factor is most important in crowd control.

Urban police departments have used horse patrols in parks, water-fronts, and beaches quite effectively. For example, patrolling large parks on foot is obviously impractical, and in an auto it is difficult to travel on surfaces other than the paved arteries. The horse can move from one point to another in a straight line, thereby reducing response time. Additionally, if the horse-patrol officer is equipped with a walkie-talkie for constant communication, his total patrol technique is improved.

Because of the officer's height while on horse patrol, he is able to observe traffic problems others would miss. This ability to pinpoint congestion increases his impact on the safe and smooth flow of traffic.

Disadvantages

The horse and the officer require special equipment, and the officer's uniform wears out quickly, especially the trousers.

It is necessary to have costly special housing for the horses. Stables, hostlers (people to tend the horses and stables), and food are extra items required of a mounted section.

There is a health problem caused by the odor and cleanliness factor.

Training must be provided for the horse, officer, and the horse and officer together.

The total process tends to cause permanency in assignment of officers.

Conclusion

During the May Day 1972 demonstrations in Washington, D.C., hundreds of scooters were used by officers in crowd-control situations. The author observed the skilled officers manipulate crowds of people rather effectively. They were excellent in performance. This demonstration has taken some of the edge off the argument that horses are invaluable in crowd control.

Each police department must determine for itself the need of mounted patrol. It is clear that budget restrictions will demand justification based on cost/effectiveness. The limited activity of horse patrol will be considered by most elected officials as essential to their considerations. Either horse-patrol tasks increase in number and effectiveness or economic restrictions will phase them out.

NOTES

1. O. W. Wilson and Roy C. McLaren, *Police Administration,* 3d ed. (New York: McGraw–Hill, 1972), p. 357.
2. Chicago Police Department Training Bulletin, vol. 13, no. 36, September 1972.
3. Crime in the United States, Uniform Crime Reports, Federal Bureau of Investigation, Washington, D.C., 1971.
4. Ibid.
5. Public Relations Department, Metropolitan Police Dept., London, England, January 1972.
6. Mayor William J. Burns, *The Lakewood Story,* published by Hughes Tool Company.
7. Sheriff Peter J. Pitchess, The Sky-Knight Project Report, published by Sheriff's Department, Los Angeles County, 1968.
8. Ibid., p. 96.
9. Mayor William J. Burns, op. cit.
10. Aerial Patrol, Kansas City Metropolitan Police Department, Planning and Research Unit, 1967.
11. Study of 24 Hour Patrol, Indianapolis Police Department.

patrol planning

Planning may be defined in several ways: outlining a course of action to achieve an objective, the process of developing a method or procedure, or an arrangement of parts intended to facilitate the achievement of a defined objective. Whatever definition you may use do not forget that planning has a direct effect on crisis-oriented leadership. To put it another way, move hindsight up to foresight and minimize second-guessing or Monday-morning quarter-backing.

A patrol administrator must realize that in order to bring about results that justify the position, planning must be done in a calculated, methodical, analytical, and realistic manner. Progressive police agencies have been shown the way by knowledgeable chiefs to systematic means of determining what is to be accomplished and the route that should be taken to achieve the objective.

When a police agency has been permeated with the value of good planning, the results appear in an obvious manner:

1. Decrease in complaints against officers
2. Innovative ideas from all levels
3. Increased apprehension rates
4. Decrease in Index Crime
5. Increased community stability
6. Improved relationships with government at all levels
7. Better coordination within the Criminal Justice System
8. Accolades from all regarding the manner in which the department responds to demonstrations, disorders, parades, athletic contests, barricaded persons, hostage situations, assassinations, and ambush

Patrol especially must act before the fact, or else events of the future, which may have been anticipated, will be left to chance. If a housewife goes shopping without planning her list of what to buy, usually she will come home forgetting some articles and so, another trip to the store. The same theory applies when we (1) take a trip, (2) begin a detailed investigation, (3) begin patrolling a beat, (4) assign work to men as supervisors, (5) develop alternatives to resolve a crime problem, (6) allocate and distribute manpower, (7) write orders or procedures, and (8) plan tactical operations or administrate a department, division, etc.

In most police agencies today resources are limited. Therefore, each member of the agency must contribute to the fullest in order to accomplish the mission. One contribution in particular, which entails little if any material resources, is to develop the ability to do your own planning. Patrol leaders should be familiar with completed staff work, writing general orders (or at least the first draft), and communicating ideas and opinions for culmination of reports. Even though the formal planning unit (if one exists) will assist all other writers in planning, when needed, this most basic management function should be done by all parts of the police organization. It is recommended that the planning process become a part of and be taught to recruit and in-service training officers. No one at this time can predict the results this effort would have on the total police operation.

WEIGHING ALTERNATIVE PLANS

"Planning is fundamentally choosing, and a planning problem arises only when an alternative course of action is discovered."[1] There is hardly any decision that needs to be made by patrol administrators which does not have an alternative, yet these same administrators accept recommendations made by subordinates which are incomplete and do not include alternatives. The tendency to select the first solution to a problem, or develop only one course of action to an anticipated problem (when some planning has been done), is what the author calls *lazy planning*.

To offset this type of decision-making these factors must be considered: (1) changes from traditional policing that the way things were done years ago is still good for today; (2) wasting time when doing any planning at all; (3) assuring the selected course of action will offend fewer people both within and without the department; and (4) not allowing an attitude of the formal planning unit to be godlike; e.g., "We have made a study and recommend solution A" (there were probably no alternative solutions considered).

Response to these influences should be made by appropriate personnel to the chief in order to bridge the gap between good and mediocre planning.

JUSTIFICATION FOR PLANNING UNIT

Since most police departments around the country are small in size and are limited in manpower and resources, the justification for a formal planning unit must be analyzed very carefully. The administrator must weigh the investment versus the dividend. If the planning concept can be communicated in a very real sense to all personnel (especially supervisors), then the need for a formal planning unit will decrease. The first step in planning is recognition of need. With proper orientation, the department already has the personnel needed to accomplish the first step. This includes all officers and the use of the suggestion box or the extension of the planning and inspection function. In most cases, the administrator in a small department realizes that each officer is like a precious gem and must be utilized to his fullest. The decision to combine the planning and inspection function into one unit with the minimal assignment of specialized officers may be appropriate. In taking this route, the need for training as many officers as possible in understanding the amount of effort necessary for each member of the force to contribute to the planning and inspection function should be realized.

In larger departments (200 men or more), there is little question about the need of a formal planning unit. Manpower allocation and distribution become so important on a broader scale, that in-depth workload analysis must be part of the planning process. The formal planning unit should attempt to project an image of assistance to the operating units.

An example of projecting such an image could be the introduction of a new reporting system into a police department. Training for the new system should be systematic and complete. All affected personnel should be introduced to the new method, the reason for the new system explained, and the results expected clearly stated. In other words, the planning unit should demonstrate to operating personnel that the introduction of the new reporting system was planned, and the who, what, when, where, how, and why were answered. Additionally, members of the unit should be on hand around the clock to assist the operating unit in a smooth transition. This will enhance the planning unit's acceptance throughout the department in a more positive way.

Solicitation from the affected units to participate in the planning of new procedures, revised rules and regulations, computer formats, information retrieval, activity sheets, evaluation reports, and personnel action memos will cause the principle of participatory management to permeate all units coming into contact with the planning unit. When people are consulted with regard to operations that must be carried out by them, the knowledge that they participated in the decision will make any change more readily acceptable and cause the implementation to be a smooth and coordinated effort. For a police organization to function properly, all steps should be taken to avoid crisis management. This can only be done through planning.

WHY PLAN?

1. To achieve objectives, help clarify and implement policy by defining the immediate objective or purpose. Specify when the plan will be implemented. Where is the best place to start the implementations? What will be the cost of the implementation of the plan? These questions are important and should be considered. In identifying our plans, we should include the fact that they are reasonable and attainable. Obstacles must be considered and priorities set. Primary and secondary missions and goals must be developed in order to include realistic approaches. The plans must be consistent with the policy and organizational objectives.

2. We plan to put ideas to work. Creativity and imagination are most important parts of the planning process. In an organization where individuals in key positions are limited only by their own imagination, they usually develop their individual abilities and contribute to the accomplishment of the total goal of the organization. Timing is most important when we speak of planning. If ideas are to be put to work, there must be an awareness of the proper time to implement.

3. Plan to make things happen. If the chief of police gives an assignment to a patrol administrator and expects it to be done in two

weeks, the first task is to outline the plan of action. Questions such as, What has to be done? Who will do it? How will it be done? When is the best time to do it? Where to start? Will it be necessary to make a schedule? What equipment will be needed? Materials? How much money will it cost? How much manpower should be included? The answers to these questions are essential if the deadline is to be met.

4. Plan to be prepared to act before the fact. In acting before the fact through proper planning, crisis management is avoided. To act before the fact, assign activities to people according to their skills, knowledge, motivation, and interests. This points up the need for administrators to be able to recognize talents of individuals because it is directly related to planning a projected course of action. That projected course of action will include deciding, looking ahead, thinking through, assembling, and evaluating.

5. Plan to cope with change. Alvin Toffler states in *Future Shock*: "Change is the process by which the future invades our lives." In coping with change it is necessary to adjust and adapt to the change that is taking place in law enforcement. Individual abilities should be developed to entertain constructive criticism. Knowledge of when people are criticizing constructively is important. Proper planning and explanation while proceeding will dissolve some of the problems that cause difficulty in adapting and adjusting. Disagreement to ideas is not inherently negative; however, review and analysis are necessary to justify positions.

6. Plan to maintain control. It is said that power is having the ability to make things move a specific way. It is highly improbable and almost impossible for things to go your way in terms of power if you do not plan, outline your steps, and approach the movement in a very analytical way. When considering change, remember that power really means controlling the rate and direction of change. Making organizations capable of changing is most important and directly related to proper planning.

PRINCIPLES OF PLANNING

1. Take time to plan. Take time to think. Everyone should allot a certain amount of time each day to think. This basic requirement of planning is fundamental, yet it is forgotten by many administrators. In taking time to think, areas of disagreement should be considered and alternatives developed.

2. Planning can be top-down and bottom-up. In an organization everyone should plan. Managers plan to manage, policy-makers plan for policy, middle management plans for implementation, patrolmen plan operational activity.

3. Involve and communicate with those concerned. The involvement and communication must begin at the beginning to be effective. Change in the implementation of plans has a much better chance of succeeding when the persons affected by the change are involved in the initial planning stages. Consider line and staff relationships and a possibility of the domino theory taking place. Change in one unit in an organization usually affects other units within that organization. By involving people you enhance participatory management and the democratic philosophy of managing by objectives.

4. Plans should be flexible and dynamic. Plans should include preparations for adjustments by having alternative courses of action. Lazy plans should not be accepted. Lazy planning means selecting the easiest solution to the problem, which may not always be the best.

5. Evaluate and revise. As in staff studies, the initiating staff officer must follow up on the procedure, plan, etc. to determine its effectiveness. After the documentation and evaluation, revision should take place to obtain the best possible results and determine new objectives. No plan can be complete without evaluation, revision, and documentation.

STEPS IN THE PLANNING PROCESS

1. *The need for the plan must be recognized.* Apparent needs must be verified by investigation and analysis. Police should be alert to discover common events that may impose unusual burdens upon them. The following are some of the needs that should be recognized when planning.

(a) The need for good intelligence. The patrol force must have quality intelligence because it affects manpower planning, a most valuable asset, and in some cases can be a matter of life and death where patrol officers are concerned. In the assignment of your manpower, intelligence will help the administrator decide what areas have the potential for several incidents occurring at the same time, the possibility of false calls, the number of marked cars, unmarked cars, uniformed officers, plainclothes officers, suspicious calls, the need to provide a new system of responding in dangerous situations, the number of men to assign to an individual police unit, the amount of communications equipment necessary for a given area, the type of back-up tactics that should be available, and the effect that quality intelligence has on the total operation of the department.

(b) There is a need for good inspection, both line and staff. Inspection should be closely related to the planning aspect of patrol administration because inspection should point out the deficiencies where there is a need for adjustment and planning to overcome these deficiencies. Good line and staff inspections are very positive and should produce an end product enhancing the professional attitude and performance of the department, especially the patrol function.

(c) Recognizing the need for liaison between police and government. The ability to utilize resources within local government through recognition of needs and the knowledge of where these agencies within local government can contribute to crime reduction is of tremendous value. There is a need for liaison between police and community groups within a locale. Recognize the need for liaison between police and activists throughout the community. If a dialogue can be developed between persons who are demonstrating, who sincerely believe in what they are doing, and an understanding of how they wish to accomplish their purpose is developed, the plan that results can be a tremendous saving in manpower.

The need for understanding and mutual cooperation between police and the business community is also very important. The recognition of the need for a plan, especially in the downtown business section during the Christmas holidays, can develop great respect for the police agency. Good planning will use manpower effectively. Increased patrol coverage in the business area at peak shopping periods improves the feeling of safety for citizens shopping during the holidays. This type of planning increases support for the law-enforcement agency.

Recognizing the need for a planned liaison between the police and other law-enforcement agencies is imperative. During the riots of 1968 in many areas the need for metropolitan assistance was obvious, yet not too many plans of that type were available. By communicating mutual problems facing metropolitan areas the need for plans that will enhance the total contribution to law enforcement within that given area will be recognized. Maintaining liaison between the police officers and courts can affect time wasted in court while cases are postponed or delayed. Cases that were lost due to poor prosecution or improper testimony can be analyzed critically. Specific training can be provided to upgrade the capabilities of officers to give testimony compatible with proper presentation and prosecution.

Liaison between the police and correctional officials should result in plans being written for response by local police agencies to jails, penitentiaries, and prisons throughout the country. Patrol administrators would do well to consider close communication with prison officials in order to develop appropriate plans for combating any potential riot situations in the prison system. Additionally, the recognition of need for a plan to be developed between police and campus or school authorities is obvious because of developments over the years.

Warning Signals. When incidents occur, a critique of the response to these incidents should be undertaken to determine if there is a need for adjustment. There are several warning signals that should alert patrol administrators to the need for possible adjustment in existing plans or for the initiation of a plan where one does not exist. Some of these signals are (1) injury to officer, (2) injury to innocent person, (3) escape of a prisoner, (4) loss of property in police custody, (5) analysis of factual data, (6) analysis of existing plans after somewhat successful operations, (7) planning and inspecting, (8) reviewing the many valid and viable ideas received from the level of execution and first-line supervisors that may lend an improvement to the operation and possibly prevent any actions that might adversely affect the operation.

Plans should be filed so that effective review can take place and plans updated. Review and proper filing may save many hours of unnecessary research.

2. *The second step in planning is the statement of the objective.* An accurate definition of the problem is necessary before the objectives can be stated. Problem definition involves time and effort but once it is done, the objective can be stated very clearly. The statement should, if possible, incorporate the answer in general terms to the question: e.g., objective—apprehend the criminal. He may be apprehended by increased patrol or selected coverages of potential victims. Many times the best solution will not be known until data has been collected.

3. *The third step in planning is the gathering and analyzing of relevant data.* In order to provide an estimate of the situation on which to base our decisions, we must gather and analyze data relevant to the situation. Operational plans are affected greatly by the analysis of relevant data. The type of data, the course of the collec-

tion, and the tabulation analyses will vary according to the purpose of the plan. In most cases the question of what, where, when, who, how, and why must be answered. The answer to these questions must also be related to the basic problem and its solution. The total basic data for planning is so voluminous it cannot be stated here. The information needed for an all-inclusive reorganization plan may be found in Appendix A of *Police Planning* by O. W. Wilson, second edition, page 284. However, it would be significant to quote that basic data designated by Wilson to be used for the patrol division.

Patrol Division

a. Personnel strength arranged by shifts and assignments.
b. Basis used in the establishment of shift hours.
c. Basis used in the organization of motorized beats.
d. Basis used in the organization of foot beats.
e. Number of shifts.
f. Number of beats on each shift covered by one-man patrol cars and by two-man patrol cars.
g. Number of foot beats on each shift.
h. Average daily number of motorized patrolmen on actual patrol on each shift during the past six months.
i. Average daily number of foot patrolmen on actual patrol on each shift during past six months.
j. Duties of patrolmen (distinguish between foot and motorized if there is a difference) in:
The enforcement of traffic regulations
The enforcement of vice regulations
The supervision of juveniles
The investigation of crimes
The search of crime scenes for physical evidence
The investigation of traffic accidents
The checking of the security of commercial establishments
The inspection of taverns, bars, dance halls, and other licensed recreational establishments
k. How many minutes before the beginning of their shift are they required to report for duty?
l. Do any patrolmen report on or off duty from call boxes without reporting at headquarters?
m. Are evidence technicians, equipped and trained to search crime and accident scenes for physical evidence, assigned to the patrol division? to other divisions? [2]

4. *The details of the plan must be developed.* Organization of personnel and equipment must be considered, procedures must be outlined, orders must be drafted, and schedules must be completed.

For example, if large numbers of men are grouped together to meet a particular situation, include in the plan a schedule indicating when the 8-hour tour of duty is up so that officers can be properly relieved. Continuation past the 8-hour tour of duty would entail a cost factor that should be considered in the plan. If plans are developed in a manner whereby most men are working at critical times, a reduction in manpower and costs can be achieved. However, these details should be included in any plan that is written. Whenever possible the plan should be written in enough time to allow the information to be disseminated throughout the personnel involved so that objections to the plan may be resolved. In considering the objections a better plan will develop out of the initial one. Concurrences and nonconcurrences to the plan should be reviewed and wherever necessary the answer to the nonconcurrences should be made so that the chief can make his decision based on pros and cons of any question.

5. *Concurrences and nonconcurrences must be obtained.* You must prepare your planning reports and, wherever necessary, completed staff work in relation to the preparation of your final report for the chief should be included. In developing the details of the plan and disseminating the information to the persons involved who must implement the plan, the chances of the plan being accepted by the chief are improved. If modifications are suggested with concurrences from the staffing process, the modifications should be considered and included if they improve the total concept of the plan. Before submitting the final recommendation to the chief, insure that the developed plan is current. Plans written for response to correctional facilities especially need to be updated since there are different problems occurring today than there were a year ago. Consideration of outside factors that may influence the plan is important. If the cooperation of other community agencies is necessary for the success of the plan, take the initiative to solicit this cooperation, and present an intelligent, factual background of the reasons for the plan. The planner must participate in a staff capacity during implementation. In cases of patrol planning, and depending on the type of plan whether it be operational, tactical, etc., the officer or supervisor responsible for planning should be on the scene. Wherever the initiator of the plan is located within the organization, he is responsible for the implementation of the particular plan.

6. *The last step includes the revision of the plans or modification wherever necessary.* This step is needed so that the initiator of the plan can document, monitor, and evaluate the implementation of the

plan. The initiator may suggest change after a short period of time, or an extended period. The initiator should also be willing to admit the plan has been less than successful in reaching the objective. Crisis management can be a thing of the past for the patrol administrator, but only if intelligent planning is incorporated into the daily routine of the particular department.

INTERNAL POLITICAL PLANNING

The word "political" is used in this book in several places. The definition given by the dictionary is "characterized by shrewdness; tactfully and skillfully contained; sagacious in devising or promoting a policy." This is exactly what the patrol administrator must have in mind with regard to the internal planning process. All members of the department are on the same team, yet each has a different personality. Each of the commanders of the staff and other line operations controls the support necessary for the patrol commander to accomplish the mission. The art of lateral communications includes being artful in address and procedure. Planning your communications and the method or procedure you are going to use to put it across are as important as the content of the message. You cannot be lazy, you cannot assume that everyone knows or should know your message, and you cannot deliberately embarrass if you wish to be successful in gaining internal cooperation and support. There is no substitute for sincerity when attempting to promote a policy change or procedure that will benefit the patrol force. In most cases the lateral communication will be one of either pointing out an error on the part of a member of the support unit, or initiating a procedure that will take the burden of a task from the patrol officer. Usually the task was given to the patrol officer some years ago when no one would speak up in his behalf. The task may very well be performed more efficiently by the support unit.

In the case of the former, the responsibility of the patrol leader to point out nonsupport (intentional or unintentional) is as basic and important as any other characteristic of leadership. After the identification of the error, the approach taken to correct it becomes relevant. Additionally, after the correction is made and a disposition agreed upon, the patrol leader would be remiss if he does not report to the person identifying the problem and advise him of what action was taken. This type of support enhances the credibility aspect of leadership for the patrol commander (see section on leadership in Chapter 4).

The latter situation makes the patrol leader an initiator of change. Thus he must consider all aspects of the situation and the steps for implementing change before making the initial approach. The basic steps of the planning process should be known. With this completed, the leader of the support unit can be approached with the best method available, showing the expected results for the good of the department as a whole. It is a mistake to give the impression of wanting a procedure changed just to enhance one's own unit in the eyes of the chief. Honesty of intent must accompany the approach, or cooperation between units will not be forthcoming. Nothing can replace mutual respect and understanding between patrol and all other units in the department. It is incumbent upon each to make decisions for the good of the department, even at the risk of personal gains or temporary divisional disruptions.

The patrol administrator will develop credibility of fairness, objectivity, and honesty through demonstrated activity. Situations will arise when the patrol force will be guilty of errors and the shoe will be on the other foot, so to speak. It is at this time that cooperation in the future will be decided. Constructive criticism and corrective action must be taken as well as given. Also, the corrective action taken must be fed back to the commander of the support division to complete the cycle.

One patrol commander reports that while attending roll call one day, one of the officers was complaining bitterly about the dispatcher in the communications unit. The officer's complaint was valid, but he misunderstood the reasons for the delay of necessary information. The patrol commander allowed the officer to spend one tour of duty with the dispatcher at his desk. When the patrol officer found out about the responsibilities and amount of work involved with efficient dispatching, his outlook changed and he was a better officer for it. Being a member of the peer group, the officer informed other patrol officers of the dispatching operations and a better team effort resulted.

The internal political-planning process is not meant to be deceiving, because all members are on the same team. But the approach of one member to another has to be planned if optimum results are to be expected. The goals of the department must be the goals of each member of the force, but especially the leaders of the different units and divisions, since they are expected to have a more complete understanding of the total operation and its interacting parts.

EXTERNAL POLITICAL PLANNING

Keeping politics out of the police department is still a valid goal when it means avoiding interference in administering a professional organization, or when it means that the administration promotes personnel because of political influence, compromises ethics and is intimidated by political pressure. *External political planning* for the patrol administrator means responding to the needs of the duly elected officials of the community in which he serves. The response to the elected officials does not mean that the patrol administrator will play partisan politics, since the response shall be to local and state elected officials, regardless to which party they belong. The goal of the patrol administrator is to respond to the needs of the people of his jurisdiction. By utilizing the elected officials as true representatives of their constituents, the patrol administrator can swiftly resolve problems before the fact. If this is not possible, then immediate reaction after the fact may distinguish a potentially explosive issue within the community. Either way, good communication is necessary.

The art of planning as a politician by the patrol administrator thus means being skillful in diplomacy, tactful and clever, initiating action to reduce chances of explosive issues, and opening lines of communication between elected officials and the patrol commander. Planning courses of action to achieve objectives then becomes all-inclusive, since the community and the department participate in whatever procedure is selected.

An example of this association between the elected official and the patrol commander might be as follows: Each patrol commander would be responsible for knowing what areas of his command were represented by which official, both local and state. (There is no need to include federal officials for this type of political planning, although responsiveness to federally elected officials would not be lessened.) Using a map of the command, outline the federal, state, and local boundaries as appropriate. The patrol commander would then initiate communication between himself and each representative located within the boundaries. A mutually beneficial common ground can be established, always keeping in mind the goal of better service to the citizen and a procedure for contact set-up. This procedure would include a 24-hour a day contact, which means the availability of each would have to be considered. Private telephone contact should be established and the trust and confidence necessary for success would then be initiated. Honest communication is very important, and complete understanding of the enormity of the many problems to be discussed must be solidified.

The theory behind this type of planning is that these two important people, having common community interests, are working in harmony in order to act before the fact. No problem will be solved easily if allowed to fester and grow. A concentrated and cooperative effort on the part of the elected officials and the patrol commander lessens the opportunity for misunderstanding, misuse of and underutilization of resources, and false rumor. The intelligent pooling of authority, communication, information, contacts, and knowledge of the area should help prevent disharmony that might prevail between the police and the community.

The support of the elected officials is a place for gaining support of the total community. Patrol administrators should be aware of what community support means to the patrol operation. Without it, the patrol commander can accomplish very little; with it, the patrol commander can accomplish much.

PLANNING CAREER ROTATION

Over the years the police recruit has been accepted into the club with some reluctance. When the recruit proved himself, then it was all right to talk to him. The credibility factor may have been part of it, but not all of the acceptance came from the officer's proving himself. Some of the reluctance came from the insecurities of older officers who thought that these new officers might do a little too much work or have just a little edge in education and intelligence—thus, "Don't tell them anything, let them learn the same way we did." Thankfully, most department personnel have abandoned this attitude. The prevailing thought today is that the sooner the new officer can learn, the more assistance he will be when the going gets rough. As the new officer develops, certain skills will surface and should be recognized. At the same time, deficiencies should also be noted so corrective action can be taken promptly for the benefit of all.

Attitude and behavior make or break any police agency. Attitude of the patrol officer and patrol administrator are of prime importance because the first line of defense is also the first view of the department by most of the citizens of the community. If police work generally, and patrol specifically, is to become a profession, then the work of patrol must be viewed as such, and the criteria included in the making of a professional must be attained in order to earn the term.

James Ahern in his book *Police in Trouble* states, "The policeman's task, as it is now performed, is by definition the kind of work that is performed in our society by professionals."[3]

James Q. Wilson, former director of the Joint Center for Urban Studies at M.I.T. and Harvard University, writes:

> Occupations whose members exercise, as do the police, wide discretion alone and with respect to matters of the greatest importance are typically "professionals"—the medical profession, for example, The right to handle emergency situations, to be privy to "guilty information," and to make decisions involving questions of life and death or honor and dishonor is usually, as with a doctor or a priest, conferred by an organized profession. The profession certifies that the member has acquired by education certain information, and by apprenticeship certain arts and skills, that render him competent to perform these functions and that he is willing to subject himself to the code of ethics and sense of duty of his colleagues (or, in the case of a priest, to the laws and punishments of God). Failure to perform his duties properly will, if detected, be dealt with by professional sanctions—primarily, loss of respect. Members of professions tend to govern themselves through collegial bodies, to restrict the authority of their nominal superiors, to take seriously the reputation among fellow professionals, and to encourage some of their kind to devote themselves to adding systematically to the knowledge of the profession through writing and research. The police are not in any of these senses professionals. They acquire most of their knowledge and skill on the job, not in separate academies; they are emphatically subject to the authority of their superiors; they have no serious professional society, only a union-like bargaining agent; and they do not produce, in systematic written form, new knowledge about their craft.
>
> In sum, the order-maintenance function of the patrolman defines his role and that role, which is unlike that of any other occupation, can be described as one in which *subprofessionals, working alone, exercise wide discretion in matters of utmost importance (life and death, honor and dishonor) in an environment that is apprehensive and perhaps hostile* [italics added].*[4]

We are not and cannot be all things to all people. The performance of all tasks now assigned to police as a professional matter using the traditional methods, is quite impossible. The total resources of government should be employed: e.g., the police should not specialize in crisis intervention for family trouble calls, but call upon the expertise of the social agency within governments to follow up on these family counseling problems. Police should be trained to handle the initial contact of family cases using the generalist concepts and provide a procedure that allows for follow-up by the social agency. The police role should be defined and then performed professionally. The patrol administrator must work to this end. Words are fine, theories are good, but it is at the actual implementation phase where the critical issues are won or lost relative to professionalism. A beginning, based on the President's Crime Commission Task Force Report *Police* (1967), is the police-agent program. The police-agent program attempts to develop career rotation for those officers possessing the education and potential for expertise in selected areas of police work.

Table 3.1 is an example of how several officers can be monitored during their career. At some point in time, promotion is attained or the appropriate career niche is located which allows for parallel goals between the individual and the organization.

CAREER ROTATION

POLICE AGENT PROGRAM

Agent	Date of Appointment	Date of Completion of Entrance-Level Training	First Assignment	Second Assignment	Time in Assignment	Third Assignment
Adam	1-1-70	5-1-70	Patrol—foot High Crime	Patrol Research	6 months	Personnel Recruitment
Thomas						
Charles						
Peter						
Edward						
Frank						
George						
Harry						
Ivan						
John						

TABLE 3.1 Career Rotation and Chart for Police Agents

Responsibility for Career Rotation

There are two areas of responsibility for career development; one lies with the department, and the other lies with the individual officer.

Individual Officer. The U.S. Marine Corps has a motto of always being ready. The officer who desires career development should always be ready if he wishes to take advantage of opportunity. Remember, responsible administrators always try to select the best man for the job. In making this selection, education, background, initiative, participation and activities of law-enforcement organizations that enhance professionalism are all part of the criteria used in deciding whom to select. The officer who has the answers (because he has studied the appropriate material, or because he has gone to school to expand his mind), who can intelligently communicate, who demonstrates the ability to produce in his present position, is likely to be the one selected for new challenges, new horizons, and career development. All of these can be accomplished by the individual officer.

In other words, the officer should be specific in identifying his personal objective, and should delineate a strategy for reaching it.

The following Career Launching Checklist may help:

1. Do I know the things I do best?
2. Have I found some things I like to do very much?
3. Do I work better by myself or with other people? What sorts of other people?
4. Do I know what talents I do not have?
5. Do I know the things I very much dislike doing?
6. Have I gotten professional advice on the fields of work I ought to consider for myself?
7. Does my education prepare me for these fields, or do I need further education or specialization courses or some sort of internship before making a full-fledged beginning?
8. How hard am I willing to work physically and mentally? Can I work long hours?
9. What are my work habits? Short bursts of very intense effort? Or a steady pace?
10. Have I talked with people doing jobs I think I might or should be interested in so that I have first-hand information on what they do, how they do it, and what a typical day is like for them?[5]

The Department. The department and the patrol administrator have a primary responsibility to develop people, the most precious resource. The patrol administrator must be aware of the talent exist-ing within his command.

> When recruits are properly selected they bring to the job consid-erable native ability but little knowledge or experience to police work. In a short time, they must be prepared to operate alone on the streets under a variety of conditions that call for knowledge of laws and ordinances, legal procedures, police practices, and human relations. As they progress, they must not only acquire more of the same kind of knowledge but also should develop some specialized understanding of investigative techniques and scientific crime de-tection. This will enable them to conduct initial or preliminary in-vestigations and to preserve vital evidence for a specialist who will assist them on difficult cases.[6]

Initial training with a recruit begins at the police academy or education and training center. After this it is the responsibility of the supervisor, middle-management, and the patrol administrator, at least in the area of the patrol function, to develop the individual tal-ents and abilities of the officers working with him.

Lateral Entry

If law enforcement is to be truly professional, then some form of lateral entry in all phases (operations, administration, and ser-vices) must be implemented. Law enforcement should spell out its desires to the legislature and the community in order to gain under-standing and decrease the possibility of law prohibiting the imple-mentation of lateral entry. There are additional concerns regarding lateral entry within the police community. First, the men in the field who have started at the bottom feel that it is unfair if the promotions go to people from the outside. The career officers of the individual departments think the years of hard work in that department should be rewarded from within. Second, there is a fear that the best quali-fied officers of the smaller departments would move to the larger departments where there would be higher pay and improved fringe benefits. This fear should be rejected because the local communities would learn to appreciate the need for qualified personnel. The com-munity will demand professional police officers and be willing to pay the appropriate wages to recruit and retain this caliber of personnel. Quality is not commensurate with size.

Additionally, there would be a decrease in the disparity between wages paid in the smaller departments and the larger departments as a conclusion to this type of lateral entry. Third, there would be a need for at least statewide job classification and requirements. This would certainly parallel what is going on today in the field of law enforcement in many states. Minimum standards set by state training commissions certainly are congruent with the thought of having a job classification, job requirements qualifications, and minimum standards on training, written at the state level. This is certainly a first step in preparing to have lateral entry and transfer within a state and between states.

In addition to the fact that professionalization will not come until law enforcement has lateral entry on a broad scale, several observations should be considered. An intimate view of a department where lateral entry has been experienced has shown lateral entry can work, it will work, and has enhanced the department as a whole. New York City and San Francisco are departments involved in exchanging officers of equal rank within their departments. These officers are gaining experience, knowledge, and exposure in those individual departments and have both learned and contributed to the department to which they have been assigned. The concept of lateral entry creates incentive for personnel to pursue education, to expand the thought process, and to make them more capable to be promoted or gain reward within their own levels of supervision. The competition that would exist between all members of the law-enforcement community and outside the law-enforcement community would be a positive one.

The National Advisory Commission on Criminal Justice Standards and Goals summarizes the concept in their report, "Police," Standard 17.4, Administration of Promotion and Advancement:

> Every police chief executive, by assuming administrative control of the promotion and advancement system, should insure that only the best-qualified personnel are promoted or advanced to positions of greater authority and responsibility in higher pay grades and ranks. Agencies that have not developed competent personnel to assume positions of higher authority should seek qualified personnel from outside the agency rather than promote or advance personnel who are not ready to assume positions of greater responsibility.
>
> 1. The police chief executive should oversee all phases of his agency's promotion and advancement system including the testing of personnel and the appointing of personnel to positions of greater responsibility. The police chief executive should make use of the services of a central personnel agency when that personnel agency is competent to develop and administer tests and is responsive to the needs of the police agency.

2. The police chief executive should consider recruiting personnel for lateral entry at any level from outside the agency when it is necessary to do so in order to obtain the services of an individual who is qualified for a position or assignment.[7]

Although studies have shown that an increase in pay, future potential, living conditions, challenge, and loss of seniority are obstacles to lateral entry and transfer, it appears that the pension factor itself is really the major obstacle to transferring an officer from one department to another throughout the country. However, the studies also reveal that if existing obstacles to the lateral transfer were removed there would be a surge for members of the law-enforcement community to develop new skills and capabilities that would cause them to be considered for promotions.[8]

The Teachers' Insurance and Annuity Association operates a central retirement fund that local authorities join. It may not be the exact answer to the obstacle of pension rights and funds; however, it shows that there are models which may assist in solving problems.

After Lateral Entry

One of the major problems, and probably the most important problem needed to be resolved regarding lateral entry after someone enters a department, is the question of credibility. Individuals both within and without the law-enforcement community may be hired by a given police organization. The background and credentials possessed by the individual may be outstanding and relevant to the position for which the person was hired. However, the background and credentials are not a panacea to obtaining credibility. Developing trust and confidence, having meaningful relationships, and projecting sincere dedication will enhance credibility and acceptance by the other members of the department.

The credibility can be developed in different ways. One way is for the lateral entrant to be put in a position where decisions need to be made, especially in the field, and the person without hesitation makes his decision and projects an image of someone who does know what is going on and has the ability to make decisions that are correct. Second, credibility can be developed by an individual possessing the talents of an analytical mind, who is a good planner, goal-oriented, and demonstrates these talents by giving support to the operational units. When this person is a staff officer responsible for contributing to the total goal of the department and uses the aforementioned talents to their fullest, he will support his claim for credibility by action. The projection of a feeling of sincerity to contribute even to the smallest detail, in any way possible, will be felt by other members of the department and help gain that much-needed respect.

Other individual qualities that will develop credibility for persons selected for lateral entry within a department are similar to the qualities of any good leader: firmness, fairness, empathy, dependability, and enthusiasm. The road to acceptance is not easy. Developing credibility is not easy, and the knowledge of how, when, and where to project those qualities that will accumulate trust, confidence, and credibility for the individual is most important. Persons entering other departments through lateral entry would do well to analyze the what, when, where, how, and why when searching for the right methods to demonstrate individual abilities.

PATROL-PLANNING COUNCIL

The patrol-planning council is an innovation designed to include participation of all ranks in the operation of the patrol function, the use of completed staff work as an individual planning tool, problem-solving conference, and brainstorming (applied imagination techniques) conference in resolving planning problems.

The council should only be formed after a serious selection process takes place. Members included in the council are patrolmen, sergeants, lieutenants, captains, and majors, along with the patrol administrator. (The make-up depends upon the size of the organization.) Members should be solicited in a practical way, placing emphasis on voluntary participation, serious review and evaluation of the program, freedom of expression, constructive criticism, and practical application. All members should be willing to accept the assignment of completed staff studies as appropriate and any part of the other types of conferences.

The goal of the planning council is to carry out the function of patrol in the most professional, efficient, and effective manner possible. Democratic leadership involving participatory management in the problem-resolution area is essential. The patrol administrator should be prepared to act as chairman of the conference and must be knowledgeable in order to insure a consensus resolution to the problem. Additionally, the patrol administrator should attempt to have every supervisor under his command aware of the planning process through the completed staff work, problem-solving conference, and brainstorming (applied imagination) procedure. The techniques applied are not commands alone, but they can be used at every level of supervision within the department.

Usually staff studies are assigned to an individual or a group of individuals when the time limit is not a critical factor. (For example, if an analysis of a particular crime problem necessitates one month's investigation in order to develop valid data, the staff study method could be used.)

If a problem has existed for some time but has erupted in the patrol unit recently, then the problem-solving conference should be used. (For example, fleet safety. The problem of accidents had existed in the unit and their efficiency had not equaled the national average with regard to fleet safety. But in the last two days the unit had experienced an unacceptable number of accidents while on routine patrol. The patrol administrator would want an answer as soon as possible, but would want the problem thought out; therefore, invite the appropriate members to participate.)

If the problem had not existed, or the problem had existed but had not presented itself before, and there was a need for immediate resolution, then the brainstorming session would be utilized. (Example: the taking of hostages during a holdup would call for a new response procedure and time would be of the essence.)

When the patrol administrator includes all levels of patrol as a part of the operation of the patrol function, the unit develops its ability to be capable of change. The strategy and techniques of change are used in that the persons affected by the change are involved in the planning and implementation of that particular change. The patrol administrator thus becomes a change agent or an initiator of change, hopefully to the benefit of the total department.

STANDARD OPERATING PROCEDURES

Contrary to all that may have been said, written, or expected from police officers, they are human, make mistakes, and are imperfect. A structure of organization in policing exists today whereby most of the decisions made by the officer, or at least the more important decisions, are reviewed and evaluated by supervisors.

Policy may be defined as the general direction of an organization within which the activities of the personnel and units must operate. It contains principles that guide the actual work of the department.

Usually policy is stated in general terms and is used to attain objectives. In effect, it provides guidelines upon which procedures, rules, and individual actions may be based, leaving room for individual interpretation, directions, and initiative. We must have policy in order to have innovation and creativity.

Rules, on the other hand, tell subordinates exactly what to do in a prescribed situation. All organizations must have rules, especially the essential feature of flexibility. Coordination and complete compliance are necessary in certain situations. Whenever the development of a plan reveals the need for training, standard operating procedures, or rules and regulations, the department should reduce to writing and disseminate information that will help officers save time and react professionally as appropriate.

Standard operating procedures are a must. Without them, there would be no team effort, and unlikely achievement of the objectives of the Patrol Operation. Not long ago an officer who worked in the Evidence Technicians Unit stated that no matter how much experience he had, he would still use the procedure as written, step by step, to insure uniformity of performance. He added, "I don't care what anyone says about me going by the book, I know I won't ever perform differently and I won't leave anything undone." Naturally if the officer had to testify in court, he could use the same procedure and overcome any defense objection. Additionally, if officers read the Miranda warning from a card issued by the department, they will not have to worry about giving the suspect his rights as prescribed by the Supreme Court. Procedures on conducting line-ups, booking prisoners, etc. must be standard in order to comply with the law in certain cases, and to produce satisfactory performance among all divisions throughout the police department.

All patrol leaders should participate in recognizing areas where standard operating procedures would improve the department or prevent a fellow officer from being injured. The range of help that is possible is wide and varied. Therefore, alert and aware patrol administrators must attempt to infuse the patrol division with the planning concept. A sergeant, while watching one of his officers testify in a lower court, observed that the officer was standing alongside the defendant with his weapon on the side closest to the defendant. Just a flip of the small leather strap and the weapon could have been in the defendant's possession. Result, standard operating procedures: all officers (when testifying) will stand on the side and slightly to the rear of prisoners with their gun side away from the prisoner.

Sloppy or careless police work should never be acceptable. However, plans or procedures should not be implemented for picayune tasks that might reduce innovation and initiative.

WRITTEN DIRECTIVES

Written directives means exactly what it says. From all practical experience, the chief who puts his policy in written form provides the department with sound direction and projects himself as a leader who wants good communication and dissemination of information. Written directives are all General Orders, Special Orders, Personnel Orders, and Memoranda. Directives are used to clarify the purposes and objectives of the department and of the subordinate elements within it so that all activity is conducted toward a single purpose.

General Orders

General Orders are written directives that pertain to the permanent policy and procedures for the indefinite future of the police department. Examples of proper subjects of General Orders:

1. Institution of permanent procedures, rules, policies and manuals related thereto.
2. Permanent changes in organization.
3. Installation of permanent programs that affect more than one unit subordinate to the issuing authority; e.g., citizen complaint, internal affairs procedure, etc.
4. Permanent personnel policies and procedures including recruiting, hiring, training, and promotion policies, but not including changes of status, such as transfers and promotions.
5. Use of public facilities and equipment.

Special Orders

Those directives affecting a specific unit, a specific event, or circumstance of a temporary or self-canceling nature or involving only specific segments of activities. Examples of proper subjects of Special Orders:

1. The assignment of individual duties to public gatherings or parades.
2. Seasonal change of uniforms.
3. Annual budget preparation and special instructions for this year completed.
4. Assignment of police vehicles.

Personnel Orders

Includes a change in position, transfer, promotion, etc.

1. The appointment of new personnel.
2. The assignment or transfer of members from one unit to another.
3. Promotions.
4. Commendations.
5. Suspension and dismissal.
6. Resignation or retirement.

Memoranda

Written information not warranting a formal order. Used to direct any segment or all of the department personnel in specific situations or to inform them of coming events. Examples of proper subjects of memoranda:

1. Date, time, and place of "Police Week."
2. Available schooling.
3. Court decisions and opinions by the legal officer.

Authority

General Orders are usually issued by the chief of police. Special orders are usually issued by the chief or with his approval. This would include the patrol commander desiring to issue a directive affecting units other than his own, who would have to forward the directive to the chief for his approval. In many cases the directives would be staffed (gaining concurrences and nonconcurrences from appropriate personnel) before being issued at the direction of the chief. Personnel Orders should be prepared by the personnel officer and issued at the direction of the chief. Memoranda may be issued by any level of command at the direction of the chief. It is most important for all members, especially at the supervisory level, to understand the authority for issuing orders. Unity of command can become broken and confusing if the system is nebulous or assurance of understanding is not completed.

Distribution

Consideration should be given to each type of order. Who receives a copy of an order is important to improve efficiency and economy.

For example, a copy of an order affecting an individual patrolman should be sent to him. Additionally, a copy of the personnel order should be sent to the patrol officer's commander to keep him informed.

Other considerations concerning standard operating procedures, etc., and which the patrol administrator should completely understand, are preparation, indexing, general format, cancellations, and amendments. Experience has shown that orders and procedures which are read and clearly understood will benefit the total department.

Patrol commanders should be aware of what it takes to prepare standard operating procedures. For example, when the United States Supreme Court ruled that a suspect be advised of his constitutional rights of representation by counsel at any line-up in which he is made to appear, procedures needed to be developed to insure standard operation with respect to compliance of the mandate.

The first step in planning is recognition of need, which becomes rather obvious from the decisions in United States vs. Wade, Gilbert vs. California, and Stovall vs. Denno (reported in *U.S. Law Week,* June 1967, p. 4597). The objective: prepare appropriate instructions and information necessary for understanding and executing courses of action to be taken when persons are to be placed in line-ups, and insure proper dissemination in the form of a standard operating procedure. Data needs to be gathered relevant to the objective, and includes (1) legal questions, (2) persons represented by counsel, (3) persons not represented by counsel, (4) indigent persons, (5) emergency line-ups, (6) waiver of right to presence of counsel, (7) responsibility for conducting the line-up, (8) preparation of appropriate forms to implement waiver of right to counsel.

The next step: answer the who, what, when, where, why, and how with the collected data. The procedure or final draft, as it is commonly called, would then be written so staffing can take place. In this example, staffing with the following persons would be beneficial: (1) attorney general of the state; (2) district or state's attorney; (3) chief judge of the circuit court; (4) chief judge of district or local court (if the names of the judges do not apply to your area, it would mean those judges who would rule or judge the admissibility of the procedure used by your department for conducting line-ups); (5) legal advisor (if applicable); (6) public defender (if applicable); (7) local bar association; (8) all operational commanders, because of the importance and effect the procedure would have on the outcome of criminal cases; (9) especially the operational commanders directly responsible for conduct of line-ups; (10) any unit that may be affected by the procedure. The procedure should be practical, feasible, written in a way so it will be easily understood, and should include any information that might be helpful for implementation. For example, Schmerber v. California, 348 U.S. 757, 772–779, where the court held that compelling a suspect to submit to a withdrawal of a sample of blood for analysis for alcoholic content and the admission into evidence of the analysis report did not abridge the privilege against self-incrimination; Holt v. United States, 218 U.S. 245 (this case supports the Schmerber decision). In this case a question arose as to whether a blouse belonged to a defendant. A witness testified at the trial that the defendant put on the blouse and it had fit. The defendant argued that the admission of the testimony was erroneous because compelling him to put on the blouse was a violation of privilege against self-incrimination. The court rejected the claim as an extravagant extension of the Fifth Amendment. The Fifth Amendment privilege offers no immunity from fingerprinting, photographing, measurement, appearance in court, or a requirement that the accused stand up or make a gesture. In other words, these things do not abridge the privilege against self-incrimination. This information is given to support and explain that part of the procedure which advises the force: It is not a violation of the Fifth Amendment privilege against self-incrimination to require a suspect to participate in a line-up. The suspect who refuses to do so may nevertheless be required to do so as long as counsel is present. The in-depth example is given to point out the type of effort needed when completing staff work for standard operating procedures. (Note: a review of all orders that may need to be amended or rescinded must take place to avoid any conflict.

TACTICAL PLANNING

Tactical planning is the kind of planning that should be done when you are confronted with circumstances at designated places when you have time to anticipate problems and develop the best solution. This type includes planning for disasters, planning for strikes, especially if your department faces picketing on a regular basis, and major crimes such as bank robberies, and plans for prison riots (see Chapter 10).

Tactical plans are flexible in that they are developed to meet needs but they can be adjusted at any time. The flexibility will be developed optimally if the basic tactical plan is a good one. The basic plan should be well thought out to achieve a smooth, coordinated performance at the time the plans are implemented. Standards of excellence in planning result in tactical task forces operating with precision and efficiency.

Let's consider a hold-up or robbery in progress at the main bank in your town, which would be a major crime. The use of force or fear is present, and it is safe to assume the perpetrator is dangerous. As in the case of good officers no matter what the rank, an assessment of the situation should take place in which you will decide what course of action you are going to follow. Take a position out of the line of sight and the line of fire. Put something—the building, police vehicle or door—between you and the suspect. Determine if there is a need to consider the victim regarding injury or potential danger, or if medical aid should be on the way. The next check-off would entail a quick review of action for confrontation. Remember, sloppy or careless police procedure has cost officers their lives. Be careful to avoid any surprise tactics that will not give you complete command of the situation. Partial success at this point could lead to injury to the victim or yourself, plus the fact you may be catalyst to the victim and become hostage yourself.

If your assessment reveals no danger to the victim and the suspect is not aware of your presence, you should remain outside and select the most advantageous position to secure the premises and await the arrival of assisting units. In this case, time is on your side. You should attempt to have the superior position so that when the suspect comes outside you are in command. Additionally, by waiting outside and the suspect not being aware of your presence, it is less likely hostages will be taken or injury to the victim will occur. If the suspect is gone on arrival, then those parts of the preliminary investigation that have not taken place should be completed.

The responsibility for completing the preliminary investigation would be department policy as a matter of procedure. Deciding if patrol or criminal investigators are responsible, and to what extent, will be determined by the chief; however, the command officers should have input. The definition of the preliminary investigation that follows is placed here to improve continuity for the tactical planning of major crimes:

1. Proceed to the scene with safety and dispatch. Emphasis should be placed on safety, since there is no help whatsoever if you do not arrive.
2. Aid the injured if required.

3. Determine what crime has been committed, if any. This becomes most important in that many officers are awaiting information to help them determine their approach of the suspect, if encountered.
4. Arrest the perpetrator, if possible.
5. As soon as you can, advise the dispatcher of a description of the suspect(s) and their method and direction of escape.
6. Protect the crime scene and cause the proper collection of evidence.
7. Locate witnesses and get identification and all other information concerning the victim, suspect, and incident.
8. Write your report clearly and accurately, remembering you may need the information to testify in court and also that other people have to read your report. Reproduce the incident as close to the real thing as possible. Usually at this point the investigator will continue the investigation.

The management by objective concept emphasizes to the patrol administrator the need to accomplish the mission no matter what the situation. Plans that have been written and are available to meet anticipated emergencies best fulfill that need. Whether the department be large or small, have night commander, inspectors, duty officers, or a platoon commander in charge after the regular working day, each should be held responsible for knowing how to implement such plans.

One such plan would be a riot or civil disorder plan. The type of information required for this plan would include:

1. Coordination with outside agencies, such as:
   a. Fire department
   b. Health department
   c. Transit and traffic
   d. American Red Cross
   e. Public worker
   f. Medical examiner
   g. Medical society
   h. Civil defense and disaster
   i. Local, state, and federal authorities
2. Internal information
   a. Call-up system
   b. Location of necessary equipment (including emergency equipment)
   c. Communication
   d. Command and supervising assignments
   e. Instruction on effective implementation
   f. Feeding and housing of personnel
   g. Arrest and detention procedures (emergency)
   h. Security of buildings
   i. Staging areas
   j. Transportation

The list could go on and on. However, the important aspect is to learn the relationship between good planning and achieving the objective in emergency situations.

Planning for special events differs from the emergency planning in that good intelligence and communication are a matter of cooperation between the police and the person(s) responsible for producing the event. Rapport should be developed between the officials and police, and meetings should be held where issues can be discussed. The importance of these meetings cannot be overemphasized, because it is at these meetings prior to the event that police manpower becomes the patrol administrator's primary concern. The patrol commander realizes his primary function and should contribute to the fullest as a participating member of the committee. However, he should always be thinking about using resources of other agencies to achieve the objective without using a police officer (e.g., in many cases the use of equipment to block off street access can be used just as well as a police officer). The other question to be considered regarding the use of police manpower is the policy of the department concerning the use of police vs. private security for situations that require security, but which are privately run and profit-making. Some departments have a policy of allowing officers to work at these events, but the organization must pay the officer. Other departments do not allow officers to moonlight and in these instances, the organization must hire private security. Additionally, some departments will supply officers for events only where police authority is required, and then the private organization must pay for the officers' time. The decision becomes a matter of priorities, manpower, and other resources.

If the responsibility falls completely on the police, or even if the police are only partly responsible, they should be interested in the following information:

1. Type of Event
   Political rally   Kentucky Derby
   Athletic contest   Rose Bowl
   Local holiday celebration   Rock 'n roll dance
   July 4th parade
2. Location
   Football or baseball stadium   Civic center
   Exposition hall   Parade route
3. Time
   Date(s)   Time of unusual features
   Time beginning   (You may need to change deploy-
   Approximate duration   ment of personnel from place to
   Time ending   place as special features occur.)

4. Approximate Number of People
   Attending
   Vehicle traffic
   Pedestrian traffic
5. Parking Facilities
   VIP
   Press
   Picture mobile command vehicle (if used)
6. Communications
   Call numbers: decision must be made to use regularly assigned call numbers or special call numbers used for special events.
   Prepositioned telephone lines should be checked to insure means for private conversation.
7. Traffic Control
   Vehicle
   Pedestrian
   Perimeter of event
   Normal flow for other areas
8. Government Agencies
   Fire department (ambulance)
   Water department
   First Aid (Who is available?)
   Public works
9. Other Agencies
   Telephone company
   Gas and electric company
10. Restricted Areas
    Unauthorized persons
    Unauthorized vehicles
11. Arrest Considerations
    Holding area for prisoners
    Transportation of prisoners
    Location to be taken (The location may be different from normal location due to circumstances.)
    Central location to be advised of persons arrested for press and relatives' notification.

Each event has certain aspects that call for adjustments in your plan even to the point that actions change while the event is taking place. Yearly events usually have basic problems that will allow the use of a master plan that can be implemented routinely. Usually there are areas where improvements can be made. This is brought out when a critique of the operations for strengths and weaknesses is completed.

Most police departments have responsibility for at least a few yearly events. The principles of planning for those events apply no matter how large the crowd or what type of event. The Sugar Bowl and Mardi Gras in New Orleans are repeated each year, and plans must be prepared in order to provide protection of life and property and a safe, smooth flow of vehicular and pedestrian traffic. The Kentucky Derby in Louisville, Kentucky, and the Preakness in Baltimore, Maryland, are also examples of parades—yearly events for which appropriate planning must take place. In both cases, no permit is needed for the horserace, but the parade that precedes the race must have a permit. Information should then be obtained about the time and location of each, anticipated size of the crowd, parking, medical aid, etc. From this, information and instructions can be disseminated to the appropriate personnel of the police agency.

APPROVAL OF PLANS

Approval of the plans would be determined by the number of divisions or units involved that may have to commit manpower. For example, if members of patrol, traffic, and criminal investigation units are assigned responsibilities, approval for implementation of the plan would have to come from the commander of the operation bureau or his equal, depending on the size of the department and title. In the case of the Kentucky Derby, officers from all bureaus are involved; therefore, approval would come from the chief. Coordination by the commanders of the respective units would be necessary, or the formation of a committee with individual responsibility assigned for producing a final plan will suffice.

The plan could be written as follows (*Note.* This does not reveal actual plan used by the Louisville Division of Police.):

21st ANNUAL KENTUCKY DERBY PARADE
AND RACE

Location:	Churchill Downs Race Track
Date & Time:	Saturday, May 5, 1973
	Appropriate police coverage shall begin at 0900 hours and continue until completion of the event and the securing of the detail, which will be approximately 1900 hours.
Purpose:	The purpose of the police detail would be:
	1. Provide for the smooth flow of vehicle and pedestrian traffic.
	2. Protect parked vehicles from vandalism and theft.
	3. Provide assistance where necessary with adequate patrol coverage including receipt of complaints. (This can be done by having one or more well-known locations at the racetrack.)

4. Have a reserve force available which could be used to alleviate potential disruptions.

Attendance:

| Parade Route | 100,000 people |
| Race | 80,000 people |

Parking:
Official parking
Public parking
Reserved parking
Prohibited parking
Buses, taxicabs
Emergency vehicles
This information would aid in coordination and flow of traffic.

Barricades: and/or Signs:
Locations should be selected as appropriate with saving of manpower but also achieving the objective.

Responsibility:
Name of ranking officer in command
Name(s) of assisting officers and area of responsibility

Required Action:
Traffic Unit
Indicate the number of supervisors and officers
Assignment (traffic control, etc.)
Location of assignment
Reporting time (adjusted to need)
If assignment changes by time and location, a chart showing the changes should be made available.
Similar instructions would be given by unit—e.g., patrol, criminal investigation, special operations. (Plainclothes pickpocket squad.) Appropriate uniforms and equipment necessary should be part of plan.

General Information:
Information that would be of importance to all personnel and of a general nature would be placed here such as:
1. Location of command post
2. Telephone number of command post
3. Location of medical facilities
4. Fire apparatus available, location and phone number
5. Lost person and property disposition
6. General prohibited areas
7. Locations in need of frequent inspections
   Lavatories would be one location where vendor-robbing and pickpocketing could take place.
8. Maps of the areas showing the parade route
9. Charts showing individual officers and exact location of assignment

Alternate plans and routes should be developed depending on conditions, weather, intelligence, and police hazards.

Five-year Plans

All plans are only as good as the department's ability to implement them. Most police departments around the country have not and do not concern themselves with five-year plans for a variety of considerations. Those departments which do know the painstaking effort that goes into producing a report that outlines the goals and approaches. With experimentation taking place throughout the country in all facets of the criminal justice system, but especially in law enforcement, five-year plans will become more prevalent.

We need only look at regional criminal-justice planning to realize the necessity of multi-year and annual planning. A review of the importance of regional criminal-justice planning points up many factors that are basic to planning, but also points out to the patrol administrator the very important aspect of developing a broad, comprehensive outlook on his position as related to state and local government, county government, city and county managers, Model Cities, OEO programs, manpower development and training, Health, Education and Welfare, Highway Safety Act, and the Juvenile Delinquency Prevention and Control Act. As an example of the interrelationship between other government agencies and the patrol administrator, the Department of Housing and Urban Development had a report prepared by the Rand Corporation of Santa Monica, California, entitled *Guide to Decision-making in Police Patrol*.

Regional criminal-justice planning begins by identifying problems, priorities, alternatives, and goals. The patrol administrator must understand his position relative to these goals and determine what resources are necessary on his part to become an active participant (even if it is through his chief) in problem resolutions, innovations, and attainment of the objectives. Planning, budgets, and statistical analyses are next on the agenda. From here, organization must take place, and money, personnel and material must be distributed. The planning agency advises that 40% of the resources shall go to local centers of government. Developing plans, setting goals and subgoals, and collecting data relative to crime in the inner city, suburban, and rural area will involve patrol administration, no matter what size department, or whether the agency is a state, county, or a municipal police organization.

As pointed out earlier, the understanding and skill of the patrol commander becomes tremendously important when the allocation of funds is based on costs, risks, benefits, feasibility, and political and community factors. The patrol administrator must be able to cope with the relationships between all other persons involved and himself.

Finally, regional criminal-justice planning uses documentation, evaluation, and multi- (in many cases this is a five-year plan) and annual plans to go forward. Implementation is not easy. Potential obstacles should be considered, especially the difficult obstacle of planning at a regional level and implementing at a local level.

What better discussion on a five-year plan than to consider an actual introduction of this type of planning and review of the considerations as done by a municipal police department? The importance of the questions, Who are we? Where are we going? and, How are we going to get there? strikes the very heart of five-year planning. The Dallas Police Department issued its five-year plan in March 1973. The foreword of the plan as written by the Chief of Police Frank Dyson is presented here. The points to dwell upon are reflections on past and future, effective police service, efficiency, human development and growth, partnership with government and community, personal commitment, and administrative expertise.

Foreword . . . a message from the Chief

In seeking to develop a comprehensive plan to guide the activities for the Dallas Police Department in the next five years, it has been critically necessary to dwell in-depth on what this Department is all about—its reason for being, its role in the community, the mistakes of the past, and hopes for the future. This plan is an initial step into our future and its ramifications are many. First, the community will receive the direct benefits of increased excellence in the rendering of effective police service. Second, the city government will realize economy of the highest order through police capability of weighing its operations in terms of cost/effectiveness. Third, each of the personnel of the Department will be able to realize his own maximum potential in terms of personal advancement in an enhanced career path, to perform as a total policeman on the front line of the attack on crime, and to achieve recognition as a community professional in the true sense.

The Dallas Police Department, in close partnership with the community and the city government, is now ready to bring implementation of a new era. We will proceed with that necessary degree of caution inherent in applying change and innovation. Research, experimentation, evaluation, and planning must precede action. A total commitment to optimum police effectiveness on a massive scale as outlined in this plan must be carefully implemented.

I am personally committed to the future of this Department and believe that, through close cooperation and a unity of effort, we will set trail-blazing precedents which will truly be turning points in law-enforcement history.

To all of you reading this report, I would like to add two important words of caution: First, the report and its summary should be read and quoted in context. The plan is an integrated and interrelated effort and undue emphasis placed on any single item could be both misleading and detrimental to the global effort. Second, a plan for change is only as good as the mechanisms it provides for feedback of information and adjustment based upon incremental results. The plan should not be considered as ultimate and unchangeable. It can and will be adjusted to meet needs which are identified as we progress. [Signed] Frank Dyson.[9]

Generally speaking, the Dallas Police Department began with an operational concept and listed major features. The specifics are important mostly because they deal with those features in the area of patrol across our nation, that will earn for policing total acceptance from the citizens. For this reason the Dallas Police Department's five-year plan is presented.

The Dallas five-year plan includes the following (note these are partial descriptions of the major features):

1. Decentralization of police service.
2. Development of generalist/specialist police officer: perform all general functions of the line officer plus develop a specialty expertise in the number and types required for total range of required services (photography, investigation, drug abuse)
3. Operations of generalist/specialist officer in team-policing.
4. Development of resources-tracking and information-delivery system to provide predictive resource allocation.

The next step is to set department goals, such as:

Goal I: Reduce crime to five (5) index offenses per 1,000 population.
Goal III: 90% of all Dallas homes and businesses enrolled in computer-identification system.
Goal V: Traffic injuries at 300 per 100,000 population.
Goal VIII: Zero loss of personnel due to lack of career opportunity.

Acceptable progress toward each goal is then spelled out in a series of posture statements. This is done in order to determine where the department is at any given time and also to revise acceptable goal gradients.

The next consideration is to be realistic and review the limitations or constraints that the department will face. Included among the restrictive features would be competition from industry for qualified personnel, pension systems that make lateral entry prohibitive, appropriate timing, and attitudes, both within and without the department—specifically, the role of the police as viewed by the other facets of the criminal-justice system and governmental agencies.

STRATEGIES

There is no way to implement a five-year plan unless there is developed a strategy or technique that considers change and the most advantageous method to accomplish the change. Change can and will usually affect other government agencies, the community, and the criminal-justice system. Two strategies that should be included are information and participation. Disclosing to other parties what you are doing and allowing them to participate in decisions affecting them will definitely enhance the ability of the department to succeed. Patrol administrators should be intimately involved in communicating the changes to these other agencies.

CONCEPT DEVELOPMENT

Most programs cannot be implemented in their entirety and result in complete success. It is therefore necessary to experiment in order to work out the bugs. Limited implementation by a pilot project calling for a total operation on a limited basis, or limited operation but on a total basis, is helpful; e.g., decentralize one whole precinct, or implement team-policing throughout the department. In either case, the experimentation and in-depth demonstration should provide the information necessary to decide, at critical stages, if adjustments are necessary.

HUMAN RESOURCES

A conversation with a Ph.D. several years ago resulted in the following answer to the question, Where can private funds help most in the development of law enforcement?: Help develop the people in law enforcement, because without good people, all the science and technology are useless.

There is no intention to demean our brothers since the team concept is necessary to go forward, but the human relations of law enforcement necessitates the development of human resources first and foremost. The foresight shown by Chief Frank Dyson and those involved in developing this five-year plan in Dallas should be commended. Increased rewards at the patrolman level are a must for law enforcement if professionalism is to be a reality. Horizontal growth at the patrol-officer level is essential.

Human Resources Development

Middle-management overload is a major problem presented when a vertical career path is the only achievement potential. Under such a reward system personal advancement tends to take expertise away from the street and builds unrealistic layers of supervision. Figure 3.1 shows how this middle-management layer may be redistributed by availability of vertical and horizontal career paths with appropriate monetary and career awards along both paths. Figure 3.2 reflects the combined vertical and horizontal career-path structure that will permit:

1. Monetary and status rewards along horizontal paths; personal growth and incentive to remain in field services.
2. Utilization of noncommissioned personnel at a lower pay scale to perform more routine functions.
3. Lateral entry at any level of organization with no threat since individual growth opportunity minimizes competition for vertical growth.

The plan identifies specific action to support the development of such an organizational structure and man it properly. These efforts are generally concerned with three ideas:

1. Know what the job is
a. Job-requirements identification
b. Role-definition
c. Task and function analyses
d. Improve training programs

2. Know and select the right person for the job
a. Selection-system improvements
b. Continuous selection-criteria validation
c. Continued emphasis on minority recruitment

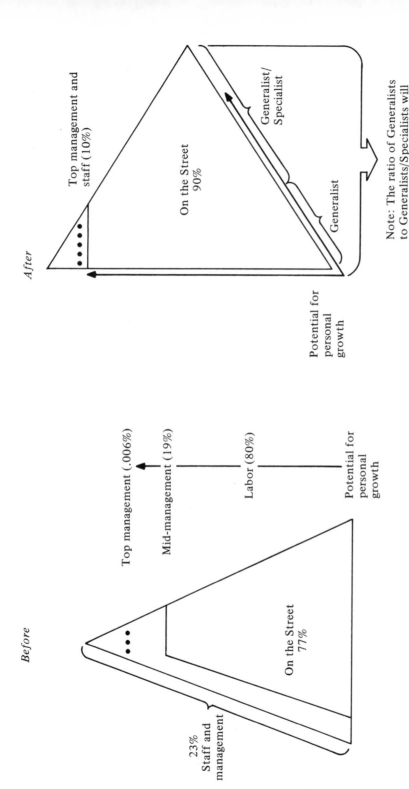

FIGURE 3.1 Concept of Redistribution of Police Personnel.

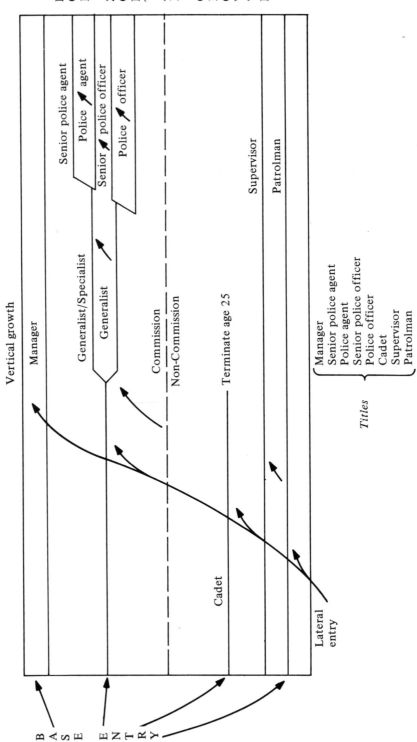

FIGURE 3.2 Proposed Organizational Structure.

d. Continued experimentation with women in police service
e. Lateral-entry opportunity development
f. Human-resources tracking and forecasting development.

3. Retain the right person in the job

a. Current human-resources assessment
b. Transitional assignment plan
c. Career-path development—vertical/horizontal
d. Positive disciplinary system implementation

SYSTEMS RESOURCES

In this day and age technology must be provided in the form of computers and information-delivery systems. The hardware and software necessary to supply the data for decision-making relative to performance, efficiency, costs, and effectiveness must also be included in order to evaluate.

Support

It is well known that the communication center of police agencies is the heart of the operation. Proper support by staff in the areas of planning and budgeting and providing a physical facility to carry on the program is as important to law enforcement as logistics is to the army.

Summary

Five-year plans will have a tremendous impact on law enforcement. The answers to where we are, where we are going and how we intend to get there can only be obtained by this type of planning. Departments which develop the in-house ability or outside assistance to accomplish this planning will be more prepared to cope with the future. Patrol administrators around the country should not be afraid to communicate with each other in order to be helpful. Knowledge of operational concepts, department goals, objectives, constraints, management plans, operational plans, support plans, manpower, equipment, and facility resources along with master-programs understanding is available and waiting for interested and dedicated police commanders.

PLANNING FOR MAXIMUM EFFECTIVENESS

Patrol planning for maximum effectiveness by the administrator simply means that by setting a good example of planning for his unit, the patrol administrator can permeate his unit with this principle of administration and also affect all other units within the department. Each level of authority, from himself to the level of execution, will have the proper direction and specific guidance to accomplish the patrol mission.

The patrol administrator views the total picture of increases and decreases in crime, crime rates, community stability, and internal esprit de corps. It is his responsibility to develop the ability to view the component parts of the picture, because it looks different to the patrolman, sergeant, lieutenant, and captain. The problem, the resolution of the problem, and the planning of that resolution requires the patrol administrator to consider manpower (his most valuable resource) and equipment. In order to achieve maximum effectiveness, it will be necessary to analyze the problem in terms of time of day, day of week, location of occurrence or occurrences, and the specific crime (robbery, burglary, auto theft) or school disruptions, rock and roll dances, etc. Assignment of the specific number of personnel and equipment will be determined by the enormity of the problem. In the case of school disruptions or rock and roll dances and similar operational problems, the patrol commander can gain some help from intelligence, both overt and covert. No leader should ever be afraid to ask the patrolman on the beat to give his estimate in order to help the department.

This advice should also apply to each level of supervision. Many times the supervisor mistakenly believes that because of his time on the job he automatically knows more about a situation, but anytime a leader tries to sit in an ivory tower and plan operational action, failure is more likely to result. Nothing is more important for the patrol administrator than to keep in contact with every level of authority under his command. When the patrol commander makes his decisions concerning the implementation of an operational plan of action, he should have considered all personnel input and empirical data relevant to the problem. This helps pinpoint potential problems. The result is maximum effectiveness because only the amount of manpower and equipment necessary to achieve the objective is used.

It is possible for this type of planning to be done by all personnel in patrol, which should result in little wasted time and effort. For example, if a patrol sergeant is working a sector containing eight beats and a problem of robbery arises on one beat at a location adjacent to a second beat, or very close to it, good planning could result in almost constant coverage of that particular location without disrupting the total sector (see Figure 3.3). If the sergeant and the men of his sector plan properly, by analyzing the robberies by beat, by time of day (a), by beat and location (b), and by beat by day of week (c), together they can develop an irregular schedule where cars number 102, 104, and 105 can assist car 101 in inspecting the police hazard. As the figures indicate, the problem exists on Thursday and Friday between 1600 hours and 1800 hours. This does not mean there should not be a plan for the other days of the week, but by being selective in the patrol procedure, the sergeant and his men can obtain maximum results from within their own sector of operation.

This type of planning does not mean assistance will not be needed if the problem continues or enlarges beyond the control of the sergeant, but it does mean that the teams of men have contributed their best efforts in attempting to resolve the problem without additional resources. The enlightened patrol commander would be aware of the problem and knowledgeable about the plans and efforts of the sergeant and his men. Consequently, the commander would be ready to assign the additional resources to resolve the problem at the appropriate time.

Communication between all levels is important because of timing and not allowing any area of the community to receive any less service and protection than required. The principle here is the same as in civil disorders: do not call all of your forces to the location of the disruption because you may leave an area unprotected, thereby suffering greater losses in that unprotected area. Emphasis is placed on communication, team effort, and total planning.

The next phase of this operational planning would have to do with the effect of patrol-planning for maximum effectiveness on other units within the department, outside of patrol. The goal of this type of planning is to resolve the problem without duplicating effort and to utilize the expertise of all units involved in the plan.

Facts indicate that narcotics addicts must commit crime in order to maintain their habit. To what percent this group has contributed to the crime problem is immeasurable at this time. We can safely say it is substantial. Crime reports have also borne out the fact that young

Beat #	1600	1700	1800	1900	2000	2100	2200	2300	2400
101	X	X	X X	X					
102									
103									
104	X								
105							X		
106									
107								X	
108									

X = Robbery

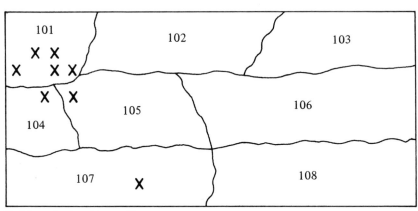

Robbery by location — Pin map

	Sun	Mon	Tues	Wed	Thurs	Fri	Sat
101					X X	X X X	
102							
103							
104							
105							
106							
107							
108							

FIGURE 3.3   Robbery, Sector #1, Watch 4-12

people are involved in more crime now than at any time since the beginning of records. This leads to the realization that cooperation, coordination, and good planning are essential between units of the police organization if specific crime problems are to be resolved.

Let's, for example, take a situation where a given area of the community is plagued with burglaries of dwelling houses. Analysis of the crime reports of this area reveals the approximate time of day, day of week, modus operandi, and all other information relevant to the crimes. First, we know it is a problem for patrol since it is the first line of defense. Second, it is a problem for the investigation section since the follow-up of felonies will most likely be made by the investigator. Depending on what is being stolen in the burglaries (more than likely it will be appliances, radios, TVs, etc.), if anything is learned in subsequent investigations (information will probably reveal that young people are involved). Third, the youth division will be concerned with the problem. And fourth, for a total effort, members of the narcotics unit would be included. To plan for maximum effectiveness in this case, the following procedure is recommended:

1. Chart the burglaries on a pin map. The problem of dwelling burglaries can be plotted over a period of weeks. A comparison can be made by the week to determine the trend by locations. In analyzing burglaries it is difficult to place the time of occurrence specifically because of the hours that people are away from home. Preliminary investigations will help, but in-depth follow-up will be necessary to close the gap when trying to determine the exact hour the crime took place. More than likely, selective enforcement will be necessary to combat dwelling burglaries. This is because most departments change shifts at 0800, 1600, and 2400 hours or 0700, 1500, and 2300 hours. In departments where permanent shifts exist, the time of shift change is more than likely the same. The burglary problem will not coincide with these shift changes; therefore, selective enforcement is necessary for time of occurrence.
2. Determine by the hours, as close as possible, when the burglaries are being committed.
3. Glean the reports of the burglaries to obtain as much information as possible about the incidents (method of entry, exit, items taken, etc.).
4. Prepare a presentation that will disseminate the information to all concerned.
5. Contact the commander of the other units you believe can assist in resolving the problem.
6. Request a meeting to include the patrol, criminal investigation, youth, and narcotics units as participants.
7. Explain the problem and request suggestions on the plan of attack.
8. Remember, patrol is the primary unit of prevention, so the patrol commander should first inform the citizens of the area where the burglaries are occurring and implement a program of awareness and involvement

from the community. Inviting representatives from the community to the police district to show them exactly what is occurring in the area where they live is a very good start. Sincerity and openness on the part of the patrol commander in presenting the problem is a positive factor.

9. Prepare a team plan utilizing the expertise of each unit, avoiding duplication of effort.

This kind of planning and cooperation between units is essential in any progressive police agency. When the individuals involved in achieving the objective are involved in the planning and told the reason why they are doing something, success is more likely to occur. It is grass-roots participatory management.

In the category of auto theft, because of the mobility it may be necessary for the crime-analysis unit to keep a pin map for the entire city. This is necessary in departments that are decentralized because the location of theft may be in one district and the location of recovery in another. In departments that are centralized, one pin map charting the location stolen and location recovered is all that would be needed, since all officers report to the same location for roll call. In either case the same procedure for pinning the map would be used, the difference being that in larger departments, which are decentralized, the crime analysis unit would be responsible for advising the different districts of related offenses. Stolen-auto pin maps would reveal the following:

City X

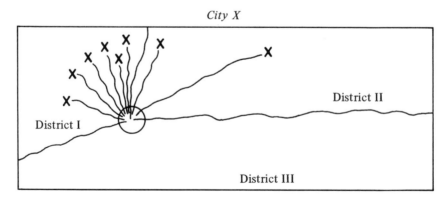

FIGURE 3.4 Stolen-auto Pin Map

X = Location of stolen auto
Y = Location of recovered stolen auto

The letter X indicates the location where the auto was stolen. The letter Y indicates where the auto was recovered. On a pin map, these letters would be indicated by a different color pin. Additionally, if the pin map was prepared for a given month, the date (i.e., 12, 14, 19, 21) could be put on the top of the pin to reveal the date. From this you could determine if most days were on weekends, which may indicate joy-riding. The next step would be to use a rubber band from the location stolen to the location recovered. If the rubber bands show a pattern, it may indicate the autos are being stolen in different parts of the city but abandoned in the same area. If this is the situation, selective and effective enforcement can take place at the location of recovery and probable routes between the theft and recovery.

A good reporting system, based on integrity under Uniform Crime Reporting, is a must for a law-enforcement agency to be effective in planning and resolving crime problems. Reporting systems that contain procedures for daily read-outs of crime for the previous twenty-four hours, posting of the crimes by time of day, day of week, and location on pin maps, and controls that insure the dissemination of this information to patrolmen by patrol supervisors are excellent. Second, when the crime patterns are plotted to reveal a comparison between, say the first two weeks of a watch and the second two weeks, supervisors are able to judge the success or failure of the patrolman, the method of patrol being used, and whether assistance is needed. Computer print-outs will substitute for pin maps wherever this technology is available.

To achieve the objectives in patrol, it is necessary to get the information to the person most responsible for achieving that objective, the patrolman. A pin map maintained in a current status, easily accessible and presented clearly, is a valuable tool and a good way to allow all levels to participate in the common goal of crime prevention and apprehension.

Each member involved in the patrol function should have an interest in the product. When responsibility, authority, and accountability are present, then interest will follow. When a patrolman is held accountable for the beat and the procedure is available to show his production (this means all aspects of policing and not just arrests), he and all levels know they are part of the organization.

Goal-Oriented Statistical Data

Besides the use of pin maps that deal with specific crimes, a goal-oriented statistical data form can be an important tool to the patrol administrator (Appendix B). The name of the game for patrol is to achieve a decrease in the part-one or index crimes of murder, rape, robbery, aggravated assault, burglary, larceny over $50, and auto-theft. Additionally, the crime rate is equally important and deals with the index crimes in two categories: (1) violent crimes, which include murder, rape, robbery, and aggravated assault, and (2) property crimes, which include burglary, larceny over $50, and auto theft. To measure the increase or decrease in crime, you simply count the number of part-one crimes for the present year and compare them with the number of part-one crimes for the previous year.

For example, if the total part-one crimes for the year 1972 was counted to be 4,440, and the total part-one crimes for the year 1971 was 4,195, then your results for the year would be an increase of 5.8% in crime. The increase or decrease in crime is calculated the same way for each month, quarter, six months, nine months, and then finally for the year. The crime rate is determined by the number of crimes per 100,000 population.

In most departments, a 24-hour summary sheet is reviewed by the patrol commander each morning. This sheet will reveal the total number of index crimes, broken down into as many subunits (district, watch, sector) as might be needed to provide the information. It will also reveal the number of violent crimes and property crimes for the previous 24 hours. The patrol commander can compare this data with the data from the previous year, month, and week, which will give him an idea as to the trend of the total crimes. This analysis will keep the patrol administrator on top of the situation and help make the daily decisions for his areas of responsibility. The Goal-oriented Statistical Data form will be produced for the patrol administrator one each week during the present month. This form will be charted by part-one crime category, by area of responsibility, by number of crimes for this month to date, this month last year, this week, and projected total crime for the present month (see Appendix B, Tables B.1–B.4).

If we review the table for the first week of the month (Table B.1), we see the immediate problem of crime as being in the area of Larceny over $50 with a projected increase of 23.5%. This means that if the trend of the first week continues as it has, the end result for the month will be an increase in that category of Index Crime of 23.5%. The patrol administrator plus commanding officers and on down the line would be informed of the condition, which would act as an early warning to give personnel a chance to change the trend. The goals would be (1) a decrease in crime in all categories; (2) reverse the trend as best as possible in any category indicating a projected increase. In this way goals can be set for all levels of authority including the level of execution on the beat. Also noted on the form will be the projected increase of 3% in the Burglary category caused by Sector I of District I, and Sector II of District II.

All personnel through patrol would be apprised of the situation. The individual sector leaders and their supervisor would have the same information. The sector supervisor would attempt to develop a plan to combat the problem with existing resources, and the patrol commander would be aware of his responsibility to give support as appropriate after the sector supervisor and his men have done all possible to resolve the problem. This attitude and total planning for maximum effectiveness is enhanced through the use of the Goal-oriented Statistical Data Form. Those categories revealing a projected decrease are not forgotten; it's a matter of setting priorities, being aware of changing conditions and crime replacements (actual decrease or prevention as opposed to moving the crime from one area to another—displacement), and developing the appropriate enforcement patrol method to do the job.

In reviewing Appendix B, Table B.2, we see the problem of Larceny over $50 has not changed to any great degree except that Sector III of District I has had a decrease for the first week to the second week. Sector I of District I has had an increase for the first week to the second week. Also in the Robbery category, Sector III of District II has had an increase from the first week to the second week and if the trend continues, this will be an increase in the crime of robbery for the month (31 for first week, 44 for second week, for a total of 75 for the two weeks). Notice also the category of Robbery for District III, all sectors. Robbery is a problem in this district, but for Sector III of District III, it has gotten worse from the first to the second week. In the category of Burglary, the first week revealed a projected increase of 3%. On reviewing the second week, we see a projected increase for the month of 16.4% if the burglary trend continues. In-depth analysis would be necessary to determine the best method of patrol, and also the inclusion of the other units, capable of giving assistance, in the planning and resolution of the problem.

The third and fourth week forms (Appendix B, Tables B.4 and B.5) indicate the continuance of a particular problem. The forms and information are easy to produce without the help of a computer and supply a tremendous amount of information for operational planning. Naturally, if the same information can be produced by a computer print-out, it would require less manpower. The key for the computer print-out would be the timeliness of the report, which will allow officers to act before the fact or immediately after the fact. Information must be available on a current basis.

Managing by objectives, or goal-oriented management, is the purpose of the tool (Goal-oriented Statistical Data Form) and should be used as such. Figures as indicated are not exact and have been used only to display the actual use of the forms. When all levels within patrol are aware of the goal and have something to strive for, knowing the team effort exists, paralleled by responsibility, authority and accountability, achieving that goal becomes more realistic.

The patrol administrator should not stop his planning for maximum effectiveness with the internal organization. There are agencies in the criminal justice system and other government agencies that should be included in any planning, especially if their assistance or acceptance of a responsibility will have an impact on crime. Good planning and cooperation between federal, state and local law-enforcement agencies resulted in the development of the National Crime Information Center. One police department, through the assistance of the Bureau of Narcotics and Dangerous Drugs, was able to develop a total operational attack on the drug-enforcement program by coordinating a three-day seminar for over 2,000 members of the force, resulting in an increase of arrests for narcotics violations of over 300% in one year. With good planning, one department resolved the problem of feeding police personnel during civil disorders by cooperating and coordinating efforts with the Office of Civil Disaster.

Patrol commanders should be keenly aware of their personnel each time they have to detail an officer to a specific duty. When proper planning negates the assignment of personnel to a duty that can be handled by nonsworn internal employees or other agency employees, the saving in manpower alone is good management. In today's police departments young patrolmen are asking more questions like, Why do we do it this way? and, Couldn't we do it a better way? Consequently, morale is a factor. These young officers resent performing a function that can be done by equipment or other personnel if proper planning and procedures are developed.

Under the new concept of the criminal-justice system, each of the agencies (law enforcement, prosecution, courts, corrections) is a component of a system, so to speak, and the parts must work in smooth harmony for the system to achieve its goals. Therefore, it is most important that the components of the system communicate and plan with each other to achieve the optimum in the administration of criminal justice.

This concept is intimately involved with the patrol commander, especially at the lower court level. If any department hasn't developed the ability to conduct meetings between judges, prosecutors, and patrol commanders and resolve problems and develop plans, try it, even on a limited basis. The potential exists, for the parts of the system can work together for the good of the community. The understanding, awareness, appreciation of the other guy's problems, and increased communication developed from this type of dialogue will go a long way toward destroying any stereotypes that might be held by one or the other.

In some areas of the country departments consist of only five or ten police officers or sheriffs. Planning between these departments can resolve the need for additional manpower during times of crisis. Mutual-cooperation pacts have been formed, and metropolitan narcotics-enforcement units are operating as a result of regionalization and consolidation. So many problems can be resolved by good planning and communication, to the extent that failure on the part of any police agency due to lack of planning, personal jealousies, or lack of communication is unacceptable management.

Included in the staff-study concept of problem-solving is a part for staffing. This means that concurrences and nonconcurrences are considered by the initiating staff officer before submitting the plan to the chief. Answers to the nonconcurrences are put in the form of rebuttal. This allows the chief to review other thoughts on the proposed procedure before signing his approval. When dealing with other agencies the same principle applies. Before any plan is placed into action, outside agencies should have the opportunity to review any discussions or conclusions that may have been drawn as a result of meetings between the interested parties. In this manner criticism, which might have developed after implementation of the plan, can be avoided.

Results of Good Planning

The results of good planning are apparent in the fact that administration will accomplish the objectives or goals. Planning, directing, and controlling are in the forefront, with organizing, coordinating, staffing, reporting, and budgeting rounding out the responsibilities of the patrol administrator. The patrol administrator is a department head, and as such, he takes the resources supplied by the chief of police and utilizes these resources in a way that produces a superior product of service for the community. The police chief uses planning to implement policy, define policy specifically, state the purpose and objectives of the policy, and set forth the procedures that he believes best to achieve the objective. The patrol administrator must have input into the policy, have the input considered, but after approval, accept the decision and make every effort to implement that policy as if it were his own. Patrol is the largest division in the police department and also has the greatest potential for disgruntled employees; therefore, an affirmative action image by the patrol administrator would help greatly in providing a well-coordinated organization. Moving out into the field, speaking at roll calls, explaining policy, showing the total patrol operation how planning and preparation result in an efficient implementation of a program is good patrol administration.

When management plans properly, then it can be expected that good planning will be something of value for everyone in the department. If the chief comes in to work in the morning and growls at the assistant, you can expect the impression to be passed on to the other subordinates. The same holds true with planning. If the chief and patrol administrator plan properly, captains, lieutenants, sergeants, and patrolmen will plan accordingly. Result: anticipation of future events and the development of methods to resolve these events to the advantage of the department.

BUDGETING: A PLAN OF ACTION

It has been said that a budget is nothing more than a plan of action, usually for the coming year. Budgeting is a good example of the tremendous results that may be accomplished from good planning. The Planning Programming Budgeting System points out planning and budgeting relationships.

> Budget . . . a statement of the financial position of a sovereign body for a definite period of time based on estimates of expenditures during the period and proposals for financing them; a plan for the coordination of resources and expenditures; the amount of money that is available for, required for, or assigned to a particular purpose.[10]

A budget calendar shows a suggested budget preparation calendar on a calendar-year basis. The planning and preparation are obviously essential to the program. The chief administrator, department heads, and finance officers are involved in the final decision, but the patrol administrator must submit the preliminary information

TABLE 3.2   Suggested Police Department Budget Preparation Calendars on Fiscal Year Basis[11]

What Should Be Done	By Whom	On These Dates
Issue budget instructions and applicable forms	City Administrator	November 1
Prepare and issue budget message, with instructions and applicable forms, to unit commanders	Chief of Police	November 15
Develop unit budgets with appropriate justification and forward recommended budgets to planning and research unit	Unit Commanders	February 1
Review of unit budget	Planning and Research Staff with Unit Commanders	March 1
Consolidation of unit budgets for presentation to chief of police	Planning and Research Unit	March 15
Review of consolidated recommended budget	Chief of Police, Planning and Research Staff, and Unit Commanders	March 30
Department approval of budget	Chief of Police	April 15
Recommended budget forwarded to city administrator	Chief of Police	April 20
Administrative review of recommended budget	City Administrator & Chief of Police	April 30
Revised budget approval	City Administrator	May 5
Budget document forwarded to city council	City Administrator	May 10
Review of budget	Budget Officer of City Council	May 20
Presentation to council	City Administrator & Chief of Police	June 1
Reported back to city administrator	City Council	June 5
Review and resubmission to city council	City Administrator & Chief of Police	June 10
Final action on police budget	City Council	June 20

Schedule is for a large department requiring 8 months to develop and process the budget and gain administrative and council approval for it. Other major departments may be on different schedules as a matter of convenience for the administrator and council.

concerning his needs, and should be prepared to appear before governmental bodies to justify requests. The anticipation of critical questioning and probable responses is a must for the enlightened patrol administrator. He must communicate effectively and present himself as an aware and knowledgeable leader.

Planning Programming Budget System (PPBS)

In PPBS there is interchangeable vocabulary. For example, an "objective" may also be a goal, subgoal, ultimate objective, program objective, or subobjective. Before continuing, let's look briefly at examples of the other types of budgeting.

1. Line-item budget: A line-item budget emphasizes input (money in) by organizational units and amounts allocated to an object of expenditure within the unit. It is the simplest system of accounts.

LINE-ITEM BUDGET EXAMPLE

Police Department (Organizational Unit)

Salary (object of expenditure)	$183,000
Printing & office supplies	3,000
Uniforms	6,000
Photo supplies	450
Gas & oil	7,000
Heat	600
Miscellaneous	2,500
Protection equipment	1,800
Auto—Rent	1,560
Auto—Buy	4,000
Auto repair & maintenance	3,600
Building repair & maintenance	500
Radio	1,250
Rent	600
Insurance	1,800
Training	6,000
TOTAL	$223,660

2. Performance budget: A performance budget may be difficult for the layman to apply to most police activities. The major emphasis is on input (money in) to output (what additional performance will be achieved). This application is not difficult to use in areas as shown in the example but becomes more difficult in areas of crime related activities: i.e., What do you expect from the addition of one patrolman to a department?

PERFORMANCE BUDGET EXAMPLE

Transportation
One position is provided at the Central Garage to meet workload resulting from maintenance requirements on electric starters, now standard equipment on motorcycles.

  1 Auto Electrician
      Salary
         General $ 5,468.

One position is added to the First Division Garage where the ratio of vehicles to maintenance personnel is so high as to require constant relief from the Central Garage.

  1 Mechanical Helper
      Salary
         General $ 4,284.

Increasing use of automobiles and motorcycles results in an annual increase in fleet mileage of approximately 1,000,000 miles. This increase is followed by the need for additional petroleum.
      Expense $18,797.

    3. Program Budget: A program budget focuses attention on programs of work and the cost of these programs. The full cost of a program is reflected in dollars and therefore allows for broad cost planning.

PROGRAM BUDGET EXAMPLE

Administration		*Cost*
Salaries	$ 18,118	
Salaries—overtime pay	10,000	
Contractual services	3,453	
Materials and supplies	4,100	$ 35,671
Detective bureau		
Salaries (new: one detective)	126,821	
Contractual services	800	
Materials and supplies	156	
One listening device	2,000	
Two desks	288	
Two chairs	142	$130,207
Youth bureau		
Salaries	40,982	
New typewriter	360	$ 41,342
Accident investigation and traffic control		
Salaries	202,835	
Salaries—overtime for		
serving warrants	3,000	
Contractual services	750	
Materials and supplies	5,750	
Two Stephenson radar units	1,400	$213,735

School traffic protection

Salaries and wages	44,620
Contractual services	60
Materials and supplies	395
Safety patrol picnic	500 $ 45,575

PPBS Planning Programming and Budgeting System (PPBS): A PPBS is a combination of the other three types of budgets into a systematic approach of using budgeting as a decision-making tool. PPBS focuses on fundamental objectives and identifies costs and benefits of major alternative courses of action.

Since the impact of budgeting in the organization is so important and the PPBS is management by objectives, the process has been shown here briefly to indicate the proper planning process. The patrol administrator must have a working knowledge of the budget process. In most police departments, the line-item budget is used. However, as police departments and local governments learn the advantage of the PPBS, more and more agencies will use the management by objective approach in their management planning. Justification, which is the essential word in budgeting, will be integrated with the objective. It must be understood that evaluation and progress measurement need continued study in order to become more meaningful.

a. *Objectives.*[12] The central term of the PPBS structure. A police agency must develop explicit objectives to make possible a genuine agency-wide understanding and a common approach toward their achievement. These objectives should provide specific grounds on which to base the answers to three key questions:

1. What services must be provided? (primary and secondary services)
2. What group is each service intended to satisfy? (juvenile, traffic, etc.)
3. What specific need or goal of the group is the service intended to satisfy?

If this process is correctly applied, the objectives developed consistent with the answers to the questions should become standards for the agency.

b. *Programs.*[13] A program is a package of each and every one of the agency's efforts to accomplish a particular objective or a like group of objectives. If the objective was to reduce crimes against persons within a given area, the program would be composed of all agency activities and expenditures put to that purpose. In a PPBS system there are no recognized objectives except those that can be identified with a program specifically designed to fulfill them.

c. *Program alternatives*[14] means other possible programs besides those already decided upon. This, therefore, creates a comparison of two or more programs (i.e., two or more possible approaches) toward fulfilling the same objective.

d. *Output.*[15]   In a police agency an output should have all of the following properties:

1. It is a service.
2. It is produced by the police agency or under the agency's guidance and authority.
3. It is the result of a particular program.
4. It is the sort of service that can be appropriately singled out as an indicator of program results. It must be a program end-product, and an important one.
5. It is considered by the agency as satisfying an explicit objective or related set of objectives.

In order to be considered an output, the good or service produced must satisfy an explicit objective and must be an indicator of program results.

e. *Progress measurement.*[16]   What does PPBS regard as progress in a given program?

1. The output that had been planned has materialized.
2. The output distribution that had been intended has been completed.

An affirmative answer would be demonstrated by fulfillment of the program. Therefore, progress measurement could be:

1. How closely does the production progress match planned progress?
2. How well is the output distribution proceeding as compared with the distribution plan?

f. *Input.*[17]   The total quantity of manpower, facilities, equipment, and materials applied to the program is the program input.

g. *Alternative ways to do a given job.*[18]   Takes the program as given and raises possibilities for changing the mix of inputs and thereby redirecting the program. Alternative ways to do a given job involve operational matters, not policy questions.

1. The timing of the service, or
2. The quantity or quality of the item or service being produced, or
3. The unit or total cost of the service.

h. *Systems Analysis.*[19] A group of techniques attached to a way of approaching problems. From the standpoint of an individual police agency, two PPBS areas may be especially adaptable to benefit cost techniques.

1. The posing and evaluation of program alternatives; i.e., determining the benefit cost advantage, if any, of shifting to different output and/or distribution patterns so as to satisfy objectives better.
2. The measurement of progress in a given program; i.e., determining the benefit—cost advantage (if any) of changing the input mixed so as to produce and/or distribute the output more efficiently.

Narrative

PPBS is an administrative tool that emphasizes a systems approach to management by determining the objectives of the agency and then developing programs to achieve those objectives. In order to attain its objectives, an agency must develop a program or several programs of activities designed to achieve the desired objectives. A key to the PPBS approach to management is developing program alternatives. This allows for the consideration of programs besides the obvious or those already decided upon, and thereby allows a comparison of two or more programs or methods to achieve the objective.

In order to apply a PPBS to a police agency, one must redesign the agency according to the objectives of the agency as opposed to the more traditional organization by function. For the purpose of this segment we will define as objectives of a police agency:

Primary Objective—The control of crime.

Objectives—Prevention of crime.
Detection of crime.
Apprehension of criminals.

Therefore, in management by objective, the objectives are used to determine both the functional and hierarchical structure or organization of the department.

In traditional organization by function, the development of the agency starts with the operating units and uses these units as a hierarchical and functional means of operation. This type of agency is built from the bottom up. Functions such as patrol and traffic are grouped in a hierarchical classification; i.e., line, by like or similar activities rather than by the ability to achieve a common objective (see Figure 3.5).

In a PPBS of management by objectives the agency is built from the objectives down. The primary objective and subobjectives are determined and the structure of the organization is built from the objective down (see Figure 3.6).

Just as management by the PPBS demands specific objectives, specific objectives should be demanded of the system. What is the specific focus of the PPBS? The aim is to specify the objectives of spending programs and then to minimize the cost of achieving these objectives or to determine whether costs exceed benefits. By the (1) specification of objectives, (2) investigation of alternative means of achieving the objectives, (3) minimization of the costs or comparison of costs and benefits, and (4) systematic use of analysis, the police administrator should maximize the return to the citizens of tax dollars spent.

Systems Information

Although it does not seem consistent with the PPBS requirement of determining objectives and then structuring programs to meet these objectives, several formats are available for applying PPBS to police agencies. The format should meet the needs of the individual department and should be selected on that basis.

SZANTON'S DETAILED POLICE PROGRAM STRUCTURE [20]

1. Control and Reduction of Crime Program

    a. Prevention/Suppression
        (1) General Purpose Patrol
        (2) Special Purpose Patrol (by type of offense)
        (3) Intelligence
        (4) Community Relations
    b. Investigation/Apprehension
        (1) Crimes Involving Major Risk of Personal Injury
            (a) Murder
            (b) Assault
            (c) Rape
            (d) Armed Robbery
            (e) Burglary—Homes
            (f) Arson
            (g) Etc.

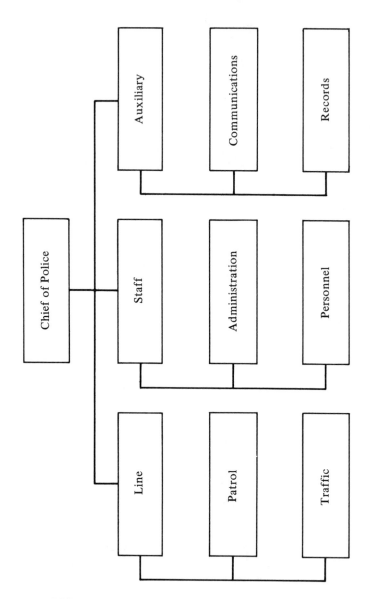

FIGURE 3.5   Traditional organization by function.

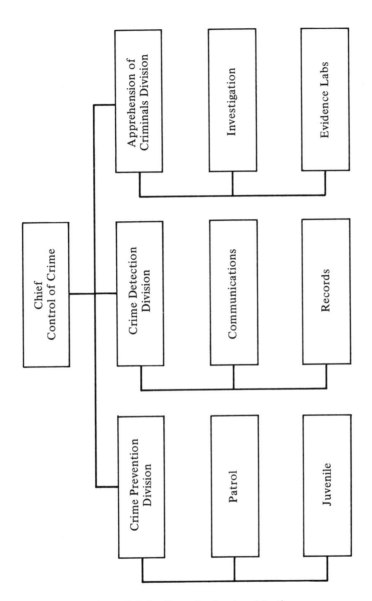

FIGURE 3.6 Organization by objectives.

These charts are not intended to represent complete organizational structures.

      (2) Crimes Not Involving Major Risk of Personal Injury
         (a) Theft
         (b) Unarmed Robbery
         (c) Auto Theft
         (d) Burglary—Commercial
         (e) Fraud
         (f) Forgery
         (g) Etc.
      (3) Vice
         (a) Narcotics
         (b) Prostitution
         (c) Gambling
         (d) Etc.

  c. Prosecution
      (1) Interrogation
      (2) Preparation for Trial
      (3) Trial

  d. Recovery of Property
      (1) Autos
      (2) Other Personal Property
      (3) Commercial Property

  e. General Support
      (1) Communcations
      (2) Records and Data Processing
      (3) Technical Services
         (a) Fingerprint
         (b) Ballistics
         (c) Polygraph
         (d) Laboratory Analysis

2. *Movement and Control of Traffic Program*

  a. Traffic Movement
      (1) Direction of Traffic
      (2) Enforcement of Traffic-oriented Parking Rules
      (3) Emergency Road Services
      (4) Weather Emergency Procedures
      (5) Identification and Reporting of Congestion Points

  b. Traffic Safety
      (1) Enforcement of Regulations
         (a) Patrol/Apprehension of Moving Violations
         (b) Enforcement of Safety-oriented Parking Rules
      (2) Driver Training
      (3) Educational Programs
      (4) Vehicle Inspections

  c. Accident Investigation

3. *Maintenance of Public Order Program*

    a. Public Events
        (1) Sporting Events
        (2) Public Ceremonies
            (a) Parades and Receptions
            (b) Public Meetings
            (c) Cornerstones, etc.

    b. Minor Disturbances
        (1) Private Quarrels
        (2) Parties
        (3) Drunkenness
        (4) Derelicts
        (5) Miscellaneous Nuisances

    c. Civil Disorder
        (1) Prevention
        (2) Suppression

4. *Provision of Public Services Program*

    a. Emergency Services
        (1) Fire
        (2) Medical
        (3) Power Failure
        (4) Flood
        (5) Civil Defense
        (6) Miscellaneous

    b. Missing Persons

    c. Lost Property

    d. Miscellaneous

5. *Administration and Support Program*

    a. Direction and Control
        (1) Direction
        (2) Planning and Development
        (3) Internal Inspection and Review

    b. Training and Personnel
        (1) Recruitment
        (2) Training
            (a) Basic
            (b) Advanced
        (3) Testing, Evaluation, Promotion

    c. Public Relations

    d. Supporting Services
        (1) Records (noncrime) and Data Processing
        (2) Communications
        (3) Budget
        (4) Property

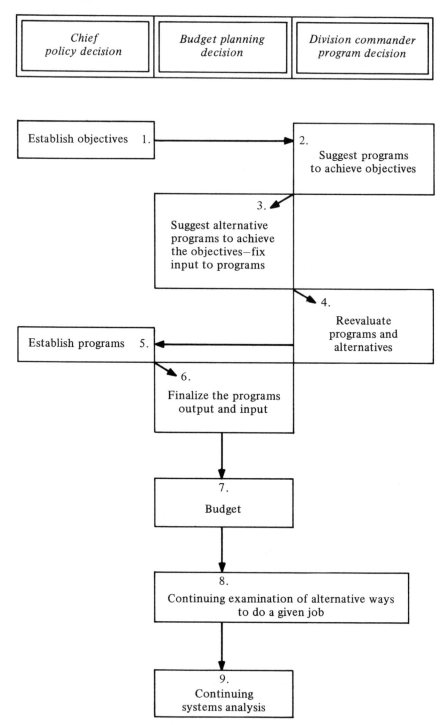

FIGURE 3.7 Plan for the development of a PPBS in a Police Agency.

RIGGS SIMPLIFIED POLICE PROGRAM STRUCTURE[21]

1. *Control of Criminal Behavior*
   a. Vice (Liquor, Narcotics, Prostitution, Gambling)
   b. Rackets (Larceny, loan sharking, organized crime)
   c. Crime against Property
   d. Crimes of Violence to Persons
      (1) For profit
      (2) Not-for-profit
   e. Youth or Juvenile Crime

2. *Public Service Activities* (primarily noncriminal)
   a. Emergency Medical Services
   b. Security in Public Buildings (city hall, courts, etc.)
   c. Traffic
      (1) Safety
      (2) Movement of Goods and Services
   d. Crowd Control (i.e., crowds at public events, athletic contests, etc.)
   e. Inspection and Licenses
   f. Control and Support (a residual category for administrative and staff units)

Program	
Administration and support	$ 515,776.00
Apprehension of criminals	857,915.00
Crime prevention	240,473.00
TOTAL FISCAL BUDGET	$1,614,164.00

FIGURE 3.8   Sample Budget.

This is not intended to represent a complete budget, but rather to demonstrate the PPBS application to a police agency.

Problems Relating to the Implementation of Planning Programs Budgeting System, Dayton Police Department[22]

The first problem that will be encountered by the police administrator who decides to implement the PPBS will be developing a program structure. It is difficult to deal with a police organization in terms of measurable objectives. The Dayton, Ohio, Police Department's program structure is the result of a time-consuming ordeal that involved an extensive period of revision. The police department initially expressed its program structure in terms of how to accomplish the police function rather than determining the objectives of the police

FIGURE 3.10

PROGRAM APPREHENSION OF CRIMINALS

Objective	Programs	Output		Input	
To apprehend violators of the law.	RESPONSE To respond to emergencies within 3 minutes & non-emergencies within 10 minutes of receipt of call 90% of the time	Calls for service Observations	45% of Patrol Div.	4 lts., 8 sgts., 63 off. 26 vehs., 6 offices	$556,315
			100% of Dispatchers	4 Dispatch, 1 office	47,100
				1 sgt., 3 off., 1 veh., 1 office	32,600
				1 lt., 1 sgt., 3 off.,1 mechanic, 1 veh., 2 copters	43,760
	INVESTIGATION AND ARREST To increase the rate of arrest by 8%	Crime scene inv. Scientific inv. Field interpretations	50% of S.E.D.	2 sgts., 9 off., 9 off.,10 vehs.	90,100
			20% Helicopter	1 sgt., 3 off., 1 veh. 2 offices	46,480
	VICE & NARCO To increase the rate of arrest by 10%	Bar checks Surveillance of organized crime activities	40% Detective Bureau 70% of Narco Detail	1 I.D. tech, 2 off., 1 photo tech, 1 clrk, 4 chemists, 4 offices, 1 veh.	29,600
	INVESTIGATION AND PROSECUTION To increase the number of solved cases by 8%	Follow up inv. Custody of evidence Court witness	30% I.D. Section 20% Training	1 sgt., 1 officer, 1 office	11,960
			Total Program Cost		$857,915.00

FIGURE 3.9

PROGRAM ADMINISTRATION AND SUPPORT

Objective	Programs	Output	Input	
To maintain a modern, well-managed, and progressive police agency	*PLANNING & CONTROL* To plan for future needs of the agency	Planning & Research	75% of Admin. Div.	$ 29,325
		Budget Control	20% Vice & Intelligence	
		Statistical Analysis	90% Admin. Commander	14,345
		Training	100% Personnel	
			3 offices	
		Administrative	95% Planning & Research	31,310
		Reports	20% Training	
	To control spending	Personnel Records	100% Payroll	15,950
		Maintain Buildings	95% Uniform Commander	14,976
			5% Patrol	7,660
			5% Traffic	8,400
			5% Helicopter	
	DEPARTMENT ADMINISTRATION To coordinate the activities of the various units of the Department.	Office Administration	100% Investigation Commander	62,035
		Payroll Processing		
		Inspectional Process		
		Records Checker		
		Improve Efficiency	100% Service Commander	13,175
		Processing Paperwork	5% Property	
	To provide general support for the various units of the Department.	Inventory & Storage of Equipment and Supplies	100% Records	44,000
			100% Maintenance	44,200
				10,400
			100% Cadets	160,600
				32,500
				26,900

Total Program Cost $515,776.00

Input details:
- 1 chief, 1 sec., 1 veh.
- 2 offices
- 1 lt., 3 off., 1 sec., 3 offices
- 1 capt., 1 sec., 1 veh.
- 1 veh., 2 offices
- 1 officer, 1 office
- 1 officer, 1 office
- 1 sgt., 1 office
- 1 clrk., 1 office
- 1 capt., 1/2 sec., 2 offices, 28 vehs.
- 1 lt., 2 sgts., 11 off.
- 2 clrks., 1 parking control, 3 offices, 12 veh.
- 1 capt., 2 clrks., 2 offices, 1 veh.
- 1 capt., 1 service off. 1/2 sec., 3 offices, 1 veh.
- 2 prop. clrks., 2 off.
- 1 lt., 2 clrk.-supvrs., 12 clrks., 4 offices
- 1 jntr., 2 mech., 2 veh.
- 11 P/T cadets

FIGURE 3.11

PROGRAM
CRIME PREVENTION

Objective	Programs	Output	Input	
To prevent violations of the law through communication with the citizenry and to deter violations of the law through aggressive police activities.	CRIME PREVENTION: To reduce the incidence of Part I and Part II crimes by 8%	Community Relations	25% Administrative Div.	$ 9,875
		Talks & Presentations Films	20% Vice/Intelligence 5% Planning/ Research	15,341
		Brochures	20% Training	798
		Youth Activities	100% Public Relations	20,275
			1 chief, 1 sec., 1 veh., 2 offices	
			1 lt., 3 off., 1 sec., 3 offices, 1 veh.	
			1 off., 1 office	
			1 off., 1 office	
	CRIME DETERRENCE: To increase the omnipresence of police by increasing the time an officer is available by 10%	Uniformed Patrol Helicopter Patrol Traffic Patrol	5% of Patrol Div. 10% of Traffic Section 65% of Helicopter	63,044
			4 lts., 8 sgts., 63 off. 26 vehs., 6 offices	
			1 lt., 3 sgts., 11 off. 3 clrks., 11 vehs.	24,670
			1 lt., 1 sgt., 3 off., 1 mechanic, 1 veh., 2 copters	106,470
			Total Program Cost	$240,473

function. The most notable example of this problem of objective determination was with the objective "Reduce apprehension time of criminal offenders." This objective was first stated as reduced response time. The police then proceeded to ask themselves why they wanted to reduce the time required to respond to a crime scene. This revealed that their real objective was to decrease apprehension time. If reducing response time did not accomplish their objective of decreasing apprehension time, they would not be concerned with reducing response time.

The development of a meaningful program structure requires the police administrator to ask continually, Why? until he has defined the police function in terms of measurable objectives.

The second problem confronting a police administrator in implementing this system will be defining what is meant by the objective and what data will have to be collected to measure that objective. This requires a police administrator to review his present data-collection system and adapt it to his program structure. The data-collection item will then go through a period of revision. Problems will be confronted during this developmental stage, such as, What is apprehension time? The Dayton Police Department decided apprehension time was the period of time that elapses after the police are notified that a crime has occurred until the perpetrator of that crime is apprehended. However, it could have been defined as the period of time that elapses from occurrence to apprehension. It is up to the police administrator to make the decision, although he should avoid assuming responsibility for objectives over which he does not have control.

The third problem of the police administrator will be the selection, training, and control of a planning team capable of using the tools of modern management. This team is essential if the police administrator is going to have the information necessary to make decisions.

The fourth problem confronting the police administrator is limiting his own expectations. The PPBS is not a substitute for an administrator's judgment, but a supplement. The system cannot be implemented overnight. It requires hard work and time to be perfect.

Lt. Col. O'Connor of the Dayton Police Department summed up the advantages of PPBS when he said that after thirty years of being a policeman, he now knows what is expected of him. Police administrators know how to do their jobs but have not had the time to relate "what is done" to "what is needed." Each citizen who picks up a telephone and requests police service, defines his idea of the police job in this relationship. Since the police administrator has limited resources, it is possible that the collective community would prefer that the police remove a seriously injured citizen to a hospital as opposed to searching for a lost house key. This question depends upon public needs and resources (tax dollars) available to the police operation.

Since the impact of budgeting on the organization is so important, and the Planning Programming Budgeting System is management by objectives, the process has been briefly discussed here to project the principle of good planning. The patrol administrator must have a working knowledge of the planning and budgeting process.

In most police departments the line-item budget is used. However, as police departments and local governments see the results of PPBS, more and more of them shall use this management by objective approach. Justification, which is the sine qua non of budgeting, will be interrelated with the objective.

The Dayton, Ohio, Police Department's experiment indicated that time and hard work are necessary for implementation, but the results are worth it: professional management.

CRITIQUE

All good planners invite critique. Just as the problem-solving conference method has a column for consequences of acceptable solutions, which forces the participants to look beyond the solution, so does the patrol administrator have to look beyond the plan. For example, if a plan is developed for response to a large disturbance at an all-girls' high school and policewomen are available, the police commander must consider carefully his decision of using men with training or policewomen without training. The use of men may bring a charge of police brutality and must be anticipated. The use of policewomen may not be as efficient (if they are not trained), but the consequences of using policewomen would be, if not positive, at least more acceptable.

The decision to use canine teams in crowd control is one where the consequences of the use of dogs in such a situation is critical. More than likely another approach would be taken because of the potential consequences.

One of the best methods of anticipating possible solutions to problems before the fact is a regular evaluation of plans and procedures. Continuous critiques, especially after using a particular plan for special events or unusual critical confrontations, keep the total patrol force updated.

After the riots of 1968 following the death of Dr. Martin Luther King, the Justice Department requested the International Association of Chiefs of Police to develop after-action reports. These reports were to document and evaluate procedures used in coping with civil disorder. Additionally, there was a need to critique the level of cooperation that takes place between federal, state, and local government; federal, state, and local law enforcement; and adjacent local law-enforcement agencies. The review would show how police had cooperated with each other in identifying problems and the solutions used to resolve these problems. Also, problems in most cases were too big for the smaller police departments and mutual aid was necessary for survival. As each of the cities was reviewed regarding its response to the civil disorders, similarities in the responses became evident.

From the events leading up to and including these disorders, it was obvious that social change was upon us. The need to adjust and cope by evaluating and reevaluating procedures used in response to civil disorders was of prime importance. History now shows that the change was met, efficiency was increased, and the challenge to law enforcement was accomplished. The author has spent many hours reviewing plans regarding disorders, demonstrations, and events and respectfully submits the great value of critique: There always seems to be some way to improve a plan or procedure.

NOTES

1. Billy E. Goetz, *Management and Control* (New York: McGraw–Hill, 1949).
2. O. W. Wilson, *Police Planning* (Springfield, Ill.: Charles C. Thomas, 1968).
3. James Ahern, *Police in Trouble* (New York: Hawthorn Books, 1972), p. 176.
4. James Q. Wilson, *Varieties of Police Behavior* (New York: Atheneum Publishers, 1970), pp. 29–30. Wilson cites Michael Banton, *The Policeman in the Community* (New York: Basic Books, 1965), pp. 105–10 as the source for this analysis of the professional role.
5. Marion S. Kellog, *Career Management,* American Management Association, Inc., p. 31.
6. The President's Crime Commission on Law Enforcement and Administration of Justice, Task Force Report, "Police" (1967), p. 137.
7. National Advisory Commission on Criminal Justice Standards and Goals, Washington, D.C., report "Police," 1973, p. 437.

8. "Portable Police Pensions, Improving Inter-Agency Transfers" (New York, N.Y.: College of Insurance, 1971).
9. Presented through courtesy of Dallas, Texas Police Department, Frank Dyson, Chief of Police, 1973.
10. *Webster's New Collegiate Dictionary* (Springfiield, Mass.: G. and C. Merriam Co., 1973).
11. National Advisory Commission on Criminal Justice Standards and Goals, Washington, D.C. 1973, Report on Police.
12. Samuel M. Greenhouse, "The Planning Programming Budgeting System: Rationale Language and Idea-Relationships," *Public Administration Review,* December 1966.
13. Ibid.
14. Ibid.
15. Ibid.
16. Ibid.
17. Ibid.
18. Ibid.
19. Ibid.
20. Ibid.
21. Ibid.
22. Gary Pence, "Problems Relating to the Implementation of Planning, Programs-budgeting system, Dayton, Ohio, Police Department," *Police Chief,* July 1971.

leadership and interpersonal relationships

The essential feature of leadership is to accomplish the mission by motivating the wished-for behavior of the people whom you are leading. There can be no leadership if there is no one to lead. Results are related to the performance of the total team. In understanding leadership, it will be necessary to evaluate carefully the basic needs of the people to be led. Second, the leader must determine what leadership style he will use to attain the desired behavior from personnel. Third, the leader must set the atmosphere wherein the members of the organization feel significantly involved to express their true feeling regarding any situation. Therefore, in any leadership capacity, it is necessary for adjustments to be made on the part of the leader and the personnel being led.

Developing the necessary qualities for effective leadership takes time and effort. Mistakes will be made on the journey to becoming good leaders in patrol. Recollecting these mistakes will also remind the potential leader of the help given by other supervisors. Discipline was necessary in keeping the organization together during a period in history when leadership was suspect to say the least. The true value of the few police leaders in America such as J. Edgar Hoover, August Vollmer, O. W. Wilson, and William Parker has yet to be fully realized. The contemporary scene has brought forth additional police leaders with a high degree of intelligence, courage, and know-how. These included Patrick Murphy, Quinn Tamm, E. Wilson Purdy, John Ingersoll, and Clarence Kelly. Time will tell who else will be included. The common denominator of effective leadership is to state the objective and then simply do all the things necessary to accomplish it.

The steps between the statement and the accomplishment require analysis, evaluation, application, and implementation.

QUALITIES THAT SHOULD BE POSSESSED

The most important quality of the patrol leader is his ability to set an example in creativity, innovation, and flexibility. He must have a fertile mind that is willing to absorb knowledge, which is power, be susceptible to new ideas, and be willing to take that extra step in achieving the goal. Other attributes include an understanding of group dynamics, motivational theory, fiscal management, and open-agency concepts, to list a few.

There are other qualities. No leader possesses all the qualities, and some good leaders of the past had different qualities, but each used the individual qualities he possessed to become a leader. Several (but not all) of these qualities are sincerity and enthusiasm, intelligence, experience, goal-orientation, courage, integrity, the ability to communicate and teach (know your direction, believe in what you are doing, and then communicate these directions clearly and unequivocally, with tact and diplomacy). Individual feelings regarding the difficulty of the task cannot be considered, since most effective decisions are these which seem the most difficult. Being people-oriented, having good judgment, humility, empathy, dependability, perseverance, decisiveness (quick mind accompanied by analytical process), and realism affect total leadership ability.

Each patrol leader must determine which of the qualities he possesses and then maximize to the fullest those particular qualities. Most police officers can remember more than one supervisor whom they would follow to the ends of the earth. It is easy to recognize that each of these effective leaders did not possess the same qualities through which leadership was demonstrated. One supervisor would be enthusiastic, intelligent, set a good example, be decisive, understanding, and pave the way with his sincerity. Another would be quiet, patient, intelligent, fair, receptive, have long experience, and guide subordinates toward the goal. Yet both were capable of leadership. Mahatma Gandhi was certainly different from Stonewall Jackson. Winston Churchill was certainly different from Charles De Gaulle. The idea is to be true to yourself and recognize the individual qualities in your makeup; utilize and expand upon the God-given talents to the limit.

Obviously, leadership is something everyone may think he possesses, but if it is not developed at the right time it may slip out of reach.

If we stipulate that all decisions must be made for the good of the department, then it must be assumed that decisions will always take into consideration the human element. It necessarily follows that the effective leader is a leader at all times. The effective leader will correct the commission of a poorly executed task whether or not it is being done within his own area of authority. Also, the effective leader feels that any decision that affects the department affects him as an individual, and he will do whatever is necessary to make that decision a positive one. He chooses to keep his outlook broad and work effectively for the welfare of the organization as a whole, leading his unit in attaining the objective that parallels the objectives of the total organization.

There is nothing wrong with setting personal or professional goals so long as they coincide with the overall goals of the organization. It is only wrong when personal goals conflict with the goals of the organization and are valued over those of the organization. This ability must be shown to subordinates or else the result will be confusion, conflict, and disintegration of the department. In a sense, a good leader will be his brother's keeper and will demonstrate concern about all those units within the department that need help. The geometric axiom that the whole is equal to the sum of its parts applies. Consequently, each unit in the department must contribute its share in moving the total organization forward.

Laurence Peter states in *The Peter Principle:* "In a hierarchy, every employee needs to rise to his level of incompetence."[1] If this is true, there is the problem of security and insecurity of mind with regard to personnel sitting in positions of authority. Such an individual, as Peter describes him, enlarges upon those little things that are of little or no significance to the organization. He has reached his level of incompetence and in most police agencies, he will not be demoted, but left alone or moved horizontally to a position of lesser importance. Such a situation frustrates the younger, more capable leaders.

It has been said that there is no real power in our urban society, there is only movement by inertia and our leaders can only slightly change the direction of the movement. Those who disagree with this say that there is an arithmetic of politics; if you can identify the right numbers and then add those numbers together, the sum is power.

Stated earlier was the belief that knowledge is power, but this is not all-inclusive: in addition to knowledge, there must be added the ability to involve others, motivate them in the performance of their duties, and be a person who is dynamic and makes things happen. You know who you are, you know where you fit in the organization, you know where you want to go, you are willing to work hard to get where you want to go, and you know how you are going to get to that goal. The total of all of these is power; they include all the necessary attributes for goal achievement.

Making things happen involves change. Change should be approached in the proper manner by being aware of policy, rules, regulations, organizational ability to change, and especially the human aspect of change. A realization that not too much can be done alone is important. In fact, there are strict limitations on what can be accomplished by any individual acting alone in any organization. Since others are needed in the department, it is imperative to have understanding between the unit leaders within a department. It is not necessary to know the communication commander's job better than he does if one is patrol commander. It does mean that each leader must have a good knowledge of what the other position involves, and know the abilities of the leaders of all other units and the relationship between each unit. It is very beneficial simply to enjoy a cup of coffee with the leader of other units. These informal meetings allow for honest expression, and real knowledge and information on both sides is given and absorbed. Under these conditions, the human element takes priority and the positive results from these stimulating, comprehensive occasions are tremendous. There is no room in a police agency for personal animosity if effective leadership and a desire to move the department forward exist. Police leaders cannot afford personal quarrels with other police leaders within the organization; later there is usually the need to obtain the cooperation of that particular leader. Decisions made by the leaders in a department must not be made for personal gain but for the good of the department. Do not take cooperation for granted. Hard work builds good will and in the long run pays off.

It is necessary to understand how to use the relationship of being a leader in a positive way. Schein brings the concept of self-actualization into better focus for us in a discussion of man and his relationship to Maslow's hierarchy of needs.

The kinds of assumptions which are implied about the nature of man can be stated as follows:

a. Man's motives fall into classes which are arranged in a hierarchy: (1) simple needs for survival, safety, and security; (2) social and affiliative needs; (3) ego-satisfaction and self-esteem needs; (4) need for autonomy and independence; and (5) self-actualization needs in the sense of maximum use of all his resources. As the lower-level needs are satisfied, they release some of the higher-level motives. Even the lowliest untalented man seeks self-actualization, a sense of meaning and accomplishment in his work, if his other needs are more or less fulfilled.

b. Man seeks to be mature on the job and capable of being so. This means the exercise of a certain amount of autonomy and independence, the adoption of a long-range time perspective, the development of special capacities and skills, and greater flexibility in adapting to circumstances.

c. Man is primarily self-motivated and self-controlled; externally imposed incentives and controls are likely to threaten the person and reduce him to a less mature adjustment.

d. There is no inherent conflict between self-actualization and more effective organizational performance. If given a chance man will voluntarily integrate his own goals with those of the organization.[2]

The personnel of the patrol force should be viewed from a new perspective. Leadership demands the ability of setting the goals of each employee and the organization to coincide. If the leader knows and understands the hierarchy of needs and is himself self-actualizing, he can contribute better to the accomplishment of self-actualization for those who are subordinate to him.

TYPES OF LEADERSHIP

Flexibility plays an important part in leadership today. Leaders must know the difference between autocratic leadership, democratic leadership, and laissez-faire leadership and when to use each. One type of leadership will not work in all situations. In *The Leader Looks at Styles of Leadership,* Warren H. Schmidt[3] points out the five most typical styles ranging from highly leader-centered to highly group-centered. These styles will be discussed, but first let's define the autocratic, democratic, and laissez-faire categories of leadership.

The *autocrat* usually makes a decision without allowing the group to participate, which means he is extremely authoritarian in that you will always know who the boss is and you will always know where you stand. The autocrat will not want his position of supervision to be questioned and usually leads through fear, which makes him a driver. He is arbitrary to a fault but he also does well in times of emergency. When there is a need for decisiveness, there is no time for participation; time is of the essence. The autocratic leader will shine under the circumstance, but because there is no flexibility to change, it will be difficult to get the best results when this type of leadership is used over a long period of time.

The *democratic leader* allows those persons who work with him to participate in the decision-making process. He understands that their ideas and suggestions will be a key to greater motivation and commitment to the decision. This type of leader does not need to be arbitrary or use extreme authoritativeness. He believes that when people are allowed to help decide issues concerning themselves and how they will be affected, they will become involved in seeing that the job gets done. The democratic leader is people-oriented. He realizes it's the little things that count. Knowing an officer's religion, family, and habits leads him to believe you are interested in him personally. Take a sergeant, for example, who supervises a squad of men and does some of the following: (1) asks an officer about his sick child, (2) knows when an officer needs extra time off and plans the work schedule to meet all responsibilities and still give the officer the time, (3) schedules officers' holidays where it really means something to each; i.e., Dr. King's birthday, St. Patrick's Day, July 4th, Christmas, and Yom Kippur. These, often thought of as minor elements, can make a big difference to the individual when he feels they indicate that the sergeant really cares about him. The results of this style of leadership are usually goal achievement, improved performance, higher motivation, and a step closer to total self-actualization for the sergeant's team.

The *laissez-faire leader* usually does not fulfill the needs of his subordinates. He pays little or no attention to what is going on and is directly opposite from the autocratic leader. He feels insecure in most areas, which is why he exercises little leadership. In other words, he does not know, so he tells his employees to do what they think is right. The other side of the coin, flexibility in leadership, allows subordinates to think for themselves in order to test their ability in this area. Laissez-faire leadership would be appropriate at this time, as long as the concept is explained to the employees performing the specific tasks.

For example, as a patrol commander you allow a group of patrolmen (part agents—[college graduates] and part experienced investigators) to work on a team-policing project. They are advised that there will be minimum supervision, expecting the team to obtain conclusions from the project. This approach allows each member to participate completely and would be appropriate leadership for this specific situation. The leader should be very careful in selecting the team participants.

STYLES OF LEADERSHIP

Continuing our exploration of the problems concerning effective leadership, Warren H. Schmidt suggests,

> When you are the recognized leader of a group, you have certain prerogatives and power. How you use these powers will affect both the productivity of the group and the freedom of the subordinates or group members. As you, the leader, use less of your authority and power, the group members gain greater freedom in making decisions; as you use more of your power, the group freedom declines.
>
> *Telling.* The leader identifies a problem, considers alternative solutions, chooses one of them, and then tells his followers what they are to do. He may or may not consider what he believes the group members will think or feel about the decision, but they clearly do not participate directly in the decision-making. Coercion may or may not be used or implied.
>
> *Persuading.* The leader, as before, makes the decision without consulting his group. However, instead of simply announcing his decision, he tries to persuade the group members to accept it. He describes how his decision fits both the interests of the organization and the interests of the group members.
>
> *Consulting.* The leader here gives the group members a chance to influence the decision from the beginning. He presents a problem and relevant background information, then asks the members for their ideas on how to solve it. He may give his tentative solution for their reaction. In effect, the group is asked to increase the number of alternative actions to be considered. The leader then selects the solution he regards as most promising.
>
> *Joining.* The leader here participates in the discussion as "just another member"—and agrees in advance to carry out whatever decision the group makes. The only limits placed on the group are those given to the leader by his supervisors. (Many research and development teams make decisions this way.)

Delegating. The leader defines a problem and the boundaries within which it must be solved. Then it turns it over to the group to work out a solution that makes sense to the implementers. He agrees to support their solution as long as it fits within the boundaries.[4]

Telling, persuading, consulting, joining, and delegating is like a continuum, the position on the continuum changing as the situation changes. Personal value systems developed over the years from home life, church, school, social and economic conditions, and total learning experience will affect the choice. These influence individual perspectives with relation to others and the job. If experience has shown aggressiveness is rewarding, attempts to obtain rewards through aggressive behavior will be made. Know thyself, attain self-actualization, be aware of similar and conflicting values from the organization, society, and other institutions in the community that may affect your ability and the ability of your subordinates to perform. A result of this awareness will be confidence in oneself as a leader. The level of confidence given each subordinate will be determined on an individual basis after the performance of tasks and an evaluation of the quality of work.

It was once said that there is nothing wrong with an egomaniac as a leader so long as he knows it and the rest of his staff or subordinates know it. However, there is a problem when the subordinates know it but the leader doesn't. The important aspect is understanding. The same applies when the leader selects his style of leadership, whatever it may be. All should understand what type is being used. The dictator-type of leader usually has a problem with the delegation aspect of leadership in that this type usually overestimates his own ability or underestimates the ability of his subordinates. In this case, he usually surrounds himself with yes-men, and the leader who surrounds himself with yes-men "is like a pilot flying blind, with instruments that tell him only what they believe he wants to see instead of their true reading. Moreover, that sort of dictator drives all strong, independent, original minds out of the organization and silences all critical discussions of his policies so that when the crash comes, there is usually no alternative policy that anyone has been formulating, and no leaders of any quality there to take over command."[5]

"When Henry Ford took over all the decision-making of his company and set spies on the managers to try and catch them making decisions on their own, he was ensuring that the crash when it came would be cataclysmic; indeed it is believed it was fifteen years before the firm showed a profit again."[6] When people say that absolute dictatorship carries within it the seeds of its own destruction, what they really mean is that it does not carry within it the seeds of its own survival.

It is not important to dwell upon the position on the continuum. What is important is to know where one is in relationship to the situation at hand. Flexibility and objectivity enhance the leadership potential. Leaders set the pace and priorities for the organization.

COMMUNICATION AND DELEGATION

It may seem strange at first to combine the ability to communicate and to delegate as one topic for discussion. However, real delegation must be communicated in a real way. Believing you possess responsibility and authority is different from truly possessing responsibility and authority. What was intended to be communicated may not be in fact what was communicated. For example, let's take this remark: "I give you the responsibility and authority to accomplish the mission." If the person (delegate) to whom this was said (1) does not have specific duties assigned, (2) must clear all actions with the supervisor, (3) cannot utilize resources as seen fit to accomplish the mission, (4) cannot make commitments on the part of the organization, (5) will not be supported by the supervisor in the use of discretion in making commitments and utilizing resources, then the communication is ineffective and is only lip-service on the part of the supervisor. Without the ability to communicate, there can be no leaders in law enforcement. Without the ability to delegate, maximum efficiency and economy will not be accomplished by the organization.

Communication

> The term *communication* comes from the Latin word "communis"
> or common. In essence, when people communicate they are attempting to share a commonness with another party or group, to
> share information, or an attitude.[7]

Briefly defined, communication is the art of transmitting information from one person to another. People who speak to each other do not always communicate in the strict sense of the term, nor do they always convey the intended message even when the listener is attentive. For a variety of reasons, messages are sent and not received, or they are sent and misunderstood.

> It is important that every citizen be capable of communicating properly; the art of communication is so critical to policemen that their whole professional world depends on it. Police officers are, first and foremost, communicators.[8]

Communication has to transfer ideas and at the same time insure understanding on the part of the recipient that results in feedback from the recipient to the sender. Because of the volume of people in his command, the patrol administrator should possess the ability to communicate. Objectives of the organization must reach the patrolman in language understood, and the feedback from patrol officers must reach the patrol administrator. In between there are levels of command and supervision that have the potential to distract the downward and upward communication. Horizontal communication is emphasized on organizational relationships. For true feedback the distortion must be minimized or eliminated completely.

Three things are important to the communication: (1) What do I intend to communicate? (2) How am I going to communicate? and (3) To whom am I communicating? Communicating is a management activity. It is a process by which a manager takes action, and it is a basic police-management problem. There are many forms of communication: talking, writing, sound, signal, gesture, time, color, and space, the latter being the silent language. There is a saying in police organization concerning those who talk about accomplishing the mission and those who accomplish it. This has a relationship to "Action speaks louder than words." One of the first things a patrol leader learns about handling riots and demonstrations is never to bluff. If a particular course of action is stated, be able to carry it out or lose face (which in this case can mean the same as losing the ability to communicate, because there is a loss of credibility).

These actions could be called the language of behavior. If a sergeant says to a patrolman in a gruff voice, "Don't bother me now," he more than likely will not be bothered at all, now or in the future. This turn-off could easily be avoided by the sergeant if he maintained an awareness about his ability to communicate.

As a part of leadership, the patrol commander takes time to know his men. Included in the knowledge is the fact that each has to be communicated to in a different way. Some men enjoy nicknames, but there are others who become indignant, especially if there is an ethnic relationship.

The use of positive or negative approaches needs to be comprehended by the leader. Behavior can be the same (gesture communication), but at two different times and two different locations, there is a receipt of a different message. If the lieutenant at roll call criticizes the actions of a man, the message may be to use the criticism as an example to the other men. However, to the man being criticized the example has lost all meaning, and the embarrassment has become the message. In this situation the lieutenant should communicate privately.

The story is told about an American scholar who was sent to Japan to teach American history to Japanese university professors. He had taught the course for some time, but since he did not speak Japanese, he wasn't sure whether they were understanding his lectures. He therefore asked for an interpreter. The interpreter advised him that the class was only understanding 50 percent of what was going on. The American was discouraged and upset, but what he didn't know was that he had inadvertently insulted the group by requesting an interpreter. In Japan a sign of an educated man is his ability to speak English. The Japanese professors felt that the American had caused them to lose face because he had implied that they were uneducated when he requested the interpreter. The delegation of questioning to the interpreter in order to determine effective communication was improper.

The patrol commander must learn how to act, when to communicate personally and when in writing and develop a sensitivity to the timing of his communications. The interpretation and comprehension of time and timing is completely different, depending on location in the communication process.

The author has been a member of oral boards for promotion in various places around the country. One aspect of communication has been pointed out as common to each of these experiences. All candidates view the length of the oral component as having a bearing on how well they did in this stage of the promotional process. Americans working for companies in foreign countries must learn a new meaning of time when dealing with officials of these countries. When asked to wait five, ten, thirty, or even forty-five minutes to keep an appointment, the Americans became insulted, not realizing that the wait is really just the beginning of the process. In Latin America, for example, business and pleasure are combined and some people take an hour to do what Americans would do in five minutes.

There are four components in the communication process: (1) the originator of the message, the person who begins the process of communicating; (2) the message (gestures, pictures, words, etc.); (3) the person to whom the message is intended (sometimes called the decoder, since it is he who must decode the message to be able to understand it); (4) the response to the message, or the action taken by the recipient of the message after decoding. If these four interact properly, the result is good communication.

All organizations have formal and informal organizations within them. Among these are the formal and the informal communication systems. In police agencies the informal system of communication or grapevine must be recognized in order to use it for the benefit of the department. The patrol administrator can have a tremendous effect on the informal communication system if he approaches the question properly. In a department that has roll-call training, the second week of a topic is usually used as time for discussion. If the patrol administrator reviews the topic, thinks about a relationship between the topic and a current item of interest in the department, he can make a roll-call become a real rap session between himself and all subordinates. The patrol administrator must be aware of the fact that all personnel can recognize sincerity. Additionally, all items of interest discussed at these formal/informal sessions will be considered important. Follow-up on the part of the patrol leader is vital to the success of this type of approach to the informal communication network.

The police leader should (1) recognize that an informal communication system exists in the department; (2) understand that it exists because all members of the department want to know what is going on and feel important if they can expand upon information to their peers that projects an image of "I'm in the know;" (3) develop credibility that will insure factual feedback; (4) identify personnel and methods for joining the communication system or cooperating in an effort to make communications effective.

If the patrol administrator wishes to act as a change agent, he can use his ability to communicate at the informal session. For example, the chief would like to attempt a change in procedure for the department and wants to get a feeling for acceptance. The patrol administrator can use the roll-call session as a sounding board to get feedback for the potential procedure. The project may be presented in a formal way, but an informal approach is used for effective communication.

There is a need to communicate by whatever means is most effective at the time. The patrol administrator must communicate in an authoritative manner for one situation, and he must communicate in a democratic or laissez-faire manner in another; and he must communicate in the third way, allowing for freer uninhibited expression in still another. He must be very careful to have his finger on the pulse of the situation with regard to each situation to be effective.

The formal communication system of the department consists of General Orders, Special Orders, Directives, Memoranda, Reports, Rules and Regulations, and Standard Operating Procedures. This system is necessary, especially in the larger police departments. The patrol commander must decide for himself when the formal, formal/informal, or informal system is the proper approach to communicate. A good sense of organization and understanding the goals of a good written directive system will help alleviate the bureaucratic red tape that prevents many organizations from moving forward. The salvation of police organizations will be the effectiveness of horizontal coordination, cooperation, and communication between the chiefs of C.I.D., patrol, traffic, records, training, and communication. Formal communication should be reviewed and evaluated to insure it succeeds in its primary purpose, the dissemination of information. Formal communication should not take place to the point of inhibiting free thought. Many chiefs complain about hallway conferences, especially when they take place after a formal conference. At this point the leader should review the manner in which communication is taking place.

Another way of evaluating effective communication is through feedback. Simply stated, observe and inspect the recipients' oral behavior and actions. The delegation of responsibility and authority also carries with it accountability, so the patrol commander must communicate, delegate, and follow up for accountability and evaluation of the communication process. This evaluation determines your ability as the initiator of the communication and also whether the message was received as intended. Be aware that tone of voice and facial expression can completely change the meaning of a message from you to the recipient. Thus when you delegate, remember the acceptance of the delegation is influenced by these factors.

Most people cannot learn anything while talking. To learn you must be able to listen effectively. A police leader should learn to be a good listener. Effective listening is necessary for the leader-subordinate relationship because it embodies respect. Some call it empathy. Whatever the word, the point is that each person wants to be heard and have his viewpoints considered. To identify with the other person increases your understanding of what he is trying to say. The police leader should remember that he was once a patrolman.

Observe the person speaking. Rank certainly has an impact on the validity of statements in police work. In most cases, the message given by a captain will be accepted more by patrolmen than if it was given by a sergeant (if not, the captain is in trouble). The same credibility is developed by the "expert" from the outside who may come into the department as a consultant. Personnel will listen more to what this expert says than to a person within the department, even though the qualifications and credentials are exactly the same. All the more reason for the patrol administrator to be a good listener and attain the credibility necessary to be an effective leader.

The following sayings, heard for many years in police organizations, are just as applicable today regarding the communication and listening process: (1) Don't assume your men know, tell them; (2) Don't assume you know how your men feel, ask them; (3) Don't assume your men understand, clarify for them; (4) Insure feedback by acting out the two-way communication principle.

Barriers to Effective Communication[9]

Two factors that complicate the process even more are the sender's skill as a communicator and the receiver's ability to translate the message. Intelligence is not the only consideration. Many apparently intelligent people have difficulty communicating with one another. Frequently difficulties stem from differences in training and experience. How many technical men, for example, have been able to convey adequately to a layman what they do on the job? The frame of reference is simply too foreign for the nontechnically-oriented person to understand, except in a very vague way.

Communication theorists also call our attention to the effects of "noise" and "filtering." Noise in this case means any distraction that tends to divert the receiver's attention from the message. This may be his preoccupation with his own thoughts at the moment, or the temporary distraction of an external stimulus. In either case, the message is blotted out or distorted by the interruption.

Filtering, as the word implies, is the technique of selective interpretation of the message according to the receiver's experience. This "experience filter" is composed of prejudices, preconceptions, and the normal human tendency to make instant judgments about the significance of any message. Its influence on our ability to interpret a given message is obviously a complex product of what that message means to us personally; in short, how it affects our own well-being.

The experience filter subtly tunes our emotions in and prevents a purely rational interpretation of the message. Depending on our experience with the questioner and our state of mind on any given day, we can react in a variety of ways to the same question. For example, the boss's query, "When will you have that report finished?" can be accepted as a simple request for a time estimate or as unbearable harassment. There are at least half a dozen possible reactions, depending on the individual experiences of the two and on their relationship with each other.

Today's patrol administrator cannot ignore the factors that might cause his intended messages to be distorted. The volume of critical situations alone demands accurate information. The department as a whole must inform its managers, who in turn must inform its middle management in order to allow for discussion and dissemination of accurate feedback, explanation of decision (the why), and improved decision-making. If the chief of a police department signs a general order implementing a procedure, only to find one week later an employee organization is submitting a grievance because no one asked the people affected by the procedure what impact it would have, and the impact is quite negative, then the person(s) responsible for ineffective communication and insensitivity should be taken to task. The art of talking to each other is a basis for human dignity and mutual respect.

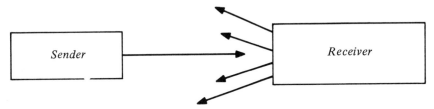

Causes of mismatch of sender and receiver

1. Lack of common background
2. Disinterest
3. Serious difference in viewpoint
4. The "generation gap"

FIGURE 4.1   The blocking of a message that occurs when sender and receiver are "mismatched."

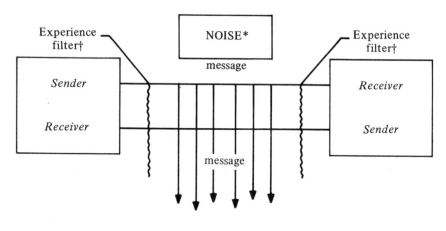

*Causes   †*Filtering*

Distractions   Selective interpretation
                                                          of a message
Limited attention spans

Our own inner thoughts

FIGURE 4.2   Both noise and the receiver's unique-experience filter adversely
affect communication.

Delegation

In today's police organization, it is impossible for a police chief to
carry out personally all the responsibilities assigned to his department. In fact, that is the reason goals are stated and the organization exists, to help the chief fulfill his responsibilities. In order to do
this properly, the chief must delegate, and he must communicate the
delegation clearly and concisely. There must be real delegation, not
a sense of delegation, and the chief should not be afraid to put it in
writing, when practicable, and assign responsibility and accountability. The chief in effect is saying: (1) Here is the goal; (2) I am
assigning you the responsibility to achieve that goal; (3) I am providing you the resources, manpower, and material, to achieve the
goal; (4) I am delegating you the authority to achieve that goal;
and (5) I hold you accountable for achieving that goal. There is,
of course, a limiting point when the chief must stop giving authority.
Decisions concerning this limited authority should be well thought
out in order to have complete understanding between the communicator and the listener.

When the chief gives the patrol administrator the aforementioned message, he should then make sure that the patrol administrator is knowledgeable about delegation and knows how to apply it. Also, it is not easy to delegate properly. It takes strength, courage, foresight, and good leadership. A failure to delegate properly contributes to the total failure of the police department. The patrol administrator cannot be insecure or afraid; unwilling to admit limitations (this aspect has no bearing on ability to perform a task); so enthralled by his own importance that he feels it is a one-man department that cannot go on without him; or an individual who must have all the answers. When Franklin D. Roosevelt died and Harry S. Truman replaced him as president, there was some concern over President Truman's ability; yet President Truman made one of the most significant decisions of World War II.

The patrol administrator should follow the golden rule of administration. The primary responsibility is developing people. Leadership should be provided to insure the continuance of operations even when the leader is not present. The team concept should prevail in all areas of the organization.

In the past it usually took months before new officers were recognized by veterans. In many cases information and good training were obtained by observation only. This is not a proper attitude and shows a sign of insecurity and lack of confidence. Hopefully, patrol administration of the present and future will provide an attitude of sharing all information and knowledge in order to provide improved service to the citizens of the community. In the case of the officer in the field, a more competent and informed officer will be of greater assistance in times of emergency than one who is less informed. Increased use of field training officers (given compensation) is recommended as a way of providing enlightened officers in volume. Recognition of the impact that veteran officers have on new officers is essential to the total well-being of the patrol force.

The patrol administrator must have courage to delegate because of the danger of potential mistakes. An important part of delegation is to give direction and then monitor the subordinate in order to evaluate his ability to perform under stress. Commanders must be allowed to learn and develop and to benefit from their mistakes. The department as a whole will benefit in the long run. The patrol administrator should not be afraid to select a delegate so long as the basis of selection is ability.

Delegating means sharing responsibility. In some cases this will be limited. The patrol administrator should be aware of the ability of the person to whom he is delegating so there is no great mismatch. Knowledge of the delegated task is important in order to make the match work. This knowledge enables the delegator to delegate the whole or part of the task according to the individual. The patrol administrator should not try to do it all himself, or delegate and not follow up. The result may be that the job never gets accomplished. If the whole task is delegated, then a clear, concise statement indicating this is in order. If part of the task is delegated, a clear, concise statement should be communicated regarding what is and what is not delegated.

Remember, Patrol Administrator, you can delegate everything except ultimate responsibility. Responsibility remains for everything performed or not performed by the personnel who work for you. Serious consideration should be given this statement in order to place the principle of delegation in its proper perspective. Delegation will bring out strength, weakness, and character, not only in the one doing the delegating, but also in the selected delegate. Careful selection is necessary. Some subordinates do not want the responsibility and this aspect should be considered.

In traditional terms, according to Louis Brownslow in a lecture given over thirty years ago,[10] there are some things that cannot and should not be delegated, although advice and aid can be solicited. Functions that can not be shoved off to subordinates include: (1) the fiscal functions, (2) the personnel functions (measuring the people to be placed into command tasks), and (3) the planning function. The third function should, however, be done by all personnel at every level.

Authority is necessary for the delegate, and usually he will need the authority for planning, supervising, performing routine tasks, organizing in his area, and for delegating to his subordinates and coordination.

To sum up regarding delegation, the following points are important:

1. Delegation should be to the most capable subordinate.
2. Similar tasks and activities should be delegated to one subordinate.
3. The delegate needs support from the delegator in the use of discretion regarding the authority he possesses.
4. Define clearly and concisely the limits of delegated authority.
5. Remember responsibility/authority/accountability.
6. Establish and define expected results.

7. Communicate to insure understanding of what is expected and what criterion will be used to evaluate the performance of the delegate.

Additionally, according to William H. Newman and Charles E. Summer, Jr. in *The Process of Management,* there are three inescapable features of delegating. These are especially true for the patrol administrator since contemporary policing is in full swing in implementing management priorities that have been used by business. Every time a manager (police captain) delegates work to a subordinate (police lieutenant), we can identify three actions that are either identified or implied.

> (1) He assigns duties; that is, the man who is delegating indicates what work the subordinate must do. (2) He grants authority. Along with permission to proceed with the assigned work, he will probably transfer to the subordinate certain rights, such as the right to spend money, to divert the work of people, to use raw materials, to represent the company (department) to outsiders, or to take other steps necessary to fulfill the new duties. (3) He creates an obligation. In accepting an assignment, a subordinate takes on an obligation to his boss to complete the job.[11]

By recognizing that no delegation is complete without a clear understanding of duties, authority, and obligation, an administrator can often save himself a good deal of trouble. These attributes of delegation are like a three-legged stool: each depends on the other to support the whole, and no two can stand without the third.

The understanding is communication. Patrol commanders should delegate authority, commensurate with responsibility, and then hold the delegate accountable.

DECISION-MAKING AND AUTHORITY

Decisions made by all levels of authority in police work should be made knowing full well that the decision may be Monday-morning quarterbacked. For the patrol officer on the beat, it will be the courts reviewing, possibly for months, his decision to make an arrest. For the sergeant or lieutenant, it will be the press and specific segments of the community regarding the decision that may have resulted in personal injury to a citizen. For example, a patrol officer has been assigned the task of executing a warrant on an individual for assault. The assigned officer calls for assistance from his partner and begins the process. When the named individual finds out the policemen are at the door he becomes excited and climbs the fire escape to the roof. Supervisors are called to the scene and a decision has to be made. Should the arrest for assault be made under the existing conditions, or should the officer retreat and execute the warrant under less stressful conditions? Would the pressure of the arrest cause a potential loss of life? The supervisors are under the gun and can feel fairly sure their decision will receive critical review.

The captain or commanding officer and a command staff officer must decide on a recommendation for disciplinary action concerning a patrol officer. These command officers must realize that all decisions must be made for the betterment of the department. In reaching a decision, many facts must be analyzed, which in most cases will reveal a need to make decisions based on the merits of the situation. Each level of authority must make decisions, and the knowledge of what it takes to make effective decisions is a tremendously important aspect of patrol administration.

Decision-making is the essence of management. Problem definition is the first step in effective decision-making. Decisiveness will be exercised according to the amount of authority possessed by the persons making the decision, timeliness of the situation, and the person(s) or group(s) affected. The number of times a patrolman uses discretion, which is the use of judgment followed by a decision, has been recognized. In police agencies especially, there must be an acknowledgement of the decision-making authority concomitant with the areas affected by the decisions. Then there can be clear policies concerning the amount of authority possessed by each in decision-making. If supervisors and administrators must delegate and in so doing relinquish authority to the delegates, it is imperative that agreement is reached and understood on how much, and to what extent, authority has been granted. Additionally, American society must clearly define how much authority they wish to give to respective police agencies.

These points are clearly identified in the report, "Standards Relating to the Urban Police Function," prepared by the American Bar Association and published in the May 1973 issue of the *Police Chief*. Even though the following is lengthy and not the complete set of standards, these standards are reported here because it is the patrol administrator, the patrol supervisor, and officers who implement policy and make the decisions relating to these standards. These standards should be reviewed and studied in-depth by students of patrol administration. They relate directly to the use of manpower and other resources available to the patrol administrator in attaining the objective.

STANDARDS RELATING TO THE URBAN POLICE FUNCTION, AMERICAN BAR ASSOCIATION

2.5 Role of the local chief executive

In general terms, the chief executive of a governmental subdivision should be recognized as having the ultimate responsibility for his police department and, in conjunction with his police administrator and the municipal legislative body, should formulate lawful policy relating to the nature of the police function, the objectives and priorities of the police in carrying out this function, and the relationship of these objectives and priorities to general municipal strategies. This will require that a chief executive, along with assuming new responsibilities for formulating overall directions for police services, must also:

(1) insulate the police department from inappropriate pressures including such pressures from his own office;
(2) insulate the police department from pressures to deal with matters in an unlawful or unconstitutional manner; and
(3) insulate the police administrator from inappropriate interference with the internal administration of his department.

METHODS AND AUTHORITY AVAILABLE TO THE POLICE FOR FULFULLING THE TASKS GIVEN THEM

3.1 Alternative methods used by police

The process of investigation, arrest, and prosecution, commonly viewed as an end in itself, should be recognized as but one of the methods used by police in performing their overall function, even though it is the most important method of dealing with serious criminal activity. Among other methods police use are, for example, the process of informal resolution of conflict, referral, and warning. The alternative methods used by police should be recognized as important and warranting improvement in number and effectiveness; and the police should be given the necessary authority to use them under circumstances in which it is desirable to do so.

3.2 Avoiding overreliance upon the criminal law

The assumption that the use of an arrest and the criminal process is the primary or even the exclusive method available to police should be recognized as causing unnecessary distortion of both the criminal law and the system of criminal justice.

3.3 Need for clarified, properly limited authority to use methods other than the criminal justice system

There should be clarification of the authority of police to use methods other than arrest and prosecution to deal with the variety of behavioral and social problems which they confront. This should include careful consideration of the need for and problems created by providing police with recognized and properly limited authority and protection while operating thereunder:

(i) to deal with interferences with the democratic process. Although it is assumed that police have a duty to protect free speech and the right of dissent, their authority to do so is unclear, particularly because of the questionable constitutionality of many statutes, such as the disorderly conduct statutes, upon which police have relied in the past.

(ii) to deal with self-destructive conduct such as that engaged in by persons who are helpless by reason of mental illness or persons who are incapacitated by alcohol or drugs. Such authority as exists is too often dependent upon criminal laws which commonly afford an inadequate basis to deal effectively and humanely with self-destructive behavior;

(iii) to engage in the resolution of conflict such as that which occurs so frequently between husband and wife or neighbor and neighbor in the highly populated sections of the large city, without reliance upon criminal assault or disorderly conduct statutes;

(iv) to take appropriate action to prevent disorder such as by ordering crowds to disperse where there is adequate reason to believe that such action is required to prevent disorder and to deal properly and effectively with disorder when it occurs; and

(v) to require potential victims of crime to take preventive action such as by a legal requirement that building owners follow a burglary-prevention program similar to common fire-prevention programs.

3.4 Legislative concern for feasibility of criminal sanction

Within the field of Criminal Justice Administration legislatures should, prior to defining conduct as criminal, carefully consider whether adequate authority and resources exist for police to enforce the prohibition by methods which the community is willing to tolerate and support. Criminal codes should be reevaluated to determine whether these are adequate ways of enforcing the prohibition. If not, noncriminal solutions to all or a portion of the problem should be considered.

PART IV. LAW ENFORCEMENT POLICY-MAKING

4.1 Exercise of discretion by police

The nature of the responsibilities currently placed upon the police requires that the police exercise a great deal of discretion. This is a situation that has long existed, but is not always recognized.

4.2 Need for structure and control

Since individual police officers may make important decisions affecting police operations without direction, with limited accountability, and without any uniformity within a department, police discretion should be structured and controlled.

4.3 Administrative rule-making

Police discretion can best be structured and controlled through the process of administrative rule-making by police agencies. Police administrators should, therefore, give the highest priority to the formulation of administrative rules governing the exercise of discretion, particularly in the areas of selective enforcement, investigative techniques, and enforcement methods.

4.4 Contribution by legislatures and courts

To stimulate the development of appropriate administrative guidance and control over police discretion, legislatures and courts should actively encourage police administrative rule-making.

(a) Legislatures can meet this need by delegating administrative rule-making responsibility to the police by statute.

(b) Courts can stimulate administrative development in several ways including the following.

(i) Properly developed and published police-administrative policies should be sustained unless demonstrated to be unconstitutional, arbitrary, or otherwise outside the authority of the police;

(ii) To stimulate timely and adequate administrative policy-making, a determination by a court of a violation of an administrative policy should not be a basis for excluding evidence in a criminal case unless the violation of administrative policy is of constitutional dimensions or is otherwise so serious as to call for the exercise of the superintending authority of the court. A violation per se should not result in civil liability; and

(iii) Where it appears to the court that an individual officer has acted in violation of administrative policy or that an administrative policy is unconstitutional, arbitrary, or otherwise outside the authority of the police, the court should arrange for the police administrator to be informed of this fact, in order to facilitate fulfillment by the police administrator of his responsibility in such circumstances to reexamine the relevant policy or policies and to review methods of training, communication of policy, and supervision and control.

4.5 Method of policy-making

In its development of procedures to openly formulate, implement, and reevaluate police policy as necessary, each jurisdiction should be conscious of the need to effectively consult a representative cross-section of citizens in this process.

PART V. CONTROL OVER POLICE AUTHORITY

5.4 Need for accountability

Since a principal function of police is the safeguarding of democratic processes, if police fail to conform their conduct to the
requirements of law, they subvert the democratic process and
frustrate the achievement of a principal police function. It is for
this reason that high priority must be given for ensuring that
the police are made fully accountable to their police administrator
and to the public for their actions.[12]

Because the patrol administrator is so intensely involved with the
performance aspect of the police agency, he must know the consequences of his decisions at each stage. Questions concerning how the
decision will affect the community, government, criminal justice system, the department as an organization, his men, and himself should
be considered. To do this he must know the interrelationships between
each person or group. It should be recognized that one's personal experience, morals, family, and values will affect his ability to make decisions. If things are "right" at home, it is more likely decisions will
be made after clear thought and analysis of the situation. If things are
not right at home, the personal complications are carried to work.
Thus a patrolman may take the wrong position when backing up a
partner on a burglary or a robbery call. The sergeant assigns the
wrong man to a beat car and then becomes sarcastic when the patrolman questions the assignment. The lieutenant conducts a raid on a
gambling operation and moves too fast or too slow resulting in a loss
of the evidence. The patrol commander fails to communicate clearly,
which results in a misunderstanding of an order and an employee
grievance. For effective decision-making, personal contentment is
necessary. Leaders cannot afford cantankerous, obnoxious attitudes.

Because most decisions cause change, especially internally, it is
important for the patrol administrator to have knowledge of his men.
For example, implementation of a manpower-distribution plan on the
15th of the month as opposed to the 22nd (which is the date for
change of shift) could result in rejection of the plan. When the personnel are informed of pending decisions and feedback is obtained,
timing will become an asset for the patrol commander. The officers
of the unit will be more likely to accept the decisions because they
were involved. They also will agree to the reporting of information
necessary to evaluate the decision.

The management by objective approach for patrol administration
can only be accomplished when periodic evaluation of the goal is

performed. If the approach taken to implement the program is found to need modification because the patrol commander made an error in judgment, then admitting the error, explaining the how and why of the error, and taking corrective action will result in respect for the commander. In this way, responsibility for decisions, right or wrong, is demonstrated. The example will do more in helping the patrol commander gain support for implementing the program than a hundred pages of explanation on why the department needs the change. Knowledge of his men—knowledge that they will make mistakes and need help in correcting their judgments—gives the commander the empathy necessary to lead.

Knowledge by the men that the patrol commander does not make decisions sitting in an ivory tower, does make mistakes, does take corrective action, is willing to change, does go to the core of the problem to obtain facts, and is willing to listen with objectivity to suggestions made by the people affected helps identify him as a leader. With this attitude, decision-making and authority will settle at the right level, just as water seeks its own level. Decisions that should be made by patrolmen should not be made by sergeants, and decisions that should be made by lieutenants should not have to be made by captains. The management by objective approach for the patrol administrator should result in improved decision-making at all levels. Knowledge of the personnel will keep him keenly aware of the appropriate level of decision-making authority in order to maintain a proper balance.

Decisions affecting the department are discussed in more detail in Chapter 5, "Organization for Patrol." The patrol administrator must have knowledge of the other units within the department, because his decisions have a domino effect. The action taken by the patrol unit will result in movement by communication, records, criminal investigator, fiscal, etc. Therefore, the consequences of the decisions should be anticipated. What may appear to be a good decision for patrol today may result in disaster for planning and research tomorrow.

Criminal Justice System

In large demonstrations or riots or any other situation when large groups of people gather, the patrol commander is usually in charge. Decisions made under these circumstances affect other facets of the criminal justice system, especially if they involve arrests. The patrol administrator must have knowledge of the system, its abilities, liabilities, and capabilities. The courts, prosecutors, and parole, probation, and correction aspects directly concern the police. Whatever impact your plan has on these partners should be considered, and effective communication should be developed between the components of the system.

Government

The patrol administrator should be aware of politics, internal pressures, special-interest groups, political organizations, and the overall impact of these on the police department. Exposure to the political scene and a study of federal, state, and local government is necessary to make effective decisions. The political questions of conservative vs. liberal, radicalism, new left, extreme right, etc. must be placed in proper context in order to make effective decisions relative to each. The police commander should know the confines of each elected official. Committee assignments and voting blocs should be documented. Government votes on operating budgets, and government is made up of individuals. The patrol administrator's decisions affect these individuals and are very important, requiring excellent judgment.

The Community

Of all the influences that affect the decision-making of the patrol administrator, none should be more important than the influence of the citizen served. The police commander must learn to develop the sensitivity necessary to act before the fact in all areas where public interest is concerned. In order to do this, feedback from all aspects of the community must be considered: business community, schools, churches, community organizations, charitable organizations, elected officials (who have a direct line to their constituents), and the press (whose independent thought and resources provide many avenues for the anticipated response). The enlightened patrol administrator will be aware of the many ways to ascertain information that would be helpful in making decisions affecting the community. This authority vested in him by the community willingly for democratic government should be guarded well.

Western philosophy on problem-solving is to act or do something in order to solve problems. This occidental philosophy, to which America adheres, says a decision must be made to do something: don't just stand there, do something, make a decision. However, there is an oriental philosophy directly opposite to this, which says that sometimes the best decision would be to do nothing and in time the problem will solve itself. When used selectively, this philosophy can be most effective. One danger should be considered. If the decision is made to do nothing concerning a problem, this decision should be communicated to the men so that the accusation of indecision is negated. The decision to do nothing is a decision in itself and should be conveyed to all concerned as a decision.

No man is an island: the patrol administrator must be aware of all influences when making a decision. The more knowledgeable he is about the aforementioned forces, the more effective his decision. If the patrol administrator considers a proper definition of the problem, gathers and analyzes the facts, considers solutions, alternative solutions, and consequences to each objectively, the right decision is more likely to be selected. Patrol administrators should realize the need to work as long and as hard as necessary to implement the programs and only after evaluation and reaffirmation of the goals can a rest be taken, and then only long enough to catch a breath.

LEADERS AS TRAINERS

The leader who realizes responsibility to subordinates in the area of training is in effect actively participating with the police chief in the primary mission of the administration, developing people. One of the many byproducts of career development upon promotion is the fact that the newly promoted supervisor will relate his previous area of expertise to the new area of responsibility and enlighten the present subordinates so as to improve their overall ability.

In most departments today some type of roll-call training is conducted. The International Association of Chiefs of Police has over 200 topics available for use at roll-call training. In the majority of cases, one officer or supervisor attending the roll-call training session will have been involved, in an in-depth capacity, in the area being discussed. The order implementing the roll-call training program should include the following:

> All persons responsible for conducting the roll-call training program shall be especially aware of personnel possessing expertise

in the area being discussed. These individuals should be utilized whenever their talents will enhance the presentation of information and knowledge.

Many times a patrolman does not take action in a particular situation because he fears making a mistake. Also, the young patrolman is afraid to call his supervisor for help because the response may be, "Don't they teach you anything at that academy?" While change is upon us and our education and training centers have improved police training tremendously, the young patrolman at first is still apprehensive. If training is good in the beginning and confidence is built by the repetition of doing, the officer begins his career in a much better position. Thus the officer responds to each incident or observation with the poise and sureness of the Green Bay Packers' football player trained by Vince Lombardi.

There is a need to continue training of officers once in the field. One method is by roll-call training. Second is the personal training given by the individual supervisor. Third is in-service training and in some areas, the training program utilizes the Matrix system in that line commanders conduct portions (leadership and supervision) of the in-service program. If the leader of the line operation teaches it, he must practice what he preaches. Fourth, there is the specialized training offered (Bureau of Narcotics and Dangerous Drugs, Federal Bureau of Investigation Administrative courses, etc., Southern Police Institute Administrative Officers Courses, Northwestern Traffic Institute) (see Figure 4.3).

The second part of the training mentioned is the one-to-one relationship between leaders and their subordinates. The leader must keep in mind his responsibility to point out the individual officer's respective areas of improvement as well as to feed back to the administrator information necessary to formulate in-service training for the department as a whole. It is one thing to correct the individual deficiency of a particular officer and something quite different to pinpoint a training need for an entire department.

A good example would be the need to emphasize the importance of protecting the crime scene. Many times supervisors are more guilty than anyone else in their curiosity, which results in the destruction of good evidence at crime scenes. This type of information is important to feed back to command and training personnel for inclusion in the in-service program.

FIGURE 4.3 Criminal Justice Center, Sam Houston State University, Hunts-ville, Texas.

Another area that brings forth the importance of personnel train-ing is observing officers while interacting with citizens.

Reviewing reports and statistics that may indicate a total review of personnel relative to a need for in-service training is also necessary. Arrests, bodily harm during arrest situations, rock and bottle throwing incidents, damage to police vehicles and other police equipment, in-jured officer, insensitivity, and complaints should be analyzed by patrol administrators to glean information indicating topics to be included in total in-service training.

Up, down, and horizontal communication should be implemented. The patrol administrator should solicit from all level of authority areas where training might improve the operation of the department. In-cluded in the areas solicited should be any and all ideas on how the training shall be conducted (methods and personnel). Upon receipt of the information, communication between the patrol administrator and the director of education and training will help solidify a meaningful in-service training program. The immediate supervisor is better quali-fied to suggest training needs due to his close observation of officers' performance of a variety of tasks. Participation in selecting the topics will enhance the value of material presented at in-service training. If the in-service program is looked upon as a wheel, with all participants (patrolmen, sergeants, lieutenants, commanders, and staff) as the spokes, then a true team effort is procured and the total product is improved.

The Learning Process

In order to instruct anyone, it is necessary to understand the learning process. Experience has shown that the majority of line supervisors at every level have neglected the training aspect of leadership. This does not mean that no individual training has been given at all, only that the identification of this aspect of the leadership responsibility has been relegated to a lower place in the list of responsibilities. It is possible that the quality of setting a good example has been viewed as fulfilling this particular need. In many cases this would be sufficient, but reviewing the fundamentals is always good procedure. Also, the ability to communicate is a part of the teaching and understanding of the learning process and its relationship to the student. Part of the following information has been taken from the text of *Techniques of Police Instruction* by John C. Klotter, dean of the School of Police Administration, University of Louisville. For anyone interested in all aspects of instruction, the text is recommended.[13]

Learning

> Learning is defined as the process of acquiring new knowledge, skills, techniques, and appreciation which will enable the individual to do something that he could not do before.

If we analyze this definition, it becomes obvious that learning anything new is an active process. When the sergeant observes a patrolman making an arrest and points out to the patrolman several points that may endanger the patrolman's life if repeated in another arrest situation, the new knowledge, technique, and appreciation of this instruction are active.

Instruction

> All of the instructor activities that contribute toward leading, guiding, directing, and controlling the thoughts and actions of the students as they learn.

This definition is synonymous with advice given a newly promoted sergeant. "You are now a first-line supervisor and you are responsible for guiding, counseling, directing and controlling your men. You're responsible for everything they do or do not do." From this statement, the first-line supervisor should be keenly aware of the many ways he can influence his men in the instructor-student relationship. First, learning by doing; second, use the five senses as the tools of learning; third, explain and then demonstrate when possible; and fourth, let the student do it again to insure that the information the sergeant has tried to impart has been assimilated by the patrolman.

Types of Learning

Knowledge. Where the student is helped to understand and retain facts, procedures, principles, and information. If the primary objective of the instructor is to teach knowledge, the approach will be different than it would be if the primary purpose were to teach skills.

Skills. The act or a series of acts which are performed instinctively without the conscious effort of thinking. Skills are not truly learned until they become almost instinctive, and they will not become instinctive unless there is much practice. Some examples of skills that are taught in police training are: driving the vehicles, operating weapons, and self-defense.

Techniques. Techniques are a way of thinking and acting based upon knowledge and often upon skills as well. Techniques are developed by applying knowledge and skills and cannot be developed adequately until there has been much practice.

Appreciation. Usually defined in terms of attitudes, ideals, interests, habits, likes and dislikes. Attitude usually determines the effectiveness of efforts.

Principles of Learning

Motivation. Since learning is an active process, the student must be motivated to learn for himself. The instructor must, therefore, create a desire to learn.

Purpose. Learning is much more rapid and effective when it is purposeful. An individual rapidly acquires skills, knowledge, techniques, and appreciation when these achievements are necessary in order to attain the realization of some purpose.

Adjustment. When the student learns either skills, knowledge, or techniques, he, to a certain extent, must make an adjustment.

Activity. This is simply learning by doing.

Association. The student associates new material with past learning. The instructor must be careful in communicating with students so the interpretation of the message is correct.

Realism. Is the material presented realistic from the standpoint of application? Is the material functional? Is the material realistic as far as the level of the student is concerned?

Incidental Learning. Incidental learning refers to the learning which occurs while the learner is doing something else. Such things as habits, attitudes, and character tactics are learned almost exclusively through this process of incidental learning. In some instances these outcomes are most important or as important as the information and skills being taught. These habits, interests, attitudes, and appreciations may be either favorable or unfavorable, depending upon the instructor. Often the student develops the same attitude toward a subject as that exhibited by the supervisor. Therefore, if the instructor takes a lackadaisical attitude toward the instruction, there is little chance that the student will consider it seriously. On the other hand, if the instructor demonstrates sincerity and enthusiasm the men will feel the same way toward the material being presented. There is no better way to develop appreciation than by example. When we consider that much of our learning is through this process, it is impossible to place too much stress on this principle of learning. The instructor teaches "the whole student, not just the subject matter."[14]

A review of these basics in the area of training generally, and being a trainer and a leader at the same time specifically, should help maintain an awareness of this particular responsibility. If we reflect on the management by objective approach, then sergeants instructing patrolmen, lieutenants instructing sergeants will realize the goals of motivation, proper attitudes, and good habits, because in achieving the goal they will be vigilant to the basics of training, especially sincerity and enthusiasm.

A valid goal for a supervisor would be to have his men say after a training session, individually or collectively, "I know where he (the patrol leader) is going and I'll follow him." At this point you are the leader and the trainer.

DISCIPLINE, MANAGEMENT'S RESOURCE

The patrol administrator who uses discipline as a resource of management is in effect saying that discipline is a function of command. As a function of command, discipline is not always negative or painful. A good leader will use discipline as a way to attain the objectives. This can be done in a very positive way so that the patrol leader and his men develop and achieve goals together. One definition of discipline has been given as follows: "Training or experience that corrects, molds, strengthens or perfects." Such discipline allows for a professionally oriented superior-performing police agency.

Bernard Baruch once said that "our freedom is the freedom of self-discipline." Self-control or self-restraint to the patrol administrator should equal power. Power means possession of the ability to influence people. One of the best ways to influence people is to set the example of self-discipline. The patrol administrator who presents an attitude of cooperation and helpfulness to his men so that they may improve and be promoted through positive discipline decreases the need for negative discipline. Negative discipline is necessary; police departments must have rules and regulations under which to operate. But the point is, if patrol commanders exert enough self-discipline to motivate the individuals working for them with the same self-discipline, they can create a desire on the part of all officers to not want to break the rules, do the right thing, obtain more freedom, need less control and supervision, and bring out a totally positive discipline atmosphere.

No one wants to be the bad guy, and one way to avoid it is to create positive discipline. However, realistically speaking, there will come a time when negative discipline must be applied. This is normal; therefore, basic ingredients of leadership, firmness, and fairness must be exuded to overcome these unpleasant situations. The patrol administrator, when meting out this type of discipline, should always develop a sensitivity to the overall consequences of the decision. Today, in the complex field of police personnel management, the patrol leader cannot make decisions concerning discipline in a vacuum. With employee organizations, court trials, and injunctions potentially facing each decision, the patrol leader should concentrate on making the decision in a fair and ethical manner, yet seek out alternatives so the best might be applied in each case. However, whenever conflict does arise, each decision must be made for the best interest of the department. Decisions made yesterday concerning a given matter may not be the same today regarding the same matter because of our changing society.

If we stipulate that positive discipline and leadership go hand in hand, we must not conclude that negative discipline means poor leadership. Both types are necessary, since no human being is perfect. The patrol leader sets goals; makes the goals realistic; shows the way, through direction and setting the example (self-discipline); and supports the methods and hard-working attempts made by his personnel to accomplish the goals. Dialogue developed between all levels of patrol;

the use of goal-oriented statistical data forms (see Appendix B); requests for reduction of 1% in the robbery category; and participatory management are examples of positive discipline. At the same time, the attitude of confidence and awareness of the ability to perform gives each man the proper perspective regarding where he fits in relation to goal achievement. How a man can contribute and knowing the amount of his contribution to the task are important to the individual. Additionally, in the example, if the patrol leader follows up at a later date and discusses the manner and direction the group is taking, offers guidance and support, especially pointing out where they are on the right track, the whole group will be motivated in the same way—goal achievement.

Documentation

Documentation regarding discipline is related to performance evaluation in that both good and bad information of a significant nature must be included. It is virtually impossible to commit to memory all incidents concerning each man. Also, it would be difficult to be objective and unemotional. Written documents are subject to inspection and therefore create a feeling of fairness. When documentation is done in a professional manner, the department and the individual benefit. It is a sad state of affairs when a patrolman attempting to obtain a promotion is knocked down in the efficiency category for poor performance when he was never told by his sergeant about the weakness and the steps available for improvement.

Many departments today are using the daily activity form for compiling information concerning work performance. Patrolmen are required to account for their time during a tour of duty. Additionally, sector sergeants and watch commanders have used the activity reports to provide information concerning supervisory performance and productivity. If at all possible, one activity report should be used throughout the operating forces wherever a man is assigned (patrol, traffic, CID, etc.). Review of the activity reports by the immediate supervisor is a proper procedure.

However, to be meaningful, the information for activity reports should be compiled, key-punched, and entered into a computer. On a monthly basis the information concerning each patrolman can be provided to the sergeant in printout form. This monthly information will provide trends, indicate areas of performance that need a close inspection by the supervisor, and produce periodic summaries of significant activity accomplishment for supervisory and command review. After the supervisor reviews the report, comments concerning the officer's performance, good and bad alike, can be written on the activity report for later retrieval. These comments, if transferred into computer language, can be forwarded to the officer's supervisor along with information concerning the activity.

With this type of documentation the supervisor can provide both the leadership discipline and the correction discipline necessary for high-level supervisors. Additionally, the printout will help the supervisor make recommendations regarding training needs, work assignment, and career development and promotional potential of the individual. Most of all, it causes supervision to communicate up, down, and laterally. The activity report is a good way to teach all personnel the value of documentation. As a patrolman is promoted to sergeant, or lieutenant, *he* observes the use of documentation by his supervisor and this effective method is highlighted all through his career.

Each level of patrol authority should possess some method of documentation on a consistent, continuing basis. Middle management has the activity reports for specific performance identification, and command has the use of the log that places emphasis on due dates and inspection. A supervisor has a responsibility to each officer to be able to indicate objectively how and when the officer can improve performance. The following are some activities that should be included in the activity report:

Name of officer(s)	Calls for service
Vehicle number	Inspection:
Day, month, year	Security
Watch, sector, beat	Building
Odometer reading	Field interviews
Finish	Foot patrol
Start	Accident investigated
Total miles	Hazardous moving violations
Vehicle condition	Number issued
Start	Felony arrests
Finish	Misdemeanor arrests
Equipment condition	Narcotic arrests
Start	Follow-up investigations
Finish	Unavailable for service (court)

Supervisor Information:

Field reports reviewed
Preliminary investigations observed
Case-preparation supervised
Administrative duties
Personal contacts

The information suggested is not all-inclusive and would necessarily be modified depending on the size of the department, resources available, and its specific needs. However, some form of documentation should be used in each police department that will enhance the potential for using positive discipline.

Patrol leaders who use positive discipline make it easier for everyone. This kind of attitude and the proper documentation will result in negative discipline being used sparingly, but effectively. Officers usually will not care as much if the supervisor doesn't believe in the goals of the department. Some police officials say, "You show me a sloppy, careless patrolman and I'll show you an uncaring sergeant." Experience has shown that no man wants to be a nonentity. If a man is made to feel that he doesn't belong, he will perform accordingly. Therefore, a supervisor must let the patrolman know that he knows the patrolman exists. In effect, the patrolman is saying, "Even if you are reprimanding me, at least I know you care, sergeant, and I am part of the department." It is most important for each supervisor to provide the necessary discipline, to maintain momentum along the road toward attaining the objective, and also to bring back into the fold anyone who strays. Where officers do stray, they need to know that a supervisor is sure to be there, and just as sure, some form of corrective action will take place. The supervisor must know the individual officer and determine the best approach to take concerning each individual officer, which will bring about improved performance in the future.

In most cases, the first step for a supervisor in patrol to take in order to attain this improved performance would be the consultation. The supervisor should talk pleasantly to the officer, attempting to find out why he may not be performing adequately. After determining why, the supervisor should offer ways in which the officer might adjust his attitude or work routine to improve the patrol effort. Counseling the officer on how to identify potential police hazards and suggested response to these anticipated problems would be one area of concern. Relating the environment to a crime problem and teaching the officer how to react to each situation on his beat would be another. If the proper attitude and approach are made by the supervisor so that the sincerity of caring is projected, it is more than likely that this guidance and counseling will be sufficient to correct any deficiency the patrolman may have. In reality, a police-patrol officer is the epitome of individualism the majority of the time. Only when he becomes a part of a squad during demonstrations or civil disorders does he give up this tremendous responsibility for discretionary judgment. Even the most active patrol sergeant will observe his patrolman only part of a tour of duty. Also, to fulfill delegation the sergeant must allow patrolmen to use discretion to improve the process of decision-making even though mistakes will occur. This is a very important part of training and development of the officers in order to become self-actualizing. This goes along with the philosophy of job-enrichment that a man should have a variety of duties and the ability to make real decisions concerning these duties. Team-policing is an approach to these principles. (Job-enrichment is discussed under the heading "Utilization of Resources" in this chapter.) Patrol officers are involved with unsavory characters on a daily basis, and this increases temptation and opportunity for neglecting their duty. Since officers are in public view almost constantly their activity is usually observed. The expectation of the citizens of the community that police officers be above reproach cannot be denied. These factors point out the need for supervision to guide and counsel the patrol officers regularly in order to maintain performance standards.

The second step, which is usually a formalization of the first, would be for the supervisor to take the officer aside in a more formal atmosphere and simply "tell it like it is." The officer should be told what he is doing and what he isn't doing. The sergeant or supervisor should remain calm so the officer will not "listen" to the supervisor's emotion, but to the message. The supervisor should think about how he is going to communicate in this setting so he does not become the catalyst that results in the officer's becoming more deficient, bringing about further negative discipline. This critical analysis of the officer's performance should be all business and should conclude with the possible consequences being explained. After the officer is dismissed from the interview, the supervisor should document the proceeding.

Such an explanation amounts to a warning. The supervisor clearly states his refusal to accept careless, below-standard police performance. Officers should be told of impending line inspections in the area of deficiency on a routine, irregular basis. The inspection should be overt. After the inspection the supervisor should contact the patrolman and let him know where he stands concerning progress. At the first sign of "no progress" the supervisor should enter the next stage.

The third step should be formal documentation. At this point, guidance, counseling, and warning have not sufficed. Again the officer should be interviewed and the good and bad of his work performance evaluated objectively. At the end of this meeting, the supervisor should hand the officer a letter addressed to the personnel officer via the chain of command. The letter summarizes the action taken by the supervisor from the beginning and should also contain the results of action to be taken if the deficiency continues. Everything at this point is formal and is entered into the personnel file of the officer.

The last step would be the actual recommendation of punishment. Each department will vary according to the organizational form and the amount of authority relative to discipline vested in the sergeants, lieutenants, captains, etc. It should be recognized that certain individuals will respond only to proactive disciplinary action. Whatever the action, dismissal (this is usually the prerogative of the chief), suspension, loss of days off, loss of vacation days, the punishment should fit the crime. How great was the deficiency? Was the deficient action willful or an honest mistake? Was the act due to laziness or sloppiness? How long has the offender been in service? What is his past record? Is there a reason for the action? Actually by this point the supervisor has gone to extreme lengths to determine the why of the performance. There are times when an officer just doesn't have it, and the kind thing to do, after all levels of supervisors and a variety of supervisors have tried to effect improvement, is to dismiss the officer from the force. These situations cause a waste of time of many good men, but most important, there is a waste of the individual's time and prevents another more qualified person from entering the force. This is the last stage, and documentation at each step is necessary.

An analogy is made regarding the range of discipline and its use. The good leader must determine when and what type (authoritative, democratic, laissez-faire) of leadership he will use in a given situation. When a riot or campus disorder is taking place, the effective leader must issue orders and expect immediate compliance. In the case of planning there is room for participatory management. The same theory applies to discipline. The good leader will use the complete range of discipline at the right time, the right place, and for the particular individual, taking all information into consideration. The good leader in patrol will not pass the buck ("Lieutenant, I brought this man to you because he wouldn't clean his vehicle") or be afraid to use any discipline whatsoever. Nor will the good leader be so insecure regarding his authority that he becomes the obnoxious, unbearable supervisor who penalizes a man for any and all infractions. The effective leader will use the leadership or positive discipline in such a way that the negative discipline will only be needed sparingly. However, everyone should be made aware of the certainty of discipline where appropriate. This is similar to the traditional deterrence of crime: the swiftness and sureness of arrest, conviction, and corrective action. The ineffective use of discipline in a police department, especially in patrol, will cause a complete breakdown in morale, indicating failure of the patrol commander to maintain internal esprit de corps.

In attempting to have the punishment fit the crime, it is important to look at the character of the offense as opposed to the results of the error. This character of the offense should also be included in the deficiencies when no bad results occur. This points up the theory of placing limited authority to discipline in the hands of the first-line supervisor. When a police department is organized in a manner where the first-line supervisor has the authority to grant vacation, extra days off, holidays, and disciplinary actions within certain guidelines, it has the ability to be an effective department. It is the sergeant who spends most time with the level of execution who in turn really achieves the objectives. The men should look to the sergeant for direction in striving to perform in an excellent manner. When the sergeant has the power to influence, he has true power, and with the proper usage he will mold and motivate his men to achieve the goal. When a sergeant has to seek approval for his every move relative to these factors, he has no real authority or powers, and therefore his ability to influence is decreased. Consequently, his ability to produce is decreased. The sergeant having a true position becomes the key supervisor. Many departments organized in this way have moved forward in effective policing in today's society.

Action becomes necessary as soon as possible after the deficiency occurs. A lesson can be learned from the parent-child relationship; correcting at the end of the day by the father when he comes home from work is less effective than immediate correction. Correct timing is necessary to make discipline effective. This does not mean dismissal or suspension for thirty days or anything so drastic. It does mean that discipline has to be firm, fair, consistent, and uniform. For this to take place, authority must be vested with the sergeant and guidelines must be written so each man is judged individually. Also, there must not be a radical difference in punishment throughout the entire department for a similar offense. For example, if two men make the same mistake, one for the first time and one for the second time, they both should be punished, but not equally.

As confidence in a law-enforcement agency increases, so will the reports of complaints by citizens concerning police action. Some of the complaints will be substantiated and result in disciplinary action; others will be unfounded or false. In either case, the police must welcome the complaints and provide a vehicle for resolution of the complaints. This should be initiated by the department. An image of openness and willingness to rid the department of undesirables will result, in the long run, in a better department. At the same time, the men of the department must be able to realize that the investigators of the complaints and decisions made from these investigations will be fair, impartial, objective, and will not tolerate false accusations without action being taken against those persons responsible. This can be done only where law permits. The rule of discipline also applies in these situations. Do not mete out discipline to an officer found guilty of an infraction (discourtesy, neglect, etc.) on the basis of results or the importance of the person who made the complaints, but on the character of the infraction.

The patrol administrator must first gain the respect of the members of his command. His most important asset in doing this is self-discipline and example-setting. The ability to communicate ideas and goals in a way that gains acceptance and causes the welding together of the unit and the individual can resolve any imbalance caused by the traditional police problems of needing rapid and willing compliance to orders and directions, yet still preserving independent thought and initiative. Innovation and creativity are key aspects of police patrol of the future and must be considered very carefully when administering discipline, no matter what kind it may be. The young, intelligent police officer of today will not accept stupid orders. If you ask supervisors around the country what happens when a directive is read at roll call, he will answer you by saying, "These patrolmen not only want to know why they have to do it, but why they have to do it a certain way."

Everyone likes to be recognized and given a pat on the back when something worthwhile is accomplished. The use of the commendation is good positive discipline. The use of praise for an individual in public should be saved for those performances that are truly outstanding. The use of praise too often reduces its effectiveness, but in private, if a man earns it, the supervisor should praise accordingly.

All patrol commanders at some time or another know the loneliness of command. This is essential if the job is to be completed. Most people, including leaders, also want to be popular. These are two different positions to attain at the same time. Respect should come first.

As a patrol administrator you should work hard, think hard, plan hard, know who you are, where you are going, and how you are going to get there in a positive way. The patrol leader sets his goals and priorities parallel to the goals and priorities of the department. The patrol leader disciplines himself first and then motivates others to do the same. When he develops these attitudes, respect will come automatically. When he implements and moves forward with this respect, sincerity, and credibility, "popularity" as appropriate, will follow. The patrol administrator's decisions, however, should not be based on popularity but on doing what is right.

PERSONAL ATTENTION, INSPECTION, AND CONTROL

In the management by objective approach to patrol administration, the police leader in patrol should consider as part of his goal: (1) making the staff-inspection unit useless with regard to patrol, and (2) acting before the fact in achieving the two added responsibilities stated in the preface to this book: maintaining community stability and enhancing internal esprit de corps. The personal-attention concept necessitates the ability to judge those situations that call for the intervention of the administrator. After determining that the situation should have personal attention, the next question to answer is to what degree the patrol administrator should become involved. First, citizens have a tendency to rate credibility and capability to perform certain tasks directly to rank. Second, the higher the rank, as it exists today, the more resources the individual has control over, therefore the broader the scope of intervention. Third, and a potential pitfall, the timing of the personal attention should not indicate a complete lack of confidence in subordinates to resolve problems. In other words, the patrol administrator must stay alert and be aware of specific situations that might enlarge into a total issue internally and externally; continue to be sensitive to the situation, watching actions and reactions; gain understanding by observing and analyzing lower level decisions; give positive suggestions on a timely basis and evaluate the outcomes of the use or nonuse of the suggestions objectively; and not wait too long after this process before personal attention is given to insure successful results.

The patrol administrator's ability to apply this principle of personal attention to inspection and control will improve as the other qualities of leadership develop. When the patrol administrator knows the individual patrol commander better, ascertains the level of ability of each to perform under stress, evaluates the method of problem-solving by each, critically analyzes the use of resources (manpower and equipment), and documents faithfully and on a continuing basis, he will have reached a point where the principle will show a positive approach to management by objective. As fundamental as it may seem, a personal log used to document and follow up is essential.

The suggestions, if used properly, will cause line inspections to permeate the entire patrol force, and this in time will cause action before the fact in resolving problems and instill the planning process to the patrolman level. It can then be said, "If the patrolman uses the principles of planning in his daily operations, it will be more probable for the objective of each to be accomplished." It follows that if the patrol administrator develops the personal goals of his leader, and these goals parallel the goals of the organization, it is more likely that the objectives of the department will be achieved. Personal attention, inspections, and control contribute directly to effective use of resources. Management is defined as getting the most with the least. An objective or goal is something to achieve. A stipulation has been made generally in law enforcement that no great increase in resources is forthcoming. Apparently this is true, and the improvement of law enforcement will come through innovation and creativity of those involved within the system and the help of scientists, educators, etc. The management by objectives approach is designed to apply these principles to obtain maximum utilization of resources.

Inspection and Control

The first step in planning is to recognize the need. Inspection is closely related, because inspection should be one of the processes through which the first step in planning is recognized. The first step can be accomplished by inspection either before or after the fact. There are cases where it will be impossible for inspection to recognize the need before the fact, but inspection should make this a goal. Inspection, when related to agencies outside law enforcement, indicates quality control. Through the joining of two words "inspection" and "control," law enforcement intends to produce a quality product, a superior service to the community. Inspection and control therefore become synonymous with the planning and directing responsibilities of the administrator. Normally, patrol is the largest unit, therefore having the largest operating budget. Consequently, patrol administrators should be keenly aware of the need for line inspection and quality control. For example, a review of a recent survey would reveal the following:

City A, Total budget	$40,627,268.00
Salary budget	$37,142,703.00
% Salary budget of total	91.4%
City B, Total budget	$21,025,220.00
Salary budget	$20,277,970.00
% Salary budget of total	96.4%
City C, Total budget	$17,320,856.00
Salary budget	$15,764,801.00
% Salary budget of total	91%

If we continued the review only in the percentage salary budget of total, it would indicate 67.9%, 86.5%, 91.5% for various police departments. The patrol administrator must reflect upon the responsibility of administering the proportion of the budget applied to the police force. In doing so, the need to apply the personal-attention principle to inspections and management by objectives becomes obvious.

The larger police departments of the country operate with a staff-inspections unit. The smaller departments cannot afford the luxury. In the case of the former, the goal stated at the beginning of the chapter is appropriate. In the case of the latter, the need for quality line-inspection is emphasized.

This method of inspection as a supervisory tool is good so long as the positive aspects are emphasized. The follow-up then becomes a reality in that those responsible for performing the tasks believe inspection will take place at each level, thereby increasing the probability of successful completion of the tasks and achievement of the goals.

Some of the objectives of the inspection process are to improve teamwork; increase production; provide superior service; anticipate future problems; resolve community and internal problems; improve maintenance regarding building, equipment, records; and finally, to achieve quality control.

Line and Staff Inspections

There are two kinds of inspection: line, or authoritative, and staff. *Staff inspections* are those performed by personnel having no direct control over the persons or things being inspected. Larger departments have a staff inspector who is usually equal in rank to those in charge of operations the inspector must inspect. Officers assigned to these units usually possess a high degree of loyalty, integrity, strength of character, technical skills, working knowledge of the department, forcefulness, initiative, tact, diplomacy, objectivity, and courage. The staff unit should project an image of openness in the inspection process, uniformity, willingness to define training needs, and cooperation with operating units for the purpose of promoting efficiency and economy for the entire department.

Line inspections (the responsibility of patrol commanders), are those made by the patrol supervisor responsible for the patrol operation. It is essential that inspections show the results of procedures used to determine the need for modifications and provide accountability and justification.

To the patrol administrator, inspection means responsibility for performance by each level between the patrolman and himself. The administrator cannot inspect each call for service, written report, or the criminal conditions of each beat, but he can and should develop a continuing inspection process in order to get a realistic accounting of each level of authority and provide personal attention where appropriate. The following checklist will assist in accomplishing this mission. It is not all-inclusive but will give some insight regarding the personal-attention principles and the amount of time and effort needed for application.

— Do you personally use the concept of anticipation?
— Do you consider in advance? Think through in advance?
— Do you ask the questions, Who am I? Where am I going? and, How do I intend to get there?
— Is my time organized to the point where appropriate reflection is given to the answers?
— What is the total Part I crime for my area of responsibility?
— What is the total Part I crime by category?
— What is the projected Part I crime for my area on a daily, weekly, monthly, quarterly, semi-annual, and annual basis? What is the comparison between last year and the present year by time?
— What does analysis reveal as the average total Part I crime for each month on a daily basis?
— Regarding the crime rate, what is the violent crime total (murder, rape, robbery, aggravated assault), and what is the property crime total (burglary, larceny over $50, and auto theft)?
— Do your subordinates complete assignments on dates as requested (due-dates)?
— What inspections have been made lately?

1. Roll call
2. Revolver
3. Foot-patrol
4. Filing systems
5. Activity reports
6. Arrests in high-crime areas
7. Mileage (This is done to prevent passing of mileage from one shift to another and also to have total mileage for a shift compatible with the beat configuration. In other words, if an officer has a beat size of 2 city blocks by 3 city blocks and recorded 50 miles of driving during his tour of duty, he would have made few critical observations. There may be exceptions; however, on an average, the size of the beat should be compatible with the crime problems and the miles of driving. Obviously, outlying beats of larger size would require more mileage during the tour of duty in order to give proper coverage.)

— Are there any areas where constant presence would resolve the crime problems? For example, if a busy intersection caused a purse-snatch problem, the application of omnipresence would alleviate the problem. Intelligent use of manpower could produce the result without disrupting the total patrol sector. Determining the time of day and day of week is necessary, and allowing the team concept between beats is helpful.

— If this approach is used, have you evaluated the effectiveness, and if successful, have you discontinued the assignment after it has served the purpose?

— Do you set the proper example in dress? Attitudes?

— Does your positive attitude permeate your areas of responsibility?

— Have you complimented anyone lately for outstanding performance?

— Do you set priorities?

— Do you inspect as you insist patrol officers patrol, in an irregular overt posture?

— Do you insist upon primary and secondary missions where appropriate? In other words, if the patrol administrator must assign manpower to a given situation but the amount of time does not constitute a full day's assignments, are these resources utilized in a secondary assignment by time of day and location?

— Have you evaluated your position on the ladder of administrative principles?

1. Do you plan, organize, etc.?
2. Do you "get the job done"?
3. Do you document?

— Are you creative and innovative?

— What have you done that is creative or innovative?

— Do you solicit imagination and creativity, or do you say, "Don't bother me with that hare-brained idea"?

— Are you sensitive to potential internal conflicts between:
Patrolmen and other patrolmen

Patrolmen and supervisors
Supervisors and commanders
Internal units
— Do you understand manpower allocation and distribution?
— Do you communicate?

Line commanders, especially patrol leaders, should appreciate the formal inspection unit, if one exists. The unit is an extra set of eyes and ears that assist the patrol administrator to act before the fact. Proper attitude and lateral communication will make the inspection process more acceptable and productive. The author realizes there will be the pressure of other duties, but believes the practice of using a log to indicate inspection time will be beneficial in the long run to the total operation. The use of the personnel board (Appendix C) will be most beneficial in this area. The analysis of crime and a review of what crime information from analysis is reaching the patrol officers through reports and pin maps will reveal answers to:

1. Are crime maps maintained on a current basis?
2. Are the maps and information accessible to the patrolman?
3. Do supervisors insure reviews of current crime information by patrol officers? If not, why not?
4. Is manpower distribution applied on a timely basis?
5. Are subordinate commanders making personal inspections?
6. Are support units producing appropriate and meaningful information at a rate which does not render it useless for operational commanders?
7. Is lateral communication taking place? If not, why not?
8. Have the personnel responsible for achieving the objective been supplied with the proper amount of resources?
9. Did the person most involved have an opportunity to express his ideas as to how the problem might be solved?
10. Is coordination taking place between operating units (patrol-CID-juvenile-special operation) to avoid duplication and wasted efforts?
11. Is any other resource possessed by the department that can be used and result in solving the problem?

The patrol administrator can help himself by using written material. As stated earlier, the internal analysis of crime will help in accomplishing "reduction of crime" and "maintaining internal esprit de corps." The other goal, community stabilization, can be assisted by reading books on police administration, formal education, and a general awareness of what is taking place around the country. This information will come from other law-enforcement agencies, intelligence reports, national newspapers, magazines, television, and radio. Additionally, reports by federal regulatory and administrative agencies such as HUD and HEW[15] can give an insight into potential pressure and influence that may come to bear on the patrol force and with which the patrol administrator should become intimately aware. A look at welfare-rights organization, availability of employment, and educational institutions reveals the extent of police involvement and the preparation necessary to meet these problems properly.

Patrol administrators take heed: in order to be prepared to meet the community-stability aspect of leadership, it is a must to stay tuned to local radio and television and review the local newspapers. It is necessary to develop personal rapport with community leaders for mutual trust and credibility. The way to act before the fact is to be in a position where citizens will bring forth their problems out of confidence and trust. Small police problems then stay small and do not become city-wide or community-wide issues. It is easy to solve the small problem; it becomes much more difficult if the problem enlarges and affects many people. The awareness of what is going on in the community and the ability to relate this to anticipated police problems are essential for effective patrol administration.

Control

Control in relationship to inspections and personal attention should be viewed as a means of maintaining a certain quality or standard of performance of which the force can be proud.

Additionally, the patrol administrator should use control as a method of helping all personnel produce a quality product and at the same time insuring that minimum deviation from standards is the order of the day. Communicate to all personnel that this positive use of control is for the benefit of the total patrol force. Quality performance reduces the need for discipline of a negative nature and enhances each individual patrol officer's chances of promotion. Repetition of quality routine activity causes the goal to be reached in an easy manner. When the patrol administrator assures personal attention appropriate to the rank and/or condition of the situation, standards of excellence should prevail in the majority of police actions taken by patrol personnel. There is a direct relationship between the patrol administrator, his personal attention, the inspection and control process, and the number of times personnel of the unit are commended or disciplined. When the proper follow-up is done by first-line supervision, middle management, and command patrol leaders, the need for discipline is reduced.

When police departments issue written policy command and supervisory personnel understand it and see to it that the level of execution understands it, then the department can move forward with common goals. Each level will be able to withstand most pressures from within and without the department. The policy and control process will help insulate the patrol leader from these unwarranted pressures and reduce temptation to enhance personal prestige. This same attitude also will help the police agency to get the team effort in achieving the goals. If personal gain is put aside, then the goals of each member of the department will be the same as those of the department. This is, in effect, a simple definition of administration. As in a field reporting system, the first administrative control is located at the sergeant or first-line supervisor level. A high degree of performance at this point reduces the need for other levels to inspect. The first-line supervisor should seek to make personal attention, inspection, and control on the part of the patrol commanders unnecessary. Quality police performance for the community can be improved by this process.

The standards of excellence should include all facets of police activity. If police leaders allow illegal searches of persons, vehicle, or similar actions, it is hard to believe that patrolmen will not use these methods to achieve the goal when pressures are placed upon them to reduce crime or stop vice. It is most urgent then that patrol commanders inspect and control through personal attention in order to accomplish the mission and at the same time insure propriety of action in the methods used to achieve the goal. The end is *not* justified by the means. The objective should be obtained by means of leadership, proven patrol techniques, experimentation and innovation in patrol, and using police ability and intelligence against the potential criminal. Effective communication, leadership, and motivation will instill in patrol personnel a desire to perform in a superior manner. Inspection and control then becomes a matter of pride. Everyone wants work inspected when a good job has been done. Preparation for inspections through education and training is necessary to fulfill the role of fully participating in the policy-making decisions of the department. The personal attention, inspection, and control process will help immeasurably to attain full knowledge of what exists within the patrol force and create effective relationships with other units.

The patrol administrator who quotes statistics of a viable nature, forecasts trends for historical data in a selective and logical manner, states grass-roots examples concerning the problem at hand, and suggests simple yet effective solutions to problems with consequences considered knows what real responsibility and authority is all about. Government officials will seek his advice, members of his command will gladly follow and seek him out for directions, the patrol effectiveness will be superior, other leaders within the organization will cooperate and coordinate in an improved manner, the potential for reaching the objective will improve, and the image of professionalism will have been projected.

USE OF RESOURCES

Since police agencies are not in the business of producing a product for profit in the traditional sense, their resources are not as easy to evaluate in terms of profit and loss. The law-enforcement product of service and order maintenance is in many ways intangible and therefore difficult to measure. However, this in no way means that the manager of a police agency should not administer as if he were actually producing a measurable product. Police leaders must use the total resources of the department as if they were their very own and insist that all others in the department do the same. Each citizen pays tax dollars that are used to purchase the resources of a police agency; therefore, it is an individual investment. All resources of a police department equate to money, so it is difficult to place a priority on any one. However, a review of each of the resource categories (manpower, material, equipment, supplies, electricity, and fuel) in terms of cost would list manpower first, since the majority of the police budget is made up of salary for police personnel. Patrol administrators should be keenly aware of using human resources as the number-one priority. This should not be to the detriment of the other resources, but the resource should be looked upon as the most precious commodity possessed: specifically, the patrol officer.

The mission of law enforcement and the function of patrol are similar to business and industry, since the principles of administration can be applied to both. The big difference, which must be completely understood, is that policing is service, law enforcement and order maintenance, not profit. As a matter of fact, the police department's existence results from the failure of certain segments of our society to live up to a fundamental role of human relations: to respect the rights, property, and lives of our fellow man. Person-to-person relations in our society are the most complex and controversial of all human endeavors, and this is the area of police work generally and patrol specifically. Patrol must mediate, counsel, and perform a repressive function in a permissive society and do it effectively and efficiently. Expanding upon the patrol function and inspecting for a minute the priorities of the police mission, there is room for reflection. Traditionally, police work has set a priority on law enforcement. Today, the priority has been challenged. James Q. Wilson points out this challenge in "Dilemmas of Police Administration" when he writes:

> The dilemmas of police administration arise out of the difficulty confronting a chief who seeks policies which can guide his men in performing the order-maintenance function and a technique which will prove efficacious in serving the law-enforcement function. The conflict over how the police should behave in order-maintenance cases results from differing expectations as to the appropriate level of public or private order and differing judgments over what constitutes a just resolution of a given dispute. In a homogeneous community, where widely shared norms define both the meaning of order and the standards of justice (who is equal to whom and in what sense), the police role is comparatively simple. But where the community, usually because of differences of class or race, has no common normative framework, the police have no reliable guides to action and efforts to devise such guides will either be half-hearted or a source of important public controversy. The conflict that arises over the performance of the law-enforcement function, on the other hand, arises out of the lack of any technique by which crime can be reduced significantly and without incurring high costs in terms of other values — privacy, freedom, and so forth. The dispute about the law-enforcement function is, unlike the dispute over order maintenance, not over ends but over means.[16]

More recently, the same topic has arisen for consideration by the American Bar Association in stating standards relating to the urban police function. See p. 240.

The patrol administrator must have full knowledge of the goals for the department in order to use the resources placed in his care to their fullest extent.

Manpower Resource

In managing the human resources of the patrol unit by objectives, the patrol administrator must realize that the goal can only be achieved through this resource and there is an interdependent responsibility between subordinates and superiors. William Bopp in *Police Personnel Administration* says:

> Succinctly stated, the manifold supervisory personnel responsibilities include (1) service on panels formed to conduct employment interviews, (2) the orientation of new employees, (3) inservice counseling, (4) training, (5) personnel evaluation, (6) recommendation of disciplinary action, (7) input or individual pay decisions for subordinates, (8) adjudication of minor grievances, and (9) the creation of a working environment conducive to productivity. In highly unionized departments, the supervisory role is greatly expanded as sergeants must often coexist with union stewards, or their equivalent.[18]

The patrol administrator has all levels of authority between himself and the level of execution as an extension of himself, and he should set the stage for efficiency and economy in management. Demonstrated success in human relations among top management will result in a similar application permeating the patrol force. Similar actions regarding other resources should produce positive results.

The management by objectives approach, as suggested in this book and expressed partly in the Patrol Planning Council, accentuates the exploration of untapped talent using all members of the patrol unit. Talent unexplored because of lack of opportunity, unsolicitation, insecurity of supervision, or lack of communication is talent wasted in the use of human resources.

In his book *The Human Organization* Rensis Likert identifies a Table of Organization and Performance Characteristics of Different Management Systems. The table indicates (column 1) an organizational variable, and then reports the relationship between the variable and four classes of systems. Likert asked several hundred managers to indicate the highest and lowest producing departments with which they were familiar. The vast majority indicated the choice toward system 4. The following are some of the statements explaining the system 4:

1. The direction of information is down, up, and with peers.
2. A very substantial amount of teamwork throughout the organization.
3. Decision-making widely done throughout the organization.
4. Decision-makers are quite well aware of problems.
5. Subordinates are fully involved in all decisions related to their work.

6. Except in emergencies, goals are usually established by means of group participation.[19]

In Chapter 4, Likert examines the effect on performance of three basic concepts of system-4 management: (1) the use by the manager of the principle of supportive relationships, (2) the manager's use of group decision-making and of group supervision, and (3) the manager's high *performance* goals for the organization.

The principle of supportive relationships is stated as follows:

> The leadership and other processes of the organization must be such as to ensure a maximum probability that in all interactions and all relationships within the organization, each member, in light of his background, values, desires and expectations, builds and maintains his sense of personal worth and importance.[20]

This interdependent responsibility and supportive relationship can be applied equally to the patrol supervisor and subordinates. When a sergeant can understand why one of his squad members reacted to a certain situation and the sergeant takes the time to guide and counsel, interaction, support, and communication has taken place. The next situation calls for praise for an outstanding achievement and is forthcoming from the sergeant. Another situation could be food arriving to a squad of policemen which has been assigned to a large disorder for an extended period of time, and the sergeant takes his place at the end of the line. Each interdependent support relationship indicates that the sergeant cares for his men. The sergeant shows how important his patrolmen are to the unit. This concept, properly implemented, is suggested for the patrol administrator as contributing to the achievement of the goal, through increased productivity.

The second concept of group decision-making and group methods of supervision, according to Likert, suggests interaction between supervisors and subordinates and assuring subordinates at each level. The author suggests that the Patrol Planning Council essentially fulfills this concept. The council is not a committee where the patrol administrator can say the group made the decision, but an effective force of using manpower resources and tapping talent in a very real sense.

The third concept, high-performance aspiration, which influences the organization, deals with performance goals. It is a matter of pride in the uniform and the department. This concept would include the needs and desires of the members of the organization, the integration of these needs and desires of their members with the shareholders, customers, suppliers and others who have an interest in the enterprise.

In applying the concept it is necessary to set objectives. Each member of the patrol unit must set objectives concurrently with supervisors. Included in Appendix B is a statistical goal form that can be used by each level of authority in the patrol function. Additionally, the goals of the police department would integrate with the goals of government, other agencies, criminal justice systems, and most importantly, the citizens of the community. The American Bar Association "Standards Relating to the Urban Police Function" recommends setting goals and priorities in a way that will achieve the goal of the particular locality.

Practically speaking, the patrol leader, no matter what rank, must implement the concepts. No one man from a squad or platoon or district should be allowed to disrupt the smooth operation of the team. Abuse of sick leave, reporting late for work, leaving an assigned task or beat unnecessarily without consideration of the goal, not answering calls promptly, failing to back up other officers as appropriate, unacceptable appearance, and obnoxious attitude are all areas where supervision must inquire and take action in order to stave off a reduction of effectiveness and a spread of negative attitude.

There should be a total understanding of the relationship between resources and money. The money belongs to the taxpayers, and they have a right to expect efficiency and economy in its use. It has been estimated that the cost of one two-man patrol car operated around the clock is $100,000 a year. The first place to realize this enormous responsibility is in the allocation and distribution of the patrol force. The second is after the distribution is made and where supervisors in patrol must apply leadership. A sector sergeant in a large police department who supervises a squad of fourteen men has a budget of approximately $250,000 a year. Similarly, a watch commander of a small department supervising fourteen district or beat cars has the same budget. In terms of the taxpayers' expectation of return on their investment, the supervisor must realize the effect of lost man-days, lost man-hours, etc. The management by objectives approach is offered for patrol so that managers in police work can assimilate their responsibilities with total expenditures and realize a profit—a high degree of excellence in performance.

In relating crime to money, here is an example. Crime analysis reveals Saturday evening as the highest crime day and time of the week. The supervisor has the authority to allow his patrolmen extra days off and in doing so, allows these days on Saturday. This is not using resources advantageously. The crimes occurring due to less coverage cost the citizen time, money, and possible personal injury.

The question of leadership regarding efficient use of manpower is basic and should not be forgotten. Another point to be understood by this example is that consistency should exist in the application as presented. When the mission has been accomplished and the crime trend changes, the supervisor must apply the same principle, even though it may appear extraordinarily advantageous to the patrol officer. Credibility can only be developed when a fair application of principles is maintained constantly. There should be no waste of manpower. The patrol administrator's use of proper planning, education, training, procedures, personal attention, inspection, and control can eliminate or reduce poor utilization of resources.

Material, Equipment, Supplies, Electricity, and Fuel

Other resources that do not make up as much of the budget as manpower, but must be adequately cared for in order to allow the manpower to operate effectively, are such things as vehicles, shotguns, buildings, radios, and revolvers. First, years of experiences with vehicle accidents reveal the following:

1. Most patrol force accidents occur while officers are on routine patrol as opposed to response to another officer in trouble.
2. The more serious occur while responding to emergency or perceived emergency situations.
3. Driver attitude is very important.
4. Many departments are guilty of in-depth training of officers to use firearms, but accept a driver's license as evidence that he is capable of driving a police vehicle.
5. Patrol officers are not instructed with appropriate policy for driving police vehicles, as they are, say, for using their service revolvers.
6. First-line supervisors have the most important role to play in developing patrol officers into good defensive drivers.
7. Attention to driving habits must be given on a continuing basis (when observed) as opposed to taking action only when accidents occur.
8. When preventable accidents occur, attention must be given to correcting that deficiency which contributes to the accident on an individual basis.
9. Education and training should be continuous in (a) recruiting, (b) correcting for errant drivers, (c) restrengthening, and will have the greatest impact on solving the vehicular accident problem in terms of lost resources, including manpower.

The above list is not all-inclusive but merely points out part of the areas to be considered when the patrol leader attempts to improve the use of vehicle resources. Another aspect is the formal inspection process connected to roll call and inspection prior to the start of a watch. The auto inspection will be included in this discussion.

The saving of money by proper attitude and knowledge in the area of equipment, supplies, fuel, etc. can be cited in the case of an officer assigned to the research and development unit. One police department had been operating under a procedure where the patrol wagon was required to make three individual trips in order to complete the arrest process when a male and female were arrested simultaneously. First, the male and female were taken to a district station from the point of arrest, at which time arrest forms were completed. Second, the female was then taken to the women's detention facility where identification forms and processes were completed. Third, the arrest forms were then returned to the district station. In reviewing the process, the officer in the system and procedure unit realized that by reversing the procedure, one step could be eliminated. The saving in manpower and fuel when multiplied by the number of arrests made under these circumstances was tremendous. Similar thought should prevail among all members of the patrol force.

Implementation of a proper roll call can cause the inspection process to involve itself in great savings regarding equipment. Additionally, watch commanders can set examples of efficiency by providing a meaningful roll-call procedure. Watch commanders should know that information given at roll call should be relevant to the officers attending, which means omitting obsolete or ambiguous information. The presentation of duplicate information tends to show the commander as unprepared. A review of available information prior to commencement of roll call would reveal that information already possessed by members of the watch should be repeated only in exceptional cases. Procedures should be written out regarding the collection of data for the oncoming watch. This data would include hot-sheets, crime maps, special attention, etc. Officers who may have been on regular vacation or sick leave should be required to update their information via written orders.

Inspection should be made by the watch commanders daily at roll call and should include uniform and personal equipment. After roll call has been completed, sergeants should accompany officers to their respective relief posts. If there is a vehicle, inspection should be made of the vehicle for damage, cleanliness, operating condition, and any equipment carried. If any abnormalities are present, reports of specifics should be made. If the vehicle is unsafe to operate it should be grounded. Minor problems due to careless inspection can result in serious consequences (oil levels directly affect the engine operation the same as rust and wear), and improper care can affect the performance of the officer's service revolver. The way to approach the issue is to consider when an officer may need to use the equipment in a life or death situation and have it fail. The result will be care of all equipment as if it were your own.

In concluding this section, several paragraphs from *Police Personnel Administration* by William J. Bopp are presented for review. The point made here is to find the best position for each individual officer's talent. The byproducts of disseminating information, paralleling individual and organizational goals, are extremely important. The author hopes this information will produce enthusiastic, sincere, realistic dialogue between students and teacher.

Summary of Los Angeles County Sheriff's Department "Career Development Program." In 1971 the Los Angeles County Sheriff's Department began what is now considered a model career-development program. The program is automated and administered by the Department's Career Development Bureau. According to agency literature, the impact of this computerized system is manifold: (1) rapid retrieval of personnel information, (2) 24-hour response to emergency personnel inquiries, (3) manpower survey capabilities, (4) comparative capabilities for evaluating departmental strengths and weaknesses, (5) accurate accounting of manpower movement, and (6) prompt, updating capabilities.

This system offers a complete index of individual training accomplishments, experience, education, special talents, personal goals, and collateral information essential to career planning, internal movement, specialization, and promotion. The initial input of information was gained from a detailed questionnaire completed by all sworn employees. Due to the comprehensive nature of the instrument, a two-week period was allowed for its completion. Each completed questionnaire represented a career profile. The forms were then collected and the data was coded and computerized.

As new employees are inducted into the department, they are required to complete the career questionnaire. In-service personnel must update their profiles on a yearly basis. Incidental updating may be accomplished more frequently when a major status change occurs, such as the achievement of a college degree. In addition to the personnel data, the system contains information on manpower levels in specialized units, projected vacancy factors, and skills, experience, and education currently desired by each unit. Deputies considering transfers to specialized components have at their disposal computer-furnished information which allows them to prepare for assignments in anticipation of the department's growth, manpower turnover, and so forth.

An important adjunct to the Los Angeles County career development plan is the career counseling program. Career counseling is a joint venture undertaken by line supervisors and a group of fulltime counselors. The functional objectives of the program are (1) to furnish deputies with career information pertinent to their situation, (2) to gather data from employees regarding personal goals, (3) to encourage officers to enter high-need areas, and (4) to assist officers with personal problems by referring them to appropriate sources of help.

In summary, Los Angeles County Sheriff's Department's Career Development Program has the following broad objectives: (1) to effectively utilize the agency's human resources, (2) to provide a system for identifying and fulfilling organizational and individual needs, (3) to improve the effectiveness of selection, placement, development, promotion, and retention of personnel, (4) to assist personnel in assessing and developing their individual abilities, (5) to achieve a more effective match between the man and the job, (6) to improve morale, (7) to decrease the rate of manpower turnover for reasons of job dissatisfaction, (8) to develop personnel at all levels of the department, and (9) to provide counseling for mobility, development, orientation (to the police academy), retirement, and personal problems.

Few police departments will be able to implement as sophisticated and as far reaching a career development program as the Los Angeles County Sheriff's Department, which is a rather large agency. But, despite the limitations of size, budget, and technology, most sizeable law enforcement agencies can implement a modified version of the plan, for the concept is sound. The extent to which a department can embark on such a program is directly dependent on the resources it can muster. The Los Angeles plan has been able to harness technology for a humanistic end which still serves the organizational requirements of a metropolitan police agency. It is an encouraging sign.[21]

PARTICIPATORY MANAGEMENT AND MOTIVATION

Although a group, which must have at least two people, has been defined as the basic structural unit of an enterprise, any group is made up of individuals. In any organization goals are achieved through congruence of individuals and the organization.

The patrol administrator should not only be able to determine the type of leadership (authoritative, democratic, laissez-faire) he will use at any given time, but also the amount of participation in managing and the amount of job enrichment (self-actualization). There should be no question about using participation as a positive factor and managing device.

The group is made up of individuals who jointly contribute their specialized services, coordinated in a manner to achieve the enterprise's purpose. This involves these concepts:

> 1. *Specialization.* The services which individuals contribute to GROUPS are always specialized services: i.e., they differ one from the other. The bases for this differentiation are the place where work is done, the times at which work is done, the persons with whom work is done, the things upon which work is done, or the method or process by which work is done.[22]

In the patrol force consider:

1. The high crime vs. the low crime areas, or the patrol function vs. the booking function.
2. The evening shift which usually contains more crime and calls for service vs. the night watch or day shift.
3. Individual officers who possess different values, backgrounds, goals, etc.
4. The selected method of patrol: foot, auto (one-man, two-man), plain-clothes, burglary, K-9, etc. Each officer is then related in a special way to each consideration and the patrol leader must identify them as such.

> 2. *Enterprise purpose.* The members of the group must accept an enterprising purpose; i.e. they must be contributing their specialized services toward the attainment of an end which is specified for them. The purpose or end of the group is its raison d'être. This purpose must change from time to time, but the purpose at any time is always the formal objective of all members of the group. However, this enterprising purpose need not coincide with the needs which induce each individual to contribute his services to the group. (This is why the patrol leader has to develop differing management tools to motivate the individual.) A football player may recognize the purpose of his team to be the defeat of an opponent; at the same time his personal reason for belonging to the team may have little to do with such defeat. In other words, enterprise purpose and individual purpose may not coincide.[23]

Some patrol officers are working in the police department only to have a job. Others are working to gain experience. (These members are those who have higher education degrees and are using the position.) Some are dedicated to law enforcement and look upon the position as a career. The patrol leader should recognize these personal reasons and insure that, whatever they are, leadership is provided to enable each to parallel his goals and objectives with those of the department.

> 3. *Coordination.* Since specialized services are being contributed by individuals for the attainment of an enterprise purpose, it is essential that the specialized service be coordinated if the purpose is to be attained. "Coordination . . . is the orderly arrangement of group effort to provide unity of action in the pursuit of a common purpose."[24] The specialized services must be so combined in mutual relations, one to the other, that harmony and balance will be achieved. Coordination involves bringing into common action, combining in harmonious action.[25] The patrol administrator is responsible for initiating the essential team effort and the managers (captains, lieutenants, sergeants) are responsible for carrying out this coordination.

Nowhere in administrative work is achievement of goals, participation, direction, and coordination more important than when determining how far the patrol officer will continue with his preliminary investigation, what offenses will be involved, and responsibility for follow-up. When to generalize and when to specialize. One view states: Specialization occurs only when patrol fails to achieve its primary responsibility of prevention. Others say that investigators are best used in follow-up work. Therefore, their presence at the crime scene is indicated only when a crime is of unusual importance, involving considerable injury to a person or high property loss.

The patrol officer should determine whether investigators are in fact needed at a particular scene. This certainly affects participation in management, the use of discretion, coordination, and achievement of goals. Patrol detectives, Youth, Research and Development, and Records should meet to discuss and participate in a decision: for example, relative to whether robberies committed by juveniles were to be followed-up by Youth, CID, or patrol units. These discussions usually result from an increase in workload of the detective unit. The active participation of captains, lieutenants, sergeants, and patrolmen is necessary since the decision directly affects their responsibilities and their individual and collective workload. Each unit has to make similar inquiries and then report to the committee. The results from this method should be coordination between units and participation in management.

Participatory management in patrol should include participation by command officers, middle management, and the level of execution (major, captain, lieutenant, sergeant, and patrol officer). If a sergeant is participating with a lieutenant, the sergeant is then the subordinate. If the sergeant is participating with a patrolman, the sergeant is then the superior. This linking system carries up and down the chain of command. However, patrol administrators must be aware of the input that employee organizations have on the participatory process. Their cooperation should be solicited when using participatory management as a managing device.

In general terms, all members of the patrol force participate in the reduction of crime. They also participate in the rewards—a proclamation of a superior performance by government, a highly complimentary cartoon in the newspaper, recognition from business and industry, professionalism, etc. This means that members of the patrol force are allowed to make decisions with management in areas where they are directly affected. Persons allowed to be involved in the decisions that affect them will be more inclined to accept and effect the necessary change, achieve the goal, and be enriched through real authority, as opposed to a sense of authority.

As Alvin Toffler defined in *Future Shock,* "Change is the process by which the future invades our lives."[26] Law enforcement must control the rate and direction of change in relationship to the criminal justice system, government, and other agencies. Law enforcement must be able to articulate and communicate desires, wishes, and goals. In order to do this, law enforcement must educate itself in the ways necessary to control the rate and direction of change. It is necessary to become open and intelligently expressive of sensitivities and frustrations.

Quoting James Ahern in *Police in Trouble:*

> The roots of police failure are buried deeply in the failures of society, and every day these roots are deepening and strengthening their hold. If the state of police is not changed, if police continue to be exploited in their weakness, then they may one day turn, and the nightmare of a police state will be upon us. Already large segments of our population — among them those whose protection should be the policeman's most cherished task — instinctively turn their heads in retreat at the sight of a police car. They have come to believe that in the eyes of the police, their very existence is a sin. Others look upon the police as so incompetent, so stupid, and so corrupt that they are no better than the criminals with whom they deal. To them, the police problem is

something far beneath them, that is manifested only in the ghettos and poverty areas of this country, and that is beneath their notice. The policeman is not insensitive to these attitudes. They merely compound his frustration and his misery and accelerate the cycle of his degradation, driving him ever more deeply into the "closed fraternity."[27]

All talent within the patrol force must be tapped. The participatory management and job-enrichment methods are only management devices. Planning, innovation, alternative solutions to problems, and effective decision-making should become routine. Communication and dissemination of information to all concerned are necessary before any participatory management can take place. The following example concerns manpower allocation and distribution for the patrol force.

Job enrichment and personal development are enhanced when officers are allowed to express their ideas and thoughts about a subject before the decision is made. For example, *Question:* Officer, what would be the best type of patrol for this beat? *Answer:* Well, Sir, the burglars appear to be working in pairs, using an auto, so from my observation and working the beat for two years, I would recommend one man on foot, and one man in a car on the perimeter. *Question:* Should they be in uniform or plainclothes? *Answer:* The offenses appear to be committed by professionals so I think we should try to apprehend them which would also prevent future offenses, therefore plainclothes. Decision: "Approved." In essence, the leader is not sharing prerogative of authority, but rather allowing participation.

Carey explains this clearly when he states, "Action initiated by the responsible head to bring his subordinates into the picture on matters of mutual concern is not a sharing of prerogatives of authority, rather it is an extension of the opportunity of participation in the development of points of view and the assembly of facts upon which decisions are made."[28]

Continuing with the example, included in manpower distribution are decisions concerning the size of sectors (worked by sergeants), size of beats (worked by patrol officers), and the configuration of both. Also, these decisions directly affect span of control and the determination of whether any motorized-patrol beat or foot-patrol beat should be one- or two-man. Participation and a feeling of belonging can best be initiated if each level is involved in planning from the beginning. Therefore, when workloads are established from computer printouts and displayed over the existing patrol configuration, it is time to communicate, disseminate, and call for participation. As the operation proceeds, patrol captains have an opportunity to express their needs and set goals and priorities for their areas of responsibility.

Additional input concerning the best approach for achieving goals is available. Lieutenants offer suggestions concerning watches, sergeants concerning sectors, and patrolmen concerning beats. The result is agreement on goals, priorities, methods, and an enhancement of internal esprit de corps.

A case in point, and continuing our example. The International Association of Chiefs of Police distributes a case study #3 titled "Manpower Allocation and Distribution." On page 7 they describe the need to make a decision concerning the assignment of one or two men to a beat. Factors to consider are:

1. The number of situations in which more than one person is arrested at one time.
2. The number of arrests involving resistance.
3. The number of arrests involving the possession of weapons (the foregoing bears a direct relationship to the frequency of disturbances, assaults, and acts of violence).
4. The frequency of calls for service.
5. Nature of area, street design, degree of congestion, etc.
6. Natural boundaries that might interfere with assistance from other police units.[29]

After careful analysis and workload study, the watch commanders and sector sergeants make recommendations covering the size and configuration of sectors. The patrolmen working the individual beats are then consulted regarding those beats that should be manned by two officers, considering the factors mentioned above. Usually these decisions need in-depth discussions, but the patrolmen point out areas of concern that are not identified when dealing with statistics alone.

Each neighborhood has its own personality and attitude. The patrolmen have an intimate knowledge and relationship with these neighborhoods and their input is significant. The concept of cooperation and participation takes into consideration the complex and changing needs of our patrol personnel. People-oriented leaders, using the several styles of leadership appropriately, can develop the patrol function into an offensive technique easily capable of accomplishing the mission. When participatory management and motivation combine, an atmosphere of innovation and creativity prevails.

Motivation

Most modern managers, when they can shift their attention from the pressure of immediate assignments, are interested in attaining similar objectives:

1. To raise the level of employee motivation
2. To increase the readiness of subordinates to accept change
3. To improve the quality of all managerial decisions
4. To develop teamwork and morale
5. To further the individual development of employees[30]

It is easy to understand why the first objective is to raise the level of employee motivation. Next, to accept change more readily, participation in the decisions affecting those employees expected to change is most important. Participatory management and motivation in the patrol unit can be implemented intelligently and can result in an extremely well managed function. There may have been times in the past when police officers accepted a man as a leader because he wore the insignia of captain or lieutenant. This man may have had grey hair, a large and elegant office and thick rugs, but none of these made him a leader. Patrol leadership today has to be merited. No longer will the appointment of an individual to a position by a higher-up automatically confer the mantle of a leader. Patrol leadership will come through the development of credibility by the accumulation of good decisions.

In order to be a motivator as a patrol leader, it is necessary to look at the several factors affecting motivation. As Herzberg, Mausner, and Snyderman point out, we must first distinguish between factors of hygiene and factors of motivation.[31] When people feel happy in their jobs, they most frequently describe factors related to their tasks, to events that indicate to them that they were successful in the performance of their work, and to the possibility of professional growth. Conversely, when feelings of unhappiness were present, they were not associated with the job itself, but with conditions that surround the doing of the job. Factors involved in these situations are called factors of hygiene. Among the factors of hygiene are supervision, interpersonal relations, physical working conditions, salary, department policies and administrative practices, benefits, and job security. When these factors deteriorate to a level below that which the employee considers acceptable, then job dissatisfaction ensues. However, the reverse does not hold true.

Motivating factors are those that deal with the needs of the individual to reach his aspirations. This approach is labeled "job factor" or "motivation," while the extra job factors are labeled "hygiene." Both are needed, but the motivations are primarily related to job satisfaction.

Jung, Adler, Sullivan, Rogers, and Goldstein state that the ultimate goal of man is to fulfill himself as a creative unique human being according to his innate potential abilities and within the limits of reality. When he is deflected from this goal he becomes, as Jung says, "a crippled animal."[32]

The top motivators with regard to self-actualization are achievement, recognition, work itself, responsibility, and advancement. The rewards attained are these, plus salary and possibility of growth. In an individual job, the less opportunity for these motivators to be applied, the more the hygiene factors are necessary for the job to be tolerable.

The patrol leader has a tremendous responsibility in determining the amount of mix necessary between participatory management and motivating factors in order to attain maximum effectiveness. The team-policing concept that has been implemented around the country is a prime example of police departments' attempts at resolving this important aspect of self-actualization. The author had many tough supervisors, but the excitement of policing and the satisfaction of achieving the goal in a challenging situation, especially if the tough supervisor recognized your efforts, made the patrol function worthwhile. It should not be overlooked, however, that money when given as a reward for performance is a reinforcement of the motivation of recognition and achievement.

It also follows that money and rewards alone are not enough. The individual must feel that he is part of the mission and the success was due partly to his ability to perform.

When a sergeant has his patrolmen volunteering to stay out on the beat until relieved on those beats because of a crime problem, he has shown leadership ability to motivate. When a captain of a watch or district has men coming back to work on their own time, not asking for compensation, to continue an investigation because the leads are hot, he has achieved the proper motivating atmosphere. When a group of patrolmen get together prior to roll call and develop a plan to present to their sergeant which they believe will reduce burglaries in their sector, that sergeant has motivated the team. These events wouldn't have occurred if the jobs themselves didn't have some interest to the individual. Police work, and especially patrol work, must keep a vigilant eye in order to prevent boredom and routinization of the patrol function. The concept of career development, as described previously in the Los Angeles Sheriff's Department's experiment, shows a realistic approach.

The patrol leader, no matter what rank, should realize the importance of allowing each officer to self-actualize. The motivating factor of recognition is direct between the supervisor and the subordinate, whether it be a pat on the back or the formal performance evaluation. Additionally, this aspect extends to others because efficiency ratings affect promotion, which means an increase in salary.

It cannot be emphasized too much how planning and organizing affect the performance of the level of execution. When the patrol leader plans and teaches his subordinates to do likewise, he raises the performance level greatly. When the patrol leader organizes, he allows the subordinates to achieve realistic assignments and thus has a motivator working. When followed by recognition of good work, and guiding, counseling, and training in work that needs improvement, another motivator is working. Modern management techniques and the application of leadership principles by dedicated police leaders is an effective formula.

Obviously, all patrol officers cannot participate in all decisions. The patrol administrator who understands the concept of centralization and decentralization as related to participation and motivation will make good decisions regarding each. Subordinates are limited in their ability to participate, and this must be recognized or else precious time will be wasted. On the other hand, the patrol administrator who uses participation at the appropriate instance and to the appropriate degree will save time. For example, crime problems that occur during different watches, but are overlapping, need the participation of each commander. The problem should be given to all concerned for recommended solutions. The diverse views and approaches should result in a coordinated resolution and simplification of the effort. Sincerity should be displayed by the patrol leader when requesting recommended action or new ideas.

Police officers will initiate ideas and offer suggestions when solicited if they believe the ideas and suggestions will be considered seriously. If they think they are being "had" by management and are being used to implement a management program, more harm than good will have been done. There must be a mutual respect and an honest exchange of ideas between the leader and officers for participation to work. Participatory management is not an absolute and therefore is used in degrees, depending on the situation at hand.

When we consider participatory management as a motivating

factor and are looking for results, we should consider attention to duty; knowledge of crime increase or decrease; watching the individual for expression of genuine concern; acceptance of responsibility (this is easily done when an officer is given a regular beat to work); the officer's willingness to work above and beyond to attain achievement; an honest expression by the officers of obstacles causing them problems (in resolving problems of crime, etc.); requesting help in alleviating the obstacles; presentations of potential conflict prior to their becoming an issue; acceptance of change as a real contribution to the total effort and not just a manipulation of subordinates to make management look good; the "why" of procedures; and acting before the fact by all levels of the patrol force. The demonstrated concern of a patrol sergeant when questioned about the increase in crime in his sector will show his acceptance of responsibility.

The same scene repeated two weeks later when the concern has changed to a smile because of participation, implementation of effective patrol methods resulting in a decrease in crime, is satisfying. The knowledge of facts, attention to duty, willingness to work above and beyond, recognition, achievement, understanding, and similar dialogue are included in the smiling face.

The patrol administrator cannot and should not use participatory management as a panacea to leadership and motivation. He should, however, know when, how, and to what degree participation will be an advantage in his leadership. An understanding of internal and external influences and their effect on him and his associates is important. Knowledge of the total environment is necessary in order to make good decisions. Understanding the limitations and capabilities of his subordinates, and the ability to be able to evaluate each as to what amount of participation he can handle and to what degree his input will affect the organization both positively and negatively, will help. The patrol administrator (leader) knows when to use which style of leadership and the planning process (solution, alternate solution, consequence of possible solution), and he should expect all members of the patrol force to use these management tools to achieve stated goals.

PERFORMANCE EVALUATION

The evaluation of performance by patrol officers throughout the United States has traditionally been attempted in one of three ways. First, there is no performance evaluation. Secondly, performance evaluation has been accomplished in a haphazard process. Third, an honest attempt has been made to evaluate personnel based on realistic factors.

Several errors have been present in the past, such as relating the number of arrests or number of traffic citations issued as an overabundant impact on the performance of an officer. Law enforcement must learn that an officer spends the majority of his time on noncriminal activities, and these activities must share a greater amount of the total evaluation. Also, there has been a lack of training for those supervisors designated as raters. The question of integrity in rating by supervisors is more a question of their not knowing how to rate objectively than of a deliberate intent to invalidate the process. Prejudice and subjectivity are other factors present in the rater and should be considered when designing the form to be used for the department.

Law enforcement hopefully has reached the point where all factors that affect the total performance of officers and supervisors will be included as part of an honest, effective performance evaluation. In fact, standards of excellence must be stated and rating based on merit is essential if police work is to continue on the road toward professionalism.

Every employee has the right to be told honestly and objectively his/her level of performance. The immediate supervisor is the most appropriate person to accomplish this task. In the patrol force, it is the sergeant, lieutenant, and captain. When the performance rating has a bearing on the position an officer places on the promotion list, it is obvious how important this evaluation becomes. Performance evaluation, promotional potential, and personal fulfillment are directly related. If we could, each of us, be objective, we would agree that we all would like to improve our performance, know that our job is vital to the success of the organization or mission, be recognized for our efforts, and know that the tasks we are performing have been done accurately and professionally. Standards of excellence for the different positions and just what constitutes satisfactory or outstanding performance as related to these positions should be clearly stated for everyone to understand. Additionally, the patrol administrator should realize that the chief sets the standards formally, and rightly so, but each level of authority also sets standards by applying degrees of compliance to the formal standard. Sergeants implement their level of performance when they give an officer an outstanding rating for accomplishing 75% of the formal standard needed to rank outstanding.

Patrol administrators would do well to insure that sergeants and lieutenants have an opportunity to express their opinions and ideas relative to standards. The standards should be realistic, measurable to a degree, relevant, attainable, surpassable, based on above average productivity, accepted by superior and subordinates, and uniformly examined. Also, effective performance evaluation will enhance the following:

1. Assigning appropriate tasks
2. Identifies strengths and weaknesses
3. Causes supervisors to allocate proper amount of time to this important process
4. Provides information for career development
5. Isolates specific attitudes and traits
6. Assists in identifying potential supervisors
7. Insures line commanders take personal interest in subordinates
8. Improves ability to solve departmental and work problems
9. Provides feedback for training purposes
10. Assists in salary decisions
11. Serves as check and balance on recruitment and selection process
12. Fulfills personal need of employee to know his level of performance
13. Improves transfer procedure (the transfers of men without proper evaluation of specifics and identification of abilities, liabilities, and communication, not only causes dissatisfaction of the officer; but disrupts the unit from which transferred and the unit to which the officer is transferred.

A study being conducted today indicates approximately 3,200 individual tasks are being performed by the police. To have written standards for this amount of tasks is illogical. Also, the vanity and complexity of police work is such that this undertaking is unnecessary. Just as the patrol administrator must learn to lead according to the existing conditions in his community and department, so should the standard of performance as related to the individual tasks on a priority basis be implemented according to position and existing conditions.

Supervision and Forms (Teaching and Rating)

The greatest asset of a supervisor is his ability to develop people. Whether or not the supervisor is aware of employee appraisal, he is continually making appraisal of each officer. If a department is to overcome to any degree the pitfalls of human beings in rating other human beings, honest effort must be made to evaluate personnel on a formal basis within the department. In order to do this, it is necessary to develop the proper form for the respective police agency. Irving B. Wicker, Jr. has suggested a five-step approach in developing the appropriate forms:

1. Determine the goals and purposes of the form;
2. Select and define, in depth, those traits to be evaluated;
3. Determine the degrees of differentiation between "poor" and "outstanding" performance;
4. Explicitly define those degrees (i.e. "unacceptable," "fail," "average," and so forth);
5. Assign weights for each degree, where appropriate.[33]

Once the appropriate form has been decided upon, explanation of departmental policy regarding the use of the form is necessary. This should be presented in the form of a general order or its equivalent. Who shall be evaluated and by whom; how the evaluation shall be performed and at what time intervals; what specific responsibilities are placed upon the sergeant, lieutenant, captain, etc.; what shall be done with the results of the evaluation; and where the final place of filing shall be located. Also, supervisors need to be trained as raters and teachers, since the improvement of the officer is most important. Realistically, supervisors cannot be trained as professional teachers, but they can train officers using the basic principle of teaching. An in-depth presentation of teaching at this time would be inappropriate; however, a couple of brief descriptions of the basic principles will add to the continuity of our discussion. One description calls for (1) explaining the task to the officer, (2) demonstrating how the job is to be done, (3) observing the officer do the job, (4) evaluating his performance.

Another way of putting it is to (1) prepare the learner, (2) present the operation, (3) try out performance, and (4) followup.[34] Whatever the case, the supervisor should plan for the training session; be sure he has the proper equipment (form, pen, flashlight, etc.) to perform the task exactly as he wants it done; try to make the training interesting (a sergeant could tell a story of his experience relating to the same task); make the situation as valid and realistic as possible by explaining, illustrating when possible; question the officer as appropriate; indicate potential pitfalls; allow the officer to perform the task fully and do it as many times as necessary until you are satisfied he knows; have him relax, and advise him you are available for help at any time; evaluate and redirect instruction as appropriate.

It is essential for the rater to be trained in rating employees.

Obstacle and objective awareness are necessary in order to make the performance evaluation meaningful and successful. The patrol administrator has a responsibility to insure that all supervisors under his command have been fully trained and maintain a lateral communication with the administration of other units within the department to satisfy his leadership role relating to standard application of the performance evaluation policy. If there is one complaint a patrol commander can bet he will receive when discussing performance evaluation, and it will be the closest thing to a sure bet, it is, "How do you expect us to rate our men objectively when the supervisors of (X) unit give their men top efficiency?"

There is no excuse for this practice if it exists. All leaders have a responsibility to review evaluation to a degree that provides information necessary to respond to the question (real or imagined) affirmatively. The first-line supervisor/sergeant is especially important when training raters. It is necessary to have formal classroom training wherein problems, problem resolution, and consensus may take place concerning the tentative procedure. One large problem coming out of the training session will concern the collection of data necessary to rate officers. The recommendation made in the section about officers' activity reports is applicable. Productivity should be gleaned and key-punched for input into the computer from the activity reports. Printouts should be supplied at least monthly to the respective supervisor to assist primarily in performance evaluation, even though other decisions regarding workload analysis and manpower deployment can be gathered from the same printout. Sergeants, who usually have a larger span of control, will especially need this type and style of information.

Pitfalls

There are several pitfalls which should be discussed by the supervisor during the training session so they will be on the same track when they rate their respective subordinates. The better supervisor will make the better rater. The less effective supervisor will carry the same traits into performance evaluation as he demonstrates in his daily leadership. Being the good guy will destroy an evaluation system. The grapevine of a police department is such that the abuse of an objective rating system by one unit will spread throughout the department and cause a decline in its value. You do not help a man by rating him outstanding if in effect he is average in a specific category.

None of us deserves "outstanding" in each category because we are human, consequently imperfect. The next pitfall is directly opposite from the good-guy approach. This supervisor just cannot be bothered with justifying his ratings of outstanding or unsatisfactory; therefore, he will place all of his men in the three columns: satisfactory, average or above average. The next pitfall is what is known as the "halo,"— the tendency of the rater to rate in terms of a very general impression rather than on the basis of specific traits.[35] The next pitfall is the misuse of authority. When the sergeant uses the performance evaluation as an ax to chop off the head of a subordinate, he is showing leadership by fear and is totally unacceptable. Objectivity, honesty, and sincerity must be projected by the supervisor or else the mutual trust necessary for valid evaluation is lost. The next pitfall is the inability of supervision to agree on the value of the categories. For example, what is outstanding to one supervisor may be poor to another.

The classroom training given at the beginning of implementation of a rating system is the place for this clarification to occur. Next, let's consider the pitfall of prejudice. It is easy for any of us to imprint in our minds certain images of people who may be different than we are. Our backgrounds and value judgments are influenced by our church, family, education, and environment. An honest effort must be made on the part of each rater to attempt objectively and sincerely to keep out any opinion based on prejudice. Very close to this is the pitfall of subjectivity. This error can be carried to the extreme. For example, when a sergeant plays golf and one of his patrolmen is a good golfer, they become a twosome on the course. At work they have similar temperaments and are easy to get along with. The natural tendency for the sergeant is to carry these factors over into the total evaluation and then give an incorrect performance rating. Additionally, when this occurs, the sergeant is leaving himself wide open for the charge of favoritism, which can affect morale in a very negative manner. Patrol commanders shall be alert to review carefully any evaluation made by sergeants who indicate a relationship giving the appearance of possible favoritism.

Pitfall of Associated Abilities. In this pitfall, the rater may confuse the factors of discipline and control with leadership. In one case, the officers of a sergeant's squad perform in an orderly manner and act well disciplined, but are doing so because of strict control and fear. The sergeant is using the authority of his position.

Pitfall of Recency. Recency error occurs when too much weight is placed on an employee's behavior immediately prior to a rating deadline. Most evaluations are intended to cover a specific time frame, such as six months or a year. If a supervisor does not keep comprehensive notes on a subordinate's activities during the evaluation period, there will probably be an inclination to overemphasize the most easily recalled behavior, which is usually the most recent behavior.

The pitfalls can be overcome if personnel are made aware and take the appropriate steps to alleviate those ingredients that cause them.

Implementing performance evaluation. To implement the program of performance evaluation by general order, the following steps should be considered.

1. Standards published for all to understand. They should be realistic and controls included for review and possible change. Policy statement outlining fact that the superior of a rating officer cannot cause the rating officer to change any evaluation mark.
2. Performance evaluation form selected and explained (using participatory management).
3. Instructions for completing the form.
4. Training (formal, roll call, individual as needed) for rated officers, rating officers, and reviewing officers.
5. Indicate the types of reports: i.e., quarterly, semi-annual, etc. and whom they affect: i.e., probationary patrolmen, patrolmen, sergeants, lieutenants, newly promoted personnel, etc.
6. State the time periods for submission of each type of report.
7. Indicate the responsibilities of the rating officer (the supervisor to whom a rated officer reports, usually the immediate supervisor). These responsibilities include review of planning the interview; avoidance of pitfalls; departmental objectives; accountability for completion of tasks; understanding discipline; data collection and demonstration; completion dates for performance-evaluation submission; consultation, guidance, and counseling techniques; instructions on completing the form, which should be signed by the rated officer indicating the fact that the evaluation procedure was consummated.
8. Indicate the responsibilities of the rated officer to accept the rating, or to disagree and state the reason for the disagreement.
9. Indicate the responsibility of the review officer (officer next in the chain of command above the rating officer) to review all performance evaluations within his authority and comment positively or negatively as necessary, and insure proper submission of reports by time, date, and location.
10. Advise each level of authority above those mentioned of the possibility, responsibility, and authority to comment as appropriate where an evaluation indicates less-than-satisfactory performance (recommend retraining, discipline, etc.)

11. Provide for evaluation to be maintained in central location, preferably the individual's personnel file.
12. Maintain confidentiality as necessary.
13. Allow for controls that will insure some type of action with regard to officers receiving unsatisfactory evaluations.
14. Include a procedure outlining the importance of the system, the recourse available for an officer who feels he has been rated unfairly, and the necessary response by the rating and reviewing officers.

Rating Methods

No police department should be satisfied with using one rating method and not reviewing other methods for possible improvement. Most methods have advantages and disadvantages, and the method selected should be tailored to fit your department. Whatever method is used, be sure to explain it fully.

Lazy method. In this case, supervisors rate their men on the basis of their memory and certain obvious characteristics that the supervisor likes or dislikes. He does not collect or document any dates on which to base his judgments. Some supervisors are able to do this, and they may do a good job, but experience has indicated a greater potential for misjudging. The core of rating is the value judgment. Patrol supervisors should always have some form of documentation available on which to rely when making these all-important judgments.

Ranking. In this method, the supervisor selects an individual in his squad and places him in a position of rank from lowest to highest based on overall performance. He is comparing each of his men with the other, sometimes using several subfactors. The problem arises when you compare Sergeant A's squad with Sergeant B's squad. The lowest ranking officer in A squad may be better than the highest ranking officer in B squad.

Paired comparison. The supervisor using this method compares each man on his squad with every other man, with the placement first to last. The final position is determined by the number of times an officer was judged to be better than all the others. A disadvantage of this method is that the younger patrolmen usually place lowest due to their inexperience, the danger being discouragement.

Proposition method. This method presupposes that in a group of men, you will have a small proportion of them fall into the upper 10%, another small percentage fall into the lower 10%, and the majority fall somewhere in between. This is similar to a professor's grading on a curve. For example, if a patrol administrator had 50 men under his command, 5 would fall in the upper scale, 5 would fall in the lower scale, and the other 40 would be proportioned on both sides of the center and the center itself.

Numerical method. In this method, the supervisor places an officer on a scale from low to high using a number of factors: i.e., judgment, leadership, quality of work, etc.

Judgment

1	2	3	4	5	6	7	8	9	10

poor   outstanding

This method is easily prepared and easy to use; however, a word of caution: Be sure to place an exact value on each number and describe the factors involved.

Word method. This is similar to the numerical method, except that the meaning of the position on the scale is given. For example, judgment in the word method would have to indicate if the judgment used by the officer was poor—needs help continuously; or good—needs help occasionally; or outstanding—makes judgment on his own and needs very little guidance.

Factor check-off method. A checklist type of evaluation form. One column has the factors (horizontally) and the other column has the value judgment (vertically). For example, for patrol, the supervisor would look for "quality of work," "initiative," "knowledge," "personal appearance" in the horizontal column, and then check the box matching his judgment on the vertical column. The vertical column may read "not satisfactory," "improvement needed," "average," "above average," "meets standards," "excellent," "exceeds standards," or "outstanding." Instructions usually accompany the form and discuss each section and block. A disadvantage of this form is the potential for having many different forms because of the variety of factors necessary to rate due to the complex duties of police work.

Narrative form. This method is not suggested for larger departments due to the difficulty of control on quality of evaluation. Smaller departments may use this method to great advantage since the supervisor can go into great detail discussing each man working for him. The supervisor must be able to communicate in writing, and in a sense, this method forces him to learn how.

Critical-incident method. This method asks the supervisor to document extraordinary good or bad performance of the essential duties during the rating period. Patrol administrators must define those areas that are essential for each rank as opposed to routine duties. The handling of these essential areas is specifically documented. For example, as a patrol administrator, if I were using this method to evaluate a patrol commander, I would look for essential areas or (1) ability to communicate: Does the commander know how to talk, and does he know how to adapt the language and content of his talk depending on the audience? This critical incident would include the ability to analyze his audience; (2) analyzing the commander's action at the scene of a barricaded person or persons: Can the commander maintain control (fire discipline)? Does he direct (lead) and not do? He may be in the front line directing supervision and officer but he is not actually doing the specific tasks. There are many more essentials that are specific but would take too much space. However, in each case, the patrol administrator would document and then at evaluation time, the discussion would involve the incident and the associated leadership qualities necessary to accomplish the mission of the position and the essential areas.

Forced-choice method. This method uses psychological scale and test construction. It must be designed for the individual department. The supervisor is asked to select two items from a group of four descriptive items. One item selected should be the most characteristic of the man and one item should be least characteristic.

Most	*Least*	
_____	_____	Temperamental
_____	_____	Everyone likes him
_____	_____	Autocratic
_____	_____	Low-key but effective leader

The supervisor doing the rating must select from a set of approximately forty. This number will vary depending on the department. Some of the sets include statements which apply to the ratee totally and others do not apply at all. This method attempts to reduce any prejudices on the part of the rater. It is best used when attempting to make an exact evaluation of the men. The system is expensive, much exploration must be given, and it takes a lot of time to complete the form. Also, supervisors sometimes feel they cannot be trusted due to the fact they do not know the relative weight of their selection in the set.

PROMOTIONAL POTENTIAL

The patrol force of any police department will stagnate if the leaders are inefficient and ineffective. The success of the patrol force will ultimately be a result of its leaders being goal-oriented and using the management by objective approach. In order to develop appropriate leadership, objective ratings of potential leaders should be included in the process of promotion within a police agency. There are excellent patrolmen and investigators who are crackerjacks in their field; however, it would be disastrous to promote them because as leaders of men they would be a failure. There are other men who are excellent patrolmen who should be promoted because of demonstrated ability to lead men, but they cannot put it in writing, or they get "uptight" before an oral board.

There is no perfect system in law enforcement for selecting those men who should be promoted. Therefore, progressive departments around the country are using a combination of written examinations, oral interviews, efficiency ratings (promotional potential ratings), and seniority. For example, a list of sergeants would be obtained from a combination of marks taken from the following process:

Written examination	40%
Oral interview	40%
Efficiency (promotional potential)	15%
Seniority	5%
	100%

As you can see, the 15% can very well make the difference between being promoted and not being promoted. In fact, practically speaking, where lists contain hundreds of men, 10% makes the difference.

The performance-evaluation and promotional-potential ratings are very close, but are used for different aspects of personnel management. In the former, we are attempting to improve performance; in the latter, we are attempting to make an evaluation concerning the employee's qualifications as they are related to the assumption of a leadership role. It therefore becomes necessary to insist upon the use of promotional-potential rating as an indication of an employee's ability to provide leadership as opposed to how well he may be performing certain required tasks. The promotional-potential rating must be taken seriously, since the input will have a direct bearing on who will be number-one sergeant on the promotion list and who will be number-ten sergeant on the list. As in the example given, it is generally agreed that the promotion-potential rating of 15% should not be given until after the written portion of the promotional process at least. Also, once the applicant has met all qualifications necessary to take part in the promotion process (physical, time in grade, application processed during time period), the steps usually follow the same pattern: (1) written test, (2) oral interview, (3) promotional potential, (4) seniority (this portion may be one point for each year in grade with each part of the year proportionately distributed; i.e., 18 months in grade would equal one and one-half points).

The author would like to point out that he completely disagrees with the concept of using seniority to any degree in the selection of leaders. There should be a probation period. For example, a newly promoted sergeant should be on probation for a period of one year, with a provision stating the probation can be cancelled any time after six months. The probation period should not be construed to equate out to seniority since this time should be used to determine the individual's demonstrated ability to handle the new position. If he demonstrated inability, he should be placed back to his previous rank.

THE NEW PATROLMAN

Leadership in the patrol force as it was known, and in some cases is still known, had an authoritative air about it because the majority of the time, orders were given with an attitude of, "Do it because I told you to." The answer to a patrolman who asked, "Why?" reflected an atmosphere of ability obtained only through experience. It was also an extension of the prevailing atmosphere that existed in our country generally and the respective locale specifically. The thought of open organization and representation through participatory management was considered radical, even to the point of being considered freakish. Every supervisor who attempted to instill pride and professionalism in appearance, attitude, behavior, etc. was ridiculed by patrolmen and other superiors alike. This discussion is meant to make patrol leaders aware that the responsibility of leadership concerning lateral and up-and-down relationships necessitates a hard look at humanistic values and needs.

Patrol officers today have a higher average educational attainment upon entrance into law enforcement and are better trained when they leave the academy for active service than at the time the described situation existed. The new patrolman also enters law enforcement when the complexity of problems are at a peak and the diversity of tasks are numerous. An awareness of the importance of law enforcement in our society makes the new patrolman a center of controversy in many instances.

The present-day task of the criminal justice system, or nonsystem if you prefer, and the position of law enforcement as the first step in this system, has thrown the new patrolman into the limelight because of the awesome responsibility he has in his use of discretion. This judgment situation has always been there, but due to the social upheaval, each decision affecting human beings can be expected to be questioned regarding the fine line between personal liberty and community security.

The new patrolman therefore must concern himself with the decisions each day in a way quite different than, say, six or seven years ago in order to prevent his actions from becoming a catalyst to mini-riots, negative police image, or disruption of community relations. This explosive atmosphere in which the patrolman works each day requires him to have an educational background in the behavioral and social sciences. The patrol officer tends to develop a human-relation approach to handling everyday tasks, yet he is better equipped through increased training to handle the various weapons necessary in law-enforcement today.

This new patrolman is recruited in many places, from military bases to college campuses to steel mills to the city street corners or poolrooms. The big sell is that law enforcement is a profession as opposed to a trade. Whether this is true or not remains to be seen. At the most, today the law-enforcement segment has professionalized on an individual basis. Self-respect in the individual usually has the greater impact in developing the professional status and pride for the officer. The author believes that dedication is still an essential factor for attaining the professional status.

In attempting to maintain his professional status, once acquired, the new patrolman has a problem with role conflict in that he must respond to differing expectations from his superior, wife, family, courts, citizens, and attorneys. (For an in-depth discussion of role conflict, see James Sterling, *Changes in Role Concepts of Police Officers.*) In one situation, the officer is expected to be fair, impartial, and rather aloof in personal contacts. In another situation, the officer is expected to be friendly. When and how to be firm, fair, friendly, courteous, impartial, and perform all the complex tasks of the patrolman calls for understanding of expectation, hopefully, a clear definition of the role, and an ability to cope or adapt to these changing roles as they appear. Sterling's research includes:

1. Residential backgrounds
2. Occupational and educational backgrounds
3. Friendship patterns
4. Intra-department aspirations
5. Personality
6. Role conflict
7. Perception of people
8. Aggregate role conception
9. Attitudinal orientation to police role
10. Essential role attributes
11. Perception of danger
12. The need for self-understanding[36]

The author would recommend this book for any student who wishes to continue his education in the field of law enforcement.

Law enforcement's new patrolman is involved in crisis intervention, conflict management, peer-group pressure in altering behavior and attitudes, team-policing as a team leader or project leader, the identification of the best type of patrol for a given community, participatory management, and a partnership with psychologist and sociologist in studying ways of attacking crime problems with new approaches. These are exciting and challenging for the officer beginning his law-enforcement career.

The challenge of a career in law enforcement as a patrolman today comes not only from involvement in testing for better methods of policing, but also from the fact that while these tests are being conducted, the officer has to exist in the present-day environment. He has in many cases lost respect and admiration from citizens, has been involved in riots, radical demonstrations, been called a pig (degrading intent), and in some areas tries to serve a hostile community. Challenging? You bet your life! However, the officer can feel good about one thing: most citizens of our country are law-abiding and do support their police agencies.

There is a general appreciation of the need for law enforcement. The officer coming on the scene today will begin his career at a time when all of law enforcement has felt the effect of the Supreme Court as it existed under Chief Justice Earl Warren. The new patrolman will enter an area where he will be taught the history of law as it existed until today, but he will not have performed his duty under the Warren court interpretation. Additionally, the Burger court has allowed the so-called pendulum to swing back to a less liberal position with regard to the rights of the accused. It appears then that the present-day officer enters law enforcement when a more realistic approach to the fine line between personal liberty and community security has been taken. This status with regard to legal restriction will lessen any possible feelings of resentment against the court by police officers, especially when compared to officers who have lived under both conditions.

The new patrolman enters police work hoping to rise on merit. New management and personnel techniques have impressed him to the point where he believes promotion will come his way as he demonstrates his ability and intelligence. There is so much available material to read on police administration, patrol operation, planning, criminal investigation, etc. that he may even be more informed than the veteran officer. In the case of college graduates with degrees in Police Administration, it is probable that the new officer is so informed with this knowledge, you add some experience and the result is that young officers ask why orders are given and insist upon being involved in change and decision-making. Where enlightened leadership does not allow participation to a degree compatible with achieving the objectives of the organization and the individual, the new patrolmen seek alliance with organized labor in order to have a say about their salary, wages, conditions of work, and policy. The new patrolman has the intelligence to have something to say. If he is not allowed to say it, he will find a way usually through the employees' organizations. These organizations include (1) The National Police Union, (2) International Conference of Police Association, (3) The Fraternal Order of Police, (4) State Research Association, (5) state employee clubs, (6) police officers clubs, (7) Police Officers' Association, (8) local fraternities, and (9) benevolent associations. The young patrolman of today has seen victory by one or more of these organizations in the area of salary, overtime, civilian review boards, etc. and finds them enticing.

These organizations have used the courts, civil suits, and executive action to resolve problems to their satisfaction. They have also demonstrated muscle in the political arena. Police departments are different for the young officer of today. Patrol commanders need to reflect on the needs, views, and values of his new patrolman in order to manage by objective properly. If being a police officer is complex and diverse, being a patrol commander is more so. Patrolmen of today will only sit by for so long to allow police leadership to do what they believe should be done. If the leadership fails, the result is internal conflict, external conflict (established authority), and community instability; none of which contributes to a professional image. Does this sound like militancy? If it does, then we must ask as William J. Bopp does in his book *The Police Rebellion,* "Why did the police become militant in the first place?" Officer Dick MacEachern, president of the Boston Police Patrolman's Association (BPPA), offers one view:

> We are sick of being thrown to the dogs. Our militancy started when everyone else's became accepted. Everyone began clamoring for their rights and, all of a sudden, the cop was left holding the satchel. The city police administration, they all began yielding to pressure groups. But who ends up the loser? The bad guy? It's the cop who's trying to represent the public and government the best he can and then finding the government isn't sure of itself. So they back step and we get the heat . . . Militancy (of the police) just had to come. There's nothing wrong with the word. What it means is that you're not sitting on your dead ass.[37]

Former Detroit Police Commissioner Ray Girardin echoes MacEachern's sentiments:

> Police these days have been on the defensive and are fighting back and they're going to the man who speaks their language . . . They feel they are handcuffed.[38]

What this means is that the officer has a view and would like the right of having that view at least considered. Patrol has the largest number of officers and the greatest likelihood of potential internal conflict.

Patrol administrators, beware, because you are leading a group of men who will not accept, "Do it because I told you to." Conflict resolution or managing conflict should be an intricate part of your education. Today, managing conflict is as difficult as managing change and has to be understood as well, to keep disrupting forces from destroying the department. Patrol leaders must be aware of what a healthy, viable patrol force consists of. It should definitely not be made up of a group of yes-men. When the allowance is made for disagreement and the disagreement is open, forthright, honest, and based upon true conviction on the part of the speaker, it must be respected and considered as an intricate part of effective decision-making. Disagreement should not be considered negativism or radicalism. As a patrol administrator, it would be good to always ask the opinion of your most outspoken patrol commander who has different viewpoints than yourself. It can be stipulated that your goals are the same; it's method that is different. When you consider all opinions (alternatives), you will be closer to the more effective decision. Sergeant, if you work a sector, a squad of men, and you lead them, "Do it because I told you to," then the only brain you're using is your own. It can become quite upsetting when you can't solve a particular problem relating to crime, community, etc. Would you like some help? Would you care for some innovative approaches? Change your style! Include your young intelligent patrolmen. Lieutenant, would you like some help? . . . Captain? . . .

ENHANCING THE ROLE OF THE PATROL OFFICER

Focus on the patrol officer and the importance of his role has been recognized by the National Advisory Commission on Criminal Justice Standards and Goals in Standard 8.2 of its "Report on the Police." The recommendations are presented here for objective discussion in class.

Standard 8.2 *Enhancing the Role of the Police Officer.*

Every local government and police chief executive, recognizing that the patrol function is the most important element of the police agency, immediately should adopt policies that attract and retain highly qualified personnel in the patrol force.

1. Every local government should expand its classification and pay system to provide greater advancement opportunities within the patrol ranks. The system should provide:
a. Multiple pay grades within the basic rank;
b. Opportunity for advancement within the basic rank to permit equality between patrol officers and investigators;
c. Parity in top salary step between patrol officers and non-supervisory officers assigned to other operational functions;
d. Proficiency pay for personnel who have demonstrated expertise in specific field activities that contribute to more efficient police service.

2. Every police chief executive should seek continually to enhance the role of the patrol officer by providing status and recognition from the agency and encouraging similar status and

recognition from the community. The police chief executive should:

a. Provide distinctive insignia indicating demonstrated expertise in specific field activities;

b. Insure that all elements within the agency provide maximum assistance and cooperation to the patrol officer;

c. Implement a community information program emphasizing the importance of the patrol officer in the life of the community and encouraging community cooperation in providing police service;

d. Provide comprehensive initial and inservice training thoroughly to equip the patrol officer for his role;

e. Insure that field supervisory personnel possess the knowledge and skills necessary to guide the patrol officer;

f. Implement procedures to provide agencywide recognition of patrol officers who have consistently performed in an efficient and commendable manner;

g. Encourage suggestions on changes in policies, procedures, and other matters that affect the delivery of police services and reduction of crime;

h. Provide deployment flexibility to facilitate various approaches to individual community crime problems;

i. Adopt policies and procedures that allow the patrol officer to conduct the complete investigation of crimes which do not require extensive follow-up investigation, and allow them to close the investigation of those crimes; and

j. Insure that promotional oral examination boards recognize that patrol work provides valuable experience for men seeking promotion to supervisory positions.[39]

NOTES

1. Laurence J. Peter, *The Peter Principle* (New York: Wm. Morrow Co., 1969).

2. Edgar H. Schein, *Organizational Psychology* (Englewood Cliffs, N.J.: Prentice Hall, 1965), pp. 56–57.

3. These materials are from the monograph, *The Leader Looks at Styles of Leadership* by Dr. Warren H. Schmidt, and is a part of the Looking-Into-Leadership series published and copyrighted by Leadership Resources, Inc., 1750 Pennsylvania Avenue, N.W., Washington, D.C. 20006. They are reproduced here by special written permission of the publisher.

4. Ibid., p. 4.

5. Anthony Jay, *Management and Machiavelli* (New York: Holt, Rinehart & Winston, Bantam Books, 1971), p. 139.

6. Peter Drucker, *The Practice of Management* (New York: Harper and Row, 1954), chap. 10.

7. Wilbur Schramm, ed. "How Communication Works" in the *Process and Effects of Mass Communication,* (Urbana, Ill.: University of Illinois Press, 1954), p. 3.

8. William J. Bopp, *Police Personnel Administration* (Boston, Mass.: Holbrook Press, 1974).

9. Roger M. D'Aprix, *How's That Again* (Homewood, Ill.: Dow Jones-Irwin, Inc., 1969), pp. 10–11.

10. Louis Brownslow, "The Administration Process," a lecture to the graduate school of the U.S. Department of Agriculture, February 1939.

11. William H. Newman and Charles E. Summer, Jr., *The Process of Management: Concepts, Behavior and Practice* (Englewood Cliffs, N.J.: Prentice Hall, 1969), p. 60.

12. American Bar Association, Standards Relating to the Urban Police Function, *Police Chief* (May 1973), p. 60.

13. John C. Klotter, *Techniques for Police Instruction* (Springfield, Ill.: Charles C Thomas, 1971).

14. Ibid.

15. See James S. Kakalik and Sorrel Wildhorn, *Aid to Decision-Making in Patrol,* a report prepared for the Department of Housing and Urban Development by the Rand Corporation, for an example of available information that may influence patrol.

16. James Q. Wilson, "Dilemmas of Police Administration," *Police Administration Review* 28 (September-October 1968), p. 412.

17. American Bar Association, op. cit.

18. William J. Bopp, *Police Personnel Management* (Boston, Mass.: Holbrook Press, 1974), pp. 80–81.

19. Rensis Likert, *The Human Organization* (New York: McGraw–Hill, 1967), pp. 3–11.

20. Ibid.

21. William J. Bopp, op. cit., pp. 94–96.

22. Chester I. Barnard, *The Functions of the Executive* (Cambridge, Mass.: Harvard University Press, 1939), p. 128.

23. Robert Tannenbaum, Irving R. Weschler, and Fred Massarik, *Leadership and Organization, A Behavioral Science Approach* (New York: McGraw–Hill, 1961).

24. James D. Mooney and Alan C. Reiley, *The Principles of Organization* (New York: Harper and Brothers, 1939), p. 5.

25. Henry C. Metcalf and L. Urwich, eds., *Dynamic Administration and the Collected Papers of Mary Follett* (New York: Harper and Brothers, 1940), p. 71.

26. Alvin Toffler, *Future Shock* (New York: Bantam Books, 1971), p. 20.

27. James F. Ahern, *Police in Trouble* (New York: Hawthorn Books, 1972), pp. 248–49.

28. H. H. Carey, "Consultative Supervision and Management," *Personnel*, vol. 18, no. 5, p. 283.

29. Copyright 1966 by IACP, Inc. Material based upon survey conducted by Field Operations Division.

30. Tannenbaum, Weschler, and Massarik, op. cit.

31. Herzberg, Mausner, and Snyderman, *The Motivation to Work* (New York: John Wiley and Son, 1967).

32. Ibid., p. 114.

33. Irving B .Wicker, Jr., "Training Law Enforcement Officers to Rate," *Police* (June 1972), pp. 47–48.

34. Thomas Riley, *Teaching an Employee to Do a New Job,* Industrial Relations Center, University of Chicago, 1964.

35. E. L. Thorndyke, "A Constant Error in Psychological Ratings," *Journal of Applied Psychology* 4 (1920), pp. 25–29.

36. James Sterling, *Changes in Role Concepts of Police Officers,* IACP, 1972, Gaithersburg, Md.
37. *Boston Globe,* June 15, 1969, p. 8.
38. Ibid., December 15, 1968, p. 88.
39. National Advisory Commission on Criminal Justice Standards and Goals, Washington, D.C., 1973, *Report on Police,* Standard 8.2, p. 195.

organization for patrol

The patrol force of a police agency traditionally has been structured as a hierarchy, which, in effect, put people in boxes like numbers or objects. But organizing human beings together in a way that produces maximum effectiveness for the organization is a rather complex problem, and job satisfaction for the individual cannot be reached if the rigidity of the traditional structure is maintained.

SYSTEMS OF ORGANIZATION

Organizational theory and leadership-motivation are needed to develop an actualized police agency. This means that a combination of the following theories must be applied to the task at hand: (1) classical (Luther Gulick); (2) bureaucratic (Max Weber); (3) scientific (Frederick Taylor); (4) informal (Hawthorne Studies); (5) systems (Daniel Katz and Robert L. Kahn)[1] and leadership (personal identity coupled with dynamic enthusiasm and dedication resolving the questions Who am I? Where am I going? and, How do I intend to get there?). In addition, behavioral science concepts should be applied: for example, (1) Rensis Likert's "Linking Pin" and "System 4"; (2) McGregor's "Theory X and Theory Y"; (3) John J. Moore and Jay W. Lorsch's "Beyond Theory Y"; (4) Chris Angyris's "Mix Model"; (5) Robert Blake and Jane Morton's "Managerial Grid"; (6) David McClelland's "Achievement Motivation"; (7) Abraham Maslow's "Needs Hierarchy" and Frederick Herzberg's "Two Factor."[2]

Leaders in patrol should seek to find the appropriate formula. No one combination can be applied to all police departments. In order to find the tailor-made approach, managers at all levels should be exposed to the various concepts. The challenge facing the patrol force is tremendous, and the management by objective approach should be used as a base from which to start to meet this challenge. This will allow for flexibility in organization and organizational concepts so the patrol force can change as the mission changes; prepare valid evaluations regarding the accomplishment of the objectives; define role expectations; allow patrol officers and leaders an opportunity to determine where they stand regarding individual performance; devise subgoals from the overall goals set for the patrol force (desire, opportunity, vulnerability of victim, physical facilities, neighborhoods); determine the amount of resources available to accomplish goals and subgoals; allocate and distribute manpower for maximum utilization; identify training and education needs, deficiencies and attributes; enhance internal cooperation through the use of goal-achievement vs. goal-failure standards; increase the opportunity for total involvement by all personnel in goal-oriented philosophies; specialize only as needed; and utilize program, project manager, ad hoc organization, and task-force concepts as appropriate to achieve goals.

The Mission

The patrol force must be flexible in order to accomplish the mission, whatever the priorities may be regarding that mission. Scholars in the field of patrol administration have stated on several occasions that a police department is number one (if police agencies were rated) if it is number one in the community served. With regard to the norm, a discussion of four views regarding the establishment of mission priority would be necessary.

View One. The usual mission as stated by August Vollmer, J. Edgar Hoover, and Bruce Smith placed priority on law enforcement:

1. Protection of life and property, which includes the prevention of criminality;
2. Reduction or supression of crime;
3. Apprehension of offenders;
4. Recovery of property;
5. Preservation of the peace through order maintenance;
6. Regulation of traffic, and performance of miscellaneous calls for service.

These are valid objectives and the order of priorities seems difficult to disagree with. However, when we look at the amount of time officers spend achieving the mission as stated, we realize that the majority of the time is spent accomplishing the order maintenance and performance of miscellaneous services.

View Two. A second view, proposed by Professor James Q. Wilson of Harvard, indicates the following:

> First, the police should recognize clearly that order maintenance is their central function—central both in the demand that it makes on time and resources and the opportunities afforded that it makes in the lives of the citizens.
>
> Hunting criminals both occupies less time (at least for the patrolman) and provides fewer chances for decisive action. How well disputes are settled may depend crucially on how competent, knowledgeable, and sensitive the police are; how fast the crime rate mounts is much less determined on the level or nature of police activity.[3]

It has been estimated that the order maintenance and service areas functions account for approximately 70% of the total police-patrol tasks. At times the percentage has gone as low as 60% and as high as 78%. This average is determined by the clientele of the community. If the community is a so-called "bedroom community," the percentage increases even higher in the areas of miscellaneous calls for service and order maintenance. If the community is high-density population, high crime, the miscellaneous calls for service decrease proportionately with an increase in the crime. When the viewpoint is analyzed by the professor and the student of patrol administration, the following aspects should be considered:

1. What proportion of training in police academies across the nation is relegated to the performance of order maintenance and miscellaneous services performance?
2. What proportion of training is relegated to the mechanics of police work?
3. Is the impression received from the percentage realistic in that the remaining 30% may be the crucial performance area? James Sterling makes the analogy between this time and the time of the surgeon. The surgeon spends most of his time diagnosing the problem, preoperative responsibilities, postoperative responsibilities, and yet the crucial time for the surgeon is the time in the operating room performing the operation.[4]
4. What do police leaders place most confidence on when the time comes

for performance and promotional evaluation? arrests? lower crime rates? courtesy? community relations? charges of misconduct?

5. Is it a valid statement to say that the only officer who causes controversy is the one who works: for example, makes arrests, has increased citizen contacts (field interrogation reports), does not patrol as though he was wearing blinders?

6. How then is the best way to reduce the crime rate? Deployment? Social advancement? Increased science and technology? Increased help in the prosecution, courts, and correctional field? Have the police advanced too far? Should the police wait for the rest of the administration of justice system to catch up? Should there be more administrative trials rather than increased criminal trials? Should the legislature reduce the number of criminal laws? Should the police begin training and education so that they can be capable of responding to white-collar crime (embezzlement, security, theft, large-scale fraud etc.)?

7. What consideration will legislatures across the country give to the recent action by government? Should the number of criminal laws be reduced?

The "cluster approach" is one method being used in response to the first three aspects mentioned above.

"Cluster Approach" to Professional Police Training

The Regional Training Academy at Independence, Missouri, which is the primary police-training facility for the five-county metropolitan Kansas City area, has adopted a type of professional training called the "cluster approach." This new concept was developed under former Kansas City Police Chief Clarence M. Kelley, who is now director of the Federal Bureau of Investigation.

This approach deviates from the traditional method of training police officers. Generally police training has concentrated upon teaching the proper techniques and procedures relating to the police function, with only a few hours relating to police-citizen relations. The cluster approach emphasizes the human-relations aspect of the police function and is introduced at the beginning of the training course. This approach hits at the heart of the 70%–80% of the time officers spend dealing with people, rather than the 20%–30% of the time where the mechanics of policing is necessary.

The Regional Training Academy concentrates the first 136 hours of training in the area of humanities and social science. The instructors for these humanities and social science courses come from outside the academy staff. Professors from the University of Missouri, Rockhurst College, Penn Valley Community College, and Central Missouri State University, including a human-relations specialist and psychologist, are among the staff members.

Courses given in the first cluster include philosophy of the constitution, sociology, criminology, psychology of personal adjustment, applied psychology, social psychology, juvenile delinquency, police ethics, liabilities of the police uniform, off-duty conduct, abnormal psychology, intergroup conflict and prejudices, history of police, stress negotiation, police discretion, and social problems. In addition to those courses directly aimed at the officer's role in dealing with people, the curriculum contains more than 80 other courses in both classroom and practical instruction. The Regional Academy includes as part of their practical instruction courses in persuasive speaking, vocabulary building, and speed reading.

Another course taught is propriety. This course is similar to the same course taught to military officers at the Wentworth Military Academy and Junior College in Lexington, Missouri. Practical instruction is used in a four-week long situational-location training. At this time entrant officers leave the classroom environment completely and move into the Academy's mock police station. From here they are dispatched in specially marked Academy police cars at locations throughout the city of Independence. At these locations, which include businesses, intersections, taverns, residences, schools, and banks, officers encounter types of calls they will face when they become full-fledged police officers. Mock situations are created in the most realistic manner possible and an instructor is assigned to each location as an evaluator. At the end of the situation a critique is made of the entrant officer's performance and further specific training is given as appropriate. In order to understand how the other person feels, each officer is subjected to both chemical mace and tear gas in order to feel the effects of these nonlethal weapons on the individual so that decisions regarding these weapons will be knowledgeable.

Only time will tell how successful this program and approach will be. However, innovations of this type and the training of our new officers in law enforcement are most refreshing, and more creative approaches should be forthcoming throughout the law-enforcement community. Research in the field of training and many other aspects of law enforcement are necessary. The Regional Training Academy in Independence, Missouri, should be complimented on its attempt to use all the resources within the community to produce an improved product from training academies. The recognition of the need to train and educate officers in the area of human relations, because this involves what officers actually do the majority of their time on duty, has arrived.

View Three.   The third mission, where the priorities would include all of those presented, is a joint statement between elected officials, the community, and the police department. The American Bar Association published in the May 1973 issue of the *Police Chief,* "Standards Relating to the Urban Police Function." The author agrees with the standard regarding objectives and priorities as expressed in the following excerpts:

AMERICAN BAR ASSOCIATION—STANDARDS RELATING TO THE URBAN POLICE FUNCTION

(2.2) Major Current Responsibilities of Police.

In assessing appropriate objectives and priorities for police service, local communities should initially recognize that most police agencies are currently given responsibility, by design or default:

- (i) to identify criminal offenders and criminal activity and, where appropriate, to apprehend offenders and participate in subsequent court proceedings;
- (ii) to reduce the opportunities for the commission of some crimes through preventive patrol and other measures;
- (iii) to aid individuals who are in danger of physical harm;
- (iv) to protect constitutional guarantees;
- (v) to facilitate the movement of people and vehicles;
- (vi) to assist those who cannot care for themselves;
- (vii) to resolve conflict;
- (viii) to identify problems that are potentially serious law-enforcement or governmental problems;
- (ix) to create and maintain a feeling of security in the community;
- (x) to promote and preserve civil order; and
- (xi) to provide other services on an emergency basis.

(2.3) Need for Local Objectives and Priorities.

While the scope and objectives of the exercise of the government's police power are properly determined in the first instance by state and local legislative bodies within the limits fixed by the Constitution and by court decisions, it should be recognized there is considerable latitude remaining with local government to develop an overall direction for police services. Within these limits, each local jurisdiction should decide upon objectives and priorities. Decisions regarding police resources, police personnel needs, police organizations, and relations with other government agencies should then be made in a way which will best achieve the objectives and priorities of the particular locality.

(2.4) General Criteria for Objectives and Priorities.

In formulating an overall direction for police services and in selecting appropriate objectives and priorities for the police, communities should be guided by certain principles that should be inherent in a democratic society:

(i) The highest duties of government, and therefore the police, are to safeguard freedom, to preserve life and property, to protect the constitutional rights of citizens and maintain respect for the rule of law by proper enforcement thereof, and thereby, to preserve democratic processes;

(ii) Implicit within this duty, the police have the responsibility for maintaining that degree of public order which is consistent with freedom and which is essential if our urban and diverse society is to be maintained.

(iii) In implementing their varied responsibilities, police must provide maximum opportunity for achieving desired social change by freely available, lawful, and orderly means, and;

(iv) In order to maximize the use of the special authority and ability of the police, it is appropriate for government, in developing objectives and problem priorities for police services, to give emphasis to those social and behavioral problems which may require the use of force or the use of special investigative abilities which the police possess. Given the awesome authority of the police to use force and the priority that must be given to preserving life, however, government should firmly establish the principle that the police should be restricted to using the amount of force reasonably necessary in responding to any situation.

The patrol administrator would be in a much better position to walk that tightrope between personal liberty and community security if these standards were followed. The American Bar Association, the International Association of Chiefs of Police, and the committee from the IACP assigned the responsibility of working with the American Bar Association should all be commended for their respective efforts in providing these standards. One can see why the patrol administrator and his organization must maintain flexibility in order to change as the mission changes and achieve the objective.

View Four. Another set of priorities for criminal justice in America was recently expressed. On August 9, 1973, President Nixon signed a bill authorizing $3.2 billion for assistance of local and state law-enforcement agencies over the next three years. On August 9, a commission of state and local officials, after a two-year study, presented a "Master Plan" designed to reduce crime and improve criminal justice during the next decade. Since 1968 LEAA has channeled

$2.5 billion into local police work. The Master Plan against crime was detailed in a 318-page report drawn up by a 22-member committee made up to study the problem, financed by a $1.5 million federal grant. A major recommendation—and one likely to raise the biggest controversy—was for prohibition of handguns. The commission urged that, no later than January 1, 1983, each state should take the following actions:

> Private possession of handguns should be prohibited for all persons other than law-enforcement and military personnel. Manufacture and sale of handguns should be terminated. Existing handguns should be acquired by states. Handguns held by private citizens as collectors' items should be modified and rendered inoperative.

The study noted that the national arsenal of privately owned handguns is reported to be as high as 30 million and is increasing by more than 1.8 million a year. "Nowhere in the world," the study added, "is the private ownership of handguns on a per capita basis as high as in the United States. Nowhere among the industrial nations of the world is the criminal homicide rate as high as in the United States."

Other Recommendations

The committee set as its goal the reduction of crimes of violence, murder, rape, aggravated assault, and robbery. Such crimes, the study said, "threaten the very existence of the humane and civilized society." It proposed four priorities for reducing crimes:

1. Prevent juvenile delinquency,
2. Improve delivery of social services,
3. Reduce delays in the criminal justice process, and
4. Secure more citizen participation in the criminal justice system.

In the section on "decriminalization" the commission recommended that the states remove from the list of crimes such offenses as vagrancy, drunkenness, and minor traffic violations. It also urged states to reevaluate their laws on gambling, marijuana use, possession for use, pornography, prostitution, and sexual acts between consenting adults in private. Such reevaluation should determine if current laws best serve the interests of the state and the needs of the public. The criminal justice system, the study said, is ill-equipped to deal with these offenses. These crimes place an unwelcome and heavy burden on law enforcement resources throughout the nation. And the laws regulating these offenses are open to abuse and to increasing constitutional challenge.

Valid Evaluation

Once the objectives have been selected, then the structure of the organization can be designed to achieve these objectives. When the community states that the priorities should be (1) law enforcement, (2) response to calls for service, and (3) order maintenance, then the resources of the department can be formulated to achieve those objectives and in the particular order of priority.

The priorities can be turned upside-down, and the distribution of the resources can be changed likewise. The patrol forces will be given the primary responsibility for attaining the objective, and each individual within the patrol function can be evaluated according to how well he contributes to attaining the goals according to the priorities. The patrol administrator can then place emphasis appropriately and evaluate each level of authority to the patrol officer.

Role Expectation

Each patrol officer should report to his tour of duty knowing exactly what role he is to play relating to the mission and the approach he should take. Professor James Q. Wilson in *Varieties of Police Behavior*[5] indicates three styles of police organization: the legalistic, nightwatchman, and service.

The author believes that most police departments today are a combination of two of the three styles mentioned. No matter what style or combination of styles used, the officer going on patrol should be aware of what is expected of him and his role in the community. Should he be aloof or friendly? View violations as black or white with no gray? Respond to human needs with officious retorts, or be the walking home of the less fortunate? Should he take $2 from his own pocket and buy food for a mother and children until the welfare check arrives, or should he call the Welfare Department and notify them of the immediate need? What will be the answer? How should he respond to the merchants on his beat? How should be respond to elected officials? How do the clientele he serves expect him to respond?

The answer to these questions may not be easy, but a clear-as-possible picture should be painted for the patrol officer concerning his role and its relationship to the community. The need for flexibility in a role is important not only for the patrol officer but for the patrol leader as well. The human situations facing the patrol force on a daily basis do not remain static. The solutions to these must change to meet each one as presented.

Individual Performance in Patrol

In meeting these different situations, it is important for an officer to know that his actions are approved and support for his decisions will be forthcoming from police officials if necessary. The policy manual published by the Los Angeles California Police Department in the January 1973 issue of *Police Chief* is a tremendous step forward in providing officers and supervisors alike with the realistic objectives and guidelines necessary to meet these situations.

Subgoals

When the goals of the patrol force are stated (e.g., reduce crime, respond to calls for service within three minutes), each patrol commander, supervisor, and officer has a chance to contribute to the objective. Patrol commanders distribute manpower as needed, watch commanders present clear pictures of problems and recommend solutions, sector sergeants spur officers on in a way that enhances team effort, and individual officers plan their tour of duty to obtain maximum use of resources in attaining the objective. In order to attain goals, planning is important.

The planning process used by patrolmen to the fullest, accompanied by participatory management, is an untapped resource for patrol forces around the country. If used by each patrol officer, it could result in the reduction of one crime per year for each officer. This statement is based upon years of experience, observation, and practical application by many patrol commanders.

The inspection procedure of recognizing a need, which is the first step in planning, would work hand-in-hand in enhancing an officer's capability to achieve goals. A sector sergeant working a squad of officers in today's patrol force would improve his potential for achieving goals if he were to instruct those officers in total planning. This is especially true in a smaller department where it is so important for each officer to contribute all of his talent in order to achieve the goals, since the patrol officer is responsible for delivering the total police service.

Available Resources

When goals have been identified for the patrol organization, and they are realistic, patrol commanders will always look to the ready manpower and equipment to determine if they have enough. In most cases, there are never enough resources. The management by objective approach analyzes beats, sectors, watches, units, and divisions to determine if assigned resources are used properly in attempting to reach the goal. The responsible commander has built-in accountability; therefore, he would use live inspection (as discussed in Chapter 4 in the section on Personal Attention) to determine if all resources are being used properly. Tours of duty that match crime by time of day and day of week become centers of attention when failure to achieve a decrease in crime is the issue. Failure of beat officers to recognize the neighborhood problem that ultimately develops into a violent confrontation causing loss of manpower, complaints against police, lower public image, etc., cries out as a failure to communicate, lead, act before the fact, and provide sensitivity. The failure to use these human resources greatly reduces the chance of goal achievement. The allocation and distribution of manpower for maximum use will be discussed in a later chapter.

Identification of Education and Training Needs, Deficiencies, and Attributes

One patrol precinct or one patrol watch of a department is doing well in the reduction of crime. Another is doing well in community involvement. Still another is achieving subgoal number 3, which is to increase merchants' installation of alarm systems and other security devices that make their businesses more difficult to burglarize (crime prevention).

The subgoal of each precinct or watch was to achieve all three, and each failed in at least one or the other. A review of not only what is wrong regarding each failure, but what is right in connection with the areas where the goals have been achieved would be necessary. Reduction in crime for one watch may have occurred because arrest and case presentation are carefully done so that convictions are higher, thus reducing the chance of a particular individual committing multiple offenses. Another watch may have an officer who, through education, is able to communicate and sell ideas to merchants. These revelations provide good feedback and can be used in helping patrol operations achieve subgoals and major goals. Methods that work well are expanded, deficiencies are corrected, cooperation and mutual desires are solidified.

Internal Cooperation

A patrol commander complains that it took a record section ten minutes to supply one of his officers with auto-theft information. The communications dispatcher describes how he tried for five minutes to raise the patrol officer on the air to assign him a call for service. These complaints will not disrupt the force if commanding officers remain objective and understanding. But if emotions and subjectivity creep in, compartmentalization and inefficiency occur. The management by objective approach helps prevent this sort of activity and reveals the reasons for not achieving goals. The opinions of officers, supervisors, and commanders of units not involved will be relegated to a backseat. The patrol force must be served by other line or service units, or else we deal in rhetoric when we allude to patrol being the backbone or patrol delivering the primary function and all other units existing to support patrol. However, it is a much smoother organization when failure to meet standards on the part of a unit is indicated by controls, rather than the commanders of patrol voicing dissatisfaction with existing operational administrative and logistical support. The management by objective approach is much more realistic when it comes to identifying responsibility, authority, and accountability.

Total Involvement and Goal-oriented Philosophy in Specialization

The need to specialize arises out of the failure of patrol to produce the total police product. When patrol doesn't prevent the crime, then someone must try to apprehend the person responsible for committing the crime. If patrol can perform its task in a satisfactory manner, there is no need to specialize. Today this is all but impossible.

The management by objective approach to patrol administration holds the patrol officer accountable for everything that occurs on his beat. This responsibility, accompanied by authority and accountability, allows him to make decisions at the level of execution, and also gives the patrolman a chance to be self-actualizing, or have a feeling of being fulfilled in the performance of his daily tasks. At the same time the patrol commander being held responsible for crime increases and decreases would have control over the investigation aspect of crime. The patrol commander has the opportunity to observe which officers really have the aptitude for investigation. These aptitudes can be defined in depth and assignments can be made by category of crime (arson, robbery, homicide) as deemed appropriate by the patrol commander. Specialization in larger departments may be necessary in the case of vice, narcotics, auto theft, bad checks, and homicide.

However, the majority of police departments in the country can be organized by the objective approach, thereby improving the chance for all personnel to be involved in goals and/or subgoals concurrent with their position in the organization.

The St. Louis Police Department has used a concept of calls for service patrol cars and for preventive patrol cars. Even the subgoals are different. All cars are under the watch commander who directs the watch in accomplishing the major goal.

In effect, the management by objectives approach attempts to hold each patrol officer, supervisor, and commander totally responsible for his area of responsibility respectively, provides resources to achieve the stated goals, allows for discretion, and documents for accountability. Doesn't this make each of these men a police chief in his own right? Won't each of them become involved in the philosophy of achieving goals? It should enhance the success of the patrol operation and reduce the need for specialization. Patrol officers should not be report-takers, responders, or mere protectors of crime scenes, but totally involved members of police work using all God-given talents each possesses to the fullest. It is necessary to look upon the patrol officer as completely capable of response, analysis, and investigation of any situation requiring police action. Continued selection, education, and training of capable men will produce the type of patrol officer that is good for policing and our country.

Students of patrol administration must be aware of police organizations as they exist today in order to change the structure as the need arises. Additionally, the principles of organization that apply must be understood so that decisions affecting the patrol function do not disrupt the department as a whole. A later chapter discusses the importance that the patrol force must attach to the team-policing concept presently and in the future.

Chain of Command

Lines of authority and channels of communication are necessary in order to have action at one point transmitted to other points within the chain. Any functioning organization uses this fundamental principle. Authority may flow only downward, but communication flows up, down, and laterally. Lateral communication is very important in the organization. (It is emphasized in the section on organizational divisional relationships.) This principle is very close to the principle of unity of command. When a patrol administrator communicates or directs an order to anyone below the level of his immediate subordinate, he relieves that immediate subordinate of any responsibilty or accountability regarding the order. This is intolerable and disrupts the organization. Additionally, the lower-level subordinate who receives the order doesn't really know to whom he should report back. Should he report back to his immediate supervisor, or should he bypass him and go directly to the supervisor who issued the order? There may be exceptions to this, such as when the middle supervisor is on vacation or medical leave, but in these cases the subordinate who receives the order has the responsibility to inform his immediate supervisor upon his return to duty. The aspect of supervision where the superior is responsible for everything a subordinate does or does not do is highlighted. Patrol leaders who issue orders to subordinates not immediately below them should show the courtesy of advising recipients that the order has been given in the absence of the patrol leader's immediate subordinates. Respect and courtesy are two-way streets: respect begets respect.

Unity of Command

Unity of command means that one supervisor has command of his squad or unit within the patrol organization. Conversely, each subordinate reports to only one supervisor. As a patrol administrator you report to the chief or deputy chief of operations. Also, your deputies as commanders report only to you.

As stated in the chain of command, if these reports bypass, or if orders bypass, then the chain of command is broken and officers do not know to whom they report. Confusion will take over. A man is frustrated when forced to say, "The captain tells me to do one thing, the lieutenant tells me to do another thing, and the sergeant tells me to do something else. I don't know who to listen to."

In certain situations the supervisor must give orders to officers who are not under his command routinely. If a bank holdup occurs and pursuit takes place, a patrol sergeant may have to issue orders to detectives in order to have a successful conclusion of the incident. Also, the detective sergeant would be remiss in his duties if he did not take action where he found a patrol officer committing a violation of departmental rules. These situations are exceptional and should not be carried over into normal operations.

Span of Control

Span of control refers to the capability of one man to direct, control, and coordinate the talents of a given number of men in attaining the objective. This includes individual ability, time and place, and the nature of the task to be performed. A patrol administrator who attempts to have too large a span of control usually makes the mistake of overestimating his own ability or underestimating the ability of his subordinates, or he lacks confidence in his subordinates.

Some administrators indicate that the ideal span of control is one to four, others say one to six, while still others say one to thirty is reasonable. Flexibility in span of control is necessary for patrol operations simply because time and area have such an impact. An excellent sergeant may be able to supervise twenty men in an urban area because of the small size of the beats. Yet their number would be impossible as soon as he removed these beats to a suburban area where the size would be multiplied by five. In a patrol force where the interrelations are simple, a patrol sergeant may supervise fifteen men, but if other factors were included (e.g., economic, community instability, political pressure) the number would have to be reduced. The patrol administrator must consider all factors before arriving at a decision that is best for his force and his department.

Span of Management

The patrol administrator of a progressive police department where commanders are of a high caliber, well-educated, and knowledgeable about administrative practices can increase his span of management. He must be careful to insure that the commanders have reached a stage of sophisticated development concomitant with the increased responsibility and authority necessary for the broadest span of management.

Responsibility, Authority, and Accountability

These aspects of the principle of organization have been discussed in the previous chapter; however, simply stated, when a supervisor delegates a responsibility to a subordinate he must also delegate the commensurate authority. Additionally, the supervisor must follow up to insure the completion of the assignment and should hold the subordinate accountable. The subordinate has an obligation to use the authority properly and should expect to be held accountable for its use. Patrol administrators should be aware of the fact that authority should be given to the appropriate level and only enough authority given to be sufficient to accomplish the mission. If delegation is used optimally, the patrol commander can use the extra time for innovativeness and creativity.

Assignment of Tasks

Even though the patrol administrator is responsible for the entire patrol force, the assignment of the tasks of patrol cannot be accomplished alone. The chief of police holds him responsible for achieving the objective of patrol. However, he assigns the accomplishment of certain tasks within patrol to members of his command. These commanders in turn assign partial responsibility for the task to the immediate supervisors and so on to the level of execution. Therefore, each member of the force is assigned a responsibility for performing specific tasks. The patrol officer's report to this may be, "If I am being held responsible for performing a certain task, I would like to be clear on what the task is." This is certainly reasonable, and an explanation should be given by the supervisor to the subordinate when the assignment is made. The definition of the task should (1) not be too rigid, (2) not be too broad, (3) allow for personal initiative, (4) consider duplication of effort, and (5) provide an avenue for honest expression of opinion by the subordinate.

Work Plan

To plan work so that maximum effectiveness for each worker is attained is a must for any organization. In the management by objectives approach to patrol administration, planning is a sine qua non in obtaining positive results. Planning how work is to be divided includes the separation by (1) function, (2) area, and (3) time.

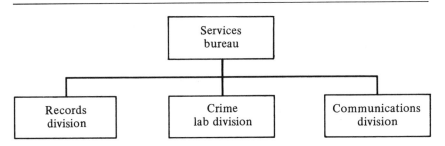

1. *ORGANIZATION BY FUNCTION*

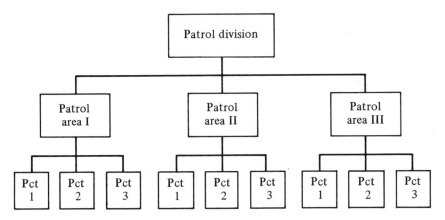

2. *ORGANIZATION BY AREA*

PATROL AREA = Each area responsible for 1/3 of community.
PRECINCT   = Each precinct responsible for 1/9 of community.

Patrol Chief

| Watch Commander | Watch Commander | Watch Commander |
| Watch I, 8 AM–4 PM | Watch II, 4 PM–12 PM | Watch III, 12 PM–8 AM |

Each watch commander responsible for patrol function for entire community for eight-hour period.

FIGURE 5.1

Also included in this separation are clientele, purpose, and level of authority. In planning the work by clientele, consideration would be given to stolen-car rings, narcotic addicts and peddlers, prostitution, juvenile offenders, etc. (In this case, clientele means the people grouped together by crime.) Also, when grouping according to clientele, the police leaders must be fully knowledgeable about specialization, its advantages and disadvantages, which will be discussed later. Questions such as the importance and value of the particular work assignments, the expediency of the situation (sniper teams, riot-control units), the amount of disruption to the total organization, degree of sophistication in development of individual personnel, and proportional needs, should be analyzed and planned for in depth. When planning by purpose, we refer to traffic control or public relations activities. Again, the need must be considered. If the purpose of traffic is to increase the enforcement index, then fragmenting the task would cause inefficiency. When organizing by purpose, do not be afraid to combine tasks to achieve the goal that is the purpose of the organization.

Specialization

The need for specialization should be based upon investment and dividend: how much return will this investment pay in terms of reduced burglary or robbery, and to what extent? What will be the effect upon the area from which the patrolman was taken? The decision should be planned for and analyzed very carefully. The advantages (specific responsibility is placed, proficiency in performance is accomplished, public support for the specialty is more easily obtained, special interests may develop additional resources) all should be weighed against disadvantages (increased complexity of the organization, compartmentalization, increased duplication, especially in records, a decrease in general interest of the specialized field, and the tendency for officers to refer citizens to the special unit for anything concerning the area of specialization).

Centralization and Decentralization

The FBI has offices around the country, and because of geographical necessity, the decentralization of operations is imperative. Where the area and population are mixed in size and density as in the case of a municipal police agency, the decision of decentralization becomes more difficult. Should all patrol officers report to the headquarters' facility and then to the beat, or should they report to the precinct and then to the beat is a question that has to be answered by each department. The patrol administrator has to consider how much time it takes to travel to each beat, the need for two roll-call sessions for each shift or watch, availability of resources, and the amount of room necessary to operate in each manner.

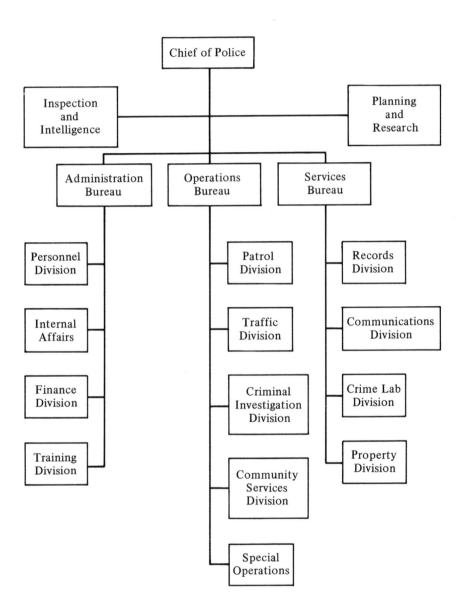

FIGURE 5.2 Organizational chart, large department.

TABLE 5.1 TABLE OF ORGANIZATION, Large Department

	Chief	Asst. Chief	Major	Capt.	Lieut.	Sgt.	Ptlmn.	Police Women	Civ.	Total
Chief of Police	1									1
Inspection & Intelligence			1		1	3	9		2	16
Planning & Research			1		2	3	6		20	32
Operations Bureau		1								3
Patrol Division			1	5	25	150	1500	10	50	1741
Traffic Division			1	2	10	25	150		10	198
Criminal Investigation			1	3	15	30	175	10	20	254
Community Services			1	2	5	15	30	5	10	68
Administration Bureau		1								3
Personnel Division			1		2	5	10	1	10	29
Finance Division			1		1	2			20	24
Internal Affairs			1		2	6	12	2	10	33
Training Division			1		2	8	5	1	5	22
Services Bureau		1								3
Communication Division			1		4	12	50		50	117
Crime Lab Division			1		2	5			25	33
Records Division			1		2	7	20		30	60
Property Division			1		2	3	20		20	46
TOTALS	1	3	14	12	75	274	1987	29	288	2683

The advantages of a centralized command are improved control, direction, and coordination. Also, communication is made easier since command officers can put the word out to all officers in the central facility. The major disadvantage of centralization is the potential for all orders to come from the chief. This stifles the initiative of commanders and prohibits the development of talent.

The advantages of decentralization are personnel assignments are closer to the actual beats, which makes shift changes easier; training is more effective because of the smaller number of men; supervision of personnel within the district is more effective; and officers have the chance to develop. The disadvantages of decentralization are difficulty for the chief to direct, control, and coordinate the department; the ability to communicate decreases; negative competition between district commanders may develop (crime reports may be manipulated); and cost.

The patrol administrator of the future must be able to manage complex organizations, conflict, change, and his own personal adaptive mechanisms to keep up with the complex society in which we live. To do this, he must know who he is, where he is going, and how he intends to get there.

TABLE 5.2 Large Department—District or Precinct Table of Organization Decentralized Command.

	Capt.	Lt.	Sgt.	Ptlm.	Ptlwm.	Civ.
DISTRICT COMMANDER	1					
Executive Officer		1				
Desk Officers			3	7		
Civilian Clerks						10
SUBTOTAL	(1)	(1)	(3)	(7)		(10)
TACTICAL COMMANDER		1				
Sector Sergeants			1			
Sector Patrolmen				14		
Tactical Sergeants			1			
Tactical Patrolmen				14		
Detective Unit			1	2	2	
SUBTOTAL		(1)	(3)	(30)	(2)	
WATCH COMMANDER		3	9			
Sector Sergeants						
Sector Patrolmen				126		
SUBTOTAL		(3)	(9)	(126)		
TOTAL	1	5	15	163	2	10
GRAND TOTAL = 196						

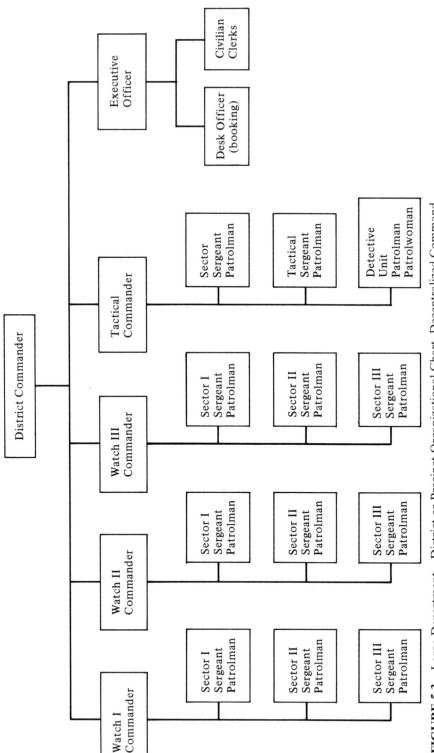

FIGURE 5.3 Large Department—District or Precinct Organizational Chart, Decentralized Command.

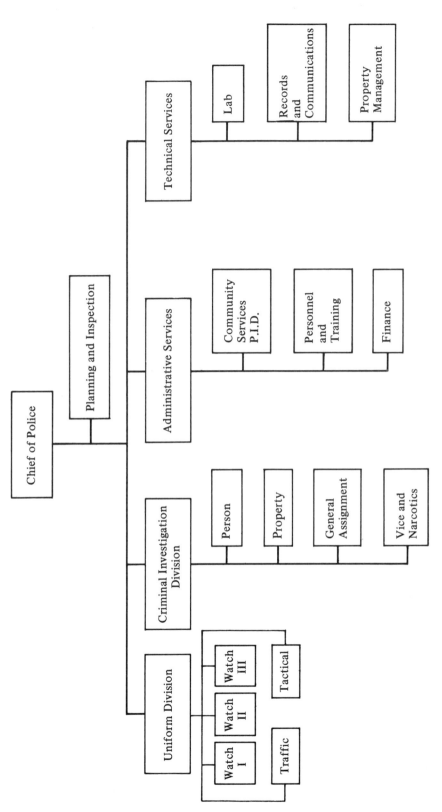

FIGURE 5.4 Organizational Chart — Medium-sized Department.

TABLE 5.3   Table of Organization — Medium-sized Department

	Chief	Capt.	Lieut.	Sergt.	Ptlm.	Civilian	Total
Chief of Police	1						1
Planning and Inspection			1	2	4	10	17
Uniform Division		1	5	10	65	5	86
Criminal Investigation		1	4	8	24	5	42
Administrative Services		1	3	4	8	3	19
Technical Services		1	2	4	12	50	69
TOTAL	1	4	15	28	113	73	234

161 SWORN
73 CIVILIAN

FORMAL AND INFORMAL ORGANIZATION

When two or more people decide to coordinate their effort and action, possess the ability to communicate in order to achieve the coordination, and agree that there is a common goal to which they will give up a certain amount of individuality to attain, a formal organization exists. The amount of effort and individual dedication each individual is willing to contribute will determine the success of the particular organization.

The patrol administrator must set the example of total commitment or at least commitment to the best of his ability. Each goal set must be realistic, attainable, and analyzed for maximum approach so that he can lead the patrol force in accomplishing these goals.

The formal organization in the patrol force will extend from the chief of patrol to the patrolmen in the vertical sense, from the watch commander on the number-one shift in district A, to the watch commander on the number-two shift in district A, and also between the leaders of middle management of different divisions or units (this aspect is discussed in organizational divisional relationships). What is essential in the formal organization is that it be able to accomplish the mission. The patrol administrator must realize that the organization should remain flexible. Priorities change. Therefore, when a renewed mission is stated, the organization should be developed in a way to best accomplish the new mission. This is the secret of the patrol administrator of the future. As the police leader develops his ability to communicate, change in mission and organization is resolved much easier because the patrol force becomes one in understanding and reacting.

Formal organizations are grouped by time, geography, service, function, and process. Jobs are well defined. Responsibility, authority, and accountability are placed and tasks are specified. Organizational charts and tables of organization are drawn and relationships between the different units through systematic policies and goals are stated.

As the organization grows, so do the complexities of the communication process and interpersonal relationships. These complexities grow at a far greater rate than do the actual number of employees. The enlightened patrol administrator will be knowledgeable about the fact that formal organizations must create informal organizations so that sincere communication can take place between all members of the organization. Respect begets respect. No matter what rank, the individual must be respected as an important component of the organization and a partner in accomplishing the mission, not be a number or a machine or impersonal object. Patrol leaders should not forget they were patrolmen at one time and realize the importance of personal choice and participation in decision-making on matters that affect the individual.

Informal organizations in police work, such as bowling teams, pistol teams, and softball teams, are not unlike those of any other formal organization. (All formal organizations have informal organizations.) The patrol leader should have a finger on the pulse of these to maintain a common purpose of mission between his leadership and the leadership of the informal organization. Patrolmen complain about the same things and usually desire a common reward and goal. Patrolmen, sergeants, etc. have their own method of communicating and will react uniformly to a threatening situation.

A patrol sergeant tells his squad they are not making enough arrests. (The amount has nothing to do with quality and reduction of crime, just statistics.) The informal leaders suggest to the squad that they patrol with blinders on. They do not look from side to side but merely drive a police vehicle or walk down the street without observing. The squad of officers makes arrests only when there is no alternative. Consequently, the number of arrests is reduced to almost nothing. The sergeant is in trouble and will have to communicate with the informal leaders to save face. The enlightened sergeant would have inquired about the arrest situation prior to making the statement. The recognition of the informal leader and the positive use of his position will reduce conflict in the goals of the organization and the individuals within it.

Patrol leaders must allow patrolmen to feel that they are an integral part of the organization and are considered as such when decisions are made about goals and methods to be used in achieving these goals. When procedures are written and implemented, open, honest communication between managers and employees will produce the necessary information to determine the effectiveness of the procedure. If change is necessary, the formal/informal communication will result in a smooth transition from one procedure to another.

There is nothing more healthy than for the chief of patrol to be in an operational room with majors, captains, lieutenants, sergeants, and patrolmen discussing honestly the whys and wherefores of specific approaches to reducing crime. The uninhibited statement of a patrolman indicating a need for an increase in arrest of narcotic addicts in a given area as the best way to reduce dwelling burglaries, showing facts and figures justifying his statement, is music to the ears of a patrol leader. A sergeant who argues his case for two foot beats in a given area as the best patrol technique to reduce robbery, then tells how he will provide the coverage without additional manpower and what the percentage reduction will be after implementation, is a thinking, planning sergeant. Healthy dialogue, objective thought, and mutual respect help coordinate the formal and informal organizations. Participatory management of this type does not take much time and will reward the patrol leader sufficiently for whatever time he provides.

The effective patrol leader realizes his people have certain attitudes and behavior patterns that usually show up in a grouping of people who have similar likes and dislikes. These groups tend to form the bowling teams, pistol teams, etc., and endure due to the fondness each has for the particular sport or social activity. There are some police officers who are fine softball pitchers and exert a great deal of influence over other policemen at work just because of their sport skill. This influence can be adjusted to enhance the goals of the organization. There are some police sergeants and lieutenants who are coaches of the softball team or pistol team who have influence over police officers formally and informally. The informal leaders may rise out of the group naturally or may be part of the formal organizational leadership as well as the informal. In both cases, there is freedom of expression and association.

The informal organization develops and responds to conditions or needs. The patrol administrator should be ever alert so he may assist the development in a manner conducive to achieving the objectives of the patrol force. Giving support, warmth, empathy, trust, respect, and confidence to the developing informal organization displays the kind of leadership that will bring together the objectives of the informal organization and the management by objectives approach to patrol administration.

ORGANIZATIONAL ATMOSPHERE

The patrol administrator is responsible for setting the tone of the patrol force. Management by objectives must reach the level of execution in a realistic manner and atmosphere. Most of us have been in situations where the "smoke was so thick, you couldn't cut it with a knife" and have felt uncomfortable. There are many ingredients of the environment within which an officer must work. Some of these forces can be controlled by the patrolman and some cannot. Patrol commanders can control a certain amount of these forces and their impact on the members subordinate to them. The forces that affect the behavior of patrol officers most are their immediate supervisors. If an officer understands the subgoals of his unit or squad and is supported by his supervisor in the quest of achieving these subgoals, this support encourages the patrol officer to move forward. Anxieties and frustrations come from not knowing exactly what the goals of the organization are and the role played by each member in helping to achieve these stated goals.

An atmosphere of confusion, weak leadership, inability to set priorities, not being able to determine when a job is well done, inadequate and unintelligent use of resources, and indecisiveness all lead to a stagnant patrol force. Patrol officers will perform according to the relationships, interaction, and conflict forces placed upon them. Usually, occupation socialization takes place first, where the majority of friends and supporters are other policemen. Next, the interrelation between themselves, their customers, their peers, and supervisors affects their behavior. The conflict comes when there is a question in their mind as to how they should present themselves to various other people or groups. For example, judges and attorneys may expect impartial and aloof approaches in the courtroom, while the officer's friends, family, clergyman and citizens in general may expect a more friendly approach. Since the patrol officer is the actual performer in attaining the objectives, the patrol commander must set an atmosphere where negative influences, over which the patrol commander has control, are reduced to a minimum level and result in minimal impact on the patrol officer.

An atmosphere that exudes a total feeling of belonging to each member of the patrol force is the responsibility of the patrol administrator. He must be careful to avoid thinking that, because he directed ten subordinates to carry out his philosophy of using their command authority to support the level of execution in reaching goals, that it will automatically be done. The patrol administrator must follow up to insure that his patrol force is permeated with an atmosphere of (1) freedom of thought; (2) open objective statements by anyone wishing to move the department forward; (3) willingness to make decisions without being afraid to make mistakes; (4) accepting disagreement as a positive force and healthy for the organization; (5) accepting change, questioning change, and managing change; and (6) putting authority in the proper perspective as it relates to the security of the individual and his relationship to others, whether they be peers, supervisors, or subordinates.

Change for change's sake is unacceptable. Criticism just to be heard or which is not constructive should be eliminated. However, disagreement should not be construed to be a negative reaction, but should be accompanied by justification for the disagreement. If the patrol administrator welcomes feedback and sets the atmosphere for honest and sincere thought by members of the patrol force, he will go a long way toward making participatory management, conflict management, and change management a reality. An atmosphere that makes all personnel feel comfortable even when discipline is meted out has to be open and above-board. An atmosphere that tends to describe the leaders as supporters of the personnel doing the job tends to increase performance quality. Support here means reduction of red tape, providing appropriate information, enhancing relations with other divisions or units that provide a service to patrol, causing an increased team effort to achieve organizational goals. Decisiveness, analysis, consensus, ability to communicate with newspaper personnel, government, other facets of the criminal justice system, and generally alleviating any aspects of the environment that might reduce the officer's ability to achieve the objective are important assets. If support such as this can be granted a patrolman, he can dedicate his total tour of duty to those patrol tasks that he is most capable of handling.

The patrol administrator who exudes confidence, knowledgeability, respect, and enthusiasm sets an atmosphere of harmony. He transmits this to the patrolmen and will make the patrolmen feel like they cannot wait to report to their tour of duty. The patrol administrator who exudes incompetence, insecurity, indecisiveness, and resorting to authority because of his inability to direct will transmit an atmosphere of anxiety and frustration that results in a "going-through-the-motion" patrol force. The student of patrol should recognize these personality traits not only of the administrator, but of each member of the patrol force. Individuals make up the organization; individuals have personalities; organizations have atmosphere.

ORGANIZATIONAL RELATIONSHIPS

Police officers educated to hold leadership positions have realized how much career development is necessary for effective leadership. Until the time is reached when most leaders in patrol have had the opportunity to experience career development, they must get this experience using their own time and effort. The more enlightened patrol administrator has a sensitivity to the needs, purpose, desires, and goals of all the other divisions within a police organization. Since the patrol administrator initiates procedures, he must know the effect upon the other units within the organization.

Good judgment is an important aspect of leadership. The more knowledge the patrol administrator has about the other units within a police organization, the more capable he will be of making good judgments. Second, the leadership necessary for his own patrol force requires that he know when to initiate communications to leaders of other divisions that require change. For example, a patrol supervisor should know the amount of response time after an inquiry made by one of his patrol officers; e.g., an officer indicates to the communications division that he is in the rear of a given address. If he is stopping a car bearing a certain license tag with several occupants, he needs to know the status of the auto (stolen or not) and the person to whom that auto is registered. The officer's performance and procedure will be affected by the length of time it takes for him to receive this type of information from the communications unit. As a patrol leader you should know the approximate length of time taken to give the requested information to your patrol officer. If this appropriate support is not effective and efficient, it is your responsibility to initiate the action necessary to correct a situation that may endanger your personnel.

INSPECTIONS AND INTELLIGENCE

Patrol administrators must have proper intelligence, with the main ingredients being quality of intelligence and accuracy. Since it has a direct effect on his manpower deployment, the patrol administrator should be aware of the procedures and tactics and techniques used by the intelligence division to gather information. He should also be able to ask valid questions, which in turn will help him to make judgments about the number of men he will commit to specific situations. If his intelligence is accurate and the need indicates the deployment of ten men in reserve status, then the intelligence unit has not only done its job with regard to gathering intelligence, but has effected the positive use of manpower. If an intelligence unit is responsible for protecting important persons who enter the community, then the quality of planning that is done by the intelligence unit will directly affect the amount of deployment of manpower by the patrol division. In this case the traffic division would also be affected due to the route and publicity given the visit of important persons.

The patrol administrator, therefore, relies heavily on the input from the intelligence section since it determines (1) the number of men necessary to accomplish the mission, (2) the method of deployment, (3) the effect on the daily operations of the department, (4) the effect on crime, (5) the assignment of responsibility, and (6) the extent to which this adjustment would disrupt the plans of the patrol force: i.e., each patrol supervisor is planning; therefore, he needs to know ahead of time if a change is being contemplated so that he can adjust his planning accordingly.

Inspections Unit

The inspections unit of a police department is naturally the eyes and ears of the chief of police. However, since most inspections include the patrol force, the patrol administrator should be aware of the purpose of inspections and the techniques used by the inspections unit. This awareness could reduce the possibility of duplication in any follow-up situation. The need for feedback from the patrol officers and their immediate supervisors to the patrol administrator concerning the subjectivity/objectivity of the inspections unit within a police organization is most important.

The ability to get the job done in an inspections unit requires that diplomacy be in the forefront of the qualities possessed by personnel assigned to that particular unit. A horrendous mistake would be for an inspections officer to state to a member of a specific unit, "Your unit is worse than that unit." Since no one enjoys being criticized, diplomacy in communicating need for improvement is primary. Members of the patrol force who must be criticized and have methods of improvement related to them must be put in a position to accept these suggestions positively. Improvement will be made and hostility will not permeate the organization when diplomatic officers are assigned to the inspection unit. Even though the inspections unit does the inspecting, they are part of the total team of a police organization and need to be projected as such. It is important to understand that the human desire for recognition and reward is a very personal thing and that commendation as well as criticism is therefore appropriate.

The patrol administrator is more likely to act before the fact if the inspections unit can provide an in-depth study of deficiencies that may have been missed during the patrol administrator's personal inspection in his areas of responsibility. A sincere cooperation between the patrol administrator and inspections unit is very desirable because of its bearing on the accomplishment of the total mission. Confidentiality is a necessary part of the inspections unit since human nature causes men to be less than perfect. There will always be some who do not perform to the fullest of their capabilities. If officers know that they can trust an inspector they will be more open in telling about procedures that need improvement and suggesting controls that might resolve the various problems.

It is the patrol administrator's responsibility to insure that the men of his command understand the nature of inspection, the need for inspection, the appropriate attitude toward the inspections unit, the results to be obtained from good inspections, and the help that they can give individual officers in the everyday trials and tribulations of patrol. If all of the units within a police department exist to support the patrol function, then it is very important for the patrol administrator to understand the maximum use of the inspection process. He must believe in it and must have his belief permeate throughout the patrol force. This can be enhanced through personal inspection by the patrol administrator. The inspection unit will assist after line inspections have indicated a need for possible city-wide inspections of the same problem found in a given area.

The relationship principle applies to Intelligence, Records, Communication, Property, Budgeting, and Research and Planning. Positive relationships with all other units assist the patrol administrator immeasurably.

EMPLOYEE ORGANIZATIONS

Organizations formed for the benefit of policemen have been in effect for many years. The Fraternal Order of Police (FOP) was founded in 1915 and has an approximate membership of over 200,000 active and associate members. It is a national organization and together with the International Conference of Police Association (ICPA) and the National Police Union (NPU) is involved in economic, social, and political activity related to police. There are also local organizations, such as police benevolent associations, police clubs, and police officers associations. Additionally, there are state organizations like the Police Officers Research Association of California (PORAC).

Whatever the employee organization, the patrol administrator must be aware of each one that exists within his force and understand its objectives, motives, techniques, and structures in order to work in harmony for the good of the department. Police chiefs will naturally develop policy regarding management and labor relations. However, most problems that develop in a police agency will have their roots in the patrol force. This is due to the environment in which the patrol officer must work. It is the patrol officer who must stand on the front line of the demonstrations, work round the clock in all kinds of weather, be subject to a change in days off or hours worked because of a crime increase or parades or athletic contests. It is the patrol officer who usually becomes the object of police-brutality charges and is exposed to the critical confrontation of riot and arrest. Other units within a department are also answerable to issues of disagreement, but not to the extent the patrol force is exposed.

The patrol administrator and patrol commander must recognize the key roles they play in using good leadership to avoid unnecessary friction between management and employee organizations. When crime situations, potential violent confrontations, or any other situation occurs requiring a buildup in manpower, it is incumbent upon patrol leaders to use their personnel wisely. They must consider amount of manpower, hours of need, support resources, and any other facts that have a bearing on the situation and an impact on the individual patrol officers. Today's patrolmen are educated and intelligent and question the procedures used in solving problems. They will not hesitate to offer suggestions concerning a different approach to solving problems which, if implemented, will improve their lot. Officers will continue to join together in their fight against negative influences on police departments. This is obvious in the case of the fight against civilian review boards where employee organizations have spent a great deal of money in defending their institution and implementation. Patrol leaders must not be the catalyst to the formation of employee organizations because of unenlightened leadership. Where employee organizations exist, management should work in harmony with them, retaining management prerogatives, to move the police department forward.

Some forward-thinking chiefs of police have formed advisory committees within the different units of their police departments to try and resolve minor complaints at the lowest level of supervision and command. The basic purpose of this type of committee is to resolve problems of a minor nature and only those problems which are parochial to that unit. Members usually consist of elected police officers for each rank in the unit. Meetings are held on a regular basis. The chairman of the committee is the highest ranking officer of the unit. For example, a patrol precinct that had a captain as a commanding officer would also have the captain as the chairman. This is natural, because he would be the one who had final say over resolving minor problems occurring within his precinct or command. Also on the committee would be a lieutenant, sergeant, and three patrolmen, one from each watch or shift. If the precinct contained detectives and civilian personnel, then one each of these would be elected to the committee. Given the proper atmosphere, this type of participation and expedient feedback has shown that small problems can remain small and be resolved easily.

Patrol administrators would do well to initiate and/or follow up on this type of employee relation in an effort to act before the fact, which in effect is using the management by objective approach in achieving goals.

There will be times when the complaints of employees cannot be resolved in the manner mentioned above. Some of these complaints will be preplanned by existing employee organizations in an attempt to test the strength of particular chiefs, command officers, including patrol commanders. A calm, friendly, firm demeanor is required when dealing with these situations. To reiterate, understanding the motives, methods, and structures of those with whom you are dealing is essential, and knowledge of departmental rules, regulations, policies, and procedures always helps in communicating the proper message at the right time. The patrol leader should not allow himself to be placed in a position where he has no exit. Absolute statements should only be made when there is no possibility of a change in policy, rules, laws, etc. Remember, most employee representatives have become very adept in the art of negotiation, compromise, bargaining, and intellectual volleyball in areas of self-improvement and collective advantages for the brotherhood. The goal is to move the department forward as a team, while at the same time providing an area of influence for management and employees that will best achieve that goal. One of the better ways to do this is by a written grievance procedure.

Grievance Procedure

Every employee wants to feel that he is a part of the department, just as every citizen wants to feel that he is a part of the country and possesses certain rights and privileges. When the individual feels that his rights and/or privileges have been violated, in his mind redress is in order. If satisfaction is not forthcoming to the individual, rational approaches become less palatable and frustration, negativism, and disruption become the order of the day. There is danger not only from the loss of the individual's contribution, but from the effect that this alleged or real mistreatment has on other employees. Personnel of the same status tend to identify with each other, especially when one seems to have been treated unfairly. When the mistreatment affects a group of personnel, the danger of disruption is expanded proportionately. Some police chiefs, to silence officers whom they consider troublesome because they have spoken out on certain conditions they believed to be unfair, transfer the officers repeatedly. The chief who uses this method has been described as being the best friend an employee organization ever had: each assignment allowed the officers to attract more men into the employee organization.

Grievance procedures for a police department should be in writing and published as a general order. In the case of a police agency where an official agreement is signed with a police-officer association, the grievance procedure should be a part of the agreement.

General orders about grievance procedures should include the following:

1. Grievance defined:
    Grievance means the claimed unjust treatment, violation, misinterpretation, or inequitable application of any of the provisions of the agreement or rules, regulations, and procedures covering working conditions applicable to the employees of the department.
2. Outline the grievance procedure.
3. Indicate that informal resolution of the grievance is encouraged.
4. Prompt resolution and action is desirable.
5. Grievance may be presented to supervisor with or without representation of employee organization.
6. A friendly atmosphere should exist, which may enhance the resolution of the grievance at this point.
7. A review of the grievance between the officer and the representative of the employee organization may take place before being presented to the immediate supervisor.
8. If settlement is not forthcoming, the grievance is then presented in writing. The grievance should contain:
    a. Nature of the grievance,
    b. Date of matter,
    c. Supervisor's reply stating facts he took into account in answering the grievance.
9. The reply should be made within a given period of time: five calendar days, ten working days, etc.
10. Acceptance or rejection of the answer is made in writing by the grievant.

The procedure is followed up the chain of command until it reaches the chief. There may be variations of the procedure when dealing with specifics, but the principle of having a procedure for individuals to voice their grievances and provision for redress is the important factor. Patrol administration involves leadership with understanding, empathy, fairness, firmness, and an open patrol force to insure harmony with employees, employee organizations, employee organization representatives, and the management of personnel. Police unions are here now and will expand into police agencies across the country. It is essential that police leaders learn the art of negotiating.

PATROL-ORGANIZATION OPERATIONAL NUMBERING SYSTEM

Patrol commanders and field supervisors should be able to identify the approximate location of any police vehicle and police personnel merely by the call number of the individual vehicle. This can be done at least within the area in which a beat car is assigned specific responsibility. Additionally, supervisors may also be identified so that responsibility at each level can be applied as is necessary.

Smaller departments having a centralized organization (one central police facility where all patrol personnel are assigned) do not have too much difficulty in identifying the individual beat car, the assigned location of the beat car, and even the name of the officer assigned the particular beat. This is due to the small number of vehicles assigned to any given shift. For example, if ten or twenty vehicles are assigned to a shift, numbering officers from ten to twenty or ten to thirty with fixed beat assignments would be simple. Even if the department uses a manpower resource-allocation system where additional vehicles and beats are added for eight-hour overlaps, the identification is easily made. Paramount in importance is the ability of patrol commanders to be able to know at any given time of the day or night where, and how many, personnel are on duty. Also, where situations require supervisory personnel, it is beneficial to be able to contact the appropriate supervisor responsible for the area concerned.

Patrol administration must be careful to insure that all other units exist to support patrol. Numbering systems must be instituted to provide the patrol commander with easily identified relationships between the number and type of vehicles and the location of the beat. The identification of the individual, to the point of knowing if the vehicle contains one man or two men, the sergeant responsible for the sector or shift, lieutenant responsible for the zone or shift are also important. Figure 5.5 is an example where the patrol force is divided by shift and sector:

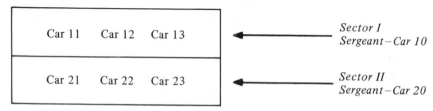

FIGURE 5.5 City X — Shift I (2400–0800).

> In this example, cars 11 and 21 could be 2-man cars. This is not difficult because of the number of cars and manpower.

The next shift, shift II (0800–1600) would change but slightly and the same assignment would occur. However, when the third shift (shift

III, 1600–2400) arrived, there would probably be an additional sector or at least more manpower added to the patrol functions. If this example were continued, it would look like Figure 5.6.

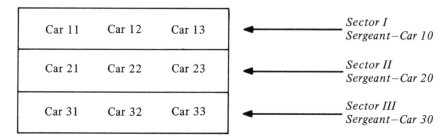

FIGURE 5.6   City X — Shift III (1600–2400).
The author realizes the small span of control and wishes to explain only the numbering and identification system.

The number from one to nine would be used for the chief of police or other officials throughout the department. The approximate size of this department would be between 75 and 100.

The real need for a systematic and practical numbering system for the small department arises when situations require all personnel to be called to duty. There may be an overlap of responsibilities and call numbers must reflect an accurate identification of personnel.

The larger, decentralized department has the difficulty on a daily basis in addition to the times when riot squads or tactical squads are called to respond in large numbers. Manpower accountability is essential to the successful solution of emergency situations. Therefore, a smooth transition must take place when a department builds from the routine application of personnel to the amount necessary to quell a serious problem. Planning is most important, and a key to this type of planning is having the normal system compatible with the unusual.

If a large department were decentralized, and the normal numbering system allowed for the accomplishment of those goals previously stated, it might look something like this: City Y is decentralized. City Y has nine districts: 1, 2, 3, 4, 5, 6, 7, 8, and 9. Each district is commanded by a captain. The call number for the captain (commander) is 100, 200, 300, etc. Simply stated, every vehicle that has a call number beginning with the first digit of the above numbers shall be located within that district. Figure 5.7 shows the city divided into districts.

District I	District II	District III
District IV	District V	District VI
District VII	District VIII	District IX

District I	=	Northwest	=	Captain (100)
II	=	North	=	Captain (200)
III	=	Northeast	=	Captain (300)
IV	=	West	=	Captain (400)
V	=	Central	=	Captain (500)
VI	=	East	=	Captain (600)
VII	=	Southwest	=	Captain (700)
VIII	=	South	=	Captain (800)
IX	=	Southeast	=	Captain (900)

FIGURE 5.7 City Y—the number of the district identifies the location within the city.

To continue, each district commander will have a given number of lieutenants, sergeants, and patrolmen under his command. These personnel should be identified by individual and location. Naturally, communities are not divided into neat little squares, but this example explains this format. Each patrol force would apply the principle to their respective departments.

The commanding officer of each district would probably have three shift commanders and an administrative and operations lieutenant. No matter which shift was presently working, the shift commander of each district would have the last two numerals the same. Therefore, to identify the shift- (watch-) commander on duty in the second district, you would call for car 201. If you wanted his contemporary in district IX, you would call for car 901; district V, 501. If you were requesting an operation lieutenant (or crime-control lieutenant) in district VIII, the call number would be 802 or district VI, 602. The administrative lieutenant of each of the districts could be assigned call number (03) which means district IV administrative lieutenant would be identified as 403.

Continuing the identification into sector and beats, let's examine Figure 5.8.

District I	District II	District III
Sector I Sgt. -110 Sector II Sgt. -120 Sector III Sgt. -130		
District IV	District V	District VI
District VII	District VIII	District IX

FIGURE 5.8   City Y.

If a patrol commander wished to contact the sergeant responsible for sector 1 in district I, he would request car 110. Similarly, if the supervising sergeant of sector 1 in district IX was being called, the number would be 910. If the call number 630 was heard conversing with headquarters, the identification would be supervising sergeant of sector 3 in district VI.

The next part of the system would be to identify the individual beat cars within the sector and district. This is somewhat difficult in terms of exact location because of the difference in configuration of sectors by district and geographic influence. However, by following the principle, identification by location can be achieved to suit the purpose for which the system is intended.

As you can see from Figure 5.9, district I, northwest section of City Y can be identified by location down to the beat car. If car 111 were to be identified, it would be in District I, sector 1 and the first car in the sector. Departments using two-man and one-man cars in patrol may want to identify the first car in the sector as a two-man car. Other departments may want to identify the first car as one equipped to transport prisoners. In any case, as long as consistency in numbering is maintained, identification is simplified. Subsequently, if car 133 were identified it would be the third car in sector 3 of district I. (northwest). If car 435 were to be identified, it would be the fifth car in sector 3 of district IV (west district).

A practical application of the principle might be used in the following situation. You are a patrol commander. The time is midnight, a dance is taking place in a school in district V which is routine

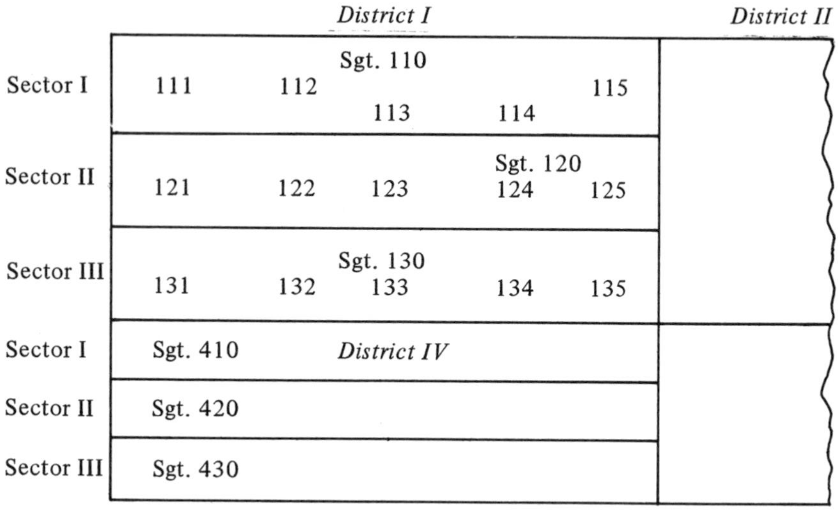

		District I					District II
Sector I	111	112	Sgt. 110 113	114	115	
Sector II	121	122	123	Sgt. 120 124	125	
Sector III	131	132	Sgt. 130 133	134	135	
Sector I	Sgt. 410		District IV			
Sector II	Sgt. 420					
Sector III	Sgt. 430					

FIGURE 5.9 City Y.

and has never been unruly in the past. As the dance ends and the youths are leaving the school, several altercations take place and erupt to the point of a small riot where rocks and bottles are being hurled at patrol cars and officers. Destruction of the school begins. You estimate a need for twenty men to assist you in abating the situation. As a patrol commander, you would not call for the needed manpower from one area and leave it unprotected. If the department policy was all first cars in each sector would be two-man cars, it would be a simple decision of calling 611, 621, 811, 821, 411, 421, 211, 221, 511, and 521. The patrol commander has requested manpower that is near his location, yet has not depleted any one of the other districts unnecessarily. Beat cars adjacent to the above cars that were responding to the disturbance would simply cover the areas vacated.

In emergency situations greater than that of the example given and when time for preplanning is available, a numbering system that identifies units from all parts of the department is easily developed. For the patrol force it is simply a matter of following the same principle transferred into the team concept. A department receives information that a demonstration to take place has the potential for developing into violence. A decision is made that 100 personnel should be readily available to respond as needed. If manpower were to be drawn from the districts, the numbering system and manpower could be developed in Table 5.4.

TABLE 5.4

District I	1 sergeant	9 patrolmen	call number 1510-11-12
District II	"	"	1520-21-22
District III	"	"	1530-31-32
District IV	"	"	1540-41-42
District V	"	"	1550-51-52
District VI	"	"	1560-61-62
District VII	"	"	1570-71-72
District VIII	"	"	1580-81-82
District IX	"	"	1590-91-92

Leadership would have to be provided in order to control and co-ordinate this amount of personnel; however, the numbering follows the routine. The leadership could be provided by the commanding officer of the district in which the demonstration is taking place. The prefix "15" identifies the team as being in a special condition, the third number identifies from which district the team has come, and the last digit identifies each car in the team; 1510, 20, 30, etc. would contain the team supervisor.

There are many variations of numbering systems that can be used, such as number and letter combinations (one adam one, one adam two). Whatever system is used by the police agency, it should meet the needs of the particular department. It is recommended that the system be designed in a manner that enhances the efficiency and effectiveness of the patrol force.

NOTES

1. A more comprehensive description of these concepts may be found in: (a) Luther Gulick, "Notes on the Theory of Organization" in papers on the Science of Administration, ed. Luther Gulick and Lyndall (New York: Institute of Public Administration, 1937), pp. 1–45; (b) Translation of Max Weber's writings on bureaucracy by H. H. Gerth and C. Wright Mills, trans., *From Max Weber: Essays in Sociology* (New York: Oxford University Press, 1946); (c) Frederick W. Taylor, *Scientific Management* (New York: Harper and Row, 1947); (d) F. J. Roethlisberger and W. J. Dickson, *Management and the Worker* (Cambridge: Harvard University Press, 1939); (e) Daniel Katz and Robert L. Kahn, *The Social Psychology of Organization* (New York: John Wiley and Sons, 1966) and Stanley Young, *Management: A Systems Approach* (Glenview, Ill.: Scott, Foresman, and Co., 1967).
2. (a) Rensis Likert, *New Patterns of Management,* (New York: McGraw–Hill, 1961) and *The Human Organization,* (New York: McGraw–Hill, 1967); (b) Douglas McGregor, *The Human Side of Enterprise,* (New York: McGraw–Hill, 1960); (c) John J. Morse and Jay W. Lorsch, "Beyond Theory Y," *Harvard Business Review* 48, May 1970, pp. 61–68; (d) Chris

Argyris, *Management and Organizational Development,* (New York: McGraw–Hill, 1971); (e) Robert R. Blake and Jane S. Mouton, "Corporate Excellence Through Grid Organization Development," Gulf Publishing Co., 1968; (f) David C. McClelland and D. G. Winter, "Motivating Economic Achievement," Free Press, 1969; (g) Abraham Mascow, *Eupsychian Management,* Irwin, 1965; (h) Frederick W. Herzberg, *Work and the Nature of Man,* World, 1966.

3. James Q. Wilson, "Dilemmas of Police Administration," *Public Administration Review* 29 (Sept.-Oct. 1968), p. 402.

4. James Sterling, International Association of Chiefs of Police Speech, October 31, 1971, "Police Community Relations: From Them and Us to You and Me," National Institute of Police Training and Community Functioning, Miami Beach, Florida.

5. James Q. Wilson, *Varieties of Police Behavior: The Management of Law and Order in Eight Communities* (New York: Atheneum Publishers, 1970).

patrol reporting, records, and information

REPORTING SYSTEMS

Any system of reporting citizen complaints to the police that does not include an effective control procedure to insure integrity in reporting is unacceptable for present-day law enforcement. Patrol administrators must understand the relationship between quality police work, manpower distribution, community sense of fear, and budgetary justification in forming an accurate picture of crime in the community. Quality police work cannot take place if citizens lack confidence in the department's ability to help control crime. When citizens call police to report all types of occurrences with a feeling that officers will respond, information will be accepted and placed into a written record, and the potential exists for possible successful results, that department has leaped the first hurdle toward knowledge of existing crime. When studies indicate that crime is not being reported, the best reaction is to produce this confidence on the part of the citizens toward your department. The patrol leader should be aware that as confidence increases and more crime is reported, the need to deploy forces more efficiently also increases. Additionally, the department must be ready for the charge of "crime wave." There is a need to communicate to the citizens just exactly what is taking place so that a false sense of fear does not take over. After this confidence is established, along with accurate reporting, historical data must be compiled in order to justify the increases in manpower and resources necessary to combat the existing crime conditions.

There are several reporting systems that can be used effectively by police agencies. One system requires the patrol officer to respond to the headquarters facility and type the report. This system has two disadvantages: (1) the officer must leave his patrol beat, and (2) most officers cannot type efficiently; therefore, much time is lost in preparing the report. The next system of reporting has the officer going to a call box and using the telephone to dictate the report to a dictating machine. This is then typed by a typist on a regular report form that can be reproduced. This system allows the officer to remain on his beat, but a typist must be hired to type the report from the dictating machine. Another system uses the same concept of transmitting the information, except that only numbered blocks are used for reports. An officer simply records information block by block into the dictating machine from a sample he has prepared, without using any narrative; in some cases, a typist is on duty to eliminate the need for a dictating machine. There is one very important disadvantage in all of these reporting systems, and that is there is no review of reports by the immediate patrol supervisor, who is responsible for the quality of performance of his patrolmen; therefore, the first administrative control is lost. Even if the officer is excellent in English and effective in writing, the advantage of discussing with an experienced supervisor the many factors of a case, the guidance, training, and counseling that would be provided on a daily basis, is lost. Also, the first administrative control is a tremendous asset when attempting to maintain integrity in a reporting system.

For these reasons a reporting system that allows the patrol supervisor possession of the administrative control involving integrity, accuracy, legibility, and effective reporting is most efficient for the modern patrol administrator. When designing a reporting system to accomplish these objectives, the patrol administrator should consider the following factors:

1. Record all citizen complaints or calls for police service on some type of radio-complaint card. This recording should include any action taken by officers in an "on view" situation. (Observing an altercation where the officer takes action to abate even though no arrests are made would be an "on view" situation that should be recorded.)
2. Record all administrative down-think such as repairs to auto, lunch, servicing auto, etc.
3. Provide a central location for these recordings to take place. The communication center is most appropriate. Calls for service should not be dispatched from decentralized facilities such as precinct or district stations.

4. Establish a staff control (records-review unit). Some police departments use a review officer within the patrol force or precinct who works for the commander and therefore is in the line unit itself. It is recommended that review officers be assigned to the staff unit.
5. Record the date and time the complaint was received, the officer who was dispatched, the time officer arrived at the location, and time returned to service.
6. If a new reporting system is being introduced, require a report for every call for police service. This may be done without too much difficulty through the use of short form where appropriate. (Some reports may be oral in nature.)
7. Establish a procedure whereby the patrol supervisor must review the reports of patrol officers and approve them as written or cause corrections or improvements to take place.

This in effect is the first administrative control. At this point the preliminary investigation should have been completed. A definition of "preliminary" as given by the Chicago Police Department is:

Proceed to the scene with safety and dispatch.
Render assistance to the injured.
Effect arrest of perpetrator.
Locate and identify witnesses.
Interview complainant and witnesses.
Maintain scene and protect evidence.
Interrogate suspects.
Note all conditions, events, and remarks.
Arrange for collection of evidence.
Report incident fully and accurately.
Yield responsibility to detectives.

8. Develop report forms that are most relevant to the department.
9. Provide for analysis and summary of information taken from the reports which can be used for personnel deployment, short- and long-range planning, budgeting, saturation patrol, random patrol, helicopter patrol, etc.
10. Provide for reproduction and dissemination of reports. A critical eye should be used in reviewing requests for copies of reports. Many times personnel in units that receive copies of reports throw them in the wastebasket without using them. Need should be the key factor when granting approval for receiving copies of reports.
11. In a decentralized posture, establish a clear flow of reports from the initiating officer through the precinct and to the records section without delay.
12. Cause the field reports to be matched with the radio-complaint cards at the review section to insure appropriate action was taken on each call for service. Also the review section should be another administrative control reviewing for accuracy, legibility, clearness, compre-

hensiveness, and completeness. The review should also insure that the proper uniform crime-reporting classification was given to the incident.

13. Provide an effective system for storage and retrieval of all information, including indexing stolen property, victims, wanted persons, etc. Many departments are going to computer systems, microfilm, ampex system, etc. for this service. Each department should use the system that best provides the achievement of goals for the department. Fiscal consideration may determine the optimum system for one department, while qualified personnel may be the difference in choice for another department.

Chapter 9 deals with manpower distribution in depth. Here we will only emphasize the need for a valid data-base from which to start effective deployment of manpower. This cannot be done if the system used to obtain the necessary information is not accurate. In an open department, citizens will be invited into the police agency to view maps indicating location of crime: high area and low. The deployment used to combat the crime for a given area can be displayed so that citizens can get a clear picture of police operations.

COORDINATED ADMINISTRATIVE CONTROL

Where decentralized operations exist, there is a need for coordination between the patrol force and the review officer of the records section. The proper classification of crime according to the Uniform Crime Reports of the FBI is understood only after study of the *Uniform Crime Reporting Handbook*. The Federal Bureau of Investigation conducts classes using the Uniform Crime Reports and explains the methods of classifying crime, clearing cases through arrests and by exception, Part I or Index Crime (murder, rape, robbery, burglary, aggravated assault, larceny, and auto theft), crime rate, property crime, violent crime, and the forms used to submit statistics to the bureau. Cooperation and assistance from the FBI have been outstanding.

After a report has been written by a patrol officer and reviewed and approved by his supervisor, the review officer of the records section provides a quality control for reporting. A system that allows the report to be returned to the patrol commander showing errors and recommending ways to improve the quality is most effective. Additionally, the patrol commander can evaluate the quality of supervision by inspecting such reports and recording the number of reports returned to any given supervisor. Identification of areas where additional training is needed can also be achieved.

There may be some conflict between the review unit and the patrol force in the classification and quality of reports. This is natural when you are dealing with conscientious officers. One solution is to form a committee of patrol supervisors and review supervisors. Questions such as interpretation and completeness of reports can be ironed out to the satisfaction of all concerned. The meetings held by the two groups become something of a retraining session concerning uniform crime reports and effective report writing. Patrol administrators naturally should concern themselves with total quality, but if personal attention is given to this factor of police work, the whole department benefits. The reason for this is simply that the more accurate and complete the preliminary investigation, the less chance for duplication of effort by the detective responsible for the follow-up investigation. Additionally, the better the report by the patrol officer, the more time the detective has to apply to the crime and the more promptly the case will be closed. Consequently, the patrol administrator who supports quality reporting is supporting the patrol force and the police department. Lip-service is not enough; the patrol administrator must review reports personally as part of his line-inspection responsibility. When the leaders of records, patrol, and detectives coordinate efforts in this area, a superior product will result. (If the Research and Planning unit is responsible for classifying, coding, and submitting Uniform Crime reports, they would also participate.)

REPORT WRITING

It is not the intention of this chapter to discuss the mechanics of report writing. However, since the ability to communicate both in writing and orally is so important to the student of patrol administration and the patrol administrator, some aspects of writing reports should be emphasized. For the patrol officer, the most important realization is the need to recount the matter being reported as close to actuality as his ability allows, and to write with the reader in mind. For the patrol leader, the most important aspect of reporting is that reports are sometimes used as a very important criteria in the appraisal of managers for promotion and increased responsibility. It is an inescapable fact that without the ability to write, you have lost one-half of your ability to communicate.

Patrol officers and first-line supervisors should understand the use of their reports in the administration of the police department, but they are primarily interested in the more immediate use: i.e., crime analysis, follow-up investigation, court presentation, property identification and recovery, and evidence.

The basic principles that should be mastered are not very difficult if the proper attitude is used when preparing written reports. The answers to who, what, when, where, why, and how are easy if the proper amount of time is dedicated to each. Also, answering each of these questions usually accounts for the gathering of all information necessary for any report. For example, *Who* was involved (witnesses, victim, suspects)? *What* occurred? *What* if any evidence is available? *What* automobiles were used? *When* did the incident take place? (Most officers are very cognizant of time, especially when court testimony is considered.) *Where* did the crime occur? (Exact locations are always important in police work and even more so when you think about a homicide.) *Where* was the body? *Where* was the gun or knife? *What* were the relationships between each location? *How* was entrance gained? *How* did the accident occur? (The answer to these "how" questions may develop a method of operation (MO)), and lastly, *Why* was the crime committed? *Why* was the particular method used?

After the officer or investigator assures himself that he has all the answers to the questions, he must check his information to insure its accuracy. If the information isn't correct, it's useless. Also, officers should never make assumptions about information, since the wrong conclusion can cause a waste of many hours of work and possibly lead to the arrest of an innocent person. Officers should always keep in mind that what they write must be used by someone else. If the follow-up officer or district attorney cannot understand what you are trying to transmit, you have not finished the report. Your words should be clear, definite, and specific so there can be no misunderstanding. Do not use unnecessary words, but get right to the point. The report should give all the information, but only the essential facts and in a manner that is clearly understood and accurate. If an officer has trouble in writing reports, he should attempt mentally, or if necessary, write, a plan for his report: outline what he wants to say in a logical, orderly manner answering who, what, when, where, how, and why, and then write it. When the report is in narrative form, remember it should have an introduction, which should indicate the information you will give in the body; a body, which describes the order of events in a comprehensive manner; and a conclusion, which tells what you have completed and any action that should be completed at a later time.

REPORT FORMS

Several forms are manufactured in a manner to allow easy reproduction by the offset process. A chemically-treated (sensitized) master report with one copy that is made while the patrol officer is writing the original report is a simple way to produce the required reporting. The master is forwarded to the records section for appropriate reproductions and distribution. The second copy may be filed in a district or precinct for a given period of time and then destroyed since the history file is maintained in a central records section.

There are several ways of determining numbers and types of forms a department needs. Whatever form is used, it would be helpful for someone to be assigned the responsibility of forms control. A forms-control person will reduce waste and duplication and improve systems procedure. Many departments use the following forms for reporting:

1. Miscellaneous Incident (noncriminal calls for service)
2. Crime Against Person (murder, rape, robbery, aggravated assault)
3. Crime Against Property (burglary and larceny)
4. Vehicle Report (stolen auto, recovered auto)
5. Accident Report
6. Missing Person Report
7. Property Report
8. Prosecution Report
9. Arrest Report
10. Prisoner Property Report

Other departments have developed multipurpose report forms in their desire to avoid duplication and improve efficiency and economy.

DISTRICT OR PRECINCT RECORDS

Departments having only one headquarters facility do not have to concern themselves with any records other than those in a central-records section. However, departments of a size where decentralization is necessary must be aware of efficiency and economy in their records system. In both cases, the central-records section should be able to provide on a timely basis any information necessary for the districts regarding crime and arrests. This information would include a crime-category file, crime-classification file, crime-location file, stolen-property file, wanted-person file, and a warrant file. To the extent the central-records section fails in providing the information on an up-to-date basis, the districts (decentralized locations) will have to maintain appropriate information. The optimum in records systems is a computerized one, where a citizen or an officer can contact one location and review any information to which he is entitled. However, this is not always possible due to budgetary problems, personnel problems, etc. Also, this does not include operational information.

One of the most important files maintained by the records section would be the master alphabetical index. This has the name of any person arrested in the jurisdiction, any person ever reporting a crime, persons wanted, and any person with a warrant outstanding —all listed alphabetically.

District station files should only include alphabetical files for a period of thirty days, and then they should be destroyed. Arrest files and copies of crime reports should also be maintained for a period of thirty days before they are destroyed. District administration files concerning disciplinary action, lateness, accidents involving officers, medical and personnel information should be maintained only if this type of information is not readily available in the personnel unit. Case files (files of a case where suspects have been arrested and continuity of the case must be maintained along with chain-of-custody records) should only be available in the district. Personal and recovered stolen property should only be held temporarily at district stations. Material should then be stored in the property section where it can be retrieved as needed.

Operational crime-analysis files, crime-category files, and any information pertaining to crime may be maintained in the district station where it is necessary to use this information in providing expedient reaction and planning to resolve crime problems. This information provided by the district assists patrol commanders in assigning personnel to the types of crime, the locations, and the time of occurrences of a particular crime in a manner that will produce maximum results.

MANAGEMENT REPORTS

A patrol administrator cannot lead effectively unless he has information passed up and down the line of the patrol force. The ability to deploy manpower optimally, direct and control, identify potential problems and issues, determine potential promotional qualities, and list assets and liabilities is enhanced by a properly designed management reporting system. In order to do this, the questions, What information is needed? Where can the information be obtained? When is it needed? How much is necessary? Why is it needed? Who is going to use the information after it is obtained? and, How is this particular individual going to use it? should be answered.

Specifically, the patrol administrator wants information concerning calls for service, use of personnel and equipment resources, average amount of time to service a call by a radio car, equitable distribution of radio calls for service, arrests (by district if decentralized) and the relationship to crime, types of crime, time of day and day of week crimes are occurring, and actions taken to resolve the problem.

Daily reports should be prepared to advise the patrol commander of immediate information concerning crime, accidents, arrests, and the number of officers available for duty.

Monthly reports are more meaningful to the patrol commander regarding crime trends, and movement of tactical personnel or special operation forces can be based upon this information.

Summary reports are of a more administrative nature. Since the patrol administrator is more concerned with operational activity, these reports are not as important to him. If summaries were to include amount of crime by location and a comparison of periods last year with the same period this year, some value would occur.

The management by objective approach to patrol administration requires wise managerial practices and considerable evaluation before goals can be stated. Also, as the situation changes due to information received through management reports, new goals must be stated and old goals must be displaced. A review of reports after goal changes is necessary in order to meet the new information requirements. Formal procedures for acquiring information must be established and a proper frequency of submission developed so that feedback to patrol commanders is timely and correlates to the problem at hand. Information provided patrol commanders should improve their ability to plan, organize for effective reactions, improve preventive maintenance and safety, inspect and identify control points, improve communication, stimulate innovations, develop potential leaders, and indicate training needs.

Management reports should be prepared carefully, keeping in mind the purpose of the particular report. Reports may reflect the individual competence of the person preparing the report. Remember, just as in public speaking, you must keep the audience in mind. Additionally, as in completed staff work, conclusions and recommendations should be stated simply and forcefully, providing supporting factual material that allows the responsible authority sufficient information to make decisions.

UNIFORM CRIME REPORTS

No one in a police agency should be more aware of Uniform Crime Reporting than the patrol administrator, clearance notwithstanding, since the commander of detectives views this aspect as paramount. One of the better ways to accomplish this awareness is to become knowledgeable about the content and procedure of the Federal Bureau of Investigation crime-reporting system. When a police agency has to account for the resources supplied by the citizens the statistical data supplied to the FBI and the returns from the FBI indicate one aspect of this accounting. Community involvement, which is so important today, can only be accomplished when a police department presents an honest, clear picture of the crime conditions as they exist within the respective community.

Many departments do not contribute to the Uniform Crime Reporting System. Some states keep records for police departments within that state in a manner similar to the FBI. The Uniform Crime Reporting System does not purport to know all the crime that occurs in the country. Several studies done lately indicate that many crimes go unreported for one reason or another (to avoid embarrassment, lack of confidence in local police, apathy, etc.). However, the Uniform Crime Reporting System is the only way today by which some type of measurement and accountability can be produced, and as such it does a real service for law enforcement. In the future, review and reevaluation may be in order so that law enforcement stays in the mainstream of contemporary American society. Victimization Rates may be a better method to evaluate crime.

The patrol commander is primarily interested in preventing crime. He relates this to the increase or decrease in the Part I or index crimes. Increases or decreases in crime are determined by comparing the number of Part I offenses occurring for a given period with the number of Part I offenses for the same period of the previous or subsequent year. (This is explained in the section on the goal-oriented statistical data sheet.) The crime rate is determined by the number of violent crimes per population and the number of property crimes in a department per population. Departments are then grouped by community population.

Each police department strives to decrease crimes. The person in the police department most responsible for a decrease in crime is the patrol chief or administrator. This goal is accomplished through a variety of patrol methods, deployment, techniques, planning, creativity, and innovation. There is a need to understand the relationship between operational application and administrative reporting so that the department maintains the professional status. Operational strategies have been stated. Administrative understanding refers to identifying the elements and classifying the incident as a particular index crime. One of the most difficult things to master is the difference in definition of the crime (say, of burglary) as defined by the law of your particular state or municipality and as defined by Uniform Crime Reporting. Remember, all attempts to commit burglary are counted as a committed burglary according to Uniform Crime Reporting. To add to the difficulty, a forcible entry or unlawful entry where no theft occurs, but where acts of vandalism, malicious mischief, etc. are committed is *not* counted as a burglary, provided the investigation clearly establishes that the unlawful entry was for a purpose other than to commit a felony or a theft.

Patrol administration should insure that as many of their personnel as possible be knowledgeable of Uniform Crime Reporting. Either request the FBI to hold classes or implement in-service training in order to train personnel in the use and understanding of Uniform Crime Reporting. A suggestion that the author found to be most beneficial for the patrol force was to make the FBI *Uniform Crime Reporting Handbook* a part of all patrol supervisors' equipment.

When patrol commanders have intimate knowledge of the goal (for example, to decrease crime or decrease crime 2%), the probability of achieving that goal becomes more realistic because the flow of communication to the level of execution is more likely to be accurate. Patrol administrators should beware of placing too much pressure on individual patrol commanders for a decrease in crime by making any threat or creating too much competition, since the fear of losing a command or not getting promoted may tempt the individual to be less accurate in reporting offenses. The goal should be achieved through effective and efficient patrol techniques, operational crime analysis, planning, and administrative and operational support. Only when a patrol commander does not apply these methods and fails to produce, should administrative guidance and counseling and probable action take place. The need for integrity and accuracy in reporting cannot be emphasized too much.

The *Uniform Crime Reporting Handbook* has complete instructions on crime reporting. If further information is needed, a handbook will be provided by the FBI upon request. Additionally, and the author had occasions to use this procedure, if an unusual case needs clarification regarding classification, the facts may be sent to the FBI Uniform Crime Reporting section for an answer.

THE COMPUTER AND PATROL [1]

One of the many technological advances being used by police is the computer. Introducing the computer as a tool into the police operations may appear on the surface to be a very difficult task. In reality, this is not so, but it does require new thinking. The combination of police-patrol operations and the management by systems approach through the use of a computer requires at least a basic understanding of the computer and its capabilities. For the patrol leader the understanding is imperative.

Figure 6.1 depicts the management function. The computer should be used in a way that allows the management function to be completed more accurately, expeditiously, and effectively. The research and development section of any police department is intimately involved in the management function, because this section usually is responsible for planning goals and objectives of the department and aids in implementing ways to achieve the objectives.

SYSTEMATICAL MANAGEMENT

Systematical management is defined as that form where all major parts of the organization are considered separate entities, but when placed together under one formal group for actual application, are considered

an organization. An example would be the solar system. All planets—
Earth, Jupiter, Mars, etc.—are believed to be self-sustaining or separate entities, but when joined together are called the solar system.
Law enforcement (solar system) has many individual police departments (planets). Each police department is a separate entity and self-
sustaining. Police records would be considered a system within a de-

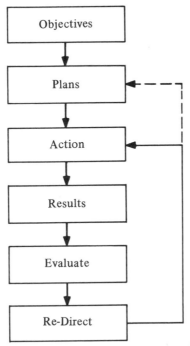

FIGURE 6.1   The Management Function.

partment. A further breakdown would classify all reporting techniques as subsystems. Arrests, accidents, and events are all subsystems within the records system. One subsystem is not dependent
on another, even though they may touch at a given point.

The nature of systematical management requires that various needs
be met prior to implementation. These needs are divided into three
categories: personnel, machines, and information. Personnel are necessary to plan, implement, supervise—achieve objectives. Machines
are needed to aid personnel in accomplishing the task easier, faster,
and more accurately. Information is needed to act as a memory and
to furnish the manager or supervisor with reports on the planned
course of action in order to measure results. The information should
be accurate and complete.

Information systems are those that supply information necessary to operate the organization and the intelligence information in a proper form on a timely basis. There are two basic types of information systems, management and real-time (on line).

The *management information system* may be described as the total method used to collect, manipulate, store, and retrieve all forms of data in order to provide managers or supervisors the proper information required to achieve the objectives of the organization. Some of this data may be placed into the real-time category. *Data* describes all forms of information received into the organization, while *intelligence* is the pertinent data organized in such a manner that it is useful to the person requiring it. Sources of such data are field operations and administration. The nature of the management information system is such that the intelligence required does not have to be received in a short time space, therefore does not require "on-line" capability. The system is designed to be operated manually, by machine, or both. Examples of the management information system include: daily activity reports; arrest reports, and property reports.

Real-time or On-line systems may be defined as those constructed to maintain information in such a way that the results of the output can be immediately available and useful to the physical operation of the organization. This type information is available twenty-four hours a day, seven days a week; in intelligence form; easily understood by the users; operated manually, by machine, or both. The National Crime Information Center (NCIC) is a real-time/on-line system.

One such system used to achieve objectives is the *logical systems cycle,* which describes the sequence of operations required to process the flow of information and documentation through a given system. It should be considered a broad view of the entire operation and include every step from beginning to end. The flow of a citizen complaint through the system is an example.

1. The event occurs.
2. The police are called.
3. The police are dispatched.
4. An investigation is made.
5. A report is completed.
6. The report is processed.
7. The report is filed.

Somewhere within the cycle consideration must be given to the use of machines. Figure 6.2 is a typical flowchart showing the flow of events and reports through a system. One important question at this

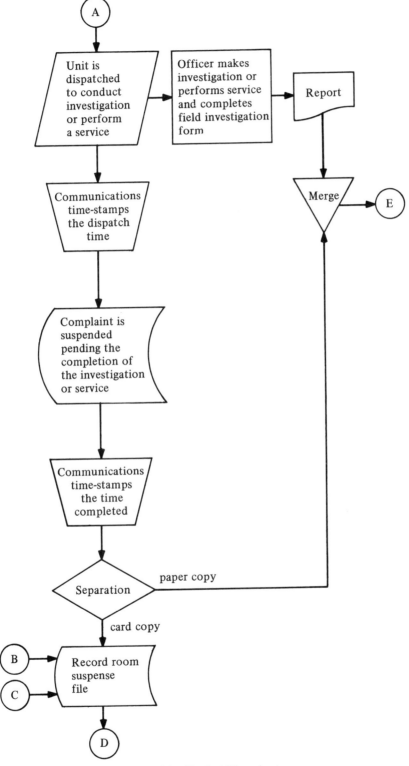

FIGURE 6.2 Typical Flowchart.

point would be, Would a data processing machine help? In order to implement the system properly, several factors should be considered. For instance, the problem area should be defined, preliminary surveys should be conducted from an interview plan, information analyzed, the system designed, personnel trained, implementation dates set, and documentation and evaluation programmed.

It's important to remember to secure the machine that will operate the system. No attempt should be made to match the system to the machine.

DATA PROCESSING

Data processing is the total concept used to process the flow of data in an organization in a systematical way so that intelligence may be extracted as required using manual, machine, or both methods. *Data* is any type of intelligence that allows two or more humans to communicate without verbal communication, or a human to communicate with a machine in a language it understands. Data is used as a form of work-information to achieve one of three things: cause an action to take place, create a memory of the action, or to report on the activity of the action. Where machines are used to process data, costs and workload are reduced and accuracy and speed are increased.

Several types of input devices are used to convert human language into machine-readable language. Some of these are the key punch, paper tape, optical scanner, and electric typewriter. Other data processing equipment includes the verifier, which checks for accuracy; the sorter, which places punch cards into any desired sequence; the interpreter, which interprets holes in punch cards; the reproducer, which duplicates; the collator, which also sequences; the accounting machine, which is a report-producing device; and the computer. The computer is actually a series of a combination of three basic sections: input, processing, and output devices. Figure 6.3 shows the sections and the function of each. Figure 6.4 shows a data processing system.[2]

COMPUTER PRINTOUTS IN PATROL

One of the greatest difficulties in using the computer in patrol operations is the time it takes to receive the printouts. Second, the format

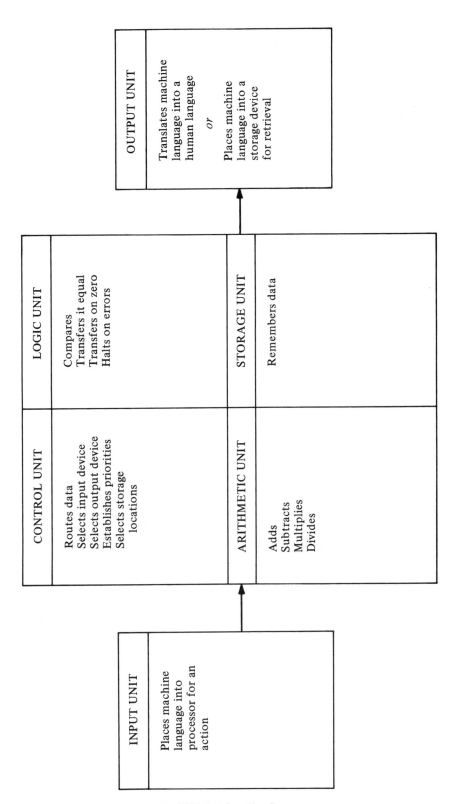

FIGURE 6.3 The Computer.

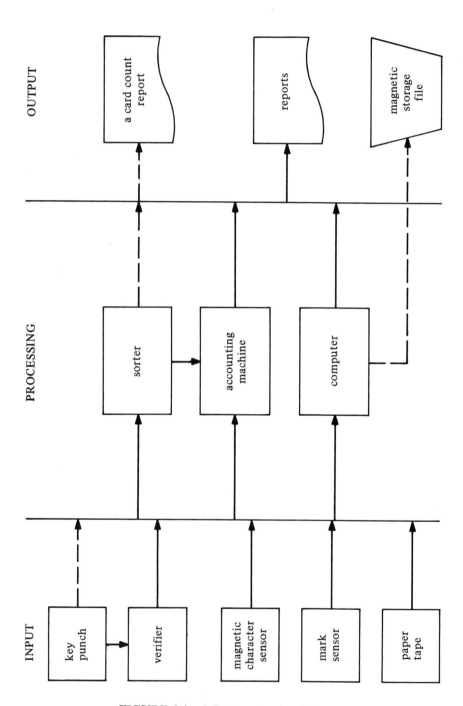

FIGURE 6.4   A Data-processing System.

used in the printout does not always provide the information the patrol administrator needs to perform the patrol function. However, the patrol commander has the responsibility of understanding the principles of the computer and the nature for which it was intended. The computer should be identified by patrol commanders as an aid in furnishing information faster, more accurately, and more completely. The operational commander must request the format; it is the computer personnel who must answer to the ability to produce as requested and, if unable to do so, suggest alternate formats that can meet the needs of the operational commanders. It is inefficient for computer personnel to allude to the possibility of producing the requested information if any doubt exists about succeeding. Patrol commanders should clearly state that crisis management can be avoided only if information is made available when needed. Management by objective requires information on time.

The primary interest of the patrol commander in real-time or on-line information should be to insure the patrol force receives this type of information immediately. Real-time or on-line information is maintained twenty-four hours a day, seven days a week and is readily available. Examples of real-time, on-line information would be stolen autos (also obtained through the National Crime Information Center), wanted-person files, warrant files, etc. In other words, the patrol officer needs to have information while he is at the scene of situations in order to make him more effective. When the computer's real-time, on-line system is working, the patrol officer can be following an auto down the street, transmit the tag number (or, in the case of an officer using the digital transmitter, he may use the machine), and within seconds be advised of the status of the vehicle. Also, after determining the identity of the driver or any person, in a matter of seconds he may be advised of the status of the individual: Is the individual wanted for any violation? Are there any warrants outstanding on the individual?

Administratively speaking, the computer information patrol commanders require comes from collection, manipulation, storage and retrieval of crime statistics. When the management by objective approach to patrol administration is used, intelligence information concerning the time of day crime occurs, the day of week crime occurs, the location where crime occurs, and all resources being utilized to combat this crime by category is necessary. In order to manage effectively, the deployment of an officer or a squad or a platoon cannot be left to mere gut feelings. A review of computer printouts and a comparison of personnel deployment should show compatibility. Preventing crime is no easy matter. If any success is to be expected at all, accurate, timely information must be provided the patrol force at all levels.

In most cases, patrol commanders will have active pin maps for all officers and supervisors to see, color-coded by category and shift. These maps are necessary to insure an awareness on the part of the patrol force concerning individual crimes and trends. When manpower distribution studies have been completed and patrol commanders have used their existing forces properly, patrol support should be forthcoming. This type of support can best be distributed where priorities regarding high-crime areas throughout the community can be clearly stated. This can only take place when information is provided in a way that develops weekly, monthly, quarterly, and yearly trends. Some departments use a time-frame of thirteen four-week periods. This may be advantageous if the printouts coincide with the change of shifts. The difficulty comes when most of the national crime reports are printed by the month or quarter year. However, it is recommended that computer printouts supply information according to the timeframe of the change in shifts or watches. Where permanent shifts are the rule of the department, the provision of data related to operational analysis is much easier. The patrolman working the same beat or the same shift month after month is much more amenable to new approaches to prevent crime when he can be shown the responsibility he has toward that goal on his beat.

Using computer printouts in patrol as an operational aid involves the decision of timeliness. A printout supplied on a daily basis may be useless. However, if provided on a weekly basis it becomes highly meaningful. A case in point would be the crime of robbery. If a computer printout was given to a patrol administrator involving the crime of robbery on a daily basis, you would more than likely find him placing an (X) indicating the robbery on the second printout at the time and beat shown by the first printout, then discard the first printout. This would be a waste, indicating that the request for a daily printout was unreasonable and ineffective. However, if a printout were provided on a weekly or 28-day basis it would be more meaningful. A sample printout on the crime of robbery might look like Table 6.1.

The offenses have been exaggerated purposely. Most crimes are occurring between 1700 and 1800 on beat A-2 and between 2200 and 2400 on beat A-9. The day of the week these crimes occur would also

TABLE 6.1 Computer Printout — Twenty-eight Day Period.

METROPOLIS POLICE DEPARTMENT
ROBBERY

DISTRICT ABLE BEAT LOCATION AND TIME PERIOD 01/01/73 –01/28/73

X = One Robbery

Beat	1600	1700	1800	1900	2000	2100	2200	2300	2400
A-1									
A-2		X X X							
A-3		X X							
A-4		X							
A-5									
A-6									
A-7			X						
A-8								X	X
A-9							X X	X	X
A-10									X
A-11									
A-12	X								

be important; thus there would be an added dimension. Patrol administration would use this printout to compare with the deployment of personnel by district Able commander. Patrol officers should be working the areas by time and location. If additional officers or a different technique of patrol or apprehension might reduce the crime, expedient action should be taken to implement those techniques. Also, if days of the week were to be included on Table 6.1, a legend with seven different codes (all meaning robbery), each for a different day of the week, could be included. This type of computer printout for patrol is meaningful and effective if produced on a timely basis and in the format presented. Tactical forces using any innovative patrol technique—saturation, random, helicopter, plainclothes (street-cleaners, repairmen, etc.)—could be deployed as needed to support the district personnel.

Effective use of computer printouts, whether it be arrest, data, documentation of court procedures affecting officers negatively, property control, calls for service, or daily activity reporting, can only be accomplished through enlightened, coordinated cooperation between patrol administrators and electronic data-processing personnel. The result of this teamwork will be the development of pertinent data presented in such a manner that it is meaningful.

NOTES

1. The major source of this section on computers and management by systems was taken from material presented at the Southern Police Institute, University of Louisville, Kentucky, by Major E. G. Columbus. Permission to use the material was graciously given by Mrs. E. G. Columbus.
2. For a more comprehensive study see Murdock and Ross, *Information Systems For Modern Management* (New York: Prentice Hall, 1973).

command and control

The term *command and control,* although used for some time by the military, is a relatively new phrase within law enforcement. It is used in the context of overseeing or dominating from a strategic position and the exercise of a restraining or directing influence over resources, both personnel and equipment. Law enforcement in general is a crisis-oriented organization and command and control of these factors must be on a dynamic or real-time basis.

Systems management, planning, and the management by objective approach to patrol administration are very compatible and necessary. Police departments inaugurating the command and control concept should begin by analyzing existing information systems, identifying problem areas and areas where improved performance can be expected. Budgeting is always an important factor, so cost-effectiveness analysis should be implemented for each stage of the systems. Alternative paths to the optimum command and control system for a particular department should receive reflection and coordination with the management by objective approach. Questions concerning the following should be answered:

1. Available fiscal resources
2. Hardware
3. Software
4. Techniques
5. Procedures
6. Training
7. Operational coordination
8. Criminal-justice system coordination
9. Information retrieval

10. Manpower distribution studies
11. Relationships between the criminal and the department's ability to prevent crime or apprehend the criminal
12. Flexibility in organization to meet goals, subgoals that may or may not change as the department reaches the different stages of accomplishment toward the complete command and control concept

Patrol administrators are confronted with decision-making that involves most of the personnel within the department. These decisions are not only administrative, but reach the lowest level of operational execution. In striving for the ability to make enlightened and effective decisions, the command and control concept shall be a tremendous asset.

In order to describe and evaluate the command and control concept effectively, it is necessary to examine it from six different, but closely related, vantage points. These are: (1) the role of the communications center, (2) the design of the communications center, (3) computer-assisted dispatch, (4) automatic vehicle-locator systems, (5) information retrieval, and (6) types of patrol communications.

ROLE OF THE COMMUNICATIONS CENTER

The communications center is at least one of the most, if not the most, important functions within a law-enforcement agency. In the parlance of police officers, it is the heart or nerve-center of the police department. The majority of calls for police service go through the communications center. It is recommended that a central location be used for all incoming calls for police service. Frequently, it is the first and sometimes the only contact that a citizen has with his police department. The treatment he receives from this initial contact will have a lasting effect on his opinion of the effectiveness and efficiency of the entire police agency. It is imperative that the communications center personnel be carefully selected and trained for this job. Unfortunately, in some cases personnel are selected to perform this function on the basis that they cannot do anything else; they are physically unable to perform in other areas of police work, due to an illness or injury, or because of some infraction of a rule or regulation (punitive action).

The patrol administrator will do well to remember that the decision made by the communications center personnel during the first few seconds after receiving a call may have a direct bearing on its successful conclusion, and possibly the safety of the officers responding. The loss of a few seconds or an incorrect decision can cause many man hours of investigation and may very well allow the escape of the perpetrator of a crime. In the case of command and control, this point is emphasized to its maximum degree.

DESIGN OF THE COMMUNICATIONS CENTER

The use of simulative exercises are very effective in coordinating and perfecting communication procedures. The design of the communications center depends upon many factors that are unique to each locale and agency. Each should be figured to satisfy the need of the agency, but several considerations are common to most, such as: (1) the size of the land area and population to be served, (2) the number of radio frequencies allocated, (3) centralization or decentralization of the departmental organizations, (4) the availability of computer-assisted dispatching, (5) availability of automatic vehicle locator, and (6) the crime problem.

COMPUTER-ASSISTED DISPATCHING

Many of the larger, more progressive law-enforcement agencies are turning to the computer for assistance in dispatching police units. As an example, the Kansas City, Missouri, Police Department has a real-time computer file that contains the address of each location where violence has occurred, such as assault on an officer or family quarrels. An inquiry is made into the computer on every call that is received for police assistance prior to the officer(s) being sent. The computer will respond with all of the information it contains relative to that address as well as identify the units available to send on the call. This system demands that the computer be updated every time an officer is sent on a call or leaves the air for any reason. The goals of computer-assisted dispatching are to lessen the potential hazards that may confront an officer at a given location by providing additional information about possible violence, and reducing response time.

There are at least two major problems with computer-assisted dispatching. First, there is a tendency on the part of the officers in the field to be lulled into a sense of complacency by thinking that if they are going to meet violence, the computer will tell them so. Officers

FIGURE 7.1   Complaint-Evaluation Unit, St. Louis Police Department Communication Center, St. Louis, Missouri.
Stationed at partitioned desks are complaint evaluators and radio clerks. The unit screens telephone calls to provide more efficient police service on emergency calls. As many nonemergency requests as possible are taken care of by phone. When the calls are urgent and require immediate police action, a car is dispatched. Photo courtesy of St. Louis Police Department.

must constantly be reminded that the computer is only a tool to assist them and that they may meet violence, even though the computer does

FIGURE 7.2   Dispatcher Section, St. Louis, Missouri, Communications Center. Officers and cadets man the three dispatchers' consoles. Each serves one of the Bureau of Field Operations areas, North, Central, and South. Car status boards on the wall indicate if a car is "in service," "available for assignment," "out of service," "on an assignment," or "dead-headed," not operating. When all department vehicles are equipped with new radios, the status boards also will show which cars are tuned to an information channel. When completed, the new communications system will provide field officers with one channel for assignments, another for information. Photo courtesy of St. Louis Police Department.

not tell them. Second, computers that are sufficiently fast and large are very expensive, and it is difficult to justify their purchase or lease unless there are other applications that need to be computerized.

Regardless of the degree of sophistication of the computer or the application, it cannot take the place of the human element. Computers are machines and can only make decisions based upon facts fed into them. They cannot make judgment decisions, so overreliance on computers can be disastrous. A clear understanding of garbage in, garbage out is necessary. If valid information is put into the computer, then it is fair to expect valid printouts. Invalid information starts a wrong base or premise and any information retrieved would also be false. After good information is put in and correct information is printed out, the patrol commander must then be able to use it. Therefore, man and machine must work together.

AUTOMATIC VEHICLE-LOCATOR SYSTEM, (FIGURE 7.3)

In order to achieve the goal of true command and control it is necessary to have an in-depth understanding of the vehicle locator. It is

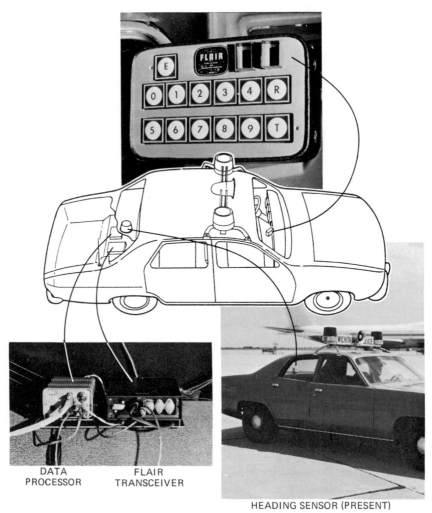

FIGURE 7.3   Vehicle Locator Unit. Courtesy Boeing Company, Wichita Division, and Wichita, Kansas, Police Department.

the most vital part of the total system. During the past few years several major manufacturers have experimented with various methods of automatically locating, identifying, and tracking vehicles. This promises to be the most significant innovation for law enforcement since the two-way radio. Many methods were tried and abandoned until 1972 when Boeing Company and the Wichita Police Department, on a joint project, developed a system that has answered all foreseeable needs. The system designed is flexible so it can be readily adapted to the unique problems of every agency with relative ease. This system has been given the acronym of FLAIR (Fleet Locating And Information Reporting).

FLAIR is a vehicle-tracking and information-reporting system that automatically updates each vehicle's location and corresponding officer's status once each second and presents this information to the police dispatcher in the command and control center. Each vehicle's location is displayed dynamically on a video map at each dispatcher's console. This gives the dispatcher a continuous picture of the deploy-

FIGURE 7.4   Computer Unit. Courtesy Boeing Company, Wichita Division, and Wichita, Kansas, Police Department.

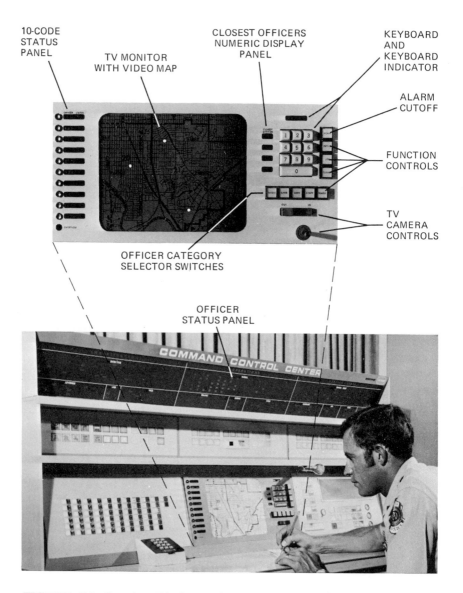

10-CODE STATUS PANEL

TV MONITOR WITH VIDEO MAP

CLOSEST OFFICERS NUMERIC DISPLAY PANEL

KEYBOARD AND KEYBOARD INDICATOR

ALARM CUTOFF

FUNCTION CONTROLS

TV CAMERA CONTROLS

OFFICER CATEGORY SELECTOR SWITCHES

OFFICER STATUS PANEL

FIGURE 7.5 Situation Display and Controls. Courtesy Boeing Company, Wichita Division, and Wichita, Kansas, Police Department.

ment of his total force, both "available for assignment" and "those out of service."

This system has two major components. First, those located at the command and control center, which are a transceiver for sending and receiving the information from the vehicles, a mini-computer (Figure 7.4), and a situation-display station (Figure 7.5). The second major

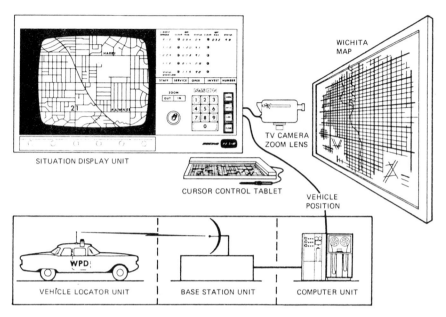

FIGURE 7.6   System Concept. Courtesy Boeing Company, Wichita Division, and Wichita, Kansas, Police Department.

component is the equipment in the field, consisting of the vehicle that has an attachment onto the odometer and electronic signal processor, a direction sensor, and a transceiver for transmitting to and receiving information from the command and control center (Figure 7.6).

FLAIR works on a basic dead-reckoning navigation principle that if the original location of a vehicle is known, its location at any future time can be determined if heading and distance change are added to its original location. The heading and incremental distance moved each second are transmitted from the vehicle locator unit to the base station unit.

System-design goals

During the initial development phase of the FLAIR system basically three system-design goals were established: (1) Vehicle location. The accuracy of vehicle location was determined to be plus or minus 50 feet. This was calculated on the formula that an automobile traveling 30 miles per hour will travel 44 feet in one second. Therefore, the vehicle reporting once each second may have traveled 44 feet since the last time he reported, assuming that he is traveling 30 miles per hour. Next it was determined that the location of all vehicles would be displayed to the command and control center personnel at all times on the display unit. (2) Vehicle information (status). In the design of the FLAIR system there were three criteria on the vehicle information. First, the system is required to identify each and every vehicle independently. Second, it must be able to report in "code" information, and third, there must be provisions for an officer's emergency call. (3) The system should be designed to allow for system playback. In order to make possible the playback of anything that happens over the system, on request, it is necessary that a magnetic tape recorder be attached to the minicomputer in the command and control center. If this is done, any situation can be reproduced in the control center to determine exactly what occurred, and for whatever time period requested.

Areas of impact

Areas of impact are five: (1) command and control, (2) communication benefit, (3) officer safety, (4) playback capability, and (5) response time.

Command and Control. The command and control capability is divided into five main categories:

1. The command and control capabilities of FLAIR permit the dispatcher to observe at all times his totally deployed force. That is, the ability to see the exact location and status of all units in the field at all times.

2. It provides for the command and control personnel the ability to readily identify and locate additional officers for emergency situations. Frequently, under stress conditions it is extremely difficult for the dispatcher to determine exactly who is available and the location of available units that could be sent on calls of an emergency nature. The FLAIR system provides this capability very well.

3. Dynamic control. The dynamic control of all units in the field is very important today due to the ever increasing calls for service and demands made upon the police service. The dynamic control is broken into four sub-categories:

a. The ability to control the units that are serving in the event of a natural or man-made disturbance. In the event of tornado, plane crash, or other unpredictable emergency, the communication center personnel can control, seal off an area, and make a determination when the area is to be sealed off and the exact locations of the areas to be sealed off.

b. Roadblock situations. Frequently on bank robberies, kidnappings, etc., it is necessary for roadblocks to be established at strategic locations. The FLAIR system allows the command and control personnel to determine exactly where and when the roadblock should be established.

c. Armed robberies. In armed robbery situations it provides a capability to command and control center personnel to establish roadblock points, to determine the paths of the units enroute to the robbery, to coordinate the arrival or to forecast the path that a fleeing culprit may take while being pursued by other officers, thereby directing secondary units to cut-off points.

d. Dignitary protection. Frequently police departments are requested to provide security for visiting dignitaries or government officials. Many times the route traveled by a dignitary must be very closely scrutinized. The location of the dignitary may be observed at all times.

4. Remote-monitoring capability. The remote-monitoring capability of the FLAIR system provides a remote monitor for appropriate bureau or district commanders. The remote monitors may be installed as is desirable and necessary in the chief of police's office, the patrol commander's office, the detective commander's office, or any other location where in the opinion of the chief administrator the monitoring would be effective.

Frequently, the patrol fleet comes under criticism for one reason or another. The FLAIR system provides the capability of showing to the public, if it becomes necessary and desirable, the fact that deployment of the police personnel is proper. This ability has a valuable public relations aspect.

5. FLAIR provides the capability of dispatching by routes. The criminal element, sophisticated as it is today, frequently avail themselves of police monitors and listen to the police broadcast to determine when the police are en route to a call. This allows the criminals to commit a crime and while doing so, monitor the police radio to determine when the crime has been reported and officers are en route to the location where the crime is being committed.

By knowing the exact location of all units in the field, command and control provide the communication center personnel the ability to dispatch units to the scene of a crime by route. As an example, officers may be advised to proceed three blocks South and two blocks West, or to make a left turn at the next corner, thereby arriving at the crime scene without forewarning the criminal possessing the monitoring capability.

Communications benefits. The communications benefits to the FLAIR system are basically the transmission of digital 10 codes or coded signals. Within each police vehicle there is located a 10-key keyboard. The provision of this allows transmission from the unit in the field to the communication picture center in the mode of 10-codes or other coded information that can be accomplished by a two-digit number. Assume for a moment that we have 100 various 10-codes, using the double zero as a number and dropping the 10 from the number itself, officers can then transmit 100 different messages by using a simple two-digit number system. This has considerable benefits as indicated in a recent study completed in Wichita, Kansas, which showed that transmission originating in the vehicle going to the communication center that could be accomplished by a 10-code system amounted to 70% of the transmissions made from the car. The police radio frequencies that are allocated today are extremely overcrowded. Most police departments face this problem and frequently an officer in the field must wait several minutes before being able to transmit from his vehicle for assistance or to advise the dispatcher that he has arrived at the scene of a call. The implementation of a system such as this will allow for a reduction in necessary transmission from the vehicle to the communications center by 70% minimally. This in effect unloads the existing frequencies for the transmission of information and requests that cannot be coded into a 10-code information system.

The transmission of digital information is much more positive than voice. The study completed in Wichita also determined that the digital transmission of information over a radio frequency is far more positive and more reliable than that of a voice.

The digital transmission of information is instantaneous. It requires a few milliseconds to complete this transmission compared to voice transmission that requires at least a few seconds to accomplish. The digital transmission of information is secure and free from monitoring by unauthorized persons. It is highly unlikely that anyone could secure a device or manufacture a device capable of monitoring the FLAIR system.

Officer Safety. The primary purpose of the automatic vehicle-locating system is for the safety of the officer in the field. There are several innovations in the FLAIR system that provide a great stride' toward achieving this goal. Within the vehicle itself is an emergency button. This button when depressed instantly notifies the command and control center personnel that the officer pushing the button has an emergency situation that prevents him from using the voice radio. In addition to the notification that the officer is, in fact, in trouble or in an emergency situation, the system also instantaneously notifies the command-center personnel the exact location of the officer and identifies the closest three officers to his location. This information is presented to the command-control center personnel in a dynamic fashion. That is, as the vehicles get closer to the officer, and the changing location of one shows him closer to the officer needing assistance, then automatically a change in their order of proximity is displayed on the dispatcher's console.

Engineering is under way as of this writing to make this emergency button portable so that the officer upon leaving his vehicle can have the choice of taking his walkie-talkie with him. It would have associated with it the emergency button or some type of voice-extending device that, if the officer should get in trouble while he is away from the vehicle, he would merely push to notify the command center of the location of the vehicle. Administrative policy would determine how far the officer could remove himself from his vehicle without having voice contact and approval of the command and control center personnel.

Playback (Figure 7.7). There are basically four purposes for having a playback capability:

1. Playback capability provides for the evaluation of a previous operation. Any time a commander wishes to review the operation (of an entire shift if desirable), the procedure could be played back to determine the path followed by each officer in the field. As an example, frequently there will be a series of burglaries within a few-blocks area. This capability provides the playing back, at increased speed of up to 100 times real time, of situations that occurred. These can be evaluated to show individual officers to determine if they have developed a pattern to their beat patrolling, or if they have in fact neglected patrolling a specified area of their beat.

2. Provide the ability to develop new tactics based upon past performance. Critical evaluation of previous actions are made possible by the playback capability.

3. Provides a tremendous device for the training of new recruit officers.

4. It should be strongly stressed at this point that the playback capability is provided for the officer's defense in the case of false allegations that may be made against him. Also, for the constructive criticism in critiquing individual performance so that improved in-service training can be provided.

Incident Response Time (Figure 7.8). *Incident response* is de-

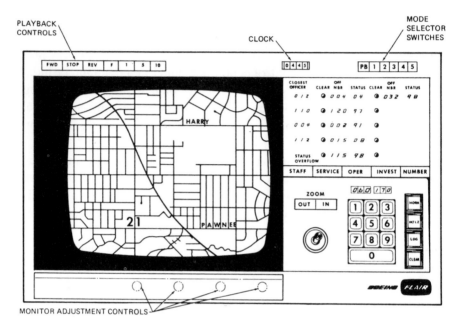

FIGURE 7.7   Playback Console. Courtesy Boeing Company, Wichita Division, and Wichita, Kansas, Police Department.

fined as the lapse of time between the time an individual (complainant) calls the police department, contacts the command and control center, an officer is assigned to the call, and the time an officer makes contact with the complainant. Additionally, the period of time required for the particular officer to return to his patrol area can also be accounted for.

The Wichita, Kansas, Police Department and the Boeing Company, Wichita Division, completed a systems-simulation study for the Wichita Police Department projecting the benefits of the FLAIR system as compared with their present operating procedures. The operating procedure for the Wichita Police Department during the year 1972 was available on punch cards for comparison. The incident response was taken from these cards and categorized into calls for service, crimes reported, etc. These calls were subdivided into calls of an emergency nature, calls of an urgent nature, and inspectional-type calls. At this point, the Wichita Police Department had a 32-beat or district setup. The systems simulation determined that under the 32-beat setup and the manual system, the Wichita Police Department had an average response time of 6 minutes.

All of the data that could be determined on the FLAIR system as

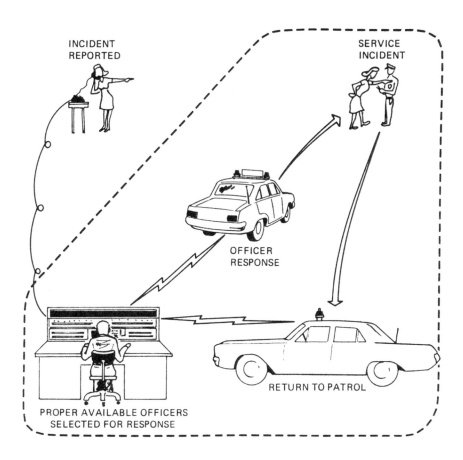

INCIDENT
REPORTED

SERVICE
INCIDENT

OFFICER
RESPONSE

RETURN TO PATROL

PROPER AVAILABLE OFFICERS
SELECTED FOR RESPONSE

PORTION SIMULATED ▬ ▬ ▬

FIGURE 7.8   Incident Response Simulation. Courtesy of Boeing Company,
Wichita Division, and Wichita, Kansas, Police Department.

to how the operating procedure would work with automatic vehicle-
locators was also fed into the computer. In a comparison made of the
two data bases, results were astonishing. The systems simulation indicated that with the addition of FLAIR and the 32-beat setup presently in operation, it would reduce the response time to 4 minutes and
15 seconds. Then the computer predicted the amount of personnel
that would be required to add to existing personnel without the addition of the vehicle-locating system and still reduce the response time
to 4 minutes and 15 seconds. The simulation showed that they would
have to double the beat size to 64 beats to accomplish, by merely

adding personnel, what the addition of FLAIR would do with existing personnel.

Within the police service, certain types of calls require more than one officer to be on the scene before service begins. As an example, a burglary in progress. If an officer arrives at the front there is a great likelihood the burglar will go out the back. This was also taken into consideration on the systems simulation and the results again were astonishing. Under the 32-beat setup in Wichita, Kansas, the multiple-officer calls response-time was 7 minutes and 45 seconds. This systems simulation showed that by merely adding manpower without the FLAIR system, the beat deployment would have to be tripled to achieve the same response time the FLAIR system could provide.

The automatic vehicle-locating system will not solve all of the problems facing law enforcement today. However, it is a major innovation that if properly and intelligently used can achieve a great deal. One cannot assume that a mechanical device or an electronic device could in any way take the place of the human element. Computer-assisted dispatch as described earlier in this chapter could be assisted tremendously by an automatic vehicle-locating system. Decisions requiring judgment must and should continue to be made through human reasoning.

INFORMATION RETRIEVAL

The teamwork between the dispatcher and the patrol officer is enhanced when information is forthcoming on a timely basis. The command and control concept provides this expeditious retrieval and transfer of important operational information. A patrol officer investigating an auto located in a secluded area with several occupants does not want to wait very long to determine the status of the vehicle. Supervisors who are conscientious about training officers in resolving conflicts and sensitive situations prefer to respond and observe calls containing these ingredients. In this manner, maximum use of the allocated time of a supervisor can be most effective. Command and control will also provide information to patrol commanders during riots and demonstrations to increase the decision-making capability regarding the movement of large numbers of personnel. Management coordination should be a prerequisite to implementation of command and control procedures. Just as the dispatcher and the patrol officer need to serve each other at this level, so do the police leaders at their level.

TYPES OF PATROL COMMUNICATIONS

Even though command and control may be seen as the communication system of the future, patrol forces will find situations when it is necessary to resort to the fundamental means of communicating. This may occur at the level of execution as well as the patrol commander level. We have discussed previously the use of digital transmissions, which is the latest type of communication used in police work. This type of transmission requires communication equipment in a police vehicle. Many departments have taken communication equipment out of the vehicles and have gone to the use of the personal transceiver, the walkie-talkie. Others have experimented with the digital system of communication and believe this method to be the best. As stated, several considerations need to be reviewed before a decision can be reached. One consideration, the number of frequencies available, is of primary importance. The patrol administrator's interest lies in the necessity to provide immediate communication for his patrol officers as efficiently as possible. Because of the frequency consideration, all types of communications should be maintained to some degree for potential use.

The flashlight, whistle, night stick, and gun are still part of the patrol officer's equipment that may be used to communicate. The modified call-box system, which can be used as a telephone, is still in existence and should be maintained on a selective basis. When radio communication becomes congested, it is necessary to have an alternative. Backup systems for computer "down" time are a must in order to maintain continuity in communication and information retrieval for operational forces. Call-box systems in some city areas are accessible to the public in order to contact a police officer when necessary. The selectivity of call-box locations should be based upon geography, crime levels, population density, traffic congestion causing auto movement to be difficult, etc. As in the selection of the proper type of patrol, flexibility is necessary so the problem can be resolved. Planning and evaluation are included and then reevaluation as needed. Lengthy conversations cannot be transmitted over a regular radio, walkie-talkie, or digital system, and should be identified as a consideration. Other considerations might be confidentiality of communications and cost factors.

The walkie-talkie has been one of the finest additions to the patrol force since the beginning of two-way communications. The use of the walkie-talkie as a communication tool assigned to the individual officer is most welcome. Patrol officers are capable of foot patrol with the added dimension of a radio car as necessary and at the same time constant communication is maintained. If appropriate frequencies are available, the optimum communication system is a combination of personal walkie-talkie, command and control, computer-assisted dispatch, and an automatic vehicle-locator system. Officers capable of making their whereabouts known on a constant basis, either walking or riding, are safer and more effective.

Patrol administrators also need public-address systems or at least "bull horns" (portable loudspeakers) when acting as field commanders during unusual situations such as riots, demonstrations, crowd control, and barricaded persons. There are many types of each; it is only a matter of choice as to which is best for the individual department, based upon review and evaluation.

No effective patrol force can be without a sound command and control communication system. The coordination of operating and support forces can achieve the goal of a law-enforcement agency if there is a complete understanding of the relationship of one to the other. Dynamic leadership can provide the total combination of the two forces.

crime prevention and community relations

If law enforcement is to deal with crime effectively, or to the best of its ability, crime prevention must be an integral part of the attack. Inherently, community relations is involved. The crime-prevention program should be designed by a police department to encourage public participation in the direct prevention of crime and to remove environmental conditions that encourage criminal acts. This involves strengthening the role of the police in direct crime prevention rather than in the traditional role of omnipresence, prevention, detection, and apprehension. This may require a philosophical adjustment in many police departments. However, a good crime prevention program will improve the ability of the police organization generally, and the patrol forces specifically, to make better use of its detection facilities and increase the rate at which criminals may be apprehended.

Crime prevention has been the goal of law enforcement since the time of Sir Robert Peel and the Metropolitan Police Act of 1829. As far back as the time of John Fielding and British Police, it was said that it was much better to prevent even one man from being a rogue than apprehending and bringing forty men to justice. Simply stated, prevention of crime should be the objective of all police direction. The security of persons and property and the preservation of the public tranquillity can be better effected by prevention than by the detection and punishment of the offender after he has succeeded in committing the crime. The true test of a police force is the absence of crime and a superior level of service.

These goals are good ones. However, modern policing has tended to evaluate police departments on the increases and decreases of crime, crime rates, and clearance rates. In 1950 British police leaders realized something more positive had to be done in the area of crime prevention. The Home Office in cooperation with some insurance companies in England produced and distributed crime-prevention material. In May 1950 the campaign was officially opened by the Home Office in various parts of the country until the autumn of 1951. In 1963 a formal training course in crime prevention was begun by the Home Office at Stafford, England. High priority was given this training. By the end of 1970 1,045 officers had attended the standard training course of four weeks' duration. Many of these officers returned to their forces to set up crime-prevention organizations to train their colleagues. Today all forces in England have facilities to give reliable advice to all who seek it about protecting themselves and their property against crime.

In 1968 the Home Office recommended that crime-prevention panels (committees) be created to develop crime-prevention programs in conjunction with the local police departments. The panels are composed of representatives of all sectors of the community—civic, commercial, and industrial—and are designed to harness local effort and awaken public responsibility about the prevention of crime. In March 1969 the Home Office published the first issue of the *Crime Prevention Newsletter,* which was designed to provide a medium for panel news covering their work, problems, plans, results, and membership. In addition, the newsletter explains the working progress of the Home Office standing committee on crime prevention and its various subcommittees and working parties.

The unique thing about the English program is its attempt to bring together the efforts of the police, the insurance industry, and the security industry and to equip the police with the means to evaluate security programs and products as they apply to the individual home owner, businessman, and industrial firm. It also includes a massive nationwide approach to crime prevention through the media and by reaching the public at all levels and all ages from grammar school to the retired.

The President's Crime Commission in "The Challenge of Crime in a Free Society" (1967) recognized the existence of such a program but did not have the time or resources to fully investigate it. John Klotter (Dean of the School of Police Administration, University of Louisville), with the help of a Ford Foundation grant, was able to make a detailed study of burglary prevention in the United States and of the English strategy in crime-prevention training. He recommended in his report that a similar type of training program be established in this country.

In 1969 the Kentucky Crime Commission recognized the validity of this approach and assisted the University of Louisville in seeking a discretionary grant to develop the pilot crime-prevention training program. The training component in the pilot project has now been completed. As a result, 60 police officers, representing 55 departments from 27 states, have been provided with uniform training in the techniques of crime prevention. Today there are thousands of graduates of the training program.

The trainees were selected from departments that had committed themselves to a crime-prevention program. Consideration was also given to the size and geographical location of the department. In accordance with the grant, two training schools were held. Officers were trained from 8 of the 20 United States cities with over 1,000 police officers. Officers were also admitted to the training program from departments with as few as 40 officers. When viewed from the impact on the total police population, departments sending officers to those two schools represented 20% of the total police population. Over 80% of the departments who sent officers to school have in fact implemented or expanded their crime-prevention efforts. This effort is continuing today and the future appears bright for an expansion of the program.

CRIME PREVENTION DEFINED

"Crime prevention is the anticipation, the recognition, and the appraisal of a crime risk and the initiation of some action to remove or reduce it." This is a definition of crime prevention developed by the Crime Prevention Training Center at Stafford, England.[1] The definition, however, requires some explanation. It has long been recognized that crime results from the "coexistence of the desire to commit the misdeed and the belief that the opportunity to do so exists." While the police and other social forces may ultimately reduce the desire to commit crime, a more vulnerable area to attack is criminal opportunity. Criminal opportunities can also be called crime hazards or crime risks. These include dark streets, unprotected buildings, inadequate locks and safes, poorly planned municipal facilities, and public and private housing developments where crime risks are heightened because of lack of security planning. Perpetrators of crime generally take the path of least resistance. Therefore, it is reasonable to believe that a relationship exists between the number of criminal opportunities at a given location and the number of criminal attacks occurring at that point. The role of the police in crime prevention is to anticipate that crime will occur where risks are high, to recognize when a high crime-risk situation exists, to appraise the seriousness of the particular risk, and then to initiate some positive action to remove or reduce the risk situation.

Police operational strategies to reduce criminal opportunity have relied almost exclusively on preventive patrol. Given enough police manpower, preventive patrol could be effective; only the irrational would venture to commit a crime under the constant surveillance of a police officer. Preventive patrol, however, has not worked effectively in the United States because increased public demands for police service in noncriminal areas have curtailed these efforts, and the patrol function does not encourage private citizens or businessmen to assist in eliminating their own crime risk.

Studies also show that citizens are confused about their role in crime prevention. They have been taught to rely too extensively on insurance for protection, are neither aware nor instructed in the available means to protect themselves or their property. Also, the tendency of both citizens and police to view crime as a police problem divorces the citizen from his role in crime prevention.

In recent years police administrators have developed more and more interest in providing services and assisting communities in planning crime prevention programs. Most programs, however, have been short-term operations or based on a special community-wide campaign at certain times of the year. Many have been developed by insurance companies, security-hardware manufacturers, or service organizations interested in the general well-being and progress of a community. The disappearance of these programs after what appears to be an initial success can be traced directly to the fact that no long-range planning took place and that operating public-service agencies had not assigned specially trained personnel to see that these programs continued.

CRIME PREVENTION CATEGORIES

One of the problems with the term "crime prevention" is that it means so many things to so many different people. But it is generally viewed as something that happens to an individual or a community after a criminal act takes place. This has also been true within the police organization, where the prevention unit works primarily with juveniles after an apprehension has taken place. In order to narrow the scope of crime prevention training to a manageable area, the National Crime Prevention Institute has adopted the crime-prevention categories (Punitive, Corrective, Mechanical) identified by Peter Lejins of the University of Maryland.[2]

(1) *Punitive*—the threat of punishment deters a person from committing an offense for which he might be punished. There has been a great deal said about the punitive approach, which appears to have been the one approach used for centuries. While there are those who argue that the punitive approach has no value, Lejins has emphasized that the threat of punishment *and the fact that the punishment will be carried out* (not the severity of the punishment) is still a major deterrent to crime.

(2) *Corrective*—major emphasis on working with the individual or social conditions in order to assure that the individual will not commit another offense or that the community environment will be such that criminal behavior is discouraged. In the corrective area we see two things: first, the emphasis on working with an individual once he has committed a crime, been convicted, sentenced, and assigned to a correctional institution or placed on probation. This approach has achieved varied success, but in any event, it takes place only after the criminal act has occurred. The other part of the corrective category deals with altering social conditions: tearing down slums, building new public housing, adding street lights—anything that can change the environment or the conditions under which crime is thought to flourish.

(3) *Mechanical*—placing obstacles in the path of the would-be offender to make committing the crime more difficult. The mechanical category of crime prevention is the most recent category to receive major emphasis on a national basis. To many people, the mechanical process of increasing security through locks, burglar alarms, and other devices is thought to be too simple; a method that does not take into consideration the so-called causes of crime. When related to opportunity reduction, mechanical crime prevention goes beyond mere devices relating directly to security. The altering of community environments through architectural planning, remodeling of old structures, increasing citizen surveillance levels, and any other program that will make criminal activity a high-risk action on the

part of the individual can be placed in the mechanical category.

Viewed according to Lejins' strict definition, the Institute's program of training is based both on mechanical prevention and the second portion of the corrective category. *Target hardening* may be a more appropriate term for that part of mechanical prevention that deals with the hardware of security.

CRITICS OF MECHANICAL CRIME PREVENTION

In the past two years a great amount of interest has developed in the area of mechanical prevention. Critics argue that mechanical prevention does not prevent crime, but only displaces it either into another geographical area or into another crime category. This is hardly an argument against the concept. As a matter of fact, the very essence of security is that you will turn the criminal from the protected premises to the unprotected. From a community point of view, security applications on the part of individuals could push criminal activities into areas of the community with previously low crime experience.

Evidence does exist, however, indicating that the bulk of criminal activities are carried out by persons who are not highly mobile and that whatever displacement occurs will force them into unfamiliar areas of operation or into types of criminal activity where they are unskilled and therefore more vulnerable to apprehension by the police. Studies by the author reveal that many criminals are arrested for committing crimes within nine or ten blocks from their place of residence.

Success in a mechanical-prevention program can be claimed if in fact a great deal of displacement does take place. Critics of mechanical prevention must bear in mind that actual lowering of crime through the mechanical approach may take several years before significant results can be shown. They should also not lose sight of the fact that very little success has been shown through the operation of punitive or corrective processes.

Other critics of mechanical prevention state that increasing security will escalate the ability of criminals to defeat security devices. It should be clear that anything devised by man can also be defeated by man, but only a limited group of highly skilled, dedicated criminals reach the stage where they can defeat technology with other than brute force. Certain parts of the security industry, recognizing the lead-time necessary to produce security devices and the time required for criminals to decipher a product, intentionally design a life span of approximately three years into improved products. It would be disastrous if crime-prevention efforts totally disregarded technology on the basis that unskilled criminals would be able to learn defeat skills faster than our scientific community could improve upon prior efforts.

The bulk of crime is committed by relatively unskilled individuals. If these persons can be prevented from criminal success, they may learn that crime is not the easiest way to achieve their desired goals and focus their attentions on more legitimate avenues to success. Patrol administrators must include this approach as part of their total program in attaining the objectives of the department.

The National Advisory Commission on Criminal Justice Standards and Goals supports this concept in their recommendation 9.1: Use of Building Design to Reduce Crime, taken from the "Report on Community Crime Prevention."

> The Commission recommends that agencies and professions involved in building design actively consult with and seek the advice of law-enforcement agencies in physical design to reduce the opportunity for the commission of crime. These agencies and firms should make security a primary consideration in the design and construction of new buildings and the reconstruction or renovation of older structures. Interaction with law-enforcement agencies and security experts should be sought during preliminary planning and actual construction to determine the effects of architectural features and spatial arrangements on building security and security costs. Careful consideration should be given to the design and placement of doors, windows, elevators and stairs, lighting, building height and size, arrangement of units, and exterior site design, since these factors can have an effect on crime.[3]

Theory of Opportunity Reduction

1. *Criminal Behavior is Learned Behavior.*

Early criminologists believed that criminals were born, and throughout the history of criminology many attempts have been made to identify those inherited characteristics that identify a person as a potential criminal. As the body of knowledge involving learning theory developed, criminologists also looked at learning theory and more and more have developed their theories to coincide with the process of learning. Most theorists, however, have explained criminal learning in terms of images that tend to condition the person's belief in the direction of criminal activity. This is certainly a vital part of learning theory, but it is also true that more important than the development of belief structures is the reinforcement of those beliefs that comes through the accomplishment of a criminal act.

A criminal act is a success if the perpetrator is not detected; but it is also successful enough to contribute to the reinforcement of criminal beliefs if, even after detection, the criminal has had ample time to consume the fruits of his illegal enterprise, if he is able through other means to escape final punishment provided under the law, or if the punishment itself can be viewed by the perpetrator as being less a personal loss than the gains he received by the criminal act itself.

2. *Reducing Criminal Opportunity Reduces the Opportunity to Learn Criminal Behavior.*

Reducing criminal opportunity not only reduces the individual's opportunity to learn about crime, but it also reduces the opportunity to receive positive reinforcements favorable to the criminal actions. Indeed, the individual's failure to achieve criminal success will provide negative reinforcement to criminal belief structures and positive reinforcement to the belief that crime is not the path of least resistance. Therefore, legitimate paths to success become more inviting to the individual.

3. *Criminal Opportunity Can Be Lessened by Improved Security Measures and By Increasing the Level of Surveillance on the Part of the General Public.* (Community Relations)

By improving security measures, we mean not only the installation and operation of more sophisticated devices, but improved applications of devices that are currently installed. A large volume of burglary, for example, is committed because entry could be achieved through unlocked doors, thus suggesting that simply locking whatever device is available would deter the beginning burglar. Criminal opportunity can be lessened by a number of ways. First of all, the environment can be designed so that the individual considering the criminal act feels that there is a good chance for him to be seen by someone who will take action on their own or call the police. Secondly, the target of his attack can be made to appear so formidable that he does not believe his abilities will enable him to reach the "forbidden fruit," and thirdly, if he actually attempts to reach the goal, the probability of his failure can be increased through the ready response of the police. The above process is the system wherein the physical environment plays part, the security devices protecting a specific target are involved, and tying it all together is the constant surveillance by both members of that particular community and the police.

4. *Long-range Crime Prevention Will Not Be Achieved Unless Criminal Opportunities Are Reduced on a National Basis.*

It can be predicted with some degree of accuracy that crime prevention applied to a small geographical area will result in considerable displacement of the activity to the adjacent areas. It can also be shown that this displacement process will tend to diminish as the area of crime-prevention activity is widened and increased effort is called for on the part of the criminal to continue his activities away from a familiar environment.

The more skilled and mobile criminal will obviously displace his activities further away from his home base for he will have the skills to relocate and create a new base of operations. Therefore, it is necessary to develop a national strategy for reducing criminal opportunity.

5. *The Police Are in a Pivotal Position and As Such They Should Be Trained in Crime Prevention and Become Involved In The Preplanning of Any Community Activity Where Their Services Will Later Be Called For.*

This statement provides the basis for all training and implementation of programs as defined in the crime prevention definition used by the National Crime Prevention Institute of the University of Louisville. It means basically that if the police are called in response to an actual crime, such as burglary, robbery, or shoplifting, they should also be concerned about reducing the crime risk that led to the commission of the overt act. Extended, this statement means that the police do not have to take a passive role in the planning process, but that they should take a positive step forward and actively solicit the opportunity to provide crime-prevention advice in the planning stages of community activity. The police possess within their records and the experience of the officers much that can be valuable to the planner when considering the safety of the community.

Any business seeking a new location of a plant site is certainly concerned with the level of criminal activity in areas under consideration. A safe community is a good community within which to work and play, and therefore a good crime-prevention program with police involvement in the planning stages can be a valuable social and economic asset to any community.

6. *Insurance, Security Hardware, and Other Areas of Business and Industry Involved in Crime Prevention Programs, Should Exchange Information With the Police.*

Security hardware and procedures, police response, and insurance make up the three levels of protection available to all citizens. At the current time very little exchange of personnel or information exists within these three areas of endeavor. It has been well documented by the Small Business Administration that insurance data and police data do not always compare favorably with each other, and there is evidence that some manufacturers of security hardware equipment do a better job of analyzing police resources as part of their marketing studies than the police departments themselves. The insurance industry and security hardware manufacturers are in business purely because of the profit motive. The police, however, are in business to provide adequate levels of service to the community and can take a leadership role in coordinating the crime-prevention efforts on all three levels of protection.[4]

THE ROLE OF THE PUBLIC

Crime is a community problem and must be viewed as such by citizens of all communities before significant crime reduction can be expected. Citizen participation in crime prevention means much more than cooperation with the police; it includes working with educational institutions, all segments of the criminal justice system, and as individuals in their homes and neighborhoods. Collective security will not be achieved unless each individual is convinced that he must protect himself from crime and also be concerned with the protection of his neighborhood.

THE ROLE OF THE POLICE

The role of the police should be one of preventing crime and not just one of detection and apprehension after the fact. However, a good program of detection and apprehension when the line of prevention has broken down is extremely important to the overall prevention process. The important thing is that the individual police officer view himself in the role of assisting the citizen to prevent crime, not one in a role that places total emphasis on crime prevention and control as an exclusive police function.

Because police deal with crime after the fact and as such are charged with the housing of records, strategies for deploying their forces, and with the 24-hour responsibility of representing community authority, they should take a leadership role and share their accumulated knowledge with members of the public. This means that some segment of the police organization (crime-prevention unit) must enable community programs to continue after the initial excitement and enthusiasm by community-spirited persons slows because of conflicts with their need to pursue activities of their own occupations.

CRIME-PREVENTION TRAINING

Upon completion of an adequate crime-prevention training school, police officers should be expected to—

1. understand the principles of crime prevention;
2. be familiar with current theories of community planning;

3. have obtained the basic skills required to conduct a premises survey and make valid recommendations regarding security devices;
4. be able to present a practical explanation of "risk management" to departmental personnel and to the general public;
5. have developed the skills required to evaluate security hardware and services offered in the community;
6. be familiar with the development of municipal security codes;
7. be familiar with proven methods of staging public exhibitions and advertising campaigns relating to crime prevention;
8. understand the basic problems of public and private crime insurance;
9. gain an understanding of architectural design and its importance to crime prevention; and
10. improve their ability to implement or advance a crime-prevention program in the department and to generate community-wide enthusiasm for crime prevention.

Training Modules

Experience has shown that training of four weeks' duration is required to accomplish the above objectives. The four weeks should be broken into three phases.

(1) *Crime-prevention Theory.* Officers attending traditional police-training schools have been conditioned through training and experience to focus their energies in the area of detection and apprehension, rather than crime prevention. It is therefore important to point out the problems associated with the detection model of policing and to introduce police officers to the concepts of security and loss prevention. The term "risk management" is introduced first during this phase because it is necessary that police officers understand the far-reaching implications of this term. A general review of the criminological literature and theories of urban planning should also be presented during this initial phase.

(2) *Crime-prevention Hardware.* The hardware phase of the crime-prevention training program should provide officers with a solid background on the development of locking devices, currently available models, their strong and weak points, and some idea of what can be expected in the future. The subject of electronic protection through the use of the various types of intrusion detection systems should be presented during this time frame.

The question of false alarms is a universal problem for police officers and special time should be set aside for a discussion of this issue. Because it is an emotional subject, experts from alarm companies, testing laboratories, and central station operations should be present for a panel discussion with the police officers. Properly moderated, this type of format can provide an effective method for exchanging information between police and the alarm industry and for solving their mutual problems.

The need for officers to contact and establish relationships with similar representatives in their home areas is important. A detailed discussion of the capabilities and limitations of safes and vaults should also be presented to the students. Students should have the opportunity to view alarm installations, the strengths and weaknesses of various methods of building construction, the problems of building design for security, and the many products available to improve lighting systems in both the public and private areas of the community. At the conclusion of the hardware phase of training, officers should have the opportunity to make a number of actual on-site surveys and provide recommendations for comment by the training school staff.

(3) *Crime-prevention Implementation.* The preparation of officers for crime-prevention implementation is an extremely important part of a training program. A program should be designed to combat the normal tendency for an officer to return from a training program full of enthusiasm for the new ideas presented to him during class sessions, only to find that he is unable to implement them in his department. Officers are advised to be patient and not expect accomplishments overnight. Such accomplishments will not happen that fast, and the officers need to be provided with some insulation against the discouragement that might lead to the abandonment of the program. They should be given a strategy for implementing the program in both their department and community. This strategy should take advantage of the many studies of organizational dynamics that have been produced by management research, both in and outside the field of law enforcement. The author has lectured on "Implementing Change" at training sessions and can verify the need for understanding change and organizational dynamics.

A training program structured in this manner and giving the proper number of hours to each of the three modules will create a learning environment leading to the successful assimilation of the knowledge required to implement a community relations crime-prevention program.

CRIME-PREVENTION IMPLEMENTATION

A successful crime-prevention program must have the support of every member of the police organization. One way to gain this cooperation is to alter the departmental reward system so that crime-prevention activities become a part of the officers' goals as well as departmental goals. While the crime-prevention officer may be considered a specialist, part of his success as a crime-prevention specialist can be measured by his ability to involve all officers, and particularly the patrol officer, in the crime-prevention community relations program. An efficient way to implement a crime-prevention program is to have it described in one of the departmental orders issued under the signature of the chief.

This order should describe the philosophy of the department regarding crime prevention, the duties of the specialized officers, the duties of officers at all ranks, and the relationship between the specialized officers and the other members of the department. (See Appendix D for an outstanding example of how crime-prevention programs have been implemented by the issuance of general orders in the Greensboro, North Carolina, Police Department.)

One of the most effective ways to implement change is through the planning and funding capabilities of state and regional criminal-justice agencies. Both the state of Texas and the state of Illinois have done an excellent job in bringing together police departments throughout their respective states and presenting to them a program of work in crime prevention. In Illinois, the SPA has placed a number of requirements on departments as prerequisites for the funding of crime-prevention programs. In Texas the Permian Basin Regional Planning Commission, under the direction of the Criminal Justice Coordinator, has designed an 11-point program that can assist the chief of police in the decision-making process when considering the advisability of implementing a crime-prevention unit. The regional commission further points out a method by which the chief can sell the crime-prevention concept to the city council and/or city manager. The selling procedures point out the necessity of stressing crime prevention rather than apprehension, the need to have an unbiased, trained officer available to give consumer-protection advice regarding security services, the possibility that community crime-insurance rates can be reduced if crime is reduced or stabilized, and how security advice to businessmen can in turn generate higher support for city services on the part of the business community. The presence of these conditions will enhance the possibility of a successful crime-prevention program. Because the crime-prevention program will generally be associated with police activity, there must be strong support from the chief of police for the establishment of the crime-prevention unit.

Local government must approve funds for crime-prevention activities as a valid investment.

Assignment of full-time officers is necessary to keep a crime-prevention program alive within a community. Crime-prevention and community relations should be viewed as an integrated process, and officers must be given detailed training in order for their information and recommendations to be based on knowledge gleaned from the security field, not merely from experiences gained in criminal investigation.

A program involving the entire community on a systematic basis must be developed.

A dynamic or feedback model of unit operations must be developed to keep the program current with community needs.

CRIME-PREVENTION OPERATIONS

The location of the crime-prevention unit in the police organization will depend on the size of the organization, the current organizational structure, and the present level of crime-prevention programs implemented in the particular police department.

It is clear, however, that the crime-prevention unit should be headed by an individual with sufficient rank and access to the chief executive. This is to insure the recognition on the part of all members of the department that the program is indeed an important one and one that is supported by sufficient departmental resources to heighten its probability of success. Experts in the field recommend that the crime-prevention unit be a major line organization and that other sections, such as community relations, juvenile, and public education, should function as a part of the crime-prevention unit. In many cases this will not be possible for some time because of the past development of community relations bureaus; however, community relations should be considered part of crime prevention.

A crime-prevention unit explains by its very name the intention of its operation to every citizen in the community. The important consideration here is not necessarily the name of the unit, but that the commanding officer be given the resources necessary to implement the program.

Scope of Activities

The scope of crime-prevention activities is limited only by the imagination of the implementing officers and the authority that they have to carry out their ideas. Managing by objective is a realistic approach. Some of the possible activities of a crime-prevention program and how it may involve the adoption of a municipal security code can be seen from the charts on the following pages.

Police/community crime-prevention programs can provide a very valuable service to the community strictly on the basis of persuasion. However, it is becoming increasingly evident that persuasion is not enough and that legislation will be required if an effective program with substantial impact on the level of crime is to be maintained. To date, the main thrust of crime-prevention legislation is in developing municipal security codes. While these may be a start in the right direction, unorganized development of these codes may lead to the implementation of ineffective legislation. Therefore, serious consideration should be given to crime-prevention legislation at the state level: specifically, the adoption of a state crime-prevention code and a companion model, a municipal security code that may be adopted by any particular community within that state.

A crime-prevention council should be established at both the state and local levels. It will be the duty of this council to research and implement crime-prevention programs both within and without the criminal justice system. At the state level this council can suggest legislation and funding for crime prevention and also provide a means for citizen evaluation of crime-prevention efforts by criminal justice agencies or agencies outside the criminal justice system. Locally, the crime-prevention council can assist the city administration in developing a security code and also with the very important task of community mobilization.

In Figure 8.1 the crime-prevention duties of a trained police crime-prevention officer have been divided into three areas: information, aid, and enforcement. The crime-prevention officer can be very effective by working with builders and getting their voluntary cooperation in the protection of the building site. The crime-prevention officer should use the security code as an opportunity to encourage architects to design innovative security concepts. In working with architects and builders and property managers the crime-prevention officer can point out that security, if it is preplanned, can save money and can provide a good sales position as well (Figure 8.2).

An extremely important part of a crime-prevention officer's duties is to increase citizen awareness of the problem of crime. This means that the crime-prevention officer must be able to relate the problem of crime to the individual citizen in his neighborhood (Figure 8.3).

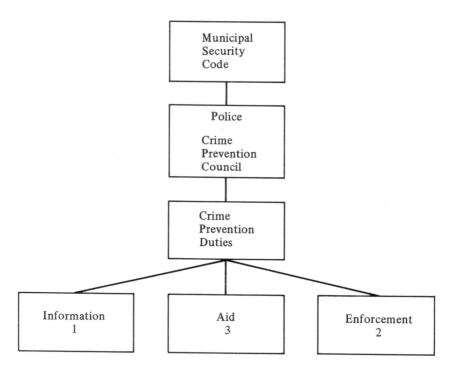

FIGURE 8.1   Police Role in Mechanical Crime Prevention

The citizen may not be able to relate the national crime problem to his home community; even crime at the state or city level may not seem personally relevant to him. A crime-prevention officer, by analyzing the community crime patterns and then opening up these records to the community, can assist in making the citizen aware of the actual problem confronting him and his neighbor on a day-to-day basis. The regular beat officer should be totally involved with this program, resulting in his identification as "Little Police Chief" community relations/crime-prevention officer.

Hopefully, an increased awareness on the part of the citizen of his responsibility for protecting himself and his neighbors should cut two ways toward effecting a lowering of the actual crime rate. First, more crimes will be reported. Second, the improved data on modus operandi should increase the probability of apprehension and therefore strengthen the deterrent effect of traditional police operations.

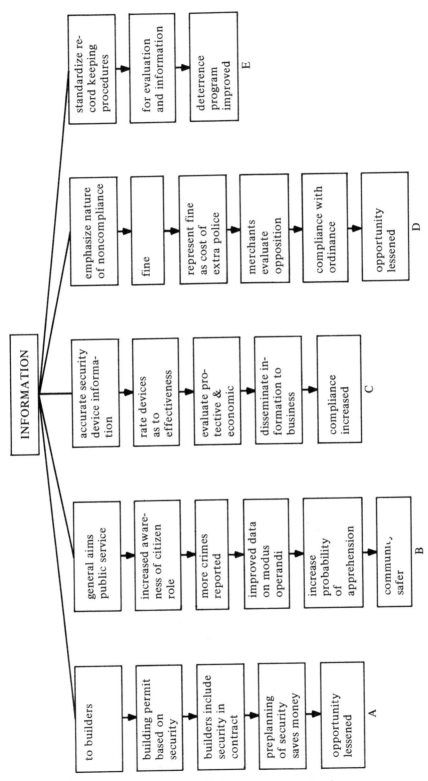

FIGURE 8.2 Police Information Services

RATINGS (Figure 8.3(a))

At present there exist no standards to permit objective evaluation for rating security devices. The rating given by police officers to products available in the community must be based on the officer's limited experience and the knowledge of what testing currently is being done in the field. Officers need not, however, wait for the ultimate answers from a sophisticated testing laboratory. By analyzing crime reports in their own city they will begin to see a pattern developing that relates directly to the effect of certain security measures.

Current experience with crime-prevention ordinances indicates a high level of compliance. However, as these ordinances are developed in a wider range of communities, some noncompliance should be expected and a program should be developed to reeducate the violator or cite him to court if necessary. There are many ways that an officer can use to encourage voluntary compliance. For example, if a merchant does not comply with the security ordinance, the probability of his being attacked is increased and the attention that must be given to his business through investigation by officers whose salary expenses are paid for by the entire community is increased. It can be pointed out to the merchant that protecting his own property may be rewarded by a reduction or at least a stabilizing level of taxes required for police protection (Figure 8.2).

An important part of a crime-prevention officer's duty is to develop techniques by which the crime picture in his community can be properly evaluated. The heart of this evaluation will be the design and standardization of reports relating to criminal attack methods (Figure 8.3(a)).

Crime-prevention officers will learn to give advice to merchants and homeowners that costs very little for the individual to implement. Officers could acquaint merchants with the buddy system (Figure 8.3) whereby connecting alarms are installed between nearby establishments with similar hours of business. When a crime is committed and the alarm is sounded in the buddy's place of business, he will be in a position to call for assistance or to gain a description of the criminal. Crime-prevention officers should also be available to make a security survey upon request of a homeowner or merchant (Figure 8.3). Unless this one-to-one relationship is established between crime-prevention officers and the person concerned with security, the proper system may not be designed to suit the particular situation. In addition to providing a valuable service, the crime-prevention officer is establishing the finest community-relations program possible, because he is displaying an expertise that will assist an individual in his own protection. It is quite often possible for crime-prevention officers to provide security hints that have nothing to do with hardware (Figure 8.3). The placement of cash registers and mirrors, the removal of valuable articles from windows, and recommendations for the safe carrying and transportation of cash are all methods by which a crime-prevention officer may assist the merchant or homeowner.

Crime insurance savings is one way to encourage the merchant to improve the security (Figure 8.3). A number of underwriter's laboratory systems can be installed and substantial savings on insurance premiums affected. Crime-prevention officers will need to develop a data base that will be meaningful both to police operations and the insurance industry before additional premium discounts can be expected.

Another recommendation is citywide standards for street lighting (Figure 8.3(a)). Complaints can be logged regarding adequate street lighting and reference made to appropriate city departments. More important, merchants and homeowners can be advised on the proper type of lighting for their own premises.

Many times other city services, such as garbage collection and street cleaning, are inefficient. This leads not only to an unhealthy environment, but one that can lead to psychological insecurity as well as immediate personal danger to a citizen (Figure 8.3(a)). As a community-relations service that will improve the psychological security of the person's home environment, officers can accept complaints about city service inadequacies and refer them to the proper departments. While it may seem to be stretching a point to relate these types of activities to crime prevention, these services can, in fact, contribute to building good feeling about the police in all segments of the community. This is important because it increases the acceptance of his preventive services and may be a factor in gaining cooperation in times of community stress.

Most police departments of any size have officers who are specially trained in the handling of juvenile problems. Unfortunately, most of these officers are only able to exhibit their skills after an act of delinquency has taken place. The crime-prevention officer can develop school liaison and educational schemes based on the traffic safety model and will encourage children from the elementary grades through high school to accept the responsibility for the protection of themselves and of their neighbors (Figure 8.3(a)).

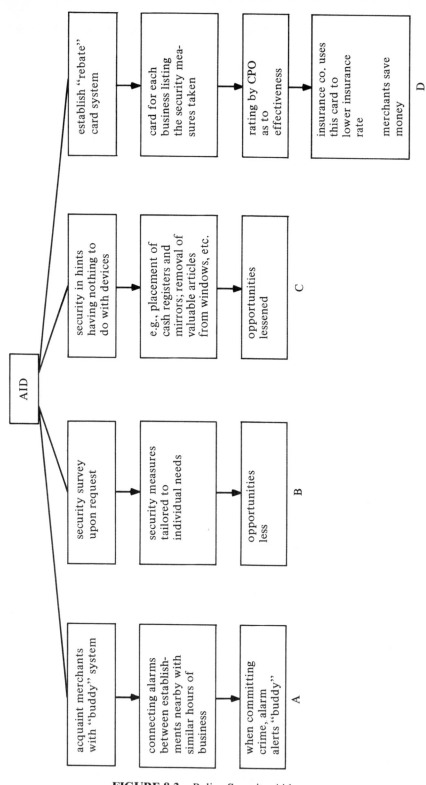

FIGURE 8.3 Police Security Aids

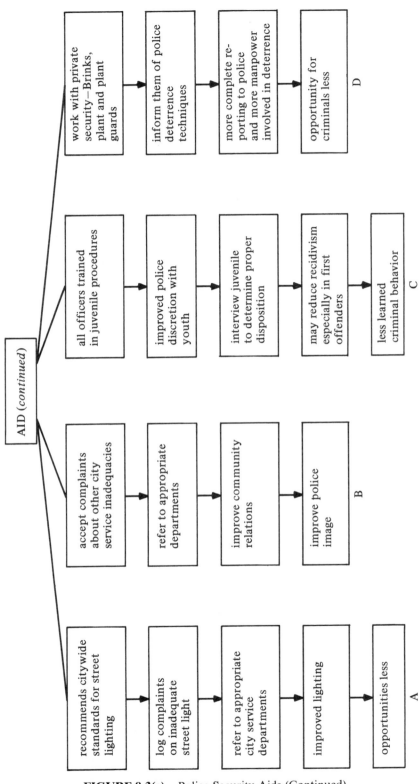

FIGURE 8.3(a) Police Security Aids (Continued)

An important part of the crime-prevention officer's job is to work with private security agencies such as Brinks, contract guard services, and in-house security (Figure 8.3(a)). In each of these cases when the criminal offense occurs, the police are called upon to assist these other agencies. Therefore, they have the right to expect to be involved in planning programs that will prevent attacks on premises protected by these private services.

Auto theft is a universal police problem. It may be attacked through public education media, the enactment and enforcement of "remove-your-key" legislation, or through the coordinated efforts of the police and insurance companies (Figure 8.4).

As more sophisticated recommendations are made by crime-prevention officers, and as the insurance industry increases its cooperation and coordination with law enforcement, it will be necessary to make periodic checks on businesses to see that they have complied with the legislation or with officers' recommendations. As in other areas of police and public-agency activities, any type of licensing system also creates its own opportunity for misconduct. To avoid this, checks can be made on a random basis to insure an even application of crime-prevention legislation (Figure 8.4).

Many activities of the crime-prevention officer directly involve the analysis of high-crime target areas and the development of strategies to prevent crime in these areas. This activity will have an impact on the entire police organization. The crime-prevention officer will have an influence on policy-making apparatus that decides when prosecutions of ordinance violations take place, and the allocation of police resources to obtain the most immediate possible response to burglar alarms (Figure 8.4).

The important thing to remember in allocating duties to crime-prevention officers is that these duties and activities, whether they are handled by specialists or by a beat officer, provide an endless opportunity for community service that will lead directly to the accomplishment of the police officer's goal: reduction of crime. The management by objective approach will develop the beat officer in crime-prevention/community-relations and planning activities.

IMPLEMENTING A COMMUNITY PROGRAM

A successful community campaign of any type does not come about without detailed planning and strategy, and crime prevention is no exception.

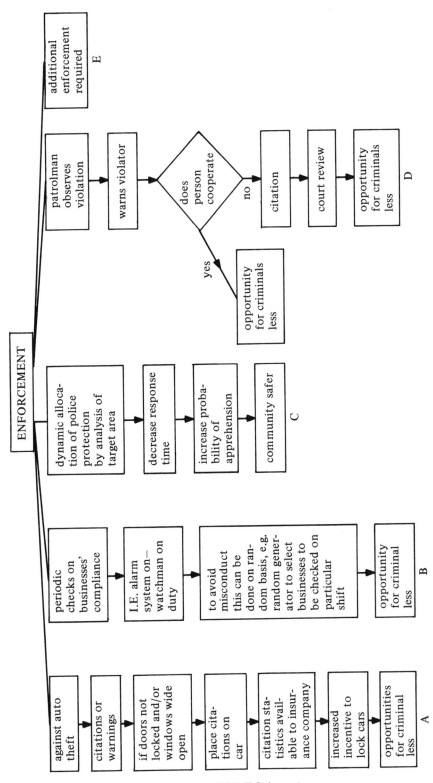

ENFORCEMENT

E
additional enforcement required

D
patrolman observes violation → warns violator → does person cooperate

no → citation → court review → opportunity for criminals less

yes → opportunity for criminals less

C
dynamic allocation of police protection by analysis of target area → decrease response time → increase probability of apprehension → community safer

B
periodic checks on businesses' compliance → I.E. alarm system on—watchman on duty → to avoid misconduct this can be done on random basis, e.g. random generator to select businesses to be checked on particular shift → opportunity for criminal less

A
against auto theft → citations or warnings → if doors not locked and/or windows wide open → place citations on car → citation statistics available to insurance company → increased incentive to lock cars → opportunities for criminal less

FIGURE 8.4

Crime-prevention lacks all the glamour of a centennial celebration, the judging of a beauty contest, and the humanistic appeal of a March of Dimes campaign. It is therefore extremely important that the entire community be involved during the planning stages of a crime-prevention program of community action. It must be developed by the community, not merely a program sponsored by the police and thrust upon the community to implement.

There is no one successful model for implementing crime prevention in a community. Such programs are still too new in the United States to judge how successful one strategy is over the other. However, we can learn from the English experience that certain elements are required to organize a community for action.

The NCPI of the University of Louisville has developed a plan for community crime prevention. While results cannot be guaranteed from following this plan, it has been accepted in a number of communities with favorable results. The heart of the plan (see Appendix E) is that someone in the community, in most cases the crime-prevention officer, will make a detailed examination of the facts concerning crime in his community. The officer will analyze the recognized community activities in the city for any given year and identify those individuals and organizations within a community whose support is necessary to get a community project under way. A list of citizens most likely to contribute to the success of a crime-prevention program will be given to the chief and city administrator, who will encourage their participation on a committee. In conjunction with the community's crime-prevention panel or committee, the crime-prevention officer will develop a strategy of implementation. The CPO will explain to a committee that patience will be required in developing the program and that it is not a one-year campaign, but a campaign that must continue through many years before the full effect will be seen in the community.

The crime-prevention committee will plan a promotional event and harness all available resources of the community to see that the campaign (at least a month in duration) will be a success. Following the campaign, the police department's crime-prevention program will swing into full operation and provide the continuing influence needed for an ongoing long-term project.

Manpower Allocations

Many times new and innovative programs receive a lot of attention and favorable comment until the point is reached where manpower allocations are necessary. It is very seldom that any police department or divisions therein will volunteer personnel to be assigned on new programs. Most divisional commanders find themselves in the position of competing for a limited number of total departmental personnel. The staffing of a new program, therefore, calls for a complete analysis of the current allocation of departmental personnel and the shifting of this personnel to meet the demands of new departmental priorities.

Thirty years or more ago, when traffic safety was a newly developing specialty, police chiefs and commanders had the same problems in finding resources and staff for a safety and traffic division. Nevertheless, these programs did develop, and now most departments of any size have a number of specialists assigned to traffic duties or at least to traffic educational programs.

With the development of the community-relations approach, the need for personnel for these new programs was again a problem. However, staffing was accomplished and now many departments have a substantial percentage of their force committed to community relations.

Today we find many recommendations calling for a reversal in what has been termed "overspecialization," and this could well apply to such areas as traffic and community relations. However, a certain core of highly trained specialists will be required in these areas if for nothing more than to plan and coordinate the activities of the entire department.

Crime prevention is no exception. While crime prevention should be the duty of every police officer, a core of trained specialists will be required to develop a department's crime-prevention program, to train officers at all levels of the department, to analyze departmental records in crime-prevention terms, and to carry out highly specialized technical surveys and recommendations regarding security problems. Each department will find it necessary to evaluate its own crime risk problems and assign officers accordingly.

Nevertheless, there are some guidelines that should be followed until enough data has been collected to establish more effective personnel recommendations. The most important requirement of assigned personnel is that they be trained in crime prevention. If officers are assigned before proper training, they may not be in a position to give accurate advice to businessmen and homeowners and may well cause the project to fail. A number of departments are recommending that a total of 2% of the personnel be assigned to the crime-prevention bureau or unit. The 2% assignment formula is a realistic future-oriented recommendation. Initially, however, departments with an authorized strength of 400 to 1,000 should strive for a goal of assigning 1% of their authorized strength to crime prevention. Departments with an authorized strength of from 100 to 400 should have a minimum of 2 officers assigned to crime prevention and departments with authorized strength under 100 men should have 1 officer assigned to crime prevention.

Personnel allocations will vary according to the activity of the department and the priority placed upon crime prevention, but unless a department is able to allocate enough officers to the crime-prevention program to make a genuine impact, the program will be doomed to failure.

Crime prevention is the type of program that must not fail. It is a program that may not meet with initial acceptance by a large segment of departmental personnel. Therefore, a poorly planned and understaffed bureau or unit would be more detrimental to the department's overall long-range goals than no program at all.

MATERIALS AND RESOURCES

The nature of the crime-prevention officer's work will require the accumulation of special equipment and supplies. As with other divisions of the police department, a certain amount of paperwork is inevitable; a crime-prevention unit should be staffed with an adequate number of clerical and secretarial personnel. A major part of the crime-prevention program will include posters, leaflets, booklets, and other printed material relating to crime prevention. Therefore, a budget allocation should be made to cover the types of printed material required in enough volume to allow community saturation with the materials.

The department should also budget adequately for the acquisition of films, slides, and other audiovisual equipment as well as projection equipment for the use of the CPO.

In the area of public information, one item generally overlooked is paid advertising. Most departments rely on public service time by television and radio for such things as spot announcements regarding crime prevention. While these may be effective, one problem is that quite often public service time is scheduled for nonprime time and therefore programs or spots may reach only a small audience. This can be resolved by using paid advertising, through radio, television, or newspaper, and some program should be designed or devised to obtain an adequate amount of funds for this phase of the project. An example of the amount of funds required for paid advertising can be seen in the federal grant allocated to the city of Cleveland for reducing auto thefts. Over $100,000 was spent in a one-year period solely on paid advertising.

In addition to the normal radios, uniforms, and patrol vehicles required of all police, many departments have found it advantageous to provide the crime-prevention officer with a special van equipped with handout literature, examples of security devices, and other items relating to crime prevention. In some departments these vans have been the VW van design. In others they have been a mobile-home type of vehicle that will accommodate visitors on the inside and provide general public relations and public information as well as a crime-prevention message. These special-purpose vehicles can range in cost from $5,000 to $25,000 according to the size of the community and the purpose for which they are designed. The community-relations/crime-prevention program can be combined in these vans.

An important resource for the crime-prevention officer is a library of books and periodicals. At the present time books on the subject of crime prevention are scarce. Nevertheless, there is a basic library that can be acquired. Also, periodicals from the security and locksmithing industry and special publications by manufacturers are a valuable asset to CPOs. Budget allocations should be considered to support the crime-prevention unit in this regard.

Crime-prevention officers should be provided with both a Polaroid camera and a camera capable of producing 35-millimeter slides. The Polaroid camera will be extremely valuable when presenting the results of a security survey to a merchant. A picture of the security hazard presented with the report can exert a strong influence on the owner of the property and increase the possibility of his remedying the crime risk. A 35-millimeter camera is essential because, in spite of prepared programs relating to crime prevention, nothing will have more impact than a program based on conditions in the officer's assigned area.

The officer should use this equipment to follow up crime-scene investigations, showing the results of criminal activities, as well as to photograph potential crime scenes for presentation to community audiences. Materials and equipment should be provided to allow the crime-prevention unit to prepare a portable exhibit for use at trade shows, PTA meetings, conventions, and other public and private meetings where the crime-prevention message should be sold.

If the department is not already involved in Operation Identification, an important resource for the crime-prevention officer will be an adequate supply of engravers to carry out this project. One of the main problems with Operation Identification is having an adequate number of engravers available at convenient points of distribution. These units should be made available not only at the police department, but at grocery stores, insurance offices, service club meetings, churches, youth groups, and any other distribution point that will encourage people to use the equipment. The city of Dallas, through both public and private funds, will have an inventory of over 1,000 engravers. They initially operated with an inventory of over 500 units and lost only one through failure of citizens to return them.

Training resources should also be made available to members of the crime-prevention unit. Besides the National Crime Prevention Institute training in this area, a number of other avenues are also available to police departments. Crime-prevention officers who are allowed to attend seminars put on by the Security World Organization, American Society for Industrial Security, the Associated Locksmiths of America, the Small Business Administration, and other public and private groups will develop a great deal of expertise and increase the crime-prevention unit's ability to deliver a complete range of crime-prevention services to the community. What greater community relations?

The crime-prevention unit should have examples of security products to be used in public demonstrations or made available in storefront community relations offices so that the public may view good security equipment. While much of this equipment will be donated by local dealers and manufacturers, a sum of money should be set aside to purchase quality items where needed. One problem with receiving donated material is that sometimes producers of poor quality items are the most anxious to have their products placed in a police exhibit. A crime-prevention officer should not feel obligated to display inferior equipment. As a matter of fact, it might be good strategy to purchase an obviously inferior product and have it available to demonstrate that fact to citizens.

A crime-prevention unit must have adequate resources with which to do a meaningful job. However, experience is showing that crime prevention can be one of the most economical programs funded by a state or local planning agency. An enthusiastic and well-trained officer is the key to a crime-prevention bureau; all other resources should be viewed as merely supportive of his personal efforts.

EVALUATION

It is important to define exactly what should be evaluated in a crime-prevention program. Projects funded on an annual basis on the premise that they must within that year show a reduction of reported crime from the year previous are doomed to failure.

Because of the generally recognized low rate of reporting, a crime-prevention program that generates new enthusiasm on the part of the public could well cause a statistical crime wave. Nevertheless, a crime-prevention unit is funded for basically one reason—to reduce crime. A system of evaluation should be designed so that the actual effect of the program can be measured at least within a five-year period. There are, however, many measurements that can be taken along the way to provide a clue as to the program's effectiveness. Some items to be considered are the following:

1. Before and after studies can be developed that determine the actual level of crime reporting in the community.
2. The effects of an anti-auto-theft campaign can be immediately measured because it is the one crime that is, in fact, overreported.
3. Statistical evaluations can be made of the public information effort to see that the message of crime prevention is actually reaching the public and if the public reacts to the message.
4. Data can be maintained to determine the level of public participation from crime-in-progress calls or from leads leading directly to the apprehension of suspects.
5. Street-lighting studies can be made to show the crime reduction indicated by improved lighting. Studies can also be made to determine the relationship between improved lighting around businesses and homes, and crime in unimproved areas.
6. Evaluations can be made of an entire community program and the level of compliance with the recommendations of the crime-prevention bureau.
7. Statistical data should be kept of the changing patterns of crime to enable the crime-prevention bureau to measure the anticipated displacement after the initiation of a program. Even though crime does not reduce immediately, an obvious displacement of crime could be related to the crime-prevention program. If enough displacement occurs constantly it may be possible to move the bulk of crime to locations

and into methods of operation that lend themselves to improved apprehension capabilities. The level of on-site criminal captures should be evaluated by measuring increased citizens' calls and improved use of electronic detection devices.

8. A measurement of public support for the crime-prevention effort and the general community feeling toward police should be developed. There should be a sound program of evaluating the department's response to crime-prevention needs, and the actual or potential effect of reducing crime in the community. Wherever possible, evaluation should be based on statistical data, not merely on the basis of intuitive judgments. Evaluations should be part of the initial design so that final results are based on reasonable expectations, relevant data, and a sound evaluation technique.

CITIZEN PARTICIPATION

Blockwatchers

A *blockwatcher* is a concerned citizen who is willing to take part in a program of observing criminal activity and reporting that criminal activity to the police. This is community relations in action. It involves the police department as an organization, the crime-prevention officer and unit, the officers on the beat, and the citizens living on the beat. The ability of our country to reduce crime depends upon citizen participation in programs designed to enable citizens to become full partners in the responsibility of maintaining security of their homes, property, and lives.

The blockwatcher program is designed for just that reason. Citizens wishing to become blockwatchers contact the crime-prevention officers of the police department. Community-relations councils (if they exist) are used to disseminate information and to coordinate organization. Training is given to the blockwatchers so that they know what to observe, how to describe the observation effectively, and how to report the incident to the police. The blockwatcher is given an identification number to use when reporting incidents. Blockwatchers are advised which incidents are emergency and which are not, and how to report each. This is an effective, realistic approach to citizen participation in crime prevention.

Reserve Units

This is an excellent method of supplementing the police departments of our country with additional manpower. This type of program requires an investment of manpower for training, and possibly money for uniforms and equipment. In some departments reserve officers provide their own uniforms and equipment. Police reserves should be selected carefully; they should not detract from the professional image of the department. Reserve officers may be assigned as extra men in one-man car operations, parade details, municipal stadiums for athletic events, auditoriums, dances, and theaters. Some police agencies have had thousands of hours contributed free of charge by interested citizens wishing to participate in police reserve programs. Police commanders should give a careful look to this approach in citizen participation.

Students

Police departments in several cities have involved students in crime-prevention programs. Demonstrations have been given to college classes, and the students have organized groups such as "Concerned Students for Crime Prevention." These students have developed programs in crime prevention and presented them to elementary school children. One program includes a game of flash cards where children are shown license plates and asked to remember the letters and numbers. This will assist them in remembering the license number of automobiles that may be used in a crime.

Citizen Patrol and Escorts

New York City has a program to assist community organizations in helping themselves in crime prevention. The organizations include block, neighborhood, civic, tenant, and business associations. These associations must contribute funds to be used for collective purposes in the crime-prevention programs. Equipment purchased includes fences, whistles, flashlights, floodlights, cylinder locks, and portable radios. The radios are used in citizen patrol and escort programs for the neighborhood. The patrol and escort program is told to patrol in pairs, stay in assigned neighborhood areas, how to report crimes, and to consider themselves the eyes and ears of the police department. The goal of the program is to stimulate private investment into security improvement and to bring people together with a new spirit and understanding of community protection and closer relationships with police, which will provide togetherness in crime prevention.

An Insight

A good insight into police-citizen relationships can be gained by reviewing *Marshaling Citizen Power Against Crime,* published by the

Chamber of Commerce of the United States. Several statements included here will give the patrol leader an idea of the interaction potential between the citizen, organized community groups, and the police.

> Citizens should not be recruited for a crime-prevention program unless they have time to fulfill their assigned responsibilities and unless they are prepared to serve for reasonable periods. High turnover and do nothing . . . members spell failure."[5]

The extract below indicates some of the problems that may face the components of the criminal justice system as stated in the National Advisory Commission on Criminal Justice Standards and Goals' "Report on Community Crime Prevention," p. 21.

> In a community where street crime is a severe problem, a citizen group may organize in order to promote the hiring of more patrolmen. Robbery arrests may increase, but the courts and correctional facilities may not be able to handle the increased caseload adequately, with the result that criminals are back on the street. In this case a more desirable objective would have been better street lighting, which might have discouraged robberies without adding to arrest totals.

This highlights the need for citizen organizations to become acquainted with the components of the criminal justice system and their interrelationship before tackling projects affecting any one of these components.

Included in the book is a problem-identification checklist, "The Police." Questions are asked with regard to organization; management and policies; coordination and consolidation of services and facilities; crime prevention and control; corruption; community relations; research and statistics; personnel utilization and performance; training; salaries and promotions, etc.[6] Patrol leaders would do well to familiarize themselves with the total checklist. Knowledge of the many questions and answers will enhance the ability to act before the fact. The familiarization should include the National Advisory Commission report on Criminal Justice Standards and Goals' "Report on Community Crime Prevention."

CONCLUSION

Any strategy to reduce crime in our country must include citizen's participation in crime prevention. If we have had a strategy in the past, it has not worked as effectively as it could. Oscar Newman in his book *Defensible Space* has pointed out the real need to improve the environmental and architectural design of buildings to decrease the opportunity for criminal activity. Other programs, such as improved lighting, locks, and citizen mobilization will play an important part in opportunity reduction. The cause and effect of desire factors need to be analyzed to insure that the cure is appropriate. Another question is the victim. Should we evaluate the police impact by victimization rate? (Victimization rate-number of crimes [in a given category] per year per thousand residents [in a given category].) If so, why and what can be done to reduce the hazards?

The basic crime-fighting tactic of all American police departments —the regular patrol of the streets by uniformed men in marked cars —does not appear to prevent crime, according to the preliminary findings of a year-long experiment. This startling conclusion appears to challenge a fundamental tenet of most police officials and politicians that more policemen patrolling the streets is the answer to a city's crime problem. Law-enforcement experts estimate that half of the $4.5 billion a year spent for police protection by the cities, towns, and counties of the United States is allocated to preventive patrol.

The experiment testing the effectiveness of preventive patrol was conducted in a 35-mile square area of Kansas City, Missouri, from October 1, 1972, to September 30, 1973. Findings indicate that the random patrolling of the streets by uniformed men in marked cars does not prevent crime. Two conclusions that police officials can draw is that they should deploy their manpower on the basis of service needs to the community and that patrols should be directed on a day-to-day basis to where the needs are greatest.[7]

NOTES

1. Adapted from material prepared by the Home Office Crime Prevention Training Center, Stafford, England, courtesy of Detective Chief Inspector Ronald Dawson.

2. Peter Lejins, in *Delinquency Prevention—Theory and Practice,* William E. Amos and Charles F. Wellford, editors (Englewood Cliffs, N.J.: Prentice Hall, 1967), p. 35.
3. National Advisory Commission on Criminal Justice Standards and Goals, "Report on Community Crime Prevention," Recommendation 9.1, p. 197.
4. Wilbur Rykert, *Reduction of Criminal Opportunity,* National Crime Deterrence Council, Pittsburgh, Pennsylvania, 1971, pp. 3–4.
5. *Marshaling Citizen Power Against Crime* (Washington, D.C.: Chamber of Commerce of the United States, 1970), p. 81.
6. Ibid, p. 87.
7. "Criminal Justice Newsletter," a publication of The National Council on Crime and Delinquency, Vol. 4, No. 23 (November 26, 1973), p. 1.

NINE

patrol manpower distribution

To my mind, the patrol force is the police department. To the extent the patrol force fails to achieve the police goal, specialized units within the police agency are necessary. Therefore, patrol administrators must manage manpower as if they were in business with a profit motive. Deployment of each officer should be done in a manner that optimizes cost effectiveness. The introduction of profit orientation into patrol distribution will be welcomed by leaders of the community and exhilarate tax-paying citizens who are overburdened no matter where they live in America.

For the patrol force to succeed, studies related to manpower distribution and equalization of workload should be completed. How much time should an officer spend on preventive patrol? What effect does the arrest rate have on crime? To what extent should an officer inspect police hazards on his beat? What is an acceptable response time to a call for service: two minutes? three minutes? What size should the patrol force be to achieve its goal? What should the task priorities be for each patrol officer during a tour of duty? What should be the workload of each patrol officer in order to have an equitable distribution?

There are no exact or easy answers. However, the citizens of any community have a right to the highest level of service the police department is capable of producing. Budget restrictions, personnel competence, volume of traffic service, calls for service, and criminal activity weigh heavily on the department's ability to provide service. Thus the patrol force should be distributed according to a proportional

351

need, geographically and temporally. To accomplish this, an analysis of statistical data is necessary.

To develop a data base that has a high degree of accuracy, a valid reporting system is essential. In order to determine the distribution of manpower, all factors contributing to the deployment must be documented. Police departments who arbitrarily distribute their patrol force by assigning equal numbers of personnel to each of three shifts (watches) are not providing that community with the highest possible level of service. Two other byproducts of the manpower distribution studies for patrol deployment are: (1) administrators are able to give an equal workload to each patrol officer, and (2) by assigning officers to regular beats, accountability of total police service can be given to specific officers and supervisors alike.

Chapter 4 discusses the mission of law enforcement as related to goals and priorities. In order to achieve the goals and priorities, a formula for manpower distribution can be developed that will be concomitant with the priorities. For example, if a community wants the patrol force to respond to all calls for service within one minute, a formula devised to distribute personnel in a manner capable of doing this is possible. But it must be understood that to the extent the formula favors one priority, the other tasks will suffer. In this case, the ability to reduce crime through preventive patrol and the inspection of police hazards by officers will be decreased.

In the management by objective approach to patrol administration, the objectives of patrol manpower distribution are to place the patrol officer in the right place at the right time to prevent crime; to develop a systematic approach to determine as accurately as possible the place and time; to use a businesslike approach (i.e., investment of each officer and the dividend expected as a management concept, assignment of officers to a beat of the size and configuration that equalizes workload and allows response to calls for service at an acceptable level of proficiency); to provide the officers time to inspect police hazards; to improve community support and cooperation; and to decrease the chance of calls for police service to back up.

While there are several approaches to the manpower distribution problem, all have the common denominator of workload by time of day, day of week, shift or watch, by the month, and reporting areas or census tract. The other factor of workload, classes of events, has been weighted according to expenditures of patrol time. This weighting simply distinguishes, for example, the amount of time necessary to investigate a simple larceny as opposed to a bank robbery. Therefore, using the proportionate-need distribution, the weight for the bank robbery would be more than the weight for the simple larceny or a simple assault. These weightings are not perfect, but until an improved system is developed, the assignment of weights according to classes of events is the best available.

A modification of the basic weighting for each individual police department would be a meaningful approach. Most weighting systems have allocated a lesser weight to accidents than to Part-I crimes; however, a close analysis has shown that at minimum, the weight of accidents should be increased from two to three and possibly four. Additionally, the following procedure is based on the author's experience in distributing patrol manpower.

COLLECTION AND ANALYSIS OF DATA

Before any workload studies can be accomplished, accurate data must be collected. In order to collect the data, a reporting system that insures the recording of every call for police service must be instituted. This is done by using a radio-complaint card. Personnel of the communication center initiate the complaint card and record a complaint number, date of occurrence, location of the incident by address, time officer dispatched, time of officer arrival at scene, time of return to service, and type of incident. (In a computer-assisted dispatching system, each call is recorded in the computer and is retrieved via the computer process.) The complaint card is then sent to the records section where the report written by the patrol officer is used to verify the validity of the incident and a reporting area number is placed on the complaint card. The complaint card is then filed and used at the time of the workload study. Usually the first workload study is attempted after the first year of data collection.

REPORTING AREAS

A *reporting area* is a section of the city the size of which is based upon an estimated amount of police work. One method used to devise a reporting area is to develop two reporting areas for each 1,000 population. Another method for designing reporting areas is to align the reporting areas with census tracts in order to develop data relative to population measurements and socio-economic factors. The method selected should be that which provides data compatible with the objectives of the respective police department. The method described here is designed primarily for providing distribution according to crime needs (preventive patrol), calls for service, and inspections or back-up calls.

The first step is to place a large map of the community on the wall. Second, experienced patrol commanders outline on the map, using different colors or shadings, areas of high, medium, and low crime. This is to design reporting areas to approximate size according to density of crime. If experience has shown a high level of crime in the downtown area, reporting areas should be made smaller. In outlying areas of the community where crime is low, reporting areas should be made larger. Patrol commanders should be advised that the reporting areas will be grouped together in order to create a patrol beat. Therefore, the boundaries of these reporting areas should follow natural boundaries, such as railroad tracks, main arteries, freeways, rivers, and bridges. Third, the reporting area boundaries will not change and should be numbered. Some reporting areas may consist of five or six city blocks in a straight line. This reporting area design usually occurs in the downtown area of the community.

This procedure is used prior to any accumulation of data. Once the data has been accumulated, the following procedure is used.

SAMPLING

The original map has each reporting area outlined. Since these reporting areas do not change and analysis of the workload necessitates making figures and making adjustments, clear acetate should be placed over the map. In this way, workload may be placed into the reporting areas and beat size and configuration may be adjusted without ruining the original map.

A sampling of 20 to 25% complaint cards (source documents) is then taken. The sampling should be spread over a six-month period, using equal numbers of each day of the week. For example, if the total number of calls for service for the department in the accumulated data for the year was 100,000, then 20,000 to 25,000 complaints or incidents would be analyzed.

The analysis would first categorize each incident according to:

Part-I Crimes (Index Crimes)
Part-I Arrests

All other offenses
All other arrests
Traffic accidents
Miscellaneous calls for service

WEIGHTINGS

Weights are assigned to the specific incidents based on the amount of time necessary for the patrol officer to properly handle the incident at the preliminary investigative stage and the seriousness of the event. The following weights are used as a part of this discussion.

Type of Incident	Weight
Part I crimes	
Murder	4
Rape	4
Robbery	4
Burglary	4
Aggravated assault	4
Larceny over $50	4
Auto theft	4
Part-II crimes	3
Arrests	2
Traffic accidents	2
Miscellaneous calls for service	1

In the case of traffic accidents, it is recommended that in-depth analysis be given in order to insure the most accurate weights. The list of incidents and weights is easily understood. For example, it would take twice as long to investigate a rape or robbery as it would to make an arrest, or it would take four times as long to investigate a burglary as it would to properly handle a call such as a sanitation complaint, parking violation, or loud party.

ANALYSIS

The next step is to determine the month of the year, hour of the day, day of the week, type of incident, and location (reporting area) of each incident. This means analyzing each of the 20,000 to 25,000 sampled incidents. This information is gleaned from the source document (complaint card). The most expeditious manner to do this is by using a computer. For example, code each list of information from the complaint card, key punch, and enter into the computer. The program of the computer would do the actual work and a printout would be received showing:

1. the number of incidents multiplied by the weight in each reporting area by shift (watch);
2. workload by day of week;
3. totals by time of day in hours;
4. "within-shift" variations in workload.

Within-shift variations means the optimum arrangements of working hours by shift, or what shift- (watch-) hour arrangement would cause the least internal variation of workload. The shift hours 0800, 1600, 2400 selected should be those that have least variation in that the difference in workload between hourly peaks and valleys regarding activity is minimized. This method will allow for the assignment of officers by shift, thus reducing the possibility of having too many or too few officers on duty at any given time.

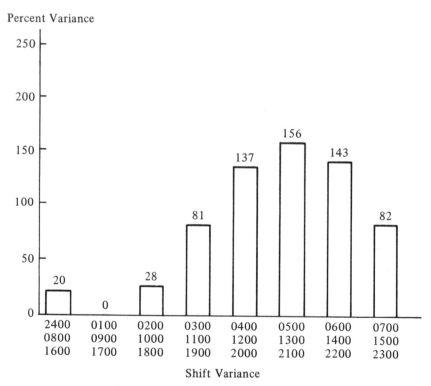

FIGURE 9.1 The least variance as indicated by the chart is when the shifts begin at 0100, 0900, and 1700. By changing shifts at this time, there is least variance from the *average* hourly workload.

SHIFT-CHANGE DECISION

When determining the basic shifts for the patrol force to operate, the decision should not be based on the within-shift variation alone. Personnel problems may arise if the selected shifts are unacceptable to the majority of personnel. Prior to announcing the new shift schedule, the potential consequences should be analyzed. For example, if the present shifts are changed at 0800, 1600, 2400, and the study reveals (as Figure 9.1 does) that the optimum change-of-shift time should be one hour later, the difference in variance may be of such a minor significance that what may be gained in efficiency would be lost in personnel/organization conflict. The decisions in the example cited would be right if either of the shift changes were selected. However, if in the same example, the existing shift change took place at 0300, 1100, 1900; or 0700, 1500, 2300; the change should be made to the 0100, 0900, 1700 because of the greater difference in variance.

Patrol administrators should not be lured into recommending decisions for the sake of efficiency alone. The production-oriented leader must keep in mind who is doing the producing. People-oriented leaders will consider the patrolman and balance decisions between people and production. The result will usually be maximum benefits in the long run.

ASSIGNMENT-AVAILABILITY FACTOR

The potential manpower for one year in a patrol force is eight hours a day for each patrol officer. A patrol officer would be assigned a beat, and the beat would be manned for a tour of duty. However, each officer will not man the beat each day because of several factors. To determine the number of officers necessary to man each beat, it is necessary to find out in hours what is potentially available and what is actually available due to the loss of officers' time because of these several factors.

The potential available hours for each officer is simply 365 days a year of eight-hour tours of duty (365 × 8), or 2,920 hours. The factors to be considered are vacations, regular days off, medical leave, training, holidays, military leave, court time, overtime, officers suspended from duty, and any other loss of time that may have a significant effect on the availability factor. Special details, officers acting as supervisors, and riot duty in other jurisdictions for extended periods should be considered in the miscellaneous category. Table 9.1 shows the calculations for one man.

POTENTIAL HOURS AVAILABLE		2,920
Vacation (10 days × 8 hours)	80.00	
Regular days off (102 days × 8)	816.00	
Medical leave (hopefully, 7 days × 8)	56.00	
Training (in-service 5 days × 8)	40.00	
Holidays (10 days × 8)	80.00	
Line-of-duty injury (?)		
Military leave (1 week × 8)	56.00	
Court time (4 days × 8)	32.00	
Overtime (?)		
Suspensions—Discipline (?)		
	1,160	
		1,160
		Remainder — 1,760

TABLE 9.1   Assignment-Availability Factor $\dfrac{2,920}{1,760} = 1.6$

Each factor in Table 9.1 should be computed on an individual department basis. Several of the factors will probably be different for many departments. For example, the question mark beside "line-of-duty injury," "overtime," and "disciplinary suspension" would be parochial to the department. Also, these ingredients may be so small they would not be significant. The vacation factor may differ, but in most cases, two weeks or ten days is usual. Two days off each week is the normal regular time off. Medical leave should be based on the average time and, hopefully, this will amount to approximately seven or eight days a year. The training factor may be different; however, most progressive departments can only afford forty hours per year for each officer.

Table 9.1 shows the assignment availability factor to be 1.6. This simply means that 1.6 officers must be assigned to each shift for every man actually on duty.

MAN-DAYS COMPARISON

In order to give the student a more realistic picture of an assignment availability factor, a patrol force of 100 officers is used as an example in Table 9.2.

Department X had 100 officers available for patrol duty during the past year. Manpower-distribution studies should be completed once each year. Therefore, the number of potential man-days for the coming year in Department X would be 100 × 365, or 36,500 man days. Using the same figures as in Table 9.1, the following computation would be made for Department X to determine the assignment availability factor.

POTENTIAL MAN-DAYS AVAILABLE		36,500
Vacation (10 days × 100)	1,000.00	
Regular days off (102 days × 100)	10,200.00	
Medical leave (hopefully, 7 days × 100)	700.00	
Training (in-service 5 days × 100)	500.00	
Holidays (10 days × 100)	1,000.00	
Line of duty (?)		
Military leave (7 days × 100)	700.00	
Court time (4 days × 100)	400.00	
Overtime (?)		
Suspension—discipline (?)		
	14,500.00	
		14,500
		Remainder—22,000

$$\text{Assignment Availability Factor } \frac{36,500}{22,000} = 1.6$$

TABLE 9.2   Department X 100-Man Patrol Force

FORMULA

Formula in manpower distribution studies refers to the amount of time the patrol administrator wants each officer to apply to the selected tasks. Some departments separate the tasks of the personnel on a shift into two distinct activities: one, responding to calls for service, and the other, to repressive or preventive patrol. The disadvantage of this method of distribution is the potential for boredom on the part of some officers and the label of "report-takers" on the part of others. Highly trained officers should not take reports of serious incidents without the opportunity to continue with the investigation at least on a limited basis. Experiments in this type of patrol assignment (separate tasks) should continue until proper evaluation can be made concerning the total patrol effectiveness.

Highly sophisticated computerized systems of manpower allocation and distribution are experimenting with forcasting assignments of patrol beats by the hour. A potential pitfall of this method is the loss of familiarity of officers who have permanent beat assignments. However, formulas that assign varying percentages of time within a tour of duty to different tasks may develop basic designs that could assist patrol forces across the country.

Another aspect of this split approach to patrol (calls for service and preventive patrol) is the potential for not developing the generalist police officer. Modifications can be made and have been made in the split approach for this aspect, but results are not yet complete regarding the total effect.

The formula used in most basic manpower distribution studies is to assign one-third of an officer's time to respond and handle calls for service, one-third of the time to be available for repressive patrol, and one-third allocated for citizen's calls to be grouped, as opposed to being equitably spaced throughout a tour of duty. (This one-third is sometimes referred to as "all other activities".)

BEAT REQUIREMENTS PER SHIFT

To determine the average time required to respond to a call for service and complete a preliminary investigation, time studies should be conducted. If it is not practical to do this, a department can use the standard average time factor of 45 minutes. The number of beats are then determined by applying (1) 45 minutes as the average for each call for service, (2) repressive patrol time and, (3) time necessary to reduce potential for cases to occur in groups.

SPECIAL ASSIGNMENTS

Other factors to consider in determining the number of beats are:
1. areas that may be of such small size and high density/volume of crime and need for service that an arbitrary decision is made in designating it a beat. These beats are usually in the high-crime, or downtown business areas and have a workload distinctly out of proportion to their size.
2. areas that are isolated (parks, lakes, etc.), and which need assignment of officers based on the distinct nature of the geographical area.
3. areas that are unique in terms of diversity, size and hazard potential. A good example of this type of area is the garment area of New York. Citizens are walking those streets with open, valuable property and an arbitrary assignment may be necessary.

Each patrol administrator in conjunction with his patrol commander can evaluate those areas of the community necessitating this type of patrol assignment. Additionally, depending upon the procedure used to transport prisoners, a wagon driver and partner may have to be assigned. Some vehicles used to transport prisoners require only one officer. These vehicles can be locked from the outside and a partner is not necessary. Another procedure requires the officer effecting the arrest to ride behind the wagon to the place of detention or holdover. Patrol administrators should review alternative procedures and select the one compatible with conditions in the community. In some cases, radio cars are equipped with screens and other equipment that makes them capable of transporting prisoners, thus reducing the need for special wagons.

The same type of decision should be made concerning assignment of station-house personnel. Desk sergeants or officers necessary for booking and turnkeys for searching prisoners and detention procedures (these officers may also be used for fingerprinting and photography procedures) are also assigned according to the need of the department. Civilian personnel and female officers are also available for assignment to desk duties.

NORMAL REQUIREMENTS

Continuing with Department X, which has 100 patrol officers available for patrol duty, the following calculation can be made using a sample number of incidents for the shifts 0100, 0900, 1700 hours. (2,100 sample incidents for Shift I, 0100 to 0900; 3,400 sample incidents for the 0900 to 1700 shift; and 4,700 sample incidents for the 1700 to 0100 shift.) The formula would be determined as follows:

SHIFT I   0100–0900

Number of incidents sampled (20% of total)	2,100
Converted to 100%	10,500 per yr.
Multiplied by .75 hours (45 minutes)	7,875 hours
Multiplied by 3 (This adds the repressive patrol time and time to reduce potential for cases to occur in groups. This is also known as "buffer time.")	23,625 hours

Divided by the number of hours necessary to man one patrol beat on one shift for one year (8 × 365 = 2,920 hours) = 8.09 or 8 beats

SHIFT II   0900–1700

Number of incidents sampled (20% of total)	3,400
Converted to 100%	17,000 per yr.
Multiplied by .75 hours (45 minutes)	12,750 hours
Multiplied by 3 (This adds the repressive patrol time and time to reduce potential for cases to occur in groups. This is also known as "buffer time.")	38,250 hours
Divided by the number of hours necessary to man one patrol beat on one shift for one year (8 × 365 = 2,920 hours) = 13.09 =	13 beats

SHIFT III   1700–0100

Number of incidents sampled (20% of total)	4,700
Converted to 100%	23,500 per yr.
Multiplied by .75 hours (45 minutes)	17,625 hours
Multiplied by 3 (This adds the repressive patrol time and time to reduce potential for cases to occur in groups. This is also known as "buffer time.")	52,875 hours
Divided by the number of hours necessary to man one patrol beat on one shift for one year (8 × 365 = 2,920 hours) = 18.1 =	18 beats

These figures do not take into account the possibility that days of the week may have large differences in workload. If this is the case, the same format would be used for those days with large volumes of workload, and assignments of beats would be made accordingly. Also, crime hazards are considered, since any incidents occurring as a result of crime hazards would manifest themselves in the total call for service statistics. Areas of high density and high-hazard locations as opposed to large residential areas and low-hazard conditions will be concurrently and proportionately covered by patrol because of the workload study of the previous year.

ONE- OR TWO-MAN BEATS

The next manpower decision to be made is the number of beats that need one-man coverage and the number needing two-man coverage. Most departments do not have enough manpower to assign two men to each beat. In most communities there are beats that should have two men assigned. Therefore, patrol administrators must make en-lightened decisions based on manpower and budgetary restrictions concerning which beats should be one-man and which should be two. When one-man beats are used, the team procedure between the dispatcher and the one-man car is essential.

The decision should be made after the following elements are considered:

1. Safety of the officer where beats are isolated due to natural barriers that preclude assisting officers from responding as back-up units in a reasonable amount of time
2. number of times arrests are made and resistance is offered by the arrestee
3. number of incidents in which multiple arrests are made
4. number of arrests where violence was involved—knife, gun, assaults
5. volume of calls for service
6. available access to area, density of population, street design, etc.
7. atmosphere of community (Does the area contain radical elements who have demonstrated attitude of dislike of police officers? Have threats emanated from the area causing belief that officers may be seriously injured?) Under certain conditions, it may be necessary to assign three-man cars or two two-man cars to the area. These conditions do not usually exist over an extended period of time; however, it is a very serious consideration.
8. the number of multiple dwellings on the beat. In high crime hostile areas, officers should not be required to be alone on upper floors. (Patrol officers should be consulted.)

Once the decision has been made regarding areas in which a two-man car should be assigned and the exact number of two-man cars, a participatory management approach is helpful. This means allowing officers and supervisors assigned to the selected areas to be involved in making the choice concerning the specific two-man beats.

TOTAL CALCULATION OF PATROL MANPOWER

After determining the number of one- and two-man cars necessary for each shift, the total number of men necessary to man each shift can be ascertained. The assignment availability factor will also be considered. If the same figures used in determining the number of beats for each shift are also used in this format, the following calculations would be made. An assumption can be made concerning the number of two-man cars on each shift: that it is necessary to have 2 two-man beats assigned to Shift I, 3 two-man beats assigned to Shift II, and 5 two-man beats assigned to Shift III.

SHIFT I—8 beats (2 two-man beats and 6 one-man beats)
The 8 beats require 4 officers to man the two-man beats and 6 officers to man the remaining one-man beats, for a total necessary strength of 10 officers. Allowing for the assignment availability factor of 1.6, it would be necessary to assign a total of 16 officers to Shift I.

SHIFT II—13 beats (3 two-man beats and 10 one-man beats)
The 13 beats require 6 officers to man the two-man beats and 10 officers to man the one-man beats, for a total strength of 16 officers. Allowing for the assignment availability factor of 1.6, it would be necessary to assign a total of 25.6, or 26 officers to Shift II.

SHIFT III—18 beats (5 two-man beats and 13 one-man beats)
The 18 beats require 10 officers to man the two-man beats and 13 officers to man the one-man beats, for a total strength of 23 officers. Allowing for the assignment availability factor of 1.6, it would be necessary to assign 36.8, or 37 officers to Shift III.

```
                    PATROL FORCE
                    Shift I   = 16
                    Shift II  = 26
                    Shift III = 37
                    Total     = 79 officers
```

BEAT SIZE, DESIGN, AND EQUALIZATION OF WORKLOAD

In order to have each officer's workload equal and so that all workloads together perform the total police mission, average workloads must be determined. This is done by shift. The first step is to total the workload for each shift by adding the weights of all the reporting areas. Then the total is divided by the number of beats for that particular shift.
For example, using the number of beats by shift in the previous illustration, the following method would be used.

SHIFT I—8 beats: If the total workload for Shift I calculated by adding the weights of the reporting area runs 8,000, then each beat should have a workload of 1,000.

SHIFT II—13 beats: If the total workload were 13,000, then each beat would have a workload of 1,000.

SHIFT III—18 beats: If the total workload were 18,000, then each beat would have a workload of 1,000.

The figures used are for explanatory purposes only; usually the workload would not be in rounded figures. The point is, that if each beat is designed to have a workload of 1,000 in each example, the officer workload will be equal. To achieve the size and design of the beat, simply add a number of reporting areas together until 1,000 is reached. In most cases, exact workload equalization is impossible. The totals in this case would probably be 990, 1,005, 1,010, 1,020, 980, etc. This is due to the fact that in high crime areas, the difference of one city block will change the workload drastically, while the same change in a low crime area will only affect the workload minimally.

Other factors to be considered in the design/workload relationship are neighborhood make-up, accessibility, a desire to have beat boundaries meet at high crime locations, and uniqueness of geography. Since population in the downtown areas of cities changes so drastically because of people going to work during the day, special attention to this factor is necessary.

Another consideration is the size of the beats in low-population areas (suburbs). If the beat is too big, even though statistical analysis indicates low workload, an officer cannot patrol it properly. It may take half an hour to travel from one end to the other, reducing the officer's effectiveness.

One beat that the author is familiar with contained 286 business establishments. Officers were required to patrol the beat on a priority basis. Businesses having alarm systems were inspected differently from those not possessing this security. This type of beat points out the real need for crime prevention through physical security. One goal of the officer on this beat was to stimulate the use of improved physical security.

In contrast to the large beat is the very small beat. Extremely high crime areas may have workloads reaching the average contained in one reporting area. In this case, the beat size is the same size as the reporting area and may be of a design one block by two blocks. If the decision is to leave the beat at this size, it should probably be a walking, bicycle, or motor-scooter beat. An alternative would be to raise the workload slightly to reduce officer boredom and allow for a larger beat, providing an automobile.

Beat size, design, and workload equalization are very real considerations, especially to the officers who are required to patrol them. Naturally, the workload study is done from statistical analysis on a scientific basis. However, if at all possible, patrol officers and patrol supervisors should be consulted on beat size and design if possible. Their in-depth knowledge of the area will supply information unavailable from statistics alone. This total approach by the patrol administrator will pay dividends for the department through employee motivation.

SUPERVISION

Span of control and unity of command are necessary principles of organization. Officers should report to one, and only one, supervisor. A supervisor should have a given number of officers working as part of his team. What is the optimum span of control? Who should lead the team when the supervisor is not there? Our example indicated 8 beats on Shift I. Should 1, 2, or 3 sergeants be assigned to the shift for supervisory purposes? A similar process for beat size and design is necessary. If sectors (supervisory areas of responsibility) are too large, supervisors will not see officers but once during a tour of duty. If sectors are too small and the workload not sufficient, then the assignment of too many supervisors would be a waste of manpower.

Each department should base the assignment of supervisors upon (1) level of sophistication of supervisory personnel; (2) level of sophistication of subordinate personnel; (3) geographical obstacles (community may be divided by natural boundary); (4) physical restrictions; (5) willingness to delegate authority; (6) patrol administrator's error in overestimating his ability and underestimating the ability of subordinates; (7) amount of support resources, communications, vehicles, etc.; (8) responsibilities regarding the number, complexity and priority of tasks (this relates to the objectives of the department, and the order of priority in which the different goals have been placed).

The number of supervisors necessary in the patrol force of evolving police agencies should be flexible and allocated on an individual department basis. As team-policing and horizontal-growth concepts progress, the new patrolman may not require as much supervision. The decision concerning the number of supervisors should be made in accordance with existing conditions.

When the decision is made, however, the assignment availability factor still exists. Shift III required 18 beats. How many sergeants are necessary to supervise that number of beats and officers? There are a total of 37 officers assigned to the shift. Should the shift be divided into 3 sectors with 6 beats in each sector? Should the number of sectors be 4 with the beats assigned 5, 5, 5, 3 respectively? All ingredients contained in the manpower distribution process must be weighed.

However, if the 18 beats were divided into 3 sectors, then 3 supervisors must be assigned. If the same assignment availability factor of 1.6 is used, then 4.8 or 5 supervisors must be assigned to Shift III. Each supervisor would then have a given number of two-man and one-man beats within his sector. Sector I, Shift III could contain 2 two-man beats and 4 one-man beats; Sector II, Shift III could contain 2 two-man beats and 4 one-man beats; while Sector III, Shift III would contain 1 two-man beat and 5 one-man beats. The assignment would look like this:

SHIFT III

Sector I	Officers	Sector II	Officers	Sector III	Officers
2 (two-man beats)	4	2 (two-man beats)	4	1 (two-man beat)	2
4 (one-man beats)	4	4 (one-man beats)	4	5 (one-man beats)	5
	8		8		7
Assignment availability	1.6	Assignment availability	1.6	Assignment availability	1.6
	12.8(13)		12.8(13)		11.2(12)

Total Assigned Patrol Officers to Shift III = 37.

Another technique requires the supervisor to select an officer of his team to replace the supervisor when he is off duty. Advantages of this method are (1) training of officer in the knowledge of supervisory responsibility; (2) understanding and awareness of supervisory problems; (3) motivation of subordinates to learn and develop themselves as individuals in job context and expand their education into other disciplines; (4) immediate feedback capable of improving supervisor performance; (5) available leader in times of emergency, riot, crowd disturbance, serious investigations, such as homicide, and injury to supervisor; and (6) budget savings in that fewer supervisors are needed. Disadvantages of this approach include (1) fewer supervisory positions may reduce incentive of officers; (2) conflict between officers selected to replace supervisor and the other officers, due to working in a supervisory capacity one day and an officer capacity the next; (3) potential jealousy between officers selected and those not selected; and (4) personnel conflict through charges of favoritism on the part of the supervisors.

If this method of distribution is used in patrol supervision, it is essential that written policy be disseminated to the force clearly outlining the procedure.

TOTAL PARTICIPATION

In order to develop the proper strength of the patrol force for each police department of the country, there must be total participation between police officers at all levels, as well as technological assistance. The most effective policies, tactics, and distributions according to time and location of patrol forces will be found through continued experimentation and research. Also, as each new method is developed, an exact evaluation must be made to determine the value for broad use by all police departments.

It is obvious to any patrol administrator that the most effective distribution of the patrol force is not equal distribution on three shifts. Proportionate need is the basis for distribution by time of day, day of week, and location. A system of weighting and calls for service has been presented in which each department modifies the procedure to match its individual needs. Emphasis must be given to good reporting so that the appropriate data may be collected, analyzed, and used accurately. The total plan must consider assignment availability factor, overlapping shifts where necessary, and the formulas for distribution. The formula selected should be based on the objectives of the department, which should be decided upon mutually between the chief executive, the community, and the chief of police.

Other methods of patrol resource allocation and distribution agree on the fundamental need for accurate reporting of crime so that data collected will reveal information of past conditions as well as data on predicted future conditions on which the allocation and distribution of manpower can be based. The reason for preferring the prediction method, as studied by those researchers who question the hazard and weighted workload method, is that these methods do not take into account interaction among factors; nor is any single factor focused upon; and they do not reflect meaningful measures of effectiveness to operational policy and are based upon past events.

Phoenix, Arizona, uses the concept differently. Three constructive innovations are used: (1) predicted calls rather than calls actually experienced in the past; (2) use of elapsed time rather than just volume of calls; and (3) allocation simultaneously by day, shift, and district rather than by district alone. However, preventive aspects of patrol are not addressed. Preliminary reports from Kansas City, Missouri, (see Chapter 7) question the value of preventive patrol.

St. Louis, Missouri, uses a method where demand for police service is predicted by hour and geographical area. A technique is then used to estimate the number of patrol cars needed to immediately answer, without dispatching delay, 85% of the predicted incoming calls for service in each geographic area by day and four-hour time periods. The remainder of the patrol force is assigned to preventive patrol. This method is limited in that role criterion used in the technique to determine the required number of response cars (i.e., the split of the patrol force into response and preventive patrol units) does not account for the fraction of calls that cannot be answered immediately by a response car. Requirements for preventive patrol are not explicitly considered when assigning cars and the question of the relative value of a car on response and on preventive assignments is not addressed.

Experiments such as that conducted in Kansas City and St. Louis, Missouri, and Phoenix, Arizona, should continue at a greater rate. There is a very real need to know if the methods of patrol deployment now being used are the most effective. New criteria upon which evaluation of patrol distribution can be based is developing. Reported crime vs. unreported crime, victimization rates, victimization probability, and simulation of patrol operations in a computer (now in progress at the Massachusetts Institute of Technology) are only part of a group of terms now being used in determining patrol deployment.

In a report prepared for the Department of Housing and Urban Development by the Rand Corporation of Santa Monica, California in 1971, the authors of the report, Sorrel Wildhorn and James S. Kakalik, recommended that research and experimentation be undertaken:

> (1) to identify the relationship between police preventive patrol activity and crime prevention, deterrence, and on-scene criminal apprehension; (2) to identify the quantitative and qualitative relationships between speed and type of police response, on the one hand, and crime rate, deterrence of crime, probability of on-scene apprehension, availability of witnesses, and the public's satisfaction with police patrol services on the other hand; (3) to predict crime and the volume of calls for police services, so that

police can be recruited and deployed based on more accurate knowledge of the need for police service in each geographic area and time period; (4) that improved methods for deploying patrol manpower be tested experimentally, modified if indicated by test results, and implemented.[1]

The authors are engineers and scientists in operations research, applying their talents to police problems. This is part of the total participation necessary to deploy our patrol forces at the right place and time to attain maximum effectiveness.

Police commanders who distribute the manpower of the patrol force in proportion to need have a ready answer to groups who exert pressure for special assignment of officers to specific areas. Proper distribution within an open police agency allows patrol leaders to present deployment practices to all citizens of the community honestly and professionally. Demands for increased patrol coverage in areas that do not show the need can be responded to with accurate data and pictorial displays. When citizens are allowed to examine police-deployment practices and professional procedures are obvious, confidence in the department is enhanced, fear of crime by the community is lessened, and support is more likely to be forthcoming. Patrol administrators who use the manpower-distribution process, make all patrol personnel aware of its goals, and allow participation, increase their ability to accomplish the leadership responsibility: "stimulate motivation of the patrol force to achieve the objective."

DEPLOYMENT SYSTEM PROCEDURES

The success of a patrol deployment system depends directly upon the support afforded by all personnel involved in the program. The active participation and willing cooperation of all personnel are greatly enhanced if representatives of all levels within the agency are included in the planning and implementation of the system.

Procedures for the implementation and ongoing operation of the system should be established and distributed in the form of agency directives from the police chief executive. These directives should provide procedural guidelines and detailed information on the need for an adequate and accurate deployment data base, the purpose of proportional need distribution of patrol personnel, and the objectives and goals of the deployment system.

Procedures should include periodic deployment-system evaluation based on timely information derived from an analysis of current patrol deployment data. Personnel allocations to geographic divisions or precincts in decentralized agencies should be evaluated and appropriately revised at least yearly. Shift, day of week, beat configurations, and personnel complements should be evaluated and appropriately revised at least quarterly.

Appropriate training programs should be established for all personnel involved in the system. The training should be tailored to the needs of personnel responsible for the various facets of the system, including the reporting, collection, and the analysis of deployment data, and the use, evaluation, and revision of the deployment system.

Provisions to insure the adequacy of deployment data and to facilitate the use of the data in allocating personnel should include the development of new forms and source documents, or the revision of existing reports, to accommodate the required information. Data source documents should be subject to supervisory review and approval to enhance the accuracy of the data base.[2]

NOTES

1. James S. Kakalik and Sorrel Wildhorn, *Aids to Decisionmaking in Patrol,* a report prepared for the Department of Housing and Urban Development, Rand Corporation. An overview of study findings by the authors was also reported in *Police* (February 1972), pp. 41–44.
2. National Advisory Commission on Criminal Justice Standards and Goals, Washington, D.C., 1972, *Report on Police,* p. 204.

TEN

special operations

Special operations are those that require flexibility in the deployment of personnel and the application of new patrol techniques to resolve complex problems facing the patrol administrator. Maximum use of personnel is developed by analyzing specific incidents which recur in a similar manner and under similar circumstances. Offensive methods of patrol should follow the analysis.

Patrol commanders, patrol supervisors, and patrol officers assigned to be the front line of special operations should have additional training in adaptability, crisis intervention, conflict, and confrontation. The critical performance of a patrol field commander is to achieve the goal when commanding an operational situation. Confrontation tactics require excellent planning and an ability to understand the people and the goals of those who may be involved. When a patrol commander resolves an explosive situation without loss of life or injury to the persons involved or to his men, he has succeeded in crisis confrontation. The ability to understand the issues (political, economical, etc.) and the persons involved in the issues comes from experience and analysis of the means and needs that might be used to achieve goals. One difficulty in the analysis comes from the intellectual dishonesty of persons involved in the issue. Patrol commanders should always be aware that words are just that, even when the words are used by persons who from all outward appearances should be trustworthy, and should be accepted objectively and with caution until credibility can be developed.

Another difficulty in the special-operations techniques of patrol is the application of responsibility, authority, and accountability. Inherent in the fact that flexibility and mobility are essential to the success of special operations is the fact that productivity must be measured in the totality of assignments, not an isolated task. Patrol administrators must require excellence in performance of all the assignments. Since these assignments change more quickly than, say, regular patrol operations, documentation of performance becomes quite complex. If, for example, special-operation forces are involved in saturation patrol to resolve a robbery or burglary problem and a school disruption or prison riot occurs, there is a movement of forces to the immediate school or prison problem. The particular problem may continue for days; therefore, continuity for evaluation purposes is lost. Special-operation forces (some departments may use the name "tactical," "task force," or "crime-control force") should be evaluated on the basis of their effect as it pertains to the assignment at hand, and their ability to move from one assignment to another maintaining swift superior response and activity. This does not mean that personnel should not be held accountable for each assignment. When squads are assigned to a high crime area, either prevention of the crime by decreasing crime incidents of the particular category or the arrest of perpetrators is, and should be, expected. Documentation of special-operation forces for accountability purposes is a must.

Commanders and officers of the special-operation forces should be highly skilled in tact and diplomacy; specific crime analysis as it relates to categories of crime (robbery, burglary, auto theft, etc.); some should have a knack for disguise, normal patrol, traffic, and investigative techniques; and the ability to adjust to the changing situations. Special training is necessary in the area of:

1. Prevention-apprehension/Prevention-apprehension theory
2. Individual officer vs. team-officer concept
3. Riots and related crowd control
4. Mob psychology
5. Small, large, and campus demonstrations
6. Squad formations, wedge, diagonals, etc.
7. Racial and ethnic groups
8. Chemical agents
9. Special weapons, including nonlethal
10. Labor relations; strikers, picket lines
11. First aid
12. Barricaded persons and snipers
13. Youth-oriented performances
14. Primary-secondary mission concept

15. Pyramid of forces
16. Mobile and stationary stake-outs
17. Mobile command posts
18. Disaster control
19. Prison disorders

PREVENTION, APPREHENSION/PREVENTION, APPREHENSION THEORY OR 23-HOUR, 59-MINUTE THEORY

The traditional theory of prevention for patrol and apprehension for detectives should be reviewed in today's police world because of the concepts of team policing and special-operations forces. Jealousy and mistrust between these two operating units should be ended and total teamwork become the byword of all police departments. Many departments are using the policy of placing information transferral on official reports to decrease the possibility of patrol officers losing deserved credit in solving cases. This method documents the time and manner in which information received affected the solution of a particular case. Some patrol administrations have meticulously analyzed preliminary investigations to assure that full and complete information is passed on to detectives in order to avoid duplication and wasted energy, hoping that this effort will produce a reciprocal attitude and set an atmosphere of cooperation. The other aspect, or crime prevention, was discussed in Chapter 7. The concept of apprehension prevention, or the 23-hour, 59-minute theory, is based upon the following factors: (1) Saturation patrol can prevent and assist apprehension; (2) Professional criminals, or those criminals who take the time to plan, cannot be prevented from committing crime as opposed to those criminals who are mere opportunists; (3) Police coverage of a criminal target, say a liquor store, can occur by placing a patrol officer in front of the store for 23 hours and 59 minutes and thereby prevent the store from being robbed, but the minute the officer leaves the assignment, the professional criminal who plans, will strike; (4) The cooperation of special-operations forces and the detective unit evolves from a goal of mutual benefit, caused by the zeroing in on the professional through the use of saturation patrol (both uniformed and plainclothes patrol), detective follow-up, including the technique of mobile and stationary stake-outs; plainclothes officers disguised as street cleaners, truck drivers, door-to-door salesmen (decoy squads); (5) This mutual benefit is that the arrest of the individual will cause an increase in the clearance rate for detectives and a stoppage of any further crimes being committed, thereby causing a decrease in crime (no more multiple offenses); (6) This effort, even though performed flexibly and on a need basis will enhance teamwork, since the total application is necessary in most cases; (7) Juvenile officers, who are intimately familiar with the workings of juvenile court and diversion techniques, will improve upon the team effort if persons arrested are in this category.

One method used by the author when an attack on crime involved this theory was an in-depth analysis of reports and an acting-out of the crimes in a simulated manner (stopping before the commission of an offense) by disguised police officers. An example of this method follows.

The crime of dwelling burglary, committed in an area one-half mile square, was studied. Reports indicate method of entry and egress, articles taken, vehicles used, etc. Special-operation officers would enter the area and use the same methods as could be perceived the perpetrator would use, all the while observing patrolling officers' activities. This hypothetical and simulated exercise revealed many interesting deficiencies. Additional information and training were needed to alleviate these problems. Inspection following these simulations and corrections improved officers' capability, regarding legal considerations, stop and frisk, probable cause and its development, patrol techniques and observation, maximum effectiveness while on foot patrol, etc.

It is recommended that patrol administrators use these methods in their respective areas. The results will be surprising. One patrol supervisor actually had two of his officers walk by another officer carrying a television set in order to determine the need for guidance and counseling in the area of probable cause and stop and frisk. This method should not be attempted without appropriate consideration being given to the safety of all concerned.

The goal of teamwork can be achieved with continued task force, team policing, apprehension/prevention experiments if communication, planning, understanding, and a desire for success on the part of the leaders of each participating unit are shown preceding the application and implementation.

INDIVIDUAL OR TEAM CONCEPT

From the time an officer enters a police department he is trained to operate as an individual, making individual decisions and judgments about situations as each arises. Officers are also trained during the latter part of their recruit experience in crowd control and other team-related situations. For the most part, this training is necessary and should be continued. However, it is exactly as stated: training, and will convey only so much reality.

Officers working platoons or regular patrol function on an individual basis more often than not. When compared to special-operations officers, there is a gap between the degree of adjustment necessary to change from the individual to the team-member concept. The amount of training necessary for each group will be determined by the size of the department and the number of occasions on which officers must change from the individual to the team member.

Special-operation officers are usually members of a squad made up of a sergeant and twelve patrolmen. Again, the size of the department will have an effect on the content of the squad since the smaller department may use a sergeant and ten patrolmen or a sergeant and five patrolmen.

Special-operations officers must understand the need to remain a part of the team when responding to situations requiring the team effort. An assignment for a platoon of special-operations officers may be to saturate a given area of the community to combat robbery. Planning has taken place, and team assignment and rotation procedures are in effect. Officers are responsible for specific beats and are held accountable. Individual performance is being evaluated. Sometime during the evening an explosive situation occurs where the platoon must be reassembled to act as three squads in the team concept. Officers are now required to act as a part of a four-man fire team or a part of an arrest team. Emphasis must be placed on the importance of not acting alone, but always as a member of the team. Safety of all concerned is paramount in this consideration and maximum effectiveness during these conditions is based upon the unit-team effort. Officers should be advised that where an arrest is necessary, the team should execute it. Additionally, there is less chance for resistance and less chance for anyone being injured when this concept is used. Performance of assignments while in this posture are accomplished by teams and individual performance is discouraged. It should, however, be pointed out that exceptions will be made where the saving of a life is involved.

Patrol commanders should insure that each supervisor and officer is aware of the difference and need when performing as the individual officer and as the team member. This is especially true when the commander has a situation where he decides to make arrests. The procedure used in performing the arrests under these circumstances is most important, since the success of prosecution and possibly the outcome of the confrontation may depend on efficient operations.

There have been many cases where officers have not been able to identify persons arrested on the particular violation, resulting in dismissal of the case. Arrest teams should practice arrest procedures in a simulated fashion so when the real thing arises, the goal is achieved. Persons "arrested" should be matched up with a specific officer so that reliable testimony can be given as to the time, place, and specific offense. One way is for the officer to have his photograph taken with the prisoner.

Another method is to use flexicuffs (plastic handcuffs) in the following manner. Officers would receive several sets prior to the incident. Each officer would sign his name on the cuff, and a code would be given to specific violations. The list of violations (with matching code numbers) that are more likely to occur, such as disorderly conduct, assault, malicious destruction, looting, and arson, would be disseminated throughout the force. When arrests are made, the officer would add the code, time, and location. (Officers stationed on the mobile-detention vehicles would carry the pens to mark the cuffs or arrest teams could be provided with several pens.) When the prisoners were taken to a holding facility and photographed, the officer's name on the cuffs would then be attached to the photograph along with the cut flexicuff, and filed under the name of the officer. When an officer arrived for a hearing, he would merely ask for his name and would automatically be matched with his prisoner. However, the procedure of taking the photograph of the officer and prisoner together is preferred.

These situations can be very sensitive and, if possible, teams of police photographers should be on hand to film the professional performance of the force.

RIOTS AND RELATED CROWD CONTROL

Nowhere in police work is the capability of a patrol administrator more obvious than at the time of critical confrontations involving unlawful assembly and riot. Planning, coordinating, deploying personnel, organizing, and supporting are all part of administering the patrol force in its performance during these crisis situations. Planning is the first step. Every department should possess a mobilization plan. It is recommended that the plan be written in stages in order to obtain maximum effectiveness of manpower and avoid any waste due to overdeployment.

Flexibility of forces and their ability to respond to locations promptly is a key to controlling explosive situations. Many experienced patrol leaders agree that there is a direct relationship between resolving potential civil disorders and the ability to respond and handle situations promptly, intelligently, and with the appropriate number of personnel. A practical method for evaluating the special-operations force ability is to select a location having the potential for disturbance and request special-operation forces to respond. The simulation will keep the officers in training as well as indicate possible areas of improvement. The knowledge that the patrol commander and his officers are ready and capable should instill an excellent esprit de corps.

Planning should also include the definition of each stage and its use; a call-up system that allows all off duty officers to report. Most departments use a pyramid call-up system. The procedure is based on superiors calling a given number of subordinates. For example, a sergeant with twelve (12) officers reporting to him would call three (3) key patrolmen and each of these three (3) key patrolmen would contact three (3) other patrolmen. A police-department headquarters' command post must be established and responsibilities for its implementation and conduct during the emergency clearly defined. In conjunction with this, a procedure for field-command posts and accompanying operational guidelines should be established. Consideration must be given to the initiation of twelve-hour shifts, time and shift schedule. When the twelve-hour periods begin, field commanders must be assigned and specific responsibilities for different areas of the community understood by each field commander. Additionally, locations of staging areas for officers to report and locations of field-command posts should be identified along with sensitive locations such as pawnshops, liquor warehouses, and gun dealers. In some situations the location of the staging area and the field-command post can be the same; for example, a shopping center, school playground, or athletic field, downtown street and public building.

Support planning or logistics includes: assignments of communications personnel and physical security for the police buildings; emergency arrest; booking and detention procedures; property security (personal and evidence).

Assignments must be made to accomplish military liaisons in

case National Guard or federal troops would have to be called in. Personnel assigned on military liaisons should have a working knowledge of military terminology in order to translate police and military terms, and the ability to coordinate maps between military and police indicating sensitive and explosive areas. (Civil defense liaison will be included in the section on natural disasters.)

Crowds develop at parades, athletic contests, and school dances and usually can be safely handled. At times, however, a crowd ignites into an unlawful assembly or riot. Crowds also show up at political rallies or demonstrations in different numbers and each situation must be judged on its merits. There are certain signs that patrol administrators might look for which may indicate the potential for disorder. Several assassinations of police officers took place across the country after pamphlets had been distributed saying, "Kill the Pigs." Police veterans may tell you it is an atmosphere, and you can almost feel the oncoming disorders. Some other signs of potential disorders are outright hostility toward officers, unfounded accusations of police brutality, threats of violence toward police in a general way, and an increase in the number of times officers need assistance in making what ordinarily would have been a routine arrest. All of these signs should be analyzed for hidden intent.

The patrol field commander arriving at the scene of a disturbance must not forget his mission. Protection of life and property and restoring peace and tranquility are fundamental. The assessment made by the patrol field commander will guide the optional capability of the patrol force and department. The number of personnel and the type of equipment necessary to accomplish the mission is the field commander's judgment and must be communicated immediately so that these forces can be accumulated as quickly as possible. This is the first act of the field commander. After this is done, he may resort to whatever dialogue he might think has a chance of quelling the situation without the use of force. The patrol field commander should always remain flexible and control as many alternatives as possible. This position allows the commander to reciprocate as needed.

If the assessment indicates the need to act, remember you never bluff. Before you make a move, think out the consequences of the move. If you attempt to disperse a crowd with too little personnel, the end result may be looting and arson, with your men arresting people who may be charged with disorderly conduct, while the looters and arsonists escape. You do not want the disorder to spread. Therefore, before the order to disperse is given (the use of a bullhorn is recommended because it can be carried with you), cover your flanks, have the teams available to arrest, and cordon off the area to avoid the spread of destruction. Usually the first order to disperse will cause the onlookers who have no real interest to leave. The second group who may be interested, but not to the point of arrest, will usually leave after the second order. The momentum should be carried forward and action taken at this point should result in the successful conclusion of the incident within the rule of law. Smaller departments that do not have the personnel to achieve the goal of disturbance control should formulate mutual-aid pacts with other jurisdictions adjacent to their communities.

A SOCIOLOGICAL ANALYSIS OF MOBS

Sociologically, a crowd "is a temporary, largely unorganized group of persons in physical proximity to one another and mutually influencing each other to a significant extent."

The phrase "to a significant extent" is important to the definition. Twenty men watching the construction of a new building are not a crowd. They do not have much intercommunication, and they influence each other only nominally, if at all.

Police history is replete with examples where a little training and knowledge of human mass behavior would have prevented serious incidents, and in many instances loss of life would have been prevented.

Types of Crowds

Basically, crowds may be divided into three subdivisions. The "sidewalk superintendents" gathered around a building under construction, although not a true crowd, may be classified as a *casual crowd* or a *physical crowd*.

The *expressive crowd* is usually a controlled crowd. Not all crowd behavior is spontaneous, this type of crowd requiring little policing and seldom becoming riotous.

The *acting crowd* is one that becomes organized around a particular purpose, its behavior directed toward the achievement of that objective. One example of an acting crowd is a *mob*. When a crowd becomes a mob, restraint and control are lost. Mobs are characteristically emotional and always irrational. Most members of a mob have a temporary common feeling with the other members of a mob. Certain principles apply themselves to mobs in general, and mobs, according to their intent, can usually be classified by type, and as having the following specific characteristics:

1. *An aggressive mob* riots and terrorizes, as in the case of race riots, lynchings, political riots, and prison riots.
2. *An escape mob* is in a state of fright, attempting to secure safety by flight. Panic creates an escape mob. In their panic, members of the escape mob have lost their power of reasoning and may go so far as to destroy each other unless controlled.
3. *An acquisitive mob* is motivated by a desire to acquire something. The mobs in food riots are acquisitive mobs. An acquisitive mob frequently results as the aftermath of an aggressive mob.
4. *An expressive mob* is a mob expressing fervor or revelry, such as following some religious activity, a sports event, or New Year's Eve celebration. An expressive mob is seldom of such proportions as to be capable of overpowering police forces.

Sociological Influences That Work in Favor of the Agitator

Why do peaceful people participate in mob actions? What is there about a large crowd or mob atmosphere that causes a person to react differently than he does in his normal day-to-day living? Factors contributing to abnormal behavior:

1. Novelty: When an individual is confronted by new and strange circumstances, the habits which he has formed may not be fully operative.
2. Anonymity: When an individual is with a mob, he may tend to lose self-identity, because his identity may merge with that of the mob.
3. Release from repressed emotions: In a mob, the prejudiced and unsatisfied desires of the individuals, which are normally held in restraint, are readily released.
4. Force of numbers:
   a. The size of a mob gives the individual a sense of power and a desire to use it.
5. Heightened suggestibility:
   a. a group will accept the idea of a dominant personality. Ideas spread without raising thought or objection on the part of the individuals.
   b. People in a mob action are not aware of the real causes of their difficulty, or at least are not convinced of them. Because of this lack of understanding they readily accept the ideas of a leader.
6. Emotional contagion:
   a. People are curious.
   b. People become emotionally stimulated by the actions of others even though they may not share the grievance from which the emotion originated.
7. Conformity: The urge to do what others do is always very strong.

The mob is quick to sense fear, indecision, poor organization and training on the part of officers, and will take instantaneous advantage of it. The responsibilities placed on the officer, therefore, are important if he is to maintain the public tranquility and well-being.

Riot control is not dependent upon individual acts of heroism, but rather upon perfectly executed tactics and maneuvers of a group of officers dedicated to teamwork, mutual support, and a high degree of *esprit de corps*.[1]

MOB PSYCHOLOGY

The most important thing a patrol commander must remember in confronting a mob or in crowd control is to have enough manpower available to accomplish the mission with the minimum use of force. Police action should never be the catalyst to precipitating the potential for destruction and violence into reality. Without sufficient manpower, it is more likely extra forces will have to be used later and thus cause the escalation of events. Patrol supervisors should be advised to respond to any incident where the potential for mob violence exists and remove the originating cause. If this is an arrest situation, the prisoner(s) should be removed from the area as soon as possible. This procedure should be strictly enforced.

Most situations of this type are sensitive and the proper method to use after a crowd has gathered is not absolute. Many times the number of personnel on the scene is sufficient to quell any violent action. There may be other situations where the best method is to station the majority of officers in a reserve or standby position readily available in case of need. Undercover officers who are familiar with the area and the issues can, and usually do, identify leaders of any large gathering and relate the mood and attitude conveyed. Intelligence information and experience will guide the action of the force in each situation. The enlightened patrol commander, however, will always maintain sufficient strength to meet the situation.

Other aspects to plan for in this situation would be:

1. Types of leaders and the best procedure to remove them and disperse crowd at the same time.
2. Obvious agitators, their positions in relationship to crowds (center, periphery)
3. Assessment of mood of participants.
4. Determination of course of events and at what point action would

gain maximum benefit. This is a judgment on the part of the patrol commander. If he waits too long, the course of events may reach a point where it is too late to act. If he acts too soon, the results may be chaotic with charges of violation of civil rights to peaceful assembly, etc.

5. If action is taken, what routes are to be left open for participants to leave? Streets leading to business districts would be blocked and other streets open. This will allow people to leave without tempting emotional reaction of some to break glass windows.

6. Who will use bullhorn or public address system to give the order to "move on"? It may be necessary for more than one patrol commander to do this due to the size of the group. Coordination should be planned.

7. News coverage of the incident. Progressive police agencies realize the value of accurate news dissemination to the community. Also, charges of police brutality can more easily be challenged, and openness in police procedures will enhance the professional image.

SMALL DEMONSTRATIONS

This is the age of demonstrations. Whatever the size, manpower must be assigned to insure peace. Manpower is a precious commodity, therefore should not be wasted at all. Planning for the small demonstrations should include intelligence information, intent and purpose of the demonstration, times indicated that the demonstration will take place, and identification of potential troublemakers. If at all possible, meet with the leaders of the demonstration to lay the ground rules under which the demonstration will take place. The meeting will decrease the possibility of misunderstanding and lessen the possibility of minor disagreements developing into real problems.

Deployment at the scene should be minimal, with reserve forces performing other tasks unless needed. Places for forming up into squads should be clearly understood by all so that response to the location is timely.

LARGE DEMONSTRATIONS

There is always the possibility of a large demonstration developing into a riot situation because of the lack of control alleged leaders of the demonstration hold over the many participants. What should the patrol administrator do to decrease this possibility? The first consideration is to determine if communication should be established. Past experience of policing demonstrations where the present leaders were involved will determine the need for this step. If a meeting does take place, it should be cordial and candid, and there should be no doubt in anyone's mind about the reaction of police to a given set of circumstances. These rules should be communicated politely but with firmness, so that the whole episode begins with the police commander in a position of authority.

Intelligence personnel should provide confidential, reliable, and valuable information. This information has a direct bearing on the manpower needed to provide coverage for the demonstration.

Personnel should be deployed in a manner that allows for response by a squad or a platoon or several platoons as the need requires. Patrol commanders should be briefed about the importance of communicating, at any given time, information about the demonstration concerning (1) fact, (2) rumor, (3) size of demonstration, (4) location of demonstration, (5) attitude of demonstrators, (6) attitude of leaders, (7) possible intent of groups and demonstrators in totality. Support, as stated earlier, should include arrests, and booking and detention assistance. Mobile jails can be stationed at locations that offer the greatest potential for unlawful acts that would lead to an arrest.

The patrol commander should be prepared to respond swiftly with enough force to snuff out any demonstration that develops or may develop into a riot. Planning is essential, training is a must, and decisiveness on the part of the field commander should be inspiring. A well-disciplined patrol force with special-operation personnel using the team concept and the military formation of the squad wedge, diagonal, and line, should be able to move demonstrators in a professional manner. Additional help in this area is given by officers whose personal appearance commands respect, projects a cool, mature image, shows sensitivity where applicable, and enough force when needed.

During demonstrations and riots, newsmen are all over the place seeking information. If at all possible, a public-information officer should be available. Orders instructing the force to refer all inquiries concerning the incident to the public-information officer should be disseminated. Also, updating of the public-information officer by operational personnel should be required.

CAMPUS DEMONSTRATIONS

One of the major problems in responding to campus demonstrations is being placed in the unenviable position of "bad guy." Patrol administrators should not allow indecisive school administrators to place the police in a position of "opposing force." Questions concerning the legal position of the police on campus should be answered. For example, When is someone trespassing, and Who will act as a complainant? At what stage will the police be requested to take action? Will the police be expected to be baby sitters?

Remember patrol commanders, administrative disagreements over rules, regulations, traditions, etc. between the administrators of the school and the students are just that: between the school administrators and the students. The police should not get involved in this aspect. Naturally, overt acts of destruction should not be tolerated and arrest should be swift and sure where appropriate.

The leaders of the patrol force assisting a school should meet with the campus security chiefs and school administrators to develop workable procedures. Careful analysis of the issues and possible answers and consequences are key aspects. The use of chemical agents as a primary tool is recommended for campus disorders. Because of the wide-open area of many schools, it will be necessary to have available the pepper-fogger and gas-grenade launching equipment. These tools will allow you to keep distance between the disruptive students and their goals, which will lessen the possibility of injury to anyone. As in any similar situation, action if taken should be swift and sure, always thinking about the consequences of each action and insuring that strength is available to complete the action.

BARRICADED PERSONS AND SNIPERS

Experience has shown that undisciplined firepower and confusion are readily attained when dealing with reported snipers or armed persons barricaded in a home or building. The need for fire discipline, a calm and decisive leader, and a written procedure understood by all is essential. Add to this, good weapons and training, and a successful conclusion to these explosive situations is readily achievable.

The critical confrontation between police and barricaded persons or snipers is one of the most sensitive situations challenging the patrol administrator and the patrol force.

No two situations are exactly alike, but with planned operational procedures and special-operations teams, sometimes known as SWAT (Special Weapons And Tactics), patrol commanders can minimize the potential loss of life and property. The primary officer responding to the location of a reported sniper or barricaded person should first determine the reliability of the report. If the report is true, call for assistance, evacuate innocent citizens, cordon off the area, and determine the location of the perpetrator if possible. When assistance arrives, and patrol supervision responsible for the areas should be prompt, assignments should be made in an effort to prevent escape, and a mobile command post set up. The SWAT team should be responding to the location of the incident. During this period, the senior patrol officer on the scene should maintain strict fire discipline and begin to determine if possible:

1. identification of perpetrator;
2. identification of perpetrator's relative, friends, etc.;
3. if there are any witnesses to incident and if so, interview for any pertinent information;
4. what weapons are possessed by the perpetrator;
5. if hostages are being held;
6. the mental condition and probable intent of the perpetrator.

It is imperative to remember that fire discipline is essential. Revolvers are usually inadequate during these situations, and random firing may cause serious injury to innocent citizens and possibly a fellow officer. The detailed methodical approach by a trained SWAT team is the more enlightened course of action. If the area is cleared, there will be no target for the perpetrator. If there is no target, there will be no personal injury. The makeup of the SWAT team will depend upon the capabilities and training of the special-operations force personnel and the resources available to the department.

It should be presumed that all persons involved in these situations are dangerous and extreme caution should be used. This is especially true where steps to develop a dialogue with the individual are taken. If this is a possibility, it should be done prior to the use of force. Another alternative, depending on the situation, is the use of chemical agents; therefore, gas masks should be considered along with bullet-proof vests.

The patrol commander in charge of this police action must demonstrate by example the qualities of leadership necessary to take firm command of the situation. Leadership qualities such as decisiveness, judgment, sensitivity, knowledge, and confidence should permeate the operation and cause all officers involved to respond similarly, resulting in a professional performance.

YOUTH-ORIENTED PERFORMANCES

Special-operation forces are usually the front-line officers in any explosive situation, and one of the special talents of these officers is to be able to relate to the young people of the country. Police agencies across the country are confronted with rock festivals and vacationing youths on the West Coast in California and East Coast of Florida at vacation times. Urban police forces are expected to control the thousands of young people who exit the amphitheaters of our cities in a high-pitched emotional state. All of these situations are sensitive, and tact, firmness, and good planning are necessary to reach a successful conclusion.

When force is necessary, enlightened leadership must provide the proper procedure to prevent escalation to the point of riot. One preventive measure that has proven successful in the past is to request the promoters and performers of these youth-oriented activities to slow down the tempo at the end of each performance. Those persons who have cooperated in this area have generally found a more receptive government when applying for future performance dates. When the emotional state of the youths has been low-keyed by this procedure, they usually exit in an orderly manner. Tension is reduced, and opportunity for unruly conduct is lessened by this preferable atmosphere.

Cooperation and coordination between local police and special police officers (private security) hired for these events can help reduce potential disorder. Opening of some exits and closing of others or opening of all exits, as the case may be, will automatically route pedestrian traffic into an area which reduces crowded conditions and is most convenient for the police agencies. The less time youths are milling around waiting for traffic to move, the less chance of an incident arising that may precipitate disorder.

Public transportation officials are most helpful in supplying buses for immediate service in order to reduce the amount of time youths must stay in a crowded atmosphere outside the facility. Liaison between special-operation forces and public and private transportation officials will result in a sufficient number of vehicles being ready for a prompt exit of the crowd from the area.

Planning for these performances will depend upon experiences from the past and information from the law-enforcement agencies confronted with similar situations. Special-operation forces should provide a sufficient number of personnel according to the estimate of the crowd, type of performance, and location of the performance. Provisions should be made for security of businesses if the performance takes place in or near a business area. Some departments use K-9 teams for this type security. Also, traffic personnel should be strategically placed to insure maximum effort in movement of traffic. Arrest teams and procedures for moving prisoners swiftly from the area should be available if arrests become necessary. Weather predictions should be reviewed to determine specific plans regarding the use of chemical agents (wind speed and direction) and probable change in plans due to inclement weather.

Also, one of the more important considerations would be the acquisition of additional manpower in case they are needed and determination of the lead time. (How long will it take the manpower to arrive at the scene from the time requested until the time they reach the scene?) This information should be broken down into minutes. For example, would the special-operation force commander have ten men on the scene fifteen minutes after requested? How many would respond to the scene in twenty minutes? Thirty minutes?

Youth groups are difficult to predict, and contingency plans must be completed in full.

PRIMARY-SECONDARY MISSION CONCEPT

In most cases, the primary mission of the patrol force and the special-operation forces will relate to crime. The patrol force will be distributed according to workload studies, and special-operation forces will supplement as needed at the times calls for service deluge the regular patrol and normally in the highest crime areas of the community. The decision to move the special-operations forces from their primary mission to the secondary mission of crowd control or one of the many other tasks will depend upon time, location, and manpower. If the primary mission of the special force on a given day is in the western part of the community and a youth-oriented performance is taking place in the downtown business district, clear instructions to the special forces about the time and method of transition is necessary. If the time frame for the shift is 1800 to 0200, and the exit for the performance is approximately 2300, the move from the primary mission should be made in such a manner that minimum time is lost from the primary mission but officers are at their assigned location for the secondary mission in time to fulfill their responsibility. Each officer should be used for maximum effectiveness. Careful review and assignment of tasks will allow for minimum waste of effort. The use of the primary-secondary mission concept in conjunction with the pyramid of forces allows the patrol administrator to obtain tremendous gains from the limited resources available.

PYRAMID OF FORCES

Webster's *New World Dictionary* supplies the following definition for the word "pyramid":

> To engage in a series of buying or selling operations during an upward or downward trend in the stock market, working on margins with the profits made in the transaction.

The conscientious patrol administrator realizes he is involved in work where margin is important. Increased manpower is not easily obtained. The fluctuating market of crime, crowd control, and potential disorders (schools, campuses, prisons) must be met with the special tool of flexibility and deployment to meet the changing situation. The profit in the transaction of primary-secondary mission concept and pyramiding of forces is the ability to make ten men look like a hundred. This may be somewhat exaggerated. However, it is intended to emphasize what this concept may bring about in terms of reduction of crime and meeting needs of the many tasks required of a special-operations force. For a patrol administrator to take the offensive in crime and still fulfill the other tasks, he must conduct intensive and timely research to identify those crimes most susceptible to the patrol techniques he intends to apply and then pinpoint the time and location of these particular crimes.

Another effort that must be made on his part is to coordinate the concept of saturation patrol along with the other two concepts of primary-secondary mission and pyramid of forces. This is not easy and takes an intense desire on the part of the patrol chief and each special-operations commander, supervisor, and officer. However, the impact of this type of planning and dedication cannot be measured until implemented by each patrol administrator, and the specific impact will apply to each department respectively. Personnel should be assigned on the basis of need. Manpower distribution is a way of discovering the need of the regular patrol force. Special-operations forces are usually manned as a result of need, but the exact number is difficult to reach, since there is no formula that can be equated to the flexibility necessary. Police chiefs and patrol administrators must reach the decision on an individual departmental basis. One department in a large urban area may have a special-operation force of 500 men while another department whose total complement is 100 may have a special force of only 5 men and a supervisor. Whatever the number, it is possible to make the 5 look like 50 and the 500 look like 5,000 on the offensive in crime and other complex tasks.

Here is an example to which all patrol administrators may relate, increasing or decreasing the principle and manpower according to the individual department. The special-operation force of city Y shall contain the following personnel: 1 lieutenant, 5 sergeants, and 25 officers. The span of control for the lieutenant is 1–5 and for each sergeant, also 1–5. There are 5 teams of special-operations forces. After an intensive review of crime reports, using the crime of robbery, the information shown in Figure 10.1 was gleaned.

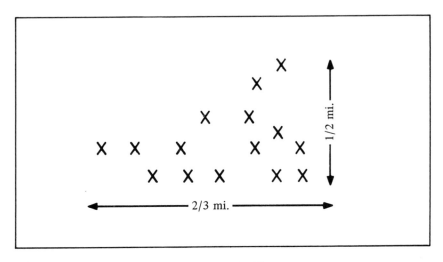

FIGURE 10.1 City Y.
X = Location of Robbery.

The attack on this problem will use the patrol method of foot, plainclothes, car, etc. One important consideration to remember is aggressive patrol officers will become bored if confined to a very small area (say the size of a regular patrol beat in a high crime

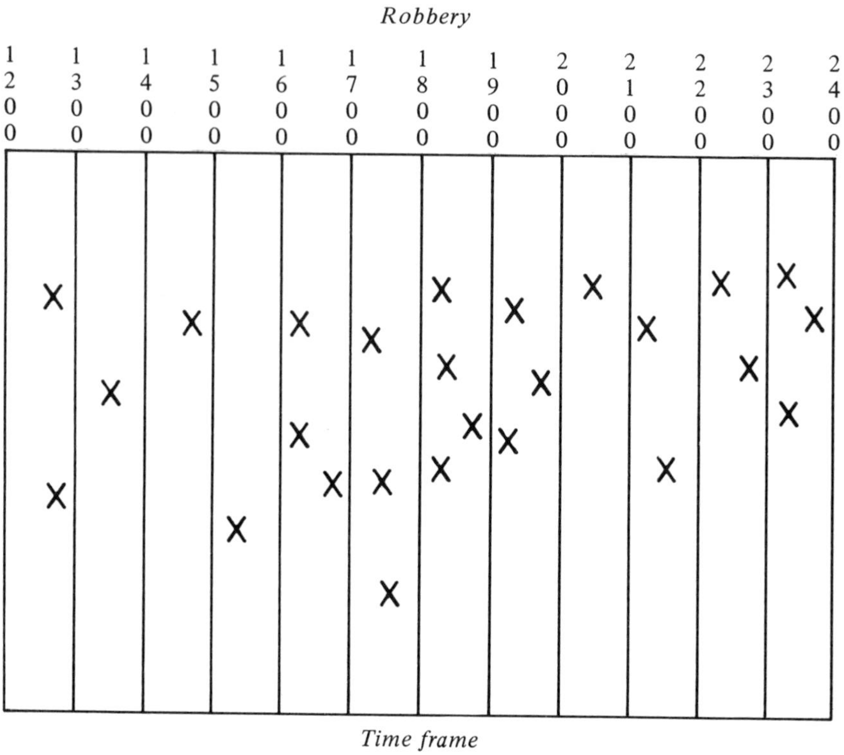

Robbery

Time frame

FIGURE 10.2

area) with nothing but prevention of crime as a goal. Second, in order to facilitate saturation patrol and the illusion of patrolling with ten times the number of men, it is necessary to identify the location and time of crime to the half-hour time frame.

With the problem as stated for the special-operation commander, and possessing the five teams, the concepts could be applied.

1. Divide the crime problem into four areas:

2. Apply a code to each area (Green I–II, Red I–II, Blue I–II).

3. Determine the time of the crime by area. For example, Green I area robberies may be occurring between 12 noon and 1400, therefore saturation of the area and method of patrol would occur there for those hours. The number of teams used in the area will depend on what time the maximum number of robberies are occurring by the hour. From the time frame we see that most are occurring between 1600 and 2000 hours. The other consideration involved is the fact that a tour of duty lasts eight hours normally.

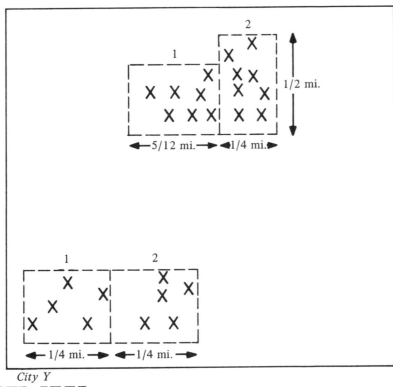

City Y

= Arbitrarily drawn patrol areas for
special operations forces

FIGURE 10.3

4. With five teams available, crime occurring on a twelve-hour period, and the majority of crime occurring between 1600 and 2000 hours, the pyramid of forces would have to be between those hours.

5. Information also shows that robberies are occurring in Red area II, the majority between 2230 and 2330 hours. Additionally, the number of robberies occurring in the Red area II are more than those occurring in Green area I between 1200 and 1400 hours.

6. To take the attack in this situation, teams A and B would begin their tour of duty at 1200 hours and saturate Green area I. (Method of patrol is the decision of the operations force commander.) Since the major portion of the Red area crime is occurring after 1600 hours and part of the Green area crime is occurring after 1600 hours and the major portion of all the robberies is occurring between

1600 and 2000 hours, teams C, D and E would report to their tour of duty at 1600 hours. Therefore, all five teams would be on duty and pyramid the special-operation force between 1600 and 2000 hours.

7. The rotation of the teams between Green area I and II, and Red area I and II would be determined by the time of occurrence of the robberies and their location. It is therefore possible for all five teams, at some period, to be saturating Green area I and II or Red area I and II, or any combination thereof.

8. The application of pyramid of forces will apply maximum manpower according to need by time and place. An additional component would be the day of week. Patrol administrators should apply the same principle, if crime is occurring by day of week in the proportion that requires the principle to be implemented. There should be no hesitation. This may entail officers to work from Tuesday through Saturday, if the information gleaned from the crime reports indicates that this deployment would produce maximum effectiveness.

9. Patrol administrators should be familiar with the *principle of mass* in mounting an attack on crime or fulfilling all other missions of this nature. This principle states that special operation forces should be committed to a problem in sufficient strength (number) at the time crime is occurring and at the location crime is occurring. It will be apparent to the patrol commander that committing forces in a piecemeal basis will not solve the problem. This also applies to the other mission of crowd control and disorder. It is the sine qua non of the effective special-operation forces. When applying this principle to crime, the usual information is necessary; i.e., time, place, MO, description, escape route, etc. Application to crowd control and disorder will entail intelligence information about attitudes of crowd, size, location, potential leaders, etc.

10. Coordination is necessary to meet the other needs of the patrol force. Continuing the example, let's suppose there is a large group of young people attending a performance in the business area of the community. Information reveals the youths will exit from the performance at about 2230 hours. The secondary mission of the special-operation forces would be to supply manpower so that an orderly exit and removal from the area will take place, since A and B teams are now off duty. A decision would have to be made concerning the remaining three teams, C, D, and E. Should all teams leave the primary mission, or should two teams leave for the secondary mission and one team remain on the primary mission? Good plan-

ning will answer these questions and the principles can reduce any potential loss of efficiency. Another consideration that proper intelligence would have an effect upon would be the potential for disorder at the youth performance. If intelligence indicates strongly that there will be trouble at the performance, then all five teams should be on duty at the time the performance ends. Decisions such as these are command decisions and the need for valid community feedback is important. It is again emphasized that good organizational relationships (Chapter 4) contribute to the effectiveness of the whole department.

11. The rotation of the teams from area to area should provide the illusion of omnipresence. The pyramid of forces and principle of mass should provide the coverage by time and place of crime control, and the primary-secondary mission procedure should emphasize the ability to be flexible in order to fulfill the many tasks assigned to the special-operations force.

MOBILE-STATIONARY STAKE-OUTS

Traditionally speaking, stake-outs are usually implemented by putting an officer or officers in the rear of an establishment and waiting for long periods of time for the perpetrator to attempt the next robbery. This is an excellent method at times and should continue to be used as appropriate. But limited manpower should stimulate patrol commanders to use different techniques and seek technological help.

Two stake-out methods that may provide an increase in effectiveness of the patrol function are the mobile and the mobile-stationary stake-out. One uses a mobile technique and the other uses technology. In the mobile technique, several teams of special-operations forces cover the many establishments requiring stake-outs. For example, if liquor establishments have been the target of holdup men and there are twenty-five liquor establishments in the community, the twenty-five would be divided up by time and location and the teams would stake these out at given times. Using the teams from the previous section, a sergeant and five men, there would be six two-man units (two teams) and create two times the amount of stake-outs available. These stake-outs may be used on the inside of the premises or on the outside. These may be covert or overt. In the covert method, the officers would be on the inside or on the outside in an unmarked car and in plainclothes. The overt method would be to have the officers of the teams well armed and make continuous and constant inspections of those establishments assigned to them for stake-outs. The word usually spreads very quickly throughout the community that special-forces officers are inspecting the particular premises in the manner described. This inspection method can permeate the total department and be used for any given target. For instance, one way to decrease bank robberies is to have officers in and out of all the banks in the community at different times. This obvious application of omnipresence and inspection will have a definite effect on bank robberies and usually is beneficial to the total community.

The second method uses technology. This is the electronic stake-out. Electronic equipment is placed in the rear of the establishment and hooked up to an alarm in the front of the store. If a holdup man enters or possibly completes the robbery, the clerk simply activates the alarm and the location of the robbery is immediately known by the police. Special-operation officers in patrol cars are patrolling the area where the electronic stake-out has been installed, and regular patrol forces are also notified of the stake-out information. The examination of new technology is necessary if law enforcement is to continue the offensive on crime, and patrol administrators should be in the forefront in their quest for alternative methods.

MOBILE COMMAND POSTS

Most departments across the country have some type of mobile command post. One department has converted a trailer that has an area large enough to hold conferences, besides the other necessary space. Smaller departments have converted station wagons, vans, buses, or any other vehicle that will fit the need of the specific department. Depending on the size, equipment can include wall maps and charts, telephones, and intricate communications systems which allow contact with any agency that may be needed during times of emergency; lighting equipment, etc. An essential consideration whenever a mobile command post is used is having complete cooperation and coordination with the normal communication center. Confusion and chaos will result if both attempt to issue instructions to field personnel. Written guidelines will help alleviate this problem.

Mobile command posts came into being for most police departments during the civil disorders of 1968. Federal troops and National Guard personnel mingled with civilian police and much talk of the CP (command post) was heard. Coordination between troops and police became complex because of the necessary increase in communication. Decentralization of control of police personnel was in order, and the mobile command post served as the headquarters for patrol field commanders. The mobile command post allowed the field commander to account for assigned personnel and deploy differing amounts of men according to each situation. At the same time, the staging area concept came into being and today these two are almost synonymous.

The *staging area* is usually that part of the mobile command post where personnel is assembled, equipped as needed, accounted for, and equipment can be stored. There may be times when staging areas are part of the command post and other times when the two are separated. As circumstances change, so does the decision concerning the location.

The field commander responsible for the area in which a mobile command post has been installed should assign a special-operations supervisor the responsibility of the command post activities. This assignment is probably best done prior to any situation and expertise should be developed through simulated exercises. The operation of a mobile command post would require a minimum of a commander, assignment officer, logistics officer, and transportation officer.

The *assignment officer* should maintain records of the number and identity of all personnel assigned to the particular post, maintain maps showing community areas involved in the situation and personnel assigned to these areas, structure zones of patrol utilizing priorities that would achieve maximum control, and coordinate activities of all concerned.

The *logistics officer* should receive, account for, and issue all personnel equipment, provide food and sanitary facilities, supervise accounting for all evidence and property recovered, and maintain liaison with central logistics.

The *transportation officer* should control parking and security of all vehicles, maintain records of vehicle assignment, supervise shift change regarding vehicles, and provide prisoner transportation and security. If there is a need to assign additional personnel to these officers, it should be done on a need basis.

It is not necessary to provide these assignments in all cases. Mobile command posts may consist of only one police car as the situation demands. However, if the problem escalates, these responsibilities should be assigned.

The patrol administrator and his patrol commanders should review strategic areas throughout the community for potential command post locations. All hazards conducive to civil disorder will affect those selected locations. This should be done in conjunction with related sites for staging areas. When the selection is completed, arrangements should be made so that once the mobile command post is implemented, immediate telephone service and related communication are available. Needless to say, without communication the procedure is ineffective. Cooperation of the local telephone company is necessary.

DISASTER CONTROL

Whenever a disaster occurs, the patrol officer is usually first on the scene. Subsequently, special operation forces will be called upon to supply the expertise, and therefore these forces should be prepared with the appropriate procedures and equipment to fulfill the police department's responsibility. The patrol administrator must plan for those disasters that are more prevalent in his specific community. Whenever it is impossible for all exigencies, the priority system can be implemented through analysis of potential disasters.

Professional approaches to disaster control require cooperation and coordination between many agencies. These agencies include all agencies of local government, telephone company, gas and electric company, American Red Cross, Salvation Army, National Guard, religious charities, and Civil Defense. The police department should draw on the expertise of all agencies in order to provide the most effective and efficient response. Simulated exercises that require all participants to take an active interest can provide the necessary communication between agencies for a "control emergency liaison communication center." All agencies practicing together will resolve the many minor problems beforehand and result in a smoothly operating disaster control procedure.

There are major disasters, both natural and otherwise. Some can be anticipated in certain parts of the country because of weather and geography. The effort of police and other public and private agencies can help reduce the potential loss of life and property.

The patrol administrator should include in his list of anticipated disasters the following: airplane crashes, earthquakes, avalanches, tidal waves, hurricanes, building collapses, cyclones, blizzards, floods, dam collapses, explosions (internal and accidental), fires (hospital, school, hotel, nursing homes), mine cave-ins, railroads, ships, gas leaks, and forest fires. An awareness of what disasters may occur will help in meeting these tremendous challenges in an enlightened and constructive manner.

Proper disaster planning will produce a calm, efficient response and add greatly to reducing potential hysteria on the part of citizens. In developing a plan for the patrol force, coordination with other agencies is paramount. However, the special-operations personnel would be called upon to supply primary control and would have to consider (1) traffic control to, from, and within the disaster area; (2) identification of victims, living and dead; (3) removal and disposition of victims; (4) mobile command post; (5) security of area to reduce possible spread of disease where applicable; (6) provision for relatives of victims to proceed to receiving area to identify dead and unite with living (this temporary facility would contain a reception area and morgue area); (7) public information office; (8) after-action reports and (9) evaluation of hazardous areas. Identification of persons who may have died as a result of a disaster is important because of personal feelings of relatives, and such legal implication as estates, insurance claims, business enterprises, and remarriage of survivors. Special care should be taken to supervise the identification to avoid any possibility of destroying articles and other paraphernalia necessary to valid identification.

Command and control of a disaster situation are essential. The prompt action of the police department in communicating the nature and extent of the disaster causing similar swift support should result in minimizing loss of life and property.

LABOR RELATIONS

No one can predict when a labor strike will occur. Strikes have reached just about all types of workers, private and public. Special-operations officers and supervisors should be well acquainted with the legal ramification of labor relations. This most sensitive area requires patrol commanders to be ever alert for situations that will involve the department negatively. Fair and impartial treatment within the rule of law is the order of the day.

What is meant by an injunction? Who is required by law to enforce the injunction? What liaisons have been developed between the police department and the organization responsible for enforcing the injunction, if it is not the police department? How much restraint will be used, if any? These questions should be answered prior to being involved in a strike situation of any magnitude. Where there is the potential for violence, or if violence is imminent, action must be swift and professional.

All personnel of the special-operations forces should be trained in this sometimes volatile area. Labor problems have evolved into arson, assaults of a serious nature, and sometimes even murder. Any labor problem should be considered important and highly skilled officers in the field of human relations given first assignment to the problem. Many times, action taken at the height of emotional stress is unnecessary and lingering resentment may result from this demonstrated judgment. Patrol commanders capable of cool, calm, and objective decisions, but with the ability to decide immediately and, if necessary, to act, are preferred as supervisors at the scene of these sensitive situations.

PRISON DISORDERS

Patrol administrators who anticipate future events will certainly develop a plan of action for fulfilling the department's obligation regarding prison disorders. The following section is presented in an effort to facilitate the patrol administrator's ability to fulfill that obligation.

> *Sample:* Emergency Response to Prison, Penitentiary, or Jail Facility (in order to maintain continuity and understanding, jail, prison and penitentiary will be presented by the phrase "Prison Facility"). The plan should presume that riots and disruptions will occur in the future as they have in the past. Also, police personnel should have some general information as to the cause of prison riots just as they needed information concerning the causes and stages of civil disorder or riots in our cities. The ability to respond intelligently with sufficient service to quiet prison riots is determined in a similar manner as response to external disorder. In order to achieve the objective, planning and prompt response are key ingredients. At this point, information regarding why prisoners riot should be written:

General Information

Information obtained from official reports and news articles usually focuses on the following reasons as why prisoners riot: (1) overcrowding, (2) poor administration, (3) insufficient financial support, (4) political interference, (5) lack of professional leadership, (6) ineffective or nonexistent treatment programs, (7) disparities in sentencing, (8) poor and unjust parole policies, (9) enforced idleness of prisoners, (10) intractable prisoners.

In addition to these reasons, psychological viewpoints focus on aggressive and acting-out personalities in the prison population. Conditions mentioned in the sociological approach exist in most prisons, yet the majority have not experienced riots.

It is therefore tenuous when attempting to identify the cause of riots where official reports or statements after the riots are considered alone. It seems the reports written during the riot give a clear picture. As reported by Vernon Fox in *Federal Probation,* March 1971, p. 9-14, "In decreasing order of validity and reliability the following material was used in making the report. (1) News stories during 20 serious riots since 1940 as reported in the *New York Times* during the action, (2) this writer's experience during the Michigan prison riot in 1952, (3) lengthy discussions with inmates involved in four prison riots, (4) conversations with prison personnel involved in seven prison riots, (5) literature concerning prison riots, (6) official reports and official statements after the riot, and (7) general literature on aggression, civil disturbance, and violence."

Causes must be divided into predisposing causes and precipitating causes. Just as in civil disobedience, there has to be a "readiness" to riot. Then, there has to be a "trigger." Too frequently, the predisposing causes have been used as causes for prison riots and the precipitating causes have been identified as causes for civil disorder. Neither is a cause in itself. The total social situation, with emphasis on the interaction or lack of it between dominant people and subjugated people, either in the prison or in the ghetto, must be evaluated to determine why people riot. It cannot be based simplistically on overcrowding, political interference, lack of treatment programs, or any other simple answer.

Riots are spontaneous—not planned—detonated by a spontaneous event. The inmates know who has the weapons and who has the force. The inmates know that no administration ever has to negotiate with them. Planned disturbances end in sit-down strikes, slowdowns, hunger strikes, and self-inflicted injury. The spontaneous event that detonates the riot may be almost anything from a fight in the yard that expands, someone heaving a tray in the dining hall, to a homosexual tricking a new officer to open his cell, as happened in the Michigan riot in 1952. Violent riots must happen spontaneously. Otherwise, they would not happen.

There has to be pressure, though, that builds up the predisposi-
tion or readiness to riot and a spontaneous precipitating event to
trigger or detonate the riot.

Riots tend to pattern in five stages, four during the riot and
one afterward. First, there is a period of undirected violence like
the exploding bomb. Second, inmate leaders tend to emerge and
organize around them a group of ringleaders who determine inmate
policy during the riot. Third, a period of interaction with prison
authority, whether by negotiation or by force, assists in identifying
the alternative available for the resolution of the riot. Fourth, the
surrender of the inmates, whether by negotiation or by force,
phases out the violent event. Fifth, and most important from the
political viewpoint, the investigations and administrative changes
restore order and confidence in the remaining power structure by
making "constructive changes" to regain administrative control
and to rectify the undesirable situation that produced the riot.

The first stage of riot is characterized by an event that triggered the unbridled violence. The first stage is disorganized among
the prisoners and, too frequently, among the prison staff as well.
It is at this point that custodial force could alter the course of the
riot but, in most instances, custody is caught by surprise and without adequate preparation so that there is little or no custodial reaction other than containment. As a result, the riot pattern is
permitted by default to move to the second stage. It is at this
point the key ingredients of planning and prompt response with
appropriate resources become essential.

The second stage is when inmate leaders emerge and the administrative forces become organized. Inmate leaders who emerge
from this violence are people who remain emotionally detached
sufficiently so that they lend stability to the inmate group. They
don't "panic." They "keep their cool." As a result they attract
around them lesser inmate leaders or "ringleaders" who similarly,
do not panic but need to be dependent upon "the boss." In this
manner, an inmate leader can gather around him probably two to
six "lieutenants," each with some delegated authority, such as
watching hostages, preparing demands, and maintaining discipline
in the rest of the inmate group. Further, the inmate leader, like
most political leaders, takes a "middle-of-the-road" position where
he can moderate the extremes and maintain communication. In a
prison riot, some inmates want to kill the hostages. Other inmates
want to give up and surrender to the administration. The inmate
leader controls these two extremes in a variety of ways and sta-
bilizes the group into a position in the center.

The third stage is a period of interaction between inmates and
prison officials. It has taken several forms, though they can be
classified generally into (1) negotiation, and (2) force or threat
of force. No administration has to negotiate with prisoners, but
the chances for negotiation are greater when the prisoners hold
hostages. The chances for force or threat of force are greater when

the prisoners do not have hostages. In either case, the decision on the part of the inmates to surrender is subject to the general principles of group dynamics. When the inmate group is cohesive and their morale is good, the prisoners will maintain the riot situation, whether faced with force or negotiation. When the group cohesion begins to disintegrate by some inmates wanting to surrender, others wanting to retaliate, and the leadership wanting to maintain the status quo, the administration may manipulate it for an early surrender. This disintegration of group cohesion may be prompted by negotiation or by force or threat of force, depending upon the situation.

In case of negotiation, the group cohesion is diminished by the administration's demonstrated willingness to negotiate and by the personality of the official negotiators who convey a feeling of trust and confidence. The group can be disintegrated, also by gas, rifle fire, and artillery shelling, all of which have been used recently in American prison riots. The less destructive approach, of course, is to await disintegration of cohesion by periods of inaction that places strain to hold the group together on the leadership by fatigue and impatience. Faced with this situation the leadership frequently has to look for an honorable way out of a disintegrating situation.

The fourth stage, or surrender, may be the inmates' giving up after being gassed and shot at, or they may surrender in an orderly way, either after force or threat of force, or by negotiation. Political interference at the wrong time in the prison riot can affect the total situation in terms of negotiation, surrender, and subsequent investigations and administrative decisions.

The fifth stage, that of investigations, consolidation of the remaining power structure, personnel and policy changes followed by political fallout, is really the most important stage, since it sets policy for the prison and the system for years to come. Editorials and news commentators suggest solutions and interpretations. Administrators have to respond to pressures from interest groups. This is why "get-tough" policies become important after riots, even though they tend to intensify the problems.

Riots do not occur in prisons or correctional institutions with exceedingly high morale. Neither do they occur in prisons where the morale is so low that the prisoners endure penal oppression in a docile manner or break their own legs and cut their own heel tendons. Riots occur in prisons where inmates have medium to high morale and where some conflict appears in the staff, probably between treatment and custodial philosophies, and probably when the program is in a state of transition from one type of procedures and ojectives to another.

Riots occur in prisons where there is a tenuous balance between controlling behavior and changing behavior. If there is a full commitment to either, riots do not occur. The riot itself, results in a political decision to control behavior. Consequently, the behavior changing in treatment forces always loses in a riot, at least in the immediate future.

There is also a direct relationship between news coverage by the mass media and incidence of demonstrations, riots, and civil disturbances. This is one reason why riots tend to cluster in terms of time.

Guidelines for Action

Guidelines for action during the riot are important. The custodial staff is frequently untrained and the administration is just as frequently caught by surprise. Action during the riot has to be planned ahead of time and modified according to the situation.

During the first stage of a riot, the disorganized inmates could well be effectively faced with force. As a matter of fact, most riots appear to have been vulnerable to custodial force in the early stages because of disorganization on the side of the inmates. If disorganization occurs on both sides, however, then the riot cannot be contained early. Immediate custodial action could have altered the course of several riots. The lack of training, preparation, or even expectation of riot has resulted in disorganizations on both sides for hours.

During the second stage, after the inmates have organized and their leadership begins to emerge, there is the question as to whether force should be used. No prison administration ever needs to negotiate with rioting prisoners. The prisoners know this. If hostages are held, then negotiation becomes a real possibility, depending upon the other factors. If the inmates holding the hostages are young, reformatory-type people with short sentences and have not already demonstrated their capability to kill, if they are psychiatric patients who cannot organize into a team, or if their majority can see parole sometime in the future, then negotiation is not necessary.

The third stage of the riot is determined by the nature of the situation. If no hostages are held, or if the prisoners holding hostages are not hardcore intractables with nothing to lose, then force or threat of force is appropriate. If the hostages are considered to be in serious danger, the administration is placed in a real dilemma in determining action because lives have to be considered in relation to public and internal reaction and consequence. If waiting for fatigue to reduce the cohesion of the rebellious inmate group will accomplish the objective, then force is not necessary.

The fourth stage of the riot is the surrender. The regaining of custodial control is all that is needed. Any further action beyond the basic need has to be for public consumption or for the satisfaction of the prison administration.

The fifth stage of the riot is the aftermath where investigation, reinterpretations, and scapegoats are involved. There is not much the prison administration can do about this because the real power lies in the political structure. Free movement of newsmen and free access to information, both inmates and staff, is the only logical approach to take during this period. In this way, the administration can demonstrate that it is attempting to hide nothing, that it recognizes it has problems and is openly and honestly seeking the best solutions.

In summary, official reaction to riot is dependent upon the situation. As in judo, the reaction is determined by the action of the adversary. No negotiation is needed where no hostages are held or where they might be held by short-term prisoners not considered to be dangerous. Outwaiting might be an approach in doubtful situations, since an overshow of force is becoming decreasingly effective in American society and it invites unnecessary derision from some segments of the public.

Discretion rather than negotiation or force is at issue while handling a riot. A basic principle of police work or any other type of social control in a democratic society is to use the minimum amount of force and destruction needed to accomplish the objectives.

The correctional officer is the key to riot prevention, although a rough and harsh custodial lieutenant, captain, or deputy warden can use policies and behavior to neutralize the good work of a hundred officers. The entire custodial force has to be treatment-oriented, just as the entire treatment staff has to be aware of custodial problems, in order to emerge with an effective correctional program.

Readiness to riot results from the predisposing causes, such as bad food, oppressive custodial discipline, sadistic staff quick to write disciplinary charges against inmates, and general punitive attitude by administration and line personnel. The precipitating cause that "triggers" the riot is very seldom the real cause. A bomb is made by constructing a strong perimeter or casing and generating pressure inside. It blows at its weakest point, but it has to be detonated. The detonation is not the "cause of the explosion," although it "triggered" it.[2]

Policy

The next part of the plan should be a policy statement from the chief of police. The statement should concern the direction of the department prior to, during, and after the prison emergency.

Responsibility and Procedure (Usually the patrol administrator will be in command at a prison riot.)

This area of the plan concerns itself with placing individual responsibilities and setting forth specific procedures responding to a prison emergency. If there is more than one prison facility location in the jurisdication of the department, a basic plan may be written with minor adjustments made for each facility. Considerations must be made regarding legal and jurisdictional responsibility.

The first step is to open up communication between the administrator of the prison and the police department. There should be a face-to-face meeting, which shall include the command staff of both agencies. Responsibility for action should be agreed upon at each step of the plan. At all times, the officer in command must be identifiable. If responsibility should include calling State Police officials or the National Guard, communication should follow with those organizations to insure a proper change of command if necessary and appropriate. This is similar to civil disorder and is most necessary. You cannot place too much emphasis on who is in command when confronted by a serious situation of this type. Once the question of responsibility at each step has been resolved, you can move on to the second step.

The second step should be to determine the authorized personnel from the prison facility who have authority to call for assistance. This avoids the problem of irresponsible reaction by lower-ranking prison authorities calling for assistance unnecessarily and causing the police to disrupt their organizations without due cause. By selecting only prison officials as authorized calling personnel, promptness, effectiveness, and coordination are enhanced. With the face-to-face meeting between the police commanders and their prison counterparts, formulation will take place and thus avoid unnecessary delay at the time of the incident.

Verification of the call for assistance is our next consideration and exchange of telephone information that can be used to validate verification enhances the operation. An exchange of pictures of the authorized officials of each agency is helpful. This information must be maintained and updated. A notification chart (Figure 10.4) and an alternate notification chart (Figure 10.5) depict the process. Circumstances existing at the time of the prison emergency will determine which planned emergency-response notification chart will be used.

As indicated by the chart, the notified member of the police who belongs to the authorized verification group will immediately verify the authenticity of the call for assistance by contacting one of the authorized prison officials. (Scheduling of command personnel leave and vacations will insure the contact of at least one member of the authorized verification groups.) This notification is done in most

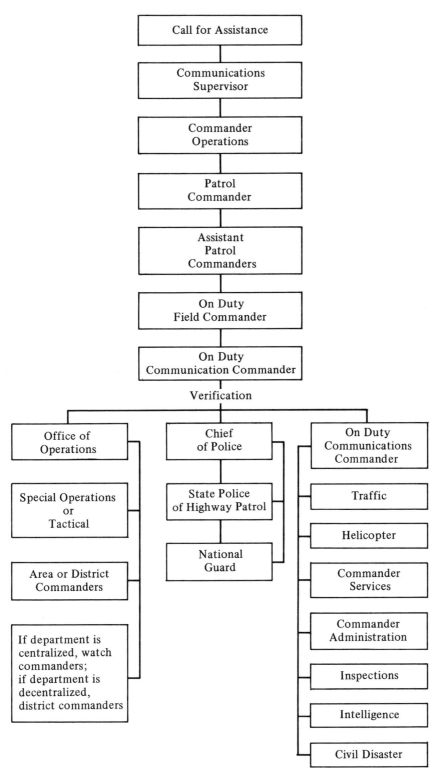

FIGURE 10.4 Planned Emergency-Response Notification Chart for Prison Facility.

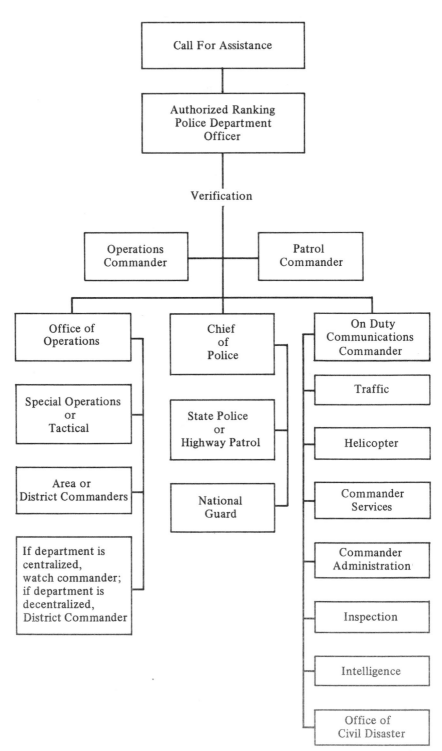

FIGURE 10.5 Planned-Emergency-Response Notification Chart for Prison Facility

cases by private telephone. (In many cases where the author was the police verification, there was no delay in contacting an authorized prison official.)

As soon as verification is made, the notified member of the authorized verification group will be responsible for notifying the chief of police and the on-duty communication commander. If the notified member of the police group is other than the on-duty communication commander, that officer should then report to the office of operations where he should coordinate notification activities. If the notified officer has duties at the scene of the prison that would supersede the coordinating activities, he would then request a replacement for that responsibility and proceed to the location of the prison.

Those authorized ranking members of the police department who receive the call for assistance and verify, should then implement the planned emergency response by properly notifying indicated personnel. As shown in Figures 10.4 and 10.5, the completion of the notification process would be automatic, and officials can then carry out their respective responsibilities expeditiously.

Prison Visit

In order to resolve any delay that might take place on arriving at the prison, police commanders who may be responsible for commanding the task force that would be assembled and respond to a prison riot should personally visit the facility. Together with the correctional officials, a tour should be taken where the many factors that need to be considered, especially if chemical agents may be used, can be discussed in depth. Some of the factors to consider would be (1) ventilation system, (2) location of potential weapons, (3) escape routes, (4) potential ingress and egress routes for police, (5) probable wind direction for a given area, (6) strength, (7) staging area inside the walls, (8) guard strength, and (9) prison population. These factors are not all-inclusive.

Communications

As in riot control, where many men are assembled, direction, coordination, and control become paramount when attempting to quell a prison riot. A decision must be made to clear all other personnel from a selected frequency that shall then be reserved for communications pertaining to the prison situation only. Communication discipline should be emphasized in any plan and subsequent orders evolving from that plan. The choice of what type of communication should be used will depend on the location of the transmitting person, the equipment available, the degree of emergency, and the confidentiality of the message. The type of communication selected can be personal messenger, telephone, or portable radio.

Certain messages may have to be transmitted by radio because of their emergency, but for which confidentiality is preferred or required. In this case the use of a code is very helpful and decreases the possibility of citizen insecurity because of misunderstood or misrepresented transmissions that may be picked up by outside agitators, the news media, or the rioting prisoners themselves who may have a radio in their possession. Also, portions of the message taken out of context, or conjecture regarding the message itself, may be used for rumor and propaganda intentionally to try to incite others on the outside.

The following is a sample of a simple code and what information you might want to be included in code transmission:

P-1 — Police injured
P-2 — Prisoners have weapons (possible to mean only guns)
P-3 — Additional personnel necessary
P-4 — Additional equipment needed
P-5 — Rioters have taken hostage(s)

The assignment of the mobile-command vehicle to a strategic position near the prison is important. Located at this position should be a prepositioned telephone hookup, which would give immediate telephone communication with the communication center. At least one radio technician should be assigned to report to the operational mobile-command post to insure immediate repair of any breakdown in communication equipment. Other responsibilities of the communications unit would be (1) to activate a central command post, (2) to maintain a log book, (3) to provide adequate personnel to keep administrative telephone lines open and, (4) to insure appropriate repair equipment for an extended siege.

Traffic

The role of traffic officers during prison riots should be examined to insure maximum use. If the situation reaches a point where traffic officers must be put directly into battle, other help would probably be on the way. In most cases when the alert is sounded, traffic personnel should be assembled and given the responsibility for handling all vehicular and pedestrian traffic within the immediate area of the prison. The traffic officers should at this time be under the command of the field-force operational commander.

Helicopter

If the police department has a helicopter unit, the plan should cause the helicopter to take a position of advantage. Flexibility of operation is primary and easily attainable for this unit; therefore, this strength is what the Field Commander would utilize.

Inspection and Intelligence

The use of these units would be determined by many factors which are specific to each department. Possible uses are recording the event for after-action review. Sensitivity to the perimeter of the facility regarding sympathizers who may be bent on disruption to show support for inmates.

Public Information

Much has been learned from the civil disorders in the past. One thing is certain: the news media should be informed of events whenever possible. Having a public information office or the equal at the scene where information can be passed on in an enlightened manner helps the total operation. In this way, operational commanders are not being interfered with by groups of people, there is less potential for conjecture and rumor, rapport between the department and news personnel is maintained, and the whole operation runs smoother. The mobile press center should be identified for the news media, and they should be told that all information will be given from the press center.

Other Service Units

Other service units, such as property, should take a posture of providing appropriate logistical support for the operational forces. If the riot continues for an extended period, feeding of police personnel shall be coordinated with other city agencies as appropriate. In some cases, this would be the office of civil disaster.

Support should be planned with any agency that might be able to supply needed services.

Prison Information

In addition to the information obtained during the prison riot, the following information should be maintained on a current level; (1) inmate population, correctional officer strength by shift; (2) strength at critical times, such as meal time, recreation time, and bed time; (3) civilian employees (this would be helpful in accounting for personnel re hostages); (4) inmate housing, dormitories, wings, block houses, diagnostic center, hospital; (5) clothing worn by inmates; (6) constant number for each location and fluctuating number of time of day and day of week as appropriate; (7) time of normal working for inmates (remember, the inmates who work in the kitchen would report to work earlier than the other inmates); (8) minimum, medium, and maximum security areas; (9) activity during evening hours, holidays, and weekends; (10) location and hours of workshops, such as the print shop, metal shop, wood shop, and laundry; (11) power house; and (12) storerooms and their contents.

As stated earlier, critical times for prison officials should be remembered by all police commanders. They should know that meal times create the greatest concentration of inmates, and historical data reveals that this is the time when most disorders take place. Another critical point is when the concentration of prisoners is at a high level and the assignment of correction officers is at a low level. Knowledge of the amount and quality of training possessed by the correctional officers regarding their ability to respond to such situations, and the volume and type of equipment possessed, will help police officers determine their optimum response. If possible, and the expertise is possessed by the police agency, arrangements can be made for training in such tactics as may be necessary to improve the ability of the prison officials to handle these situations. This training would benefit all concerned.

Operational Response

The planned emergency response notification chart would be implemented as indicated in Figures 10.4 and 10.5. At this point, all notified officers would be placed in one of four categories: (1) committed to the prison, (2) reserve status, (3) alert status, (4) function routinely. The change from one category to the next would come from orders given by the operational field commander.

The plan should then outline the number of personnel of each rank, depending on the size of the prison, inmate population, manpower available, and degree of seriousness of the situation. Whatever the case, if response is to be implemented, control, direction, and leadership exemplified by command personnel accompanied by supervisors and patrolmen in team or squad-concept will offer the best approach to prompt resolution of the problem. For example, squads of twelve patrolmen with a sergeant supervisor where the twelve men are broken into four-man fire teams are excellent to work with as a total team. Each fire team would have a unit leader, baton man, launcher man, and assistant launcher man. Each man would be equipped with appropriate fire-power which may or may not include minigrenades, CS grenades, baseball grenades, grenade launcher, launcher shells, triple chaser grenades, shotgun, etc. The team should be able to work as a unit and as close as possible to a total entity. Inspection of men should insure no loose equipment hanging from uniforms that might be taken by a rioting prisoner and used as a weapon against the officer. These precautions should be taken at the staging area, preselected for its advantage of the prison. The staging area should be large enough for congregation of personnel and have space available where proper information and instructions can be disseminated. If it is not close enough to walk to the prison, buses should be available to transport large numbers of men to the prison at one time. Armory support units should respond to the staging area in order to keep supplying the operational forces with proper equipment both in volume and complexity.

The operational commander will notify each group within the various categories in enough time so that smooth coordinated change from one category to the next takes place. This notification procedure will decrease the possibility of having confusion at the staging area. The change from routine function status to alert status to reserve status to committed status should be done on a timely basis and calls for planned decisive orders from the operational commander and his assistants.

Canine Teams

How canine teams will be used in prison riots should be considered ahead of time. They should be in the front ranks of the committed personnel as soon as assessment of the situation takes place. The operational commander has at least three important decisions to make in determining which approach to use in quelling the disturbance. Should he use chemical agents, manpower in volume with canine teams in the lead, or should he shoot plastic bullets?

All of these decisions (and there are more) will be determined by the situation as it exists in that instant. By developing options, the operational commander eases the tension and errors that might come from not knowing these options. We need only look around the country to find situations where alternate methods may have been the better solution.

When confronted by hundreds of inmates who are rioting in a prison, you will find them with headbands wrapped around their heads, towels around their faces, armed with everything from knives, guns, baseball bats, wooden poles, chairs, iron bed posts, and broken bottles. When the order is given to act, the moment of truth has arrived. The rioting prisoners may or may not obey. As the operational commander, your next move should be planned depending on the response to your order. If the order is disobeyed and action must be taken, the safety of police and correctional officers is the first consideration. Your action should accomplish the objective with minimum violence (including prisoners), remembering whatever the action, a decision must be made, and the consequence of the decision should be anticipated.

Under the conditions of a prison riot, canine teams in squads is one of the most effective weapons you can possess. In many instances, just the appearance of the canine teams will cause many of the rioting prisoners to have second thoughts about their actions, and may even be the reason for them giving up. If canine teams are used, they should be used in squads of 3, 4, 5, or 6 depending on the geography of the specific area. In smaller areas, one group of three teams could back up another group of three. If the area is open, one squad of six canine teams could back up another squad of six canine teams.

These fine animals can do the job if they are used properly. If it becomes necessary at some point during the riot to use chemical agents, the animals should be given consideration regarding their position to the chemical agents. The officers in charge of the canine team squads can easily be consulted prior to taking the specific action where chemical agents may be used. The use of this canine-team option can result in a very successful operation.

Identification of Inmates

Arrangements should be made to insure identification of inmates who might commit various violations during the riots, so prosecution can take place after the completion of the action. In most large disorders, the identification problem is one of the most difficult to solve no matter what procedure is used (taking pictures of officers with violators, using plastic handcuffs, etc.), and good planning will improve the percentage of rioters successfully prosecuted as a result of any committed violation.

Critique

In conclusion, the plan should end with a critique of the operation. Procedure should be outlined where constructive criticism is solicited. In this way improvements can be made in needed areas so that the next time the plan is implemented, a better product results.

NOTES

1. Paul F. Cromwell, Jr., Robert L. Lewis, Jr., "Crowds, Mobs, and Riots: A Sociological Analysis," *Police,* Sept. 1971. Reprinted by permission of Charles C Thomas.
2. George G. Killinger, Paul F. Cromwell, Jr., "Penology," *The Evolution of Corrections in America* (St. Paul, Minn.: West Publishing, 1973). Pp. 319–27. Reprinted by permission.

weapons in patrol

In all likelihood, discussion concerning the formulation of policy on the use of deadly force by police officers will continue. There is no escape from this important feature of police administration. The author believes that a firearm policy must be written in order to provide guidelines for officers which, in some cases, may save their lives or the lives of innocent citizens. Police officers generally, but patrol officers specifically, have a very real need to be completely clear on when and where firearms may be used. A written policy will enhance the potential for using good judgment and making accurate decisions when an officer is faced with a situation where deadly force is an alternative.

First, patrol administrators should be keenly aware of the impact that misuse of firearms may have on their ability to achieve the objective of maintaining community stability. More than once, riots have resulted from the belief by citizens that police have shot (and killed) unreasonably a member of the community. This is especially so if the victim is young. Additionally, in some cases, the citizens do not wait for a ruling, administrative or otherwise, before they take to the streets under these conditions.

Second, there is a very distinct relationship between an enlightened firearms policy and its implementation, and the patrol administrator's ability to achieve the objective of providing internal esprit de corps. When a fellow officer becomes involved in a controversy over the use of firearms, morale problems become a very real probability.

Third, the legal ramifications both in liability and politically explosive terms, can become a continuing embarrassing situation.

The object of a written policy on the use of firearms includes safety of the officers, safety of the citizens, professional performance, and a sense of social and human responsibility. Urban law enforcement especially must utilize these professional police principles in order to resolve their most complex problems.

WRITTEN GUIDELINES

Appendix F contains written instructions of the San Diego, California, Police Department regarding the carrying and use of firearms. These guidelines are an excellent example of a professional approach to the control of firearms and related incidents in a police department. There is no need to elaborate on them here. The student of Patrol Administration and the professor teaching should examine each point very carefully. A comparison could be made to the Model Firearms Use Policy printed in *Police Patrol Readings* by Samuel G. Chapman (Springfield, Ill.: Charles C. Thomas, Publisher). Additionally, another comparison could be made with the following information provided by the President's Commission on Law Enforcement and Administration of Justice, Task Force Report "The Police."

It is essential that all departments formulate written firearms policies which clearly limit their use to situations of strong and compelling need. A department should even place greater restrictions on their use than is legally required. Careful review of the comprehensive firearms-use policies of several departments and discussions with police administrators indicate that these guidelines should control firearms use:

1. Deadly force should be restricted to the apprehension of perpetrators who, in the course of their crime threatened the use of deadly force, or if the officer believes there is a substantial risk that the person whose arrest is sought will cause death or serious bodily harm if his apprehension is delayed. The use of firearms should be flatly prohibited in the apprehension of misdemeanants, since the value of human life far outweighs the gravity of a misdemeanor.

2. Deadly force should never be used on mere suspicion that a crime, no matter how serious, was committed or that the person being pursued committed the crime. An officer should either have witnessed the crime or should have sufficient information to know,

as a virtual certainty, that the suspect committed an offense for which the use of deadly force is permissible.

3. Officers should not be permitted to fire at felony suspects when lesser force could be used; when the officer believes that the suspect can be apprehended reasonably soon thereafter without the use of deadly force; or when there is any substantial danger to innocent bystanders. Although the requirement of using lesser force, when possible, is a legal rule, the other limitations are based on sound public policy. To risk the life of innocent persons for the purpose of apprehending a felon cannot be justified.

4. Officers should never use warning shots for any purpose. Warning shots endanger the lives of bystanders, and in addition, may prompt a suspect to return the fire. Further, officers should never fire from a moving vehicle.

5. Officers should be allowed to use any necessary force, including deadly force, to protect themselves or other persons from death or serious injury. In such cases, it is immaterial whether the attacker has committed a serious felony, a misdemeanor, or any crime at all.

6. In order to enforce firearms use policies, department regulations should require a detailed written report on all discharges of firearms. All cases should be thoroughly investigated to determine whether the use of firearms was justified under the circumstances.

If all departments formulated firearms use policies which include the above principles and these policies were consistently enforced, many of the tragic incidents which had a direct bearing upon community relations could have been avoided.[1]

ASSASSINATION OF POLICE OFFICERS

Police officers are being killed more at this time than at any prior time in our nation's history. Whether these killings are intended assassinations or committed while in the act of attempting another crime, police officers have fallen. The majority of officers being killed will continue to be in the area of arrests. The weapons most used will continue to be handguns. There is no way of predicting the exact situation, which might help prevent these horrible deeds. However, there are several points which patrol commanders should keep in mind regarding the performance of the force during these critical and emotional times. An awareness of individuality, preplanning, timing, and use of simulative exercises may help resolve the possibility of escalation. Additionally, intelligence, quality of intelligence, emotional state of officers, and sensitivity on the part of patrol commanders regarding impulsive actions should be evaluated. Some officers want to be transferred from the critical area while others prefer to stay. The potential for several incidents to occur at the same time; false calls; increased number of officers in one car; additional weapons; increased back-up units; a change in "procedure of response" to critical areas; marked car; unmarked car; uniformed officer; plainclothes officers; suspicious calls; increased communication in critical areas; and back-up tactics are all considerations for the leader in patrol relative to ambush and sneak attacks.

Among the factors that can be resolved during normal times are physical shape of officers and firearms training. An officer in the eastern part of the United States who was the victim of an attempted assassination is alive today because of his excellent physical condition. Officers who are overweight may not be the best partners in critical situations. Training in double action and fast draw are extremely important since many shootings occur at close quarters. Also, firearms training at night is necessary if the shootings are taking place at night.

A deterrent to police killings is the realization on the part of the potential killer that all force will be brought to bear in the attempt to bring the perpetrator to justice. There may be outcries from the community regarding the number of personnel used to solve a police killing, but nothing should stop the effort since the killing of a police officer is an affront against the very heart of our country. When a police officer is attacked, a tremor is felt in almost every citizen of the community. The citizen is afraid. If a police officer is killed, how safe is an ordinary citizen? Another excellent tool that will aid in the deterrent attempt is a good liaison with federal agencies. Open communication and rapport with the Federal Bureau of Investigation, drug-abuse agencies, and intelligence units will improve a police department's chances of solving the crime.

Who is it that is most likely to attack police officers in this critical manner? Possibly the extremists of the radical organizations. Many times the organization is too soft for these individuals. Other times, the radical organization prescribes violence to a degree where the extremist member cannot handle it mentally and must strike out. The organization then denounces the individual as not belonging any longer. Every attempt should be made to maintain communication with these groups. If at all possible, individual leaders should be identified and told of their responsibility regarding the organization and the actions of its members. Usually, leaders who may be held responsible for violence will not be so apt to preach violence that may cause other people to commit violence.

LETHAL WEAPONS

The most obvious of the lethal weapons in the arsenal of police agencies is the officer's side arm. The policy statement on the use of firearms indicates a criteria under which the side arm can be used. This applies also for the shotgun, carbine, rifle, machine guns, or any other automatic weapons. Under normal conditions, the individual police officer may be confronted by persons who may attempt to take his life or the life of another citizen, and respond with his service revolver or shotgun as the situation presents. When the situation changes to urban guerrilla warfare, snipers, or a barricaded person or persons, the other weapons (30 cal. semiautomatic carbine, machine gun, rifle) must be available in order to reach a successful conclusion of the incident. All of these weapons continue to be part of the police arsenal.

NONLETHAL WEAPONS

A *nonlethal weapon* is a coercive device or agent intended in normal law-enforcement applications not to create a substantial risk of deadly harm or serious injury to the person or persons against whom they are used.

"Nonlethal" is a relative term. All weapons, and a wide variety of objects that are not intended to serve as weapons, create some primary or secondary risk of death or permanent injury. The probable seriousness of their effects (their lethality) depends upon a number of factors, not all of which are determined by their design. Weapons not intended to kill or create permanent injury, used frequently, would undoubtedly cause some deaths because of physiological difference among those against whom they are employed, physical malfunctioning, improper utilization, and other circumstances. Thus, in the weapons context, nonlethal means substantially less lethal—designed to avoid the creation of a high risk of death or permanent injury as a primary objective, and less likely to do so in fact than a device (such as a firearm) intended to have the capability of killing.

It should also be noted that there are degrees of nonlethality. The probability of death or permanent injury from the use of particular nonlethal weapons may range from an extremely remote contingency to a relatively high likelihood. The borderline between the relatively risky nonlethal weapon and the relatively ineffective lethal weapon is a fuzzy one.[2]

Stun Gun (Kinetic-energy impact weapons)

The *stun gun* is a weapon that delivers a cartridge containing a four-inch diameter bean bag loaded with one-fifth to one-half pound of shot. It may be used as a handgun or with an extension as a shotgun. When shot, the bag hits the victim with full force as it flattens on impact and has the effect of a hard hit baseball. The stun gun is used by only a few police agencies. A West Coast police department has recently used the stun gun in a crowd situation and caused a serious injury to an individual. The significant point or characteristic of the stun gun is the very real possibility of death or severe injury if fired within 20 feet and striking the skull or an area containing a vital organ (see Table 11.1).

TABLE 11.1

Weapons	Description	Effects	Current Use or Status	Major Problems or Issues Requiring Research
A. Kinetic Energy Impact Weapons:				
Baton, Nightstick and Billy Club	Wooden stick from 12" to 36" hanging from a leather thong.	Used to administer a physical blow to immobilize or incapacitate or as a hand-held barrier.	Standard equipment for most police and other law enforcement officers for routine patrol and disorder control.	If improperly used, can cause serious injury to victim; need for improved training.
Extensible Billy Club	Measures 6" to 7" in closed position. The three telescopic sections rapidly flick open to an extended 16" to 18".	Adaptation of billy club offering concealment and surprise for personal protection or plainclothes use.	In use in Japan; in limited use in U.S.	Need to identify possible users and user needs.
Breakaway Nightstick	Billy or nightstick made of substance that will break if used incorrectly.	Adaptation of billy club to limit severe injury from misuse.	Undeveloped. Not in use.	Needs to be developed; questionable level of acceptability by law enforcement agencies.
Stun Gun	Special stun gun delivers cartridge containing a 4" diameter bean bag loaded with 1/3 to 1/2 lb. of shot. Can be used as handgun or with an extension as a shotgun.	Bag hits victim with full force as it flattens on impact. Has effect of hard-hit baseball.	Widely advertised, but used by few law enforcement agencies	If fired within 20 feet, force of impact may cause death or serious injury to skull, liver or other parts of body.

Weapons	Description	Effects	Current Use or Status	Major Problems or Issues Requiring Research
A. Kinetic Energy Impact Weapons: (Cont.)				
Broomstick Round	Wooden cylinder delivered by riot guns or by a British Army signal gun.	Normally aimed to strike at legs of rioters or at close range on ground for a ricochet effect. Produces extreme discomfort; effective dispersal agent.	Although used by foreign control forces, not used by U.S. police forces.	Possibility of serious internal injury or death because of force of impact. Field testing revealed problem of splintering.
Soft Plastic Ricochet Rounds	Polyethylene pellets ⅟₁₆″ in diameter delivered from standard 12-gauge shotgun aimed to ricochet. Available in larger sizes.	Used at short ranges (but more than 10 feet), has peppering effect. Used for personal protection.	Not in general use.	No range. Can be lethal within 5-10 feet. Beyond that, insufficient kinetic energy to be effective.
Rubber Baton	Pliable rubber cylindrical projectiles delivered from the riot gun or British Army signal gun .	Used to disperse disorderly crowds and mobs. Shot at ranges of 100 feet, impact on legs or bodies causes rioters to disperse.	Extensively used by the British in Northern Ireland.	Some U. S. police forces have experimented with and indicated desire to purchase these if British manufacturer could export enough. Some risks of internal injury or death.
Blake Impact Gun	Aluminum alloy-type, golf ball-sized projectile fitted to a bolt-action shotgun.	Stuns victim.	New; not now in use.	Possibility of serious injury or death.

Rubber Ball Rounds	Rubber ball fitted with a "Blake" attachment to shotgun. Ball can be solid or filled with liquid or gas. Various designs for point or area targets.	Effects depend on substance in rubber balls, shape and velocity.	Not in general use.	Possibility of serious injury or death, depending on the velocity and material.
Selector System Gun	Handgun designed to give a choice between three types of projectiles: (1) chemical agent, (2) marking dye, and (3) training round.	Varies depending on how loaded. Gives alternative nonlethal capabilities in one weapon.	Available from private manufacturer. Limited use to date.	Poor quality, easily broken. Forces officer to make difficult decision under pressure. Training round can be lethal if shot at too close a range.
Splatt Round (thixotropic)	Any caliber shotgun shells with grease or soft putty on tip; deforms on impact.	Flattens out on impact, making this projectile less lethal than some others mentioned above.	Not in general use.	Possibility of serious injury or death.
Water-filled Projectile	2"-3" spheres with a flexible polyethylene skin. Delivered from special adaptor on shotgun or handgun.	Designed to rupture with an orange peel effect on impact, making it less lethal than most projectiles.	Experimental.	Projectile is too large to be accurate.
Water Cannon	Mobile unit which projects a continuing stream of water.	Force of water, general discomfort and slippery surface aid in dispersing crowds.	Has been used abroad, but not often in the U.S.	Poor public image from highly publicized use of fire hoses in civil disorders in the South.

Weapons	Description	Effects	Current Use or Status	Major Problems or Issues Requiring Research
B. Chemical Weapons: (Chemicals can be disseminated by grenades, projectiles, cartridges or mechanical bulk dispensers. Effectiveness is determined by choice of proper delivery system to fit situation.)				
CN	Conventional tear gas—alphachloroacetophenone	Causes choking, ear tearing, difficulty in breathing. Odor of apple blossoms.	In use after World War I by military and many law enforcement agencies for crowd control and flushing out barricaded persons.	Affected by weather conditions. Some temporary eye and skin injury reported when aerosol dispensers used at close range. Only limited effect on some persons.
CS	Newest riot control agent—orthochlorobenzal-malononitrile	More severe, faster acting and less toxic than CN. Also more persistent because the particles cling. In high concentrations will cause nausea and vomiting. Odor like pepper.	Adopted by Army to replace CN in 1959. Used by many large police forces and institutions.	Affected by weather conditions. Less public acceptance than CN because its effects are more severe. De-contamination is a problem when used indoors.
DM	Diphenylaminechloroarsine.	Violent nausea 30 minutes after use. Smoky odor. Since reaction is delayed, it is often mixed with CN for more immediate response.	No longer in use by military, due to risk.	Effects are too violent and severe to justify civilian use.

HC	Smoke delivered by grenades or smoke pots.	Used to contain crowds by psychologically disorienting its members.	Some use by military, but little use by civilian forces.	Indiscriminate effects on users as well as victims may hinder efforts to restore order.
C. Electrical Weapons:				
Electrified Baton	Standard dimension baton which delivers an electric charge of low voltage, powered by standard flashlight cells.	Administers uncomfortable but harmless shock as a barrier or prod. Effect is like a bee sting but not as severe.	Has been used in some institutions and in a few cases for civil disorders control, but not in general use.	Poor public image. Widespread public outrage developed when it was used by control forces during early civil rights marches. Limited research on effects.
Electrified Water Jet	Mobile unit projecting a waterstream charged with high voltage, low amperage.	Proposed as barrier; also has disabling potential for crowd control or dispersal.	Concept patented but not yet developed; technology available.	Problem of public acceptance. Limited research on effects.
Taser	Fires small, barbed electrical contactors with up to 500 feet of trailing wire which snags victim's clothing. Electric charge administered through barbs.	Victim is paralyzed until electrified contacts are removed or current shut off.	Developed, but not yet in use.	Insufficient testing and research on effects. Public reaction to use unclear.
D. Systemic Drugs:				
Dart Gun	Modified shotgun or handgun in which the projectile is a drug-filled syringe activated by a small charge on impact. Wide variety of drugs available.	Drug immobilizes victim after several minutes delay.	Currently used only in capture of animals.	Amount needed for quick immobilization might be lethal dosage. Police skeptical of any weapon with delayed action.

Weapons	Description	Effects	Current Use or Status	Major Problems or Issues Requiring Research
E. Light Emission, Acoustical, Cold, and Stench Weapons:				
High Intensity Lights	High intensity light on a reflector-equipped hand-held candle holder.	Destroys night vision if blinked off and on to disorient a crowd.	Only used in relatively infrequent special situations.	Effective for only a short time period, as eyes become adjusted to light.
Teleshot	Cartridge projecting a powerful sonic device delivered by a 12-gauge shotgun.	Effect is to disorient and to disrupt communications between leadership and crowd in riot situation.	Only in experimental use.	Affects user as well as victim.
Sound Curdler	Mobile unit creating high intensity sound painful to ear.	Proposed use to break up communication in crowds and to create discomfort to precipitate dispersion.	Only in experimental use.	Affects user as well as victim. At physical distress levels serious risk of permanent impairment of hearing.
Cold Brine Projector	Delivers slug of liquid below body temperature.	Causes incapacitating shock to body.	Technology available, but undeveloped.	Impractical because portable weapon would not have required capacity. Further research needed to determine if cold actually arrests activity. May burn when used in very cold condition.
Stench	Pot or grenade which projects obnoxious odor.	Proposed for use to disperse crowds.	Not in use.	Problems of decontamination, public acceptance and effectiveness. May be physically harmful to persons with respiratory problems.

F. Miscellaneous Weapons

1. Marking Devices

Type	Description	Availability	Comments
Paint Gun	Gelatine capsule contains a marking agent which splatters on impact leaving a 3" circle and streamers from 12" to 18".	Available for commercial marking but not as a weapon.	Could indelibly mark fleeing persons for later capture.	Police have no systems for use of such a weapon. Questionable effectiveness.
Smoke Dyes	Marking dye can be added to smoke in crowd control.	Available.	Identification of rioters. Also a deterrent for anyone anxious to avoid identification.	Not specific enough. Could mark innocent bystanders as well.
Fluorescent Marking Powder	Concept envisions a fluorescent powder sprayed into crowds from pressurized container. Particles adhere to clothing and are only visible under ultraviolet light.	Available.	Could be used as proof of an individual's presence at an unlawful gathering.	Not specific enough. Could mark innocent bystanders as well.

2. Others

Type	Description	Availability		Comments
Foam Generator	Concept involves blowing air through nylon net kept wet with mixture which creates foam.	Available; not in use.	Enormous quantities of foam can be produced quickly to create a barrier which will last 5 to 10 minutes.	Difficult to control. Affects users as well as victims.
Instant Banana Peel, Low-Friction Polymers, Liquids, Etc.	These weapons create a slippery surface.	Available.	Create a barrier by making streets impassable.	Affect users as well as victims. Decontamination is difficult. Lack flexibility. Danger of injury.

Weapons	Description	Effects	Current Use or Status	Major Problems or Issues Requiring Research
F. Miscellaneous Weapons (Cont.)				
Wire Gun	Cylinder containing barbed wire coiled under tension with enough energy to propel wire 80 feet.	Creates effective barrier.	Available.	Police dislike most barriers because they lack flexibility and affect users as well as victims.
Instant Jungle, Instant Cocoon, Instant Mud.	Quick-setting sticky substances delivered by projectile or from back pack container.	Inhibits undesirable action by restricting movement.	Not available.	Questionable suitability and effectiveness for many control situations.
Rapid Rope	Nylon rope dispersed by "Archolithic Gun" using compressed air mounted on truck. Thirty cubic feet per minute.	Can be used to block off small areas such as store fronts.	Available.	Police dislike most barriers because they lack flexibility and affect users as well as victims.

Broomstick Round (kinetic-energy impact weapon)

The broomstick round is a wooden cylinder delivered by riot guns or by a British army signal gun. Possibility of serious internal injury or death because of force impact (see Table 11.1).

CHEMICAL AGENTS

In the police arsenal, chemical agents can be classified as offensive weapons. A discussion of offensive and defensive weapons follows. The principle for using chemical agents in a one-on-one situation for the patrol officer is that properly used, these chemical agents will reduce the risk of injury to the police officer and/or the person on whom it is used. The same principle applies in the crowd control situation. Where action must be taken, and it is not a life-or-death situation, it is more humane to use chemical agents than the baton, for example.

Chemical Mace

Many patrol officers across the United States now have, as part of their everyday equipment, chemical mace. This piece of equipment is a supplement to the other weapons, the baton and gun, and does give the officer an alternative. However, patrol administrators must insure that the use of chemical mace is treated with the same care, discretion, and limitations as the weapon it is designated to supplement. Officers should resort to the use of mace in situations where it is necessary to restrain an individual physically and while the officer is performing his official duties. This situation may or may not be an arrest situation. Many times in the past officers have had to deal with violent persons and had to use a baton to restrain them. The alternative of using chemical mace has helped tremendously in reducing injury to the officer and the citizen.

The author has been injured several times attempting to subdue violent persons (on calls for service to homes where individuals had been acting in a manner where they may have injured themselves or others) because the restraint in the use of force places an officer at a disadvantage. The only defensive weapon available at the time was the baton and assistance from other officers. Any time physical contact has to be made under these conditions, the possibility of injury is substantial. There are also many reports where officers have found that in handling violent persons, the use of mace has had little or no effect. However, there can be little argument against the officer possessing an alternative weapon such as chemical mace because of its design and intent to reduce personal injury. One major point to remember: once chemical mace has been used by an officer and the violent person has been subdued, there is no justification for using it further on that person.

Written procedures on the use of chemical mace should be disseminated to all officers in any department where the weapon is issued. Conditions under which mace may be used should be spelled out and procedures for treatment of persons who may have been sprayed by mace should be explicit. Flushing of the affected areas with water usually is sufficient. However, if any doubt exists, professional medical attention should be given.

Administratively, as in the case of using the firearm, written reports should always be required whenever chemical mace is used. The reports should be in sufficient detail in order to evaluate the effectiveness of the mace used under the existing conditions, as well as be a record so that potential complaints on its use may be responded to intelligently by the department.

CS-Gas (Ortho-chlorobenzal-malononitrile)

CS gas is the latest in chemical agents. It is more severe, faster-acting, and less toxic than the traditional CN (see Table 11.1). CS gas is very effective in crowd-control situations and is used by most police departments around the country in varying degrees and situations. This gas can be disseminated by grenade, mini-grenade, baseball grenade, projectile, and bulk dispenser. The method of dissemination depends solely upon the objective and the situation. What may be effective in one situation may be a total failure under different conditions. For example, mini-grenades are small—3" long, 1" in diameter—and contain CS gas. The gas is released by pressing a lever to the grenade and pulling a pin. Several may be carried in pockets conveniently. They are sufficient to disperse a small crowd in close quarters but would be totally ineffective in dispersing a crowd of twenty in an area the size of a football field. The patrol commander should be sufficiently familiar with the different methods of delivering so the proper choice can be made for the situation.

Wrong decisions concerning the use of chemical agents can infuriate otherwise uninvolved, innocent bystanders.

During the campus demonstrations of the late 1960s and early 70s, it was necessary to resolve problems in and around colleges. Many times the areas of concern were wide-open spaces. The objective of many police commanders was to clear certain areas that had been taken over by students. In attaining the objectives, it was necessary to reduce the possibility of personal contact between student and police. Mini-grenades would not assist in achieving the objectives under these circumstances. It was necessary to use the bulk dispenser (pepper fogger) that allowed large volumes of gas to cover large areas. (Remember, always consider the wind speed and direction. Your goal is not to gas innocent people.) Many times during such situations, it becomes necessary to disseminate gas in a volume not quite so large as the pepper fogger, but in more volume than the mini-grenade. Students group up and move from one area to another. For this situation, the police commander could choose the baseball grenade (grenade shaped like a baseball, which can be thrown accurately and disseminate gas at a very fast rate so that, properly placed, it can have a great degree of effectiveness), or a triple-chaser grenade fired by a shotgun with a grenade launcher attached. The triple-chaser when fired strikes the ground intermittently all the while releasing gas. It is difficult for anyone to throw back at officers, since the majority of the gas is released while the grenade is skipping across the ground and into the air alternately.

Another tactic used by students in urban areas was to block intersections causing the stoppage of traffic. The mini-grenade was very effective for this type of crowd. By distributing mini-grenades to several officers, the exact number required for the situation may be set off at different locations of the intersection. This is important since the goal is to disperse the group without lingering gas and also to alleviate the possibility of dousing innocent bystanders or motorists who have been caught in traffic.

An important consideration, which should be emphasized for patrol administration, is to review carefully the problem of return of gas by the crowd once delivered. Companies producing chemical agents should be made to demonstrate all delivery systems before a decision to buy is made. The choice to buy should be based upon the best equipment made to meet the department's needs.

A very important point that should be emphasized again and again to patrol commanders when using CS gas is to remember to consider wind speed and direction. Do not gas innocent people! Use it only to achieve the objective. The objective will determine the method of delivery and the type of dispenser.

A CONTINUING ISSUE

Whether or not a weapon is lethal or nonlethal, offensive or defensive, and whether or not the police should be disarmed, and what approaches are necessary to stop or decrease the assassination of police officers are all questions of concern and are likely to continue. In a democratic society, there are and should be different points of view so that a resultant procedure, or resolution of the question, will be one that is best for the total community. Police are part of that community and should listen carefully to what is said by the community. However, in recognizing the important role and difficult task performed by the police, the community must listen to the philosophy of their police departments and understand the approaches used to achieve objectives.

Many times chemical agents are used, after a warning has been given, in crowd-control situations, even though the only overt act up to that point has been the blocking of streets or trespassing. The question of when one citizen or a group of citizens are infringing upon the rights of the rest is a touchy one. When chemical agents are used at this time, there may be some who feel that the police have attacked when, in effect, this approach reduces the possibility of person-to-person contact between the police and citizen and is intended to achieve the objective and, at the same time, reduce the possibility of personal injury on both sides. This is the humane approach; one which is amenable to policing in a democratic society, and is used to ameliorate the potential for attack with baseball bats on the one hand and batons on the other. When chemical agents are used intelligently, fragmentation of groups of people can be achieved. When routes of egress from the locations are available, exit can be made without any personal contact. The situation has ended and no violence has occurred. The goal has been achieved. The citizens of our country should be proud of their police departments performing in this manner.

Similarly, many citizens are quite upset when they observe a group of officers arresting one or two individuals. Possibly, they view this act as one of police brutality. However, when viewed as an approach to achieving the objective, under conditions where arrests are necessary, it should be understood that the potential for violence or personal injury is reduced when sufficient manpower is used to effect an arrest. It is less likely that someone will resist when three or four officers are available to assist in the arrests. A patrol commander must always think of safety first whenever making a decision concerning his officers in critical confrontations. There may be times when no other decisions could be made and physical confrontation is necessary. However, when these situations arise, the principle of mass whereby he has sufficient forces (personnel) to achieve the objective, should be the rule. This approach, if it will not completely eliminate, will certainly reduce the potential for violence and personal injury.

Citizens of our country should be concerned. If questions about these police procedures are asked of open, progressive departments, the explanation would surely satisfy their concern. These approaches in no way should be accepted as perfect. Improved approaches should be examined and, if found, resources should be made available to implement them. Additionally, individual or group failures in implementing these procedures should be looked upon as "readily accountable" if citizens are mistreated in any way. Most police departments operating under an open system will welcome inquiries by sincere citizens. In many cases these professional departments use teams of photographers to record the performances of its patrol officers. These films are used to critique the situation and improve the quality of service and performance of the department should any similar situations arise. The success of the police depends largely on citizen involvement.

NOTES

1. President's Commission on Law Enforcement and Administration of Justice, Task Force Report: *The Police,* pp. 189, 190.
2. *Nonlethal Weapons for Law Enforcement,* Security Planning Corporation, 1972.

team policing

Of all the experiments attempted in the patrol forces of police departments in Britain and the United States, team policing is one of the most dynamic. This technique may not be a panacea to participatory management, employee representation, or a giant step forward in getting closer to the community, but it certainly is exploring these areas in an innovative manner. Police patrol should participate as full partners in developing better ways to produce a superior patrol product.

Generally, team policing involves the combination of line operations into a team with a leader. All officers involved in the team have an opportunity to perform the patrol, traffic, CID, and, where appropriate, the specialized functions of narcotics and vice and juvenile control. (Community relations as a specialization is not included, since this function is the responsibility of every police officer; therefore, one of the team's responsibilities.) These teams are assigned a permanent sector or geographic area and are totally responsible for the assigned area. Authority for internal team assignments, scheduling, and complete police service is given to the team leaders. The team is held strictly accountable for total police service. The following discussion will include different concepts of team policing and will look at the Cincinnati Com-Sec team policing in depth.

Only time and evaluation of the team-policing effort will determine the impact of this concept on the American police system. The Dallas Police Department is experimenting in the area of horizontal and vertical growth of an individual officer. This is based on the principle that not all officers are capable of promotion and many officers do not wish to increase their responsibility via this path. Horizontal growth allows personnel to remain in the patrol function and receive a reward through the merit system. This is known as the generalist/specialist concept. It is very close to team policing. Self-actualization of the individual allows the total talents of each patrol officer to evolve in achieving the patrol goal. The Kansas City, Missouri, experiments have allowed patrol officers to be leaders in patrol projects. Early results indicate valuable administrative ability on the part of these patrolmen. If talent remains untapped because of an unwillingness on the part of patrol leaders to be creative, innovative, and responsive to constructive change, policing of the future is in trouble. Present experience and innovation indicate this will not happen.

When employees are involved in decisions that affect them, the results of these decisions are usually more positive. When patrol officers, who are closest to the citizens of the community, are identified as being responsible for the police service and are granted authority and held accountable by the citizens, they become like a police chief on the beat. One of the tragedies of police-community cooperation is that citizens hold the chief of police responsible for police-related problems. Organizationally speaking, this is correct, but realistically speaking, the citizen should resolve the problem, if at all possible, with Officer A or Sergeant B or Team Leader C. These men are more intimately involved with the problem than anyone and should be given the first opportunity to develop solutions.

One of the major pitfalls of team policing is the interaction of the team members and the community, and the interaction between the members of the team. Just as problems of cooperation in the traditional sense occur between patrol and detectives, they may also occur in team policing. This interaction should be watched very carefully by the team leader. Higher authority should also observe this same cooperation between teams. Total communication between members is essential to success of any team-policing method. The transfer of information must be complete and current.

Team policing, or a modified team-policing concept (discussed under "The patrol team"), may prove to be the answer to part of the crime problem as well as improving police-community cooperation, and providing quality police service. However, one must remember that not too long ago, the President's Commission on the Administration of Justice in its Task Force Report: "The Police" indicated the need for centralization in order to gain control of the police agency. Team policing is one of the roads to decentralizing police services. Government and police have tried to provide better services in this way through the use of "little city halls" and "storefront community-relations centers." This would lead one to believe that police agencies must remain flexible, and police patrol forces being the most observable, the most flexible of all.

THE PATROL TEAM

The patrol team is discussed here as that patrol effort best-suited for providing all the police service expected of the patrol force today. In a sense, it is a modified team-policing concept in that team policing as defined previously is supplemental to the patrol team and will only replace the patrol team when it exhibits the ability to provide the total patrol service in an improved manner. Naturally, each concept will be determined by the manpower resource of the police department. Pilot projects should be used to evaluate the methods, and careful analysis on a systematic basis provided. Additionally, as previously stated, the specific goal of the project will have an impact on determining its success or failure.

The patrol team, in the modern traditional sense, contains a sergeant and a squad of men. The patrol team is responsible for a given sector (geographical area) of the community on an 8-hour shift. The size of the sector and the size and configuration of the beats contained in the sectors are determined by manpower-workload analysis studies (Chapter 9). These patrol teams may rotate shifts or remain on permanent shifts.

The team may work together in the sector and be relieved together as a sector. The sergeant and all men on his team are off at the same time and a relief team replaces them. The other approach has the sergeant replaced by one of his patrolmen when he is off duty, which maintains continuity of the team-area relationship. Also included in the approach is the assignment of a beat officer to an individual beat with fixed boundaries that he works each day he is on duty. Sergeants are given extra men in the team (availability factor) so a relief officer works the beat when a regularly assigned officer is on leave.

If the patrol team rotates, the officer remains on the same beat but at a different time of the day. This concept can be very successful if good leadership is provided because responsibility can be placed, authority can be granted, and accountability is possible. The usual advantages and disadvantages of rotating vs. permanent shifts still prevail.

Under the modified team-policing concept, an officer will want the same beat and be given all statistical information concerning his beat so he may be able to perform the total mission. Supplemental to this deployment will be a team-policing experiment. Using the guidelines given by the President's Commission, Task Force Report: "The Police," master patrolmen or police agents are part of this team. These officers (agents) possess degrees in law enforcement, sociology, psychology, business administration, etc. They are made agents after graduation from the police academy and one year of patrol service, and after passing an oral interview given by members of the command staff of the police department.

The teams consist of two police agents and three regular patrolmen. The patrolmen have experience in the investigation aspect and in vice and narcotics, and extensive patrol knowledge. A sample team would look like this:

1. Police agent, degree in sociology
2. Police agent, degree in police administration
3. Patrolman, vice and narcotics background
4. Patrolman, investigative background
5. Patrolman, in-depth patrol experience

An extensive analysis of a given area of the community (usually a high-crime area) is completed. The boundaries of the area are defined and all regular personnel assigned to the areas are briefed on the nature and goals of the teams. Communication up, down, and laterally is established to insure support for the teams as necessary. There is very little supervision and direct control. Goals are established and documentation and evaluation guidelines are written. Time schedules for the review and evaluation are on a regular basis in case goals need to be changed and new goals set. Clear lines of authority are established and coordination and cooperation are requested from all. Initially, it is necessary to document information of a proprietary nature on a daily basis so that redirection can be given on a timely basis.

Once the areas have been selected, the team's first responsibility is to contact each resident in the area and explain the concept under which the team is working and ask for assistance and cooperation. The regular officer assigned to the beat within the area accompanies the team to these introductions on an irregular basis. However, the regular officer is allowed to attend the neighborhood meeting that is set up at a later time or as a result of the work of the team. The regular officer on the beat is asked to communicate the total police picture for the citizens attending this meeting.

As the team continues to progress, the regularly assigned officer begins to meet with the citizens on his beat at one of their homes. At this time, only persons living on the officer's beat are invited to the meeting and a good in-depth dialogue is initiated. This is part of the procedure in attempting to develop the officer into a police chief for this beat. He is now being looked upon as the officer responsible for supplying the police service and must respond to the problem. At the same time, the officer is developing community support and cooperation. This support and cooperation are essential, especially in the high-density, high-crime beats of the urban police-patrol force.

After the officer develops this support, he attends church service on Sunday and is identified by the religious leaders as an important member of the community and hopefully respect will follow as the rapport between him and the community improves. The goals of improved quality of police service—crime reduction and community cooperation—cannot be attained if the patrol officer does not develop himself as being identified with that community. Sincere interest and a demonstrated action on the patrol officer's part is an important aspect of reaching this goal.

While this positive action is occurring between the regular beat officer and the community, the team is starting to define those complex problems that contribute directly or indirectly to police problems in the area. Narcotic peddlers are identified and related to the community. Pimps, gamblers, and anyone contributing to the degradation of the neighborhood are given special attention. If the team cannot be effective in any of the areas, special units are given any information the team possesses in the hopes that a coordinated effort can produce appropriate action. Additionally, the needs of the community, such as sanitation and health are passed on to the appropriate city agencies as a formal request from the police department. For example, back alleys littered with debris may hinder an officer on motor patrol from driving through them in order to prevent dwelling burglaries or apprehend persons using them as escape routes. The Bureau of Sanitation is requested to supply prompt service, and the community realizes the police are helpful and do care. Therefore, better community cooperation results and simultaneously the opportunity for better patrol is available.

Patrol personnel have been taught that crime exists because of a desire on the part of the criminal and an opportunity for successful completion of crime. Also, the patrol officer could not do anything about the desire and should supply his efforts in the area of decreasing the opportunity. However, with the recent introduction of crime prevention via the "Operation Identification" and target-hardening application (reduce criminal opportunity), police are more than just involved with prevention, patrol, and apprehension; they are involved with citizen participation in helping to achieve the goals. This is a step forward, and experimentation and implementation should continue in this area.

At the same time, team policing should experiment using different approaches. Research into the police ability to affect the desire of the potential criminal is very important. Scholars and associates have indicated a need for innovation, creativity, enthusiasm, honesty, responsibility, and a willingness to be held accountable on the part of the team/team leader/sergeant (depending on the approach) if the team-policing concept is to be a success. Patrol administrators attempting to implement the team-policing concept must be aware of the resistance to change, and be prepared to take the steps necessary to implement the change successfully.

BRITISH TEAM POLICING

Team policing was introduced in Aberdeen, Scotland, after World War II, around 1948. The concept was unique at the time. It changed the constable's role of working an individual beat with designated unchanging boundaries to his being part of a team that patrolled a section made up from several beats. Usually a sergeant and five to ten constables were assigned responsibility for providing police service to the sections. The team was supplied a car, radio, and section map. The sergeant was given the authority to deploy his men according to need and could rotate them and work in uniform or plain clothes as he saw fit. This procedure gave the team flexibility and esprit de corps and has been described as the forerunner of fluid patrol and LEMRAS (Law-Enforcement Manpower Resource-Allocation System). This is an IBM computerized system that is leased to police departments. The Aberdeen plan was used until 1963 when they returned to their old method of patrol. This plan was also tried in Tucson, Arizona, and a number of other small American cities.

The Salford (England) plan was similar to the Aberdeen team-policing system except in the amount of flexibility each possessed. Salford was a community of 180,000 in eight square miles, which can therefore be considered high density. Team policing was introduced in Salford in 1949. The city was divided into patrol districts that varied in size according to shift. As the crime situation changed, the districts changed accordingly to meet this crime change. The watch commander was given the authority to make the changes.

Under this plan, the sergeant is the team leader. He is assigned a radio car that is used as the team headquarters. Emphasis is placed on the organizational and leadership abilities of the sergeant because he must deploy his men adequately and stimulate initiative. Each sergeant has a driver assigned to the car so that the sergeant can patrol on foot but have the necessary mobility to reach the other officers of the team. The members of the team rotate their assignments; it is not unusual for a constable to be a driver one day, traffic officer the next, and investigative officer the next. The sergeant quickly becomes aware of the assets and liabilities of each man, thereby allowing him to give advice and training.

This plan produced efficient policing in Salford for the years 1949, 1950, and 1951. Clearances by arrests and decreases in offenses were significant. However, due to increased district demands, the plan was ended. Salford returned to the traditional concept of police patrol of the British police organization. The consolidation in England has caused every police constabulary to have a minimum of 600 personnel.

UNIT BEAT POLICING

British policing methods have experimented with team policing as stated and have tried closed circuit television, commando patrols, neighborhood policing, special patrol groups, and manning-up of a full division. The British have shown the way in experiments of different techniques for police patrol. They are looked upon with admiration. Unit beat policing was started as a result of the mobile patrol of Kirkby in Lancashire. The patrol increased officers' enthusiasm and brought about increased effectiveness, except in the area of clearances. Also, when mobile patrol is used, there is always some loss of the citizen-police contact.

Unit beat policing was first tried in 1966 at Accrington, Coventry. This concept is used by most U.S. police departments and is usually called "neighborhood team policing." The implementation was possible because of an increase in the number of radios and cars. The system includes a local constable who lives in his district and is a supplement to the regular mobile patrol. The resident constable need work only eight hours a day, but these eight hours should coincide with the needs of the area. He is allowed to wear his uniform or plain clothes, depending on the need. The next area of concern is making maximum use of the resident officer's community knowledge. The ability to collect in-depth information of the area is synonymous with this type of patrol. However, the information is only good if it is disseminated throughout the district, and further, if the information is necessary. For this reason, the position of collator was established. The duties of the collator are to collect, record, and disseminate information to whatever area the information may be helpful. Lastly, CID is brought into the concept by assigning one detective to a unit car beat and and two resident constables. This way, the detective is looked upon as belonging to the team.

The unit beat policing plan has to be adjusted according to geographical needs. The center city has dense population, which is mostly anonymous, while that of rural areas is the opposite. One new consideration in America regarding this plan is suburbia. In many urban areas the need for a resident constable or an identified constable who would act as one is almost imperative. Flexibility in patrol organization and techniques must be maintained.

AMERICAN SYSTEMS

In the mid 1960s the team-policing concept, American style, was developed in Richmond, California. This was simply the cohesion of a team of officers working for the same sergeant and having the same leave days and shift. However, there was no attempt to create cooperation among the teams with regard to solving the problem of the areas patrolled.

All patrol officers were team members. There were originally ten teams and the whole city was the neighborhood. Under the team plan the patrol force was organized into five basic teams to cover the 24-hour working day: two relief teams to work days when other teams were off, and a vacation team to relieve teams taking vacations. In March 1972 two additional teams were added as special crime-fighting units. Working closely with the Criminal Investigation Division, these two teams were to work in those areas of the city that might have special crime problems such as burglaries. The Richmond teams differ from others in that they do not have separate neighborhoods.[1] Chief Phelps explained: "Some people use teams policing as a geographic concept . . . A more appropriate use . . . would be to denote a functional entity—a working team—and this is the meaning of team policing . . . for the Richmond Police Department."[2]

Los Angeles Basic Car Plan

The basic car plan began in Los Angeles as an experiment in the Hollywood section in 1969, and on a city-wide basis in April 1970. Under this system, the team or basic car unit contained nine officers: one lead officer, five senior officers and three officers with less experience. The more qualified officers are selected for the basic cars. The sergeant is used as an adviser and counselor, and the team leader is primarily a coordinator. Detectives are not assigned to the team, and there is no increase in the investigative responsibility of the patrolmen. The regular assignment of the area is given to the basic-car plan patrols that are designated "A" cars. To allow for the increased workload, the "A" cars are supplemented by an overlapping car for the regular patrol force. The overlapping cars are designated "X" cars. Under this plan, the increased workload by time of day is covered since most men would be working at this time. The nine officers of the team attend monthly meetings with members of the community to improve contact with citizens.

Detroit, Michigan, Beat Commander

Under this system, the team commander has a twenty-four hour responsibility for the total policing of a given area. Usually the area is high crime and the team consists of a sergeant or beat commander and twenty-one officers. The commander is primarily an administrator and uses planning to deploy the teams based on need and analysis of crime. Officers of the team are encouraged to walk and make contact with the citizens of the area.

Cincinnati, Ohio, Community Sector Team Policing (COM-SEC)[3]

The team-policing concepts, or COM-SEC as it is known, of the Cincinnati Division of Police is presently operating in one district of the city. The district contains about 35,000 residents and 52,000 non-resident workers with an added 225,000 shoppers or tourists.

The "Golden Age" of American police work is usually thought of as a time when a friendly, well-known officer stood on the same corner, year in and year out, helping community residents manage the problems of urban life and learning a great deal about their lives in the process. In the late 1940s and early 1950s, however, reformers found this friendly officer to be corrupt and slow to respond to the scene of an emergency. To solve the latter problems they put him in a radio car. To solve the former, they transferred him so frequently that he would not, they hoped, have a chance to know people well enough to become corrupt.

The impersonal police officer created by those changes became less effective at controlling crime and maintaining order in the class and race conflicts in the 1960s. In fact, both the President's Crime Commission (1967) and the President's Riot Commission (1969) addressed the lack of community contact problem as a serious weakness of patrol operations, and recommended that officers get out of their cars more and talk with local residents. The Crime Commission, in fact, urged that "patrolmen should be considered as foot officers who possess vehicles available nearby for quick, nonfatiguing transportation from one point to another." All of these recommendations point towards a stronger orientation to a particular area served by the patrolman.

Many patrolmen resist the idea of getting out of cars to talk, largely because it is seen as a form of "appeasing" a hostile community (as well as disrupting a fairly comfortable routine). Further, they feel that their continual moving presence on the street is required to provide adequate preventive patrol. Many departments have long held that view officially, to the extent that "unnecessary" or "unofficial" conversation with the public is forbidden by department regulations. However, any crimes prevented by the passing by of a patrol car can be committed as soon as it is out of sight with the comfortable assurance that it won't return for at least five minutes. Police presence can only prevent street crime if police are everywhere at once, which they obviously cannot be.

A more effective way to increase the risk involved in committing a crime is to raise the probability of apprehension after commission of the crime. In the absence of information supplied by the community, though, apprehension is quite difficult. The only way to obtain such information is to get out of the car and talk to community residents. Police officers are generally more receptive to this idea when painted in terms of crime control. Egon Bittner has developed a theoretical justification based on his many observations:

> To give circumstantial factors their correct weight in decision-making it is necessary that they be intelligently appraised. That is, patrolmen must be able to draw on background information to be able to discern what particular constellation of facts and factors mean. In the case of the carefully deliberate policeman—by which is meant a man who organizes his activities with a view towards long-range peace-keeping and crime-control objectives in the area of his patrol, knowing that what he does from case to case can create more or less calculable advantage or liabilities for himself in the future—the background information consists of an enormously detailed factual knowledge.[4]

When one considers that crimes of violence are usually committed by people known to the victim, it becomes quite clear that a knowledge of the human relationships in a community is of immeasurable value in solving crimes. It is instructive, though, that Bittner had to note the "case of the carefully deliberate policeman" as an exception to the rule. The cultivation of area knowledge is not something that police organizations reward, perhaps because it is not seen in the United States as quantifiable. An essential element in the English unit beat scheme is the "collator," or a central recipient of area knowledge reported on a daily basis. Under the English scheme, a constable's effectiveness "will be gauged by the amount of information he feeds into the collator."

The individual officer can only gather information during his eight hours a day on duty, whereas the life of the community goes on twenty-four hours a day. Thus, an area-based team is essential to keep the area-based patrolman fully informed of events, large and small, in his area. Only full communication between all officers working in a given area can meet this need, regardless of the quality of computerized information systems or human collators.

Now let us examine the three models (past, present and future—
Cincinnati).

TABLE 12.1   Cincinnati

	Traditional	*Com-Sec I*	*Com-Sec II*
Assignment	Rotating	Consistent for some, not for others. Not everyone is a team member.	Consistent to all
Communication	Mainly through roll call	Close communications among teams, not for others	Team meetings, rolling roll call, sector information sheets, collators
Community/Police Interaction	Little or none	Sector meetings	Sector meetings, community meetings, walking beats, more time for service
Supervision	By relief, little consistency among them	Supervision indep. of teams	Supervision included in team
Policy-making Power	Minimal	Limited to team members only, no impact on others who may enter the teams area	Wide policy-making and decision-making authority at the team level
Conferences	Supervisors only	Infrequent and separate from supervisors	Regular and including as many as possible from all team ranks.
Public meetings	Only District-wide	Sector-wide	Sector-wide and community group meetings
Investigations	Carried out by centralized units	Same as traditional	Investigators are part of team
Jurisdiction	Limited to patrolling, transportation, and Part II crimes	Same as traditional	All activities except homicide investigations
Referral systems	None formalized	None formalized	At least a first effort with detoxcenter and referral agency

The basic elements of area-based team policing, as distinct from conventional modes of police operations, may be described as follows:

1. Consistent assignment of the same officer to the same patrol beat, radio car sector, or similarly small area.
2. Close communication between all officers who work the given area over the full twenty-four hours per day, seven days a week.
3. Maximum positive and informational interaction between the police and the individuals in the community served.

The Desirable Elements:

4. Unity of supervision or command over the twenty-four hour period, seven days a week, by a team commander (and perhaps some assistants), usually (all) sergeants.
5. Maximum flexibility of policy-making power given to the team and its leader in such areas as scheduling, the wearing (or not) of uniforms, priority setting and problem setting.
6. Conferences (on at least a weekly basis) attended by as many members of the team as possible, to facilitate elements #2 and #5.
7. Public meetings to discuss area police problems with the community held about once a month.
8. Combination of both patrol and investigative responsibilities within the area team, either by assigning detectives to work with the team (maintaining the investigative specialty) or by giving complete investigative responsibility to all members of the team (merging the patrol function with investigation).
9. Clearly mandated original jurisdiction of the team for all police problems in its area, giving it control over the activities within the team area of such specialized units as vice, narcotics, tactical, anti-robbery decoys, etc. (Assuming such specialties should still exist.)
10. The establishment of referral systems to other social and governmental agencies for problems brought to the attention of team members that could be handled more appropriately by other agencies (e.g., family problems, garbage collection, and even drug addiction).

Obviously, it is easy to describe what team policing should include, but it is a different matter to implement such a plan. Without going into great detail, one can expect problems with the community, other agencies, governmental bodies, the other parts of the criminal justice system, and last, but not least, within the police agency.

The problem of designing the community sector team-policing concept in Cincinnati was minimal. Implementing the plan was more difficult. First priority was the resolution of internal communication. The goal of participatory management and accepting the change that team policing was going to bring about was a test of innovative ability. Hopefully, the plan would improve the delivery and quality of police service. Attempts were made to communicate the plan via roll call, newsletter, summary copies for each member of the force, video tape recordings, liaison meetings for each unit, and chain of command. None of these communication channels resulted in total information reaching all members. Finally, the participation (peer-group) method of selecting future members of the teams to communicate the plan informally to all members was found to be the most successful. The future members were trained in role-playing, communication skills, referral techniques, technical training, and team building. After the training, each member returned to his unit and actually sold the program.

In order to prepare supervisory and management personnel to deal with change, the Cincinnati police department worked with the University of Cincinnati. Instructions were given in accepting and implementing change, and understanding oneself in relationship with others managing change. Additional training in crime-scene search, interview and interrogation techniques, and vice procedures were given to all members of the team.

The next approach to resolving the implementation problem was to involve the personnel in the planning. The participatory management aspect was defined as transferring the abstract concepts and goals into practical guidelines. To accomplish this, the task force principle was used. The task force consisted of three team leaders, six (6) assistant team leaders, three (3) investigators, and three (3) patrol officers. This task force was given total responsibility and authority to develop the practical guidelines for action. After the report was developed, it was reviewed for continuity and grammar.

Evaluation. How do you assess the efficiency of such a program? The following is an outline of the Cincinnati Police Division's approach to evaluation of the new Com-Sec model.

There are two areas of evaluation that are required by this comprehensive experiment: very simply, the short- and long-term impact of the program. The Program Management Bureau and district one are responsible for the short-term evaluation while the Urban Institute has been contracted to study the long-range impact of Com-Sec upon criminal victimization and police/community relations.

The Urban Institute of Washington, D.C., will be conducting pre and post Com-Sec surveys in the following areas:

1. Citizen victimization—to be handled by extensive surveys, both within the model district and the rest of the city. Also, the census has sched-

uled a victimization survey for 1974 that we will be able to use since the surveys are compatible.

2. At the same time as the victimization survey, citizen attitude and experiences will be surveyed.
3. In an effort to determine the attitudes of certain, more sensitized groups, surveys will be made of businesses, citizens who have requested service, and those who have been arrested in district one. While this last group is very likely to be less positive toward the police officers, they are, or have been, in a position to experience the program on a first-hand basis.
4. A survey of police attitude and experience will also be conducted in order to measure any impact the program has upon the personnel involved.

Other innovative aspects of this phase of evaluation would include:

1. The number of times an officer does not respond to radio calls in his sector
2. The number and type of citizen contacts
3. The ability of the team to make its method of operation match the problems it faces
4. The amount of citizen inputs into investigations
5. The ability of the teams to provide all police services
6. Crime patterns and statistics
7. Sector meetings
8. The performance of collators
9. The use that the Com-Sec personnel make of other agencies in responding to the problems they face
10. The quality and quantity of service to the community

It is essential that there be community and employee involvement if the change is to be given every chance for success.

The method of patrol for a community must be determined by the police department and the community and employees. This total involvement will give the change a better chance of success.

AN ADMINISTRATIVE, ORGANIZATIONAL, AND OPERATIONAL REVIEW OF TEAM POLICING

The Urban Institute of Washington, D.C., under a grant from the Law-Enforcement Assistance Administration, has presented some interesting characteristics of neighborhood team policing in its project report.[5] Table 12.2 summarizes the planning, funding, training, evaluation, and manpower in the cities studied.

TABLE 12.2 Administrative Elements*

City	Characteristics of City	Planning	Funding	Training	Evaluation	Manpower Allocation
Model City (Suggested Neighborhood Team Policing Organization)	• 80,000 to 9 million people • 100 to 35,000 officer police force	• 6 months to 1 year • Task Force representative of all levels of department • Citizen involvement in planning	• Funding for training and evaluation	• Extensive training for supervisors and patrolmen	• Preferably external evaluation using pre-post data and control groups and focused on community attitudes, police attitudes, job satisfaction, crime and quality of arrests	• Allocation of officers to teams proportional to workload • Does not necessarily require more officers
Albany Neighborhood Police Unit	115,000 residents; 400-man police force	• 6 months • Crime control co-ordinator and team supervisor—extensive analysis of community • Limited police officer and community input.	• OLEA (1968): $337,000 for 1 year for personnel, equipment, training and evaluation	• 160-hour training program for all personnel, with emphasis on social problems, referral, crisis intervention, police-community relations • Community participation in training • Officers encouraged to talk to citizens in the field	• External firm to evaluate program using police and community attitude survey at 3 points in time; police control group to be used	• Allocation based on previous workload and time for community relations work. Team strength 1½ to 2 times previous levels.

*The descriptions given in this chart are based on the first team implemented in that city unless otherwise stated.

City	Characteristics of City	Planning	Funding	Training	Evaluation	Manpower Allocation
Oxnard Neighborhood Car Plan	• 82,000 residents • 100 officer police force	• 6 month period • Chief was primary planner • Limited input from community or other police	• None	• College courses in community mental health and Spanish • Recognized need for group dynamics and ethnic studies	• Chief evaluating police attitudes, one year and two years after program • Control group of police • Crime, arrest, job satisfaction measures	• Manpower assigned based on workload —no increase in manpower • Maximum manpower at peak hours • Ten hour days-4-day week used
St. Petersburg Public Safety Team	• 240,000 residents • 350 officer police force	• 9 month period • Primarily by Chief of Planning and team commander • 3 additional officers in final stages • Some community input	• LEAA—$86,000 for one year—primarily for equipment, cars and portable radios	• First team: 80 hours • Confrontation and stress management, black history, community attitudes, investigative skills, visits to businessmen, rap groups with youth • Other teams: similar 40 hour program + M.B.O.*	• Internal evaluation—control group, pre-post, community attitudes, police attitudes, clearance rates, crime calls for service and meeting M.B.O. goals	• Manpower assigned to teams based on manpower consumption, average manpower, previous allocation, percentage of calls • Maximum manpower at peak times • Steady tours, regular days off

*Management by Objectives.

Table 12.3 summarizes the organizational and operational elements for each of the cities. At the beginning of each table is a summary of a model city that is considered to have adopted the recommendations of the project report.

These tables are reproduced here by permission of The Urban Institute, 2100 M Street, N.W., Washington, D.C. 20037.

TABLE 12.3 Organizational and Operational Elements*

City	Team Area Description	Composition of Team	Supervision	Investigative Function	Stability of Assignment to Neighborhood	Crime Analysis and Planning	Community Interaction
Model City	Team policing applicable to any area 12,000 to 35,000 population	1 Lieutenant-commander 3-4 Sergeants—Assistant Team Commander	• Commander: 24 hour responsibility for team. Authority to police area in most effective way • Assistant Commanders: supervision, training, administration and special tasks (e.g., crime analysis) • Professional Model: Patrolmen participate in decision making and call supervisor when needed	• Detectives assigned to teams • Patrolmen responsible for investigations as determined by team commander	• Commander has influence over outside units working in team area—can call on need basis • Men assigned to team for long period of time • Dispatched out of area only on emergencies	• Regular analysis of crime patterns and workload to determine scheduling and deployment—most manpower at peak hours—use of foot, plainclothes, patrol, and innovative approaches to crime control • Patrolmen participation where possible	• Patrolmen develop rapport with community. • Community input: advisors, volunteers, crime information • Service orientation—referral systems—use alternatives to arrest—follow up citizen complaints
Albany (Neighborhood Police Unit)	• Implemented July 1971 in area of 10,000 residents (50% black, poverty, street crime, unemployment, substandard housing prevalent) • Second Unit in similar area October, 1972	First Unit— • Lieutenant commander • 4 Sergeants • 31 Patrol officers Second Unit • Lieutenant commander • 4 Sergeants • 41 Patrol officers • 4 Detectives • Officers *not* representative of overall quality of personnel	• Essentially like Model City • Sergeants work permanent tours of duty, as do officers.	First Unit: All investigations handled by patrol officers. Second Unit: Detectives handle investigations, analyze crime patterns and suspect data.	• Commander has complete authority in area—*area integrity strictly upheld* • No cars dispatched into area—Unit cars seldom dispatched out • 40 percent turnover in 2 years. Does not seem to have disrupted Unit identification. • Special blazer and cars used by units.	• Deployment based on crime • Use of foot, scooter and plainclothes patrol. • Some participation in crime analysis by patrol officers. • More emphasis on crime analysis in second unit.	• Personal contact with public emphasized • Referrals made • Police act as advocate for citizen in complaints about public service • Lieutenant active in community groups • Advisory Board for second unit • Storefronts for both units manned 24 hours a day • Special blazer and cars used by units

TABLE 12.3 (Continued)

City	Team Area Description	Composition of Team	Supervision	Investigative Function	Stability of Assignment to Neighborhood	Crime Analysis and Planning	Community Interaction
Oxnard Neighborhood Car Plan	• 13,000 residents • 90 percent Mexican American • Poverty, high crime, high unemployment, substandard housing.	Lieutenant-Commander 1 Sergeant 13 Patrol officers • Selected Volunteers	• Lieutenant has responsibility for area on 24 hour basis • Lieutenant and Sergeant also take on city-wide supervision when on duty, but they are involved in planning, training and community relations • Monthly Team meetings	Team has *no* new investigative responsibility; detectives *not* assigned to team.	Try to keep in area. No information available on runs in and out.	Little emphasis on crime analysis and planning.	• Heavy emphasis on service orientation non-aggressive approach • Participation in community projects • Citizen Advisory Board of residents (not leaders of the community)
St. Petersburg Public Safety Team	• Began April 1972 • 26,000 residents • 99 percent black • Median income $5,000 • High unemployment, substandard housing • City-wide (5 teams) March 1973	• First Team: 1 Lieutenant-Commander 3 Sergeants 21 patrol officers 3 detectives 1 secretary • Under City-Wide teams, no detectives assigned to teams. • Officers representative of overall quality of personnel.	Lieutenant has 24-hour responsibility for area and authority. Sergeants are primarily responsible for supervision when needed.	First Team: Patrol officers responsible for all investigation. Detectives assisted and trained but also patrolled. Under City-wide: Patrol officers handle all investigations except homicide, robbery, rape, forgery and auto theft.	• Maintained through stacking screening, orientation. • Only Narcos operate in area without request. • Assignments to teams fairly stable. • Dispatched out only on emergencies.	Pin maps, crime by day and hour used to detect patterns and allocate men. Emphasis on foot patrol in heavy pedestrian problem areas. Lieutenant-Commander construct budget for team.	• Regular community meetings • Emphasis on non-aggressive patrol stance. • Team Commander active in community relations • Blazers, different colored cars.
Cincinnati Com-Sec (District 1)	• 35,000 residents (60 percent black) • 52,000 non-resident workers • 225,000 shoppers and tourists daily • 6 team areas, each distinctive neighborhood	Each team has, 1 lieutenant-leader 3-4 sergeants Assistant Leaders and proportion of District manpower based on workload: 1-5 detectives 11-47 patrol officers and officers (continued)	• Lieutenant has 24 hour responsibility for team area and coordination with other teams. • Sergeants have field supervision responsibilities, planning, and co-ordination of community relations.	• Team responsibility for all investigations except homicide. • Patrolmen responsible for all preliminary investigations —can close case.	• Use of community service assistants to ease patrolman workload. • Dispatched out only when absolutely necessary.	Weekly and monthly analysis of crime patterns, spot maps.	• Regular community meetings • Referral system • Complaint system • Orientation to service and alternatives to arrest, police contact with citizens (park and talk).

The Police Foundation has published "Team Policing," seven case studies, from which I have taken excerpts as a conclusion to this chapter.

Team policing has meant something different in every city in which it has been tried. But all of the team-policing programs studied for the Police Foundation's book (except Richmond, California) attempted to implement three basic operational elements that differ from conventional patrol concepts.

1. Geographic stability of patrol; i.e., permanent assignment of teams of police to small neighborhoods.
2. Maximum interaction among the team members, including close internal communication among all officers assigned to an area during a twenty-four hour period, seven days a week.
3. Maximum communication among team members and the community.[6]

The departments that were not successful in implementing these elements also had in common certain organizational supports:

1. Unity of supervision.
2. Lower-level flexibility in policy making.
3. Unified delivery of services (allows team members to determine need for specialist assistance).
4. Combined investigative and patrol function.[7]

The experience of seven cities indicates that the basic elements of team policing cannot be achieved without training. Whether the training is in the form of participation in planning, good on the job training, or formal classroom education, it is essential. Some changes in police departments can be made by fist, but changes of the nature envisioned in team policing can be made only when the patrol officers understand and support them.[8]

Four of the programs (St. Petersburg, Venice, Cincinnati, Albany) contain most of the elements of our suggested organization. Cincinnati's Planning Task is the basis for our recommendation that a task force be used in the planning process. Venice's extensive block-captain program is an example of an innovative system to involve the community in crime prevention.

The programs in Albany and St. Petersburg have demonstrated how comprehensive team-policing programs can work. In Albany, police-operated storefronts are kept open twenty-four hours a day, and police serve as advocates for residents even on complaints against the city. Although Oxnard's program is not team policing in full bloom, it does demonstrate that team policing can improve police-community relations without additional funding or manpower.

A CONCLUDING WORD, SEVEN CASE STUDIES

Team policing may not be the "end" in patrol administration, but it certainly is exciting to see members of the patrol force of this country experimenting with new approaches. The team-policing concept just might be what the author feels is the beginning of the police revolution: patrol officers working as equal partners with the business, middle class, cultural, and intellectual members of the community. The whole criminal justice system must participate fully in order to make it work, and all of the government agencies must participate to improve the effectiveness of providing total community service. Team policing involves the patrol function intimately with initiating change. Requesting many government agencies to become aware of their responsibilities and causing some to react positively is a tremendous step forward.

> Should team police officers be aggressive, stopping citizens to demand identification? Should they forsake preventive patrol and try foot patrol near their cars, talking to people in a friendly manner? Is a team member different from a regular patrol officer? If so, how? These are important questions, basic to the proper functioning of the team police officer on the street, which training programs could have addressed. The degree to which they were addressed influenced the degree to which team policing resulted in actual changes on the street and in the neighborhood.[9]
> The most critical aspect of team policing is the complex process of moving from plan to fact, from lecture hall to street.[10]
> Team policing was conceived as a means to an end—a decentralized professional patrol style. In none of the cities studied has that end yet been achieved. The many problems and obstacles experienced by team policing projects merely demonstrate the depth of the change they attempt, which cannot realistically succeed overnight. In all the team-policing cities, there were three major reasons that team-policing either failed or reached only partial success. These were:
> 1. Mid-management of the departments, seeing team policing as a threat to their power, subverted, and in some cases actively sabotaged, the plans.
> 2. The dispatching technology did not permit the patrols to remain in their neighborhoods, despite the stated intentions of adjusting that technology to the pilot projects.

3. The patrols never received a sufficiently clear definition of how their behavior and role should differ from that of regular patrol; at the same time, they were considered an elite group by their peers who often resented not having been chosen for the project.

There is at present a great concern among police forces and in American cities at large to consider changes to make police officers more responsive to the community. This concern has surfaced in many projects in addition to those labeled "team policing." Efforts to reestablish foot patrol (the pinpoint patrol program in Kansas City) or bicycle patrol (in Baltimore—originated by the author when he was chief of patrol and may be seen in May 1972 issue of *Police Chief,* New York City, and Isla Vista, Calif.) reflect the need on the part of both community and police for more personal contact between the two groups. The Urban Group in New Orleans Police Department, the Bert Committee in Dallas, and the Pilot District Project in Washington all attempt to improve community relations.

Whether a specific community should adopt team policing, however, depends first on that community's goals, and second, on that community's judgment of team policing's effectiveness within its own situation. Most of all, it depends on both the commitment and the available resources to manage a complex process of institutional and community change.[11]

NOTES

1. *Team Policing, Seven Case Studies* (Dayton, Ohio; Detroit, Michigan; New York City; Syracuse, N.Y.; Holyoke, Mass.; Los Angeles, Calif.; Richmond, Calif.), Police Foundation, 1015 Eighteenth St. N.W., Washington, D.C.
2. "Team Policing, Four Years Later," by Lourn G. Phelps and Sgt. Lorne Harmon, FBI, *Law Enforcement Bulletin,* December 1972.
3. Paper delivered at Southern Police Institute, University of Louisville, by Chief Carl Goodin. Reprinted here with permission of Chief of Police Carl V. Goodin, Cincinnati, Ohio.
4. Egon Bittner, "The Functions of the Police in Modern Society," National Institute of Mental Health, Chevy Chase, Md.
5. "Neighborhood Team Policing," 1973 Project Report to LEAA, The Urban Institute, 2100 M St. N.W., Washington, D.C.
6. *Team Policing, Seven Case Studies,* p. 4.
7. Ibid., p. 5.
8. Ibid., p. 68.
9. Ibid.
10. Ibid., p. 73.
11. Ibid., pp. 107–8.

change and the
patrol administrator

New horizons for patrol and patrol leaders require a liberal education as part of the cultural endowment necessary to manage change
and conflict. Whatever the horizons, people are the prime ingredient,
and flexibility-adaptability the prime attributes. The patrolman needs
to be flexible in performance. The organization needs flexibility to
allow performance by all employees. The patrol leader must deal
with change, change strategy or techniques, change models, change
implementation, resistance to change and change agents. Most likely,
he will be a change agent himself. Questions concerning, for instance, the extent to which women in patrol will affect the complexity
of tasks or manpower distribution, and the assignment of women
in patrol to handle the calls for service will surface. Additionally,
the interaction between the patrol force and the community calls
for understanding, mutual awareness, and careful analysis of change
strategy. Relationships between patrol leaders and employee organizations and patrol leaders and leaders of other units within the
police departments must be enhanced so that conflict does not disrupt goal achievement.

The urban patrol leader must continue to improve his ability to
relate to confrontations because his clientele will not change very
much from what it is today. People are people, and the situations
that require police intervention will not change: domestic problems,
assaults, homicides, robberies. These incidents will always need
effective and understanding response. Decision-making will be the
center of administration, and operational police ability, judgment,
and discretion highlighted in the daily execution of the patrol force.

Hopefully, the patrol administrator will realize the importance of personnel having those qualities that enable them to be good police officers. Education is an attribute but not a panacea. Once hired, personnel possessing the right qualities should be trained to perform those tasks assigned to the patrol force professionally. If tasks are presented realistically and officers are required to resolve the tasks using simulated exercises, excellent performance can result. After six months in the field, officers should be returned to the police academy to evaluate what was taught, the procedures presented, and the likeness or difference between the academy and the field.

As a manager of conflict, the patrol administrator has to be a problem solver. The ability to influence people is synonymous with power in many respects, and a real attribute to any individual who must resolve conflict. In the management by objective approach to patrol administration, knowledge of traditional organization and how to make it flexible in order to achieve goals is essential. The patrol administrator who develops his ability to think is like a sponge in his thirst for knowledge, reading and retaining everything available that is written about patrol. He will use his talent to see the forest rather than the trees. The criminal justice arena needs coordination and cooperation from all participants. This mind-expanding role should aim at saving the chief of police as much work as possible so that the chief may use his time in resolving problems and doing all those things (usually external) that no one else has the position or authority to do. The elevation of the patrol function to the position it deserves in a police department is here. Now it requires enlightened, planning patrol leaders to produce the superior change expected from it by the citizens of our country.

CHANGE

Alvin Toffler in *Future Shock* states that change "is the process by which the future invades our lives."[1] Patrol administrators must develop an ability to control the rate and direction of change as it applies to the patrol force. Knowledge of current issues, political aspects, special interest groups, legal questions, and employee-organization relationships would enhance this ability. For example, the national unions are highlighting the humanistic aspect of employer and employee relations. The principle of workers as individuals as opposed to machines or numbers has been the central issue of many negotiations. Control of one's own destiny, so to speak, is taking its place as a real part of the negotiating process. Management is being required to consider the human side of the worker in planning and implementing work organization and production. Self-actualization is becoming a reality. For example, auto workers, instead of placing a siren into position every ten seconds, now participate in building a total part of a particular car.

Team-policing in law enforcement has evolved into the generalist/specialist concept with a change in tasks for each member. The approach of using the total talent of each participant in producing the police function is on the increase in police departments around the country. The management by objective approach to patrol administration allows the personnel responsible for achieving the goals to participate in setting the goals. This is a reality for some police departments. When management takes this initiative in sharing power, there is a greater possibility for controlling the rate and direction of change for the organization.

The patrol administrator cannot look upon change as a one-time event, but rather as a continuing part of his crisis-oriented nature. Consequently, his mind must be trained to meet each crisis with effective decisions based upon his accumulated knowledge. This should consist of a broad background in political science, history, sociology, psychology, mathematics, planning, management, urban studies, labor relations, social psychology, law, and experience. This knowledge should also include being flexible, able to adapt to changing situations with the appropriate decisive response. The patrol administration must also know how to evaluate situations and programs for their effectiveness. This directly relates to goal-setting and changing goals after evaluation. Cooperation between patrol leaders and the academic and scientific community is necessary in order to determine the value of crime prevention, apprehension, as well as understand how different patrol techniques affect these goals. There should be no change just for the sake of change, but willingness to change as appropriate is essential to preclude management failure.

Change must be related to the individual organization. Patrol administrators within each department will have to reflect on the part they must play in the change in attitude, values, behavior, policies, and structure of the total police organization. Therefore, change will be tailor-made. Depending upon the priorities and goals of the department, patrol must be able to work with the resources available in order to achieve the goal assigned to it. The ability to communicate will continue to be an important factor for the patrol leader because of the need to disseminate information. Patrol officers will continue to use discretion, but management responsibility will be to provide information in sufficient amounts so that decisions made at the level of execution will be improved as a result of accurate, timely information.

History is full of examples of external forces causing police agencies to change. In many cases, police procedures have been the catalyst to these changes. These changes (especially the court decisions) have been largely for the better. One of the qualities for the police administrator mentioned by the American Bar Association "Standards Relating to the Urban Police Foundation" is "sensitivity to policing in a democratic society." The President's Commission on Law Enforcement and Administration of Justice in its report, *The Police,* has had a profound effect on law enforcement and the total criminal justice system. As a result of this report, the Omnibus Crime Control Bill, or the Safe Streets Act of 1968, has caused a great move forward in the administration of criminal justice. These examples indicate that law enforcement has been the target of change, rather than the initiator of change.

One of the realistic methods of having a voice in change decisions is to be the initiator of change. In order to develop into initiators of change, it will be necessary for law enforcement to become more sophisticated as an entity in its relationship to other institutions and agencies within and without the criminal justice system. It will also be necessary to teach the formal planning process to all members of patrol to enhance the total participation and understanding of organizational goals and assist in paralleling goals of the individual and the organization. Consequently, the entire patrol force will be working together to achieve the objective. As the first step of planning is recognition of need, so the first step in change must be to recognize the need to develop the patrol force in a manner that makes it capable of change. This awareness regarding change capability and implementation includes a sense of timing. A word of caution when introducing the planning process to all levels of the patrol force: the patrol administrator should plan the implementation so that an organized, coordinated effort will result.

Whisenand and Ferguson express this quite clearly: "Planning is the process by which the police department adapts its resources to changing environmental forces and achieves its goals. It is a highly dynamic function and must be carried out effectively so as to provide a solid foundation for the remaining managerial activities."[2] This is reinforced by Blumenthal: "The planning function in the police organization can be considered as an integrated decision system which established the framework for the activities of the organization."[3] Whisenand and Ferguson go on to say, "It is the responsibility of management planning to plan an integrated planning system that will enhance organizational performance. In other words, planning for planning."[4] Planning must not be done in a vacuum.

There are two outstanding examples of the importance of planning and change in law enforcement: the Los Angeles County Sheriff's Department's Long-Range Planning and the Dallas, Texas, Police Department Five-Year Plan. The first points out the planning process, and the second reveals the need to achieve change without disrupting the police organization, other agencies, or the community.

The Los Angeles County Sheriff's department has a grant to develop the law-enforcement long-range planning project for the California Council on Criminal Justice. The purpose of the project is to design, demonstrate, and evaluate a long-range planning process which prescribes what a large law enforcement agency should be doing today in preparation for an uncertain tomorrow.

DRAFT ARTICLE
FOR
MANAGEMENT FORUM[5]
SHERIFF'S DEPARTMENT
MANAGEMENT PLANNING PROJECT

In February 1972, the Sheriff's Department launched a time-phased, development project to enhance management planning processes throughout the Department. The Project is funded in part by a federal grant through the California Council on Criminal Justice. The overall aim of the Project is to design a formal planning system whereby top and middle management can:

— Chart the future course of the Department;
— Periodically establish and assess an integrated hierarchical set of goals and priorities on a Department-wide basis; and
— Link such planning decisions to the County budget process.

Present plans call for completing the design by June 1974, along with a schedule for instituting the new planning system during the subsequent 12 months. Some of the more important features to be incorporated in the System include:

— A capability to monitor external factors that top management views as the most critical in terms of their impact on the Department's future.
— Management by Objective practices so that each manager throughout the Department would be planning for his own area of responsibility, and further, be evaluated on goal achievement.
— A program structure so that the Department's planning efforts will complement and contribute towards the new approaches being instituted by the Board of Supervisors and the Chief Administrative Officer concerning Program Analysis and the means whereby the Board of Supervisors will examine goals, progress, and budget requests of County Departments.

The recent shifts in County budget processes provided the Department with an excellent opportunity to conduct a "real-world" test of key concepts and practices presented in a Project Training Program for management and staff personnel selected throughout the Department. Last fall, as part of the Project a Department-wide effort was launched, aimed at establishing a clearly articulated hierarchy of missions and related goals for all organizational units under the command of top and middle management. The guidelines and terminology for managerial planning, presented in the start-up training sessions and subsequently used in the Missions/Goals Program, were supportive of those set forth in the Chief Administrative Officer's January 1973 request to all Department heads for a Program and Goal-oriented analysis of budget requests. Hence, the mission and goals statements generated throughout the Department were used to formulate the Sheriff's 1973–74 Program Analysis/Goals and Objectives document presented by the CAO to the Board of Supervisors.

The fact that Project-stimulated mission and goals statements were useful in meeting the new budget request requirements illustrated the pragmatic philosophy that underlies the Project. The project approach recognizes that changes in planning practices must be incremental, evolutionary, and relevant to issues and problems facing managers in the Department. For example, in addition to designing the overall new system for Departmental planning, the Project will also produce a practical manual for step-by-step planning. The manual, scheduled for production by the end of 1973, is designed to guide each manager through the creative, deliberate thinking required as he performs his planning role within the framework of the new System.

The Department's expectations for the new planning system are realistic. The new System is not viewed as a panacea. Rather, through its use and continuous refinement, it will help managers at all levels to analyze where he is, what he wants his organization to achieve, and the steps and costs required to get there. Finally, there is simply no better form of management development than the learning-by-doing offered by results-oriented planning.

TASK II REPORT
ASSESSMENT OF PRESENT PLANNING PROCESS
SUMMARY

Data collected in the first six months of the Long Range Planning Project have been analyzed. The following are conclusions which the joint LASD/PSSI Project Team has drawn regarding the state of management planning in LASD:

No formal mechanism exists to support top management planning decisions.
The Department does not possess a clearly articulated hierarchy of missions, goals, and objectives.
The missions of many staff units are ambiguous.
New projects and new ideas are launched in a fragmented uncoordinated manner, resulting in duplication and dissipation of resources.
In many cases, LASD managers do not realize that planning is an integral part of their jobs and is not a staff activity.

LONG RANGE PLANNING PROJECT

Introduction

Under a grant from the California Council on Criminal Justice, the Los Angeles County Sheriff's Department (LASD) is conducting a Long Range Planning Project. Briefly, the objectives of the project are:

1. To design an improved long-range planning mechanism for LASD top management.
2. To develop a plan for the second year of the project so that the newly designed mechanism can be demonstrated, tested, evaluated, and refined for permanent implementation in the Department.
3. To improve the quality of planning at all levels of LASD.

The last objective, that of improving the quality of planning at all levels in LASD, is not explicit in the grant under which the project is operated. It is the belief of those involved in the effort, however, that when planning at the top management level is improved, a concomitant improvement in planning will result at all departmental levels.

Project Organization

The project embodies a joint team concept. The Sheriff's Long Range Planning Unit (LRPU) has joined with the project consultant, Public Safety Systems Incorporated (PSSI), in working toward the objectives stated earlier. A second consultant group, University of Southern California's Center for Futures Research (CFR), is providing ongoing evaluation for the project. PSSI's services are being channeled into three broad areas. During the course of the project it will:

1. Aid the Department in examining and assessing its present planning.
2. Assist the Department in increasing its current planning capability by recommending improvements in the process.
3. Help the Department to create an in-house capability to continuously improve its planning process.

Project Status

The project has reached halfway mark. The three formal tasks completed to this point constitute Phase One, which encompasses the following:

1. An appraisal by the Project Team of present goals of the Sheriff's Department.
2. An assessment of existing planning processes in LASD.
3. A survey of planning processes and techniques in use by other organizations to determine transferability to LASD.

Purpose of the Report

This report will comment on the conclusions reached by the Project Team regarding the state of management planning in LASD. Those conclusions, by themselves, will not come as revelations to members of LASD management. It is hoped, however, that as an appraisal of LASD's state-of-the-art in planning, it will lead managers at all levels to think about planning, and to give careful thought to their own requirements for an effective planning mechanism. The second phase of the project, the design of that mechanism, will require understanding, interest, and participation on the part of LASD executives.

Definitions

In order that managers of the Department can think about and discuss planning in common terms, this document establishes a basic planning terminology. Much of the management-planning literature clouds the issue because there is little semantic agreement. Confusion can be avoided if the definitions below are accepted for the context of this project.

1. *Planning* is a process whereby managers make decisions with regard to:

> Goals and objectives.
> Courses of action to achieve those goals and objectives.
> The means to continually evaluate and alter either of the above.

The definition implies three things. First, goals and objectives, whenever possible, should be measurable and verifiable so that their achievement can be recognized. The courses of action selected should represent the best use of an organization's limited resources. Finally, the means to evaluate and alter either goals and objectives or the courses of action leading to achievement requires flexibility in planning.

2. A planning mechanism is a structure or system which facilitates the planning process. Using an illustration from Robert Anthony's book *Planning and Control Systems:*

> The distinction (between "mechanism" and "process") is similar to that between anatomy and physiology. Anatomy deals with structure—what it is; whereas physiology deals with process—how it functions. The digestive system (mechanism) facilitates the process of digestion.

Therefore, the planning mechanism facilitates and supports a planning process. The mechanism consists of:

a. Decision-makers (managers)
b. Staff support to decision-makers

c. Rules, policies, and procedures which govern the actions of the "people" components.
d. An information base.

3. *Plans* are tangible results of planned decisions. They document both goals and objectives and the courses of action selected to reach them.

4. *Missions* are the enduring functions of an organization and its components.

5. *Goals* are desired end-results which are to be attained by a selected course of action. They represent guides to action.

6. When a planning mechanism is characterized as *formal,* or formalized, it has the following features: it is structured; it is procedural; and it is planned in advance. The mechanism components have explicit authorization. The rules and roles for the people involved are published. The scope of the mechanism is clearly defined so that the set of planning decisions supported is understood. The need for formality varies from agency to agency; sufficient formality is needed to make those people involved in the mechanism known to the entire agency.

7. *Long-Range Planning* is the process by which managers make planning decisions having multi-year impact. It involves the establishment of organizational goals for the future and developing plans to meet long-term requirements. The time range for which the organization plans, called the planning horizon, depends on the needs and capabilities of the specific organization.

For LASD, the most appropriate long-range planning horizon appears to be three to five years.

It should be noted that forecasting is not planning. Forecasting is a staff function which facilitates the planning process by providing managers (decision-makers) with estimates of future conditions and circumstances.

This list of terms and definitions is not comprehensive. It is sufficient, however, to deal with this project and its implications.

Factors Influencing Present LASD Management Style

The project team identified several factors which color LASD and make it the kind of organization it is. The Project Team viewed these factors as important background to any organizational analysis of LASD. The Team's efforts were directed toward identifying these factors and gauging the degree of their collective influences on the organization.

1. *Rapid Growth.* Following the establishment of the first contract law-enforcement relationship in 1954, LASD has grown rapidly. The greatest personnel increase, which occurred in the mid-1960s, was necessitated by a rising crime rate and a rapid population increase in Los Angeles County.

Those factors, coupled with the expansion of contract law enforcement, have brought LASD to its present size. Currently, LASD provides a broad range of services to a demographically diverse population.

2. *Bureaucratic Outlook.* Internally, "bigness" has led to a kind of compartmentalization. The Project Team observed that personnel in each Division tend to view other Divisions as separate entities, rather than as a part of the same organization. Proceeding through channels is a time-consuming, often self-defeating process. The result is a bureaucratic environment in which people frequently accomplish things through the informal organization. That bureaucratic posture is reinforced through external contacts with other government agencies on all levels.

3. *Quasi-military Orientation.* LASD is for the most part rooted in a rank-oriented organizational environment. The prevailing management style is authoritative. Direction by fiat is far more common than leadership through ideas. This style of management produces satisfactory accomplishment at most levels, but at the cost of some initiative and innovation. Much of the energy in any authoritative organization is expended in discovering new ways to "beat the system."

4. *Emergence of New Managers.* The Project Team perceived an emerging new manager type in LASD, reflective of changes in society. The evolving manager appears to have adopted a normative view of the organization, seeing it as it should be. Although he works within the organization as it is currently structured, he personally is less authoritarian in his leadership style. Further, he is less receptive to the authoritarian style from above. He wants to participate in decisions which affect him. This new manager is likely to have a profound future impact on the Department because he appears to be a highly promotable individual by virtue of education and awareness.

Analysis of Management Planning

In arriving at its conclusions regarding the state of management planning in LASD, the Project Team relied on information drawn from three broad sources. First, it interviewed top management personnel and over sixty other line and staff personnel throughout the Department. Secondly, it studied a range of LASD documents, including announcements, Unit Commander's letters and various memoranda and communications. Lastly, the Project Team observed various LASD activities, operational as well as managerial, in order to gain first-hand knowledge of various aspects of the LASD planning process. The comments which follow are the results of that effort.

1. No formal mechanism exists in LASD to support top management planning decisions. That is, LASD does not possess in writing an explicit, planned set of roles, rules, policies, and procedures for the planning mechanism which supports LASD top management's planning decisions. Those decisions are currently supported by an informal mechanism which acts without a unifying design or charter. There is no mechanism in LASD for coordinating and facilitating department-wide planning on an ongoing basis, analogous to the mechanism established for coordinating and facilitating the preparation of the annual budget. The following comments, drawn from interviews with LASD managers, characterize the need for more formalized, multi-divisional planning:

> . . . exchange of ideas and planning information dealing with multidivisional concerns is informal, and primarily based on the personal rapport developed . . .
> . . . a more formalized mechanism would force . . . (executives) to interact on important managerial issues before they become (major) problems.

Certainly, using the definition of planning cited earlier, planning does take place in LASD, and documented plans do result. However, the quality of that planning is highly variable and there is no consistent requirement or mechanism to relate planning in one component with planning elsewhere. As a result, plans may be developed which are contradictory or inconsistent.

2. LASD does not possess a clearly articulated, hierarchical set of goals and objectives. In order for managers at all levels of the organization to plan intelligently, they must be able to determine how their plans fit in with the goals of the total organization.

Interviewees expressed an inability to determine where LASD

is headed and how they can contribute. They appeared to be saying, "How can I tell if I'm doing what I should be?" Some of their comments were:

> Rarely is there an attempt to relate proposed major planning decisions to other major ongoing or proposed LASD efforts. There is a lack of coordination of major efforts within the Department.
> Often a commander in the LASD hierarchy doesn't know where or how his unit fits in a grand scheme or the big picture.
> LASD does not really have clear goals and objectives now. If this project does nothing else but clarify the goals of LASD, the project will be worthwhile.
> It is difficult to set goals because LASD problems and solutions vary so greatly.

Lacking a framework, managers are likely to develop plans which have merit in themselves but do not contribute to overall LASD goals, even to the point of detracting.

The comparatively new budget approach does not constitute a framework for systematically setting organizational missions, goals, and objectives. The budgeting mechanism currently employed is a major improvement over previous procedures, but the budget, which in other organizations constitutes a plan, serves only as a constraint on the men, material, and physical plant for LASD and its organizational elements.

3. The roles of staff units are ambiguous, despite a formal charter for each unit promulgated in the Manual of Police and Procedures. The charter is the result of each unit's perception of what it thinks it should be doing, based on what it has done in the past. The Research and Development Bureau compiles statements from each unit regarding its activities, then publishes them in the Manual. The role of each unit is therefore self-defined, and, in the context of the organization, unclear.

4. Staff units are assigned projects on what appears to be a random basis. Each top manager has his own preference in a staff unit, based on past work products or familiarization with unit personnel. Such assignments frequently vitiate the appropriate role of the staff unit. Many staff units appear to work with little awareness of the activities and objectives of other units. Frequently, completed staff work exists in one unit which is useful to another. The present situation does not facilitate the sharing of such staff work. It leads, instead, to persistent reinvention of the wheel and a clear waste of LASD resources.

5. In many cases, LASD managers do not realize that planning is an integral part of their job, and therefore is not a staff activity. Too few LASD managers have the time to devote to systematic planning activities, and when they do, they often lack the appropriate skills. There is a general lack of an understanding as to the nature of formal planning. Managers frequently find themselves in decision-making positions for which they are unprepared by either education or experience. Middle managers expressed genuine concern over developing qualified people for supervisory and managerial positions.

Implications for Future Direction

If a formalized planning mechanism is to be designed, there are three questions which should be addressed:

1. What should the scope of the new mechanism be?
2. Should the new mechanism include a specialized staff unit(s) as a component?
3. If there is to be a specialized staff unit, what should its role be?

Clearly, in any organization the degree of formality associated with its planning mechanism is never zero (totally informal) and never 100 percent (totally formalized in writing). Thus, when formal planning mechanisms are designed and subsequently documented, the people who are to be involved in, or affected by, its operation know how it is to work. This alleviates problems and misinterpretations that arise when people who are affected by the operation of a planning process do not have a clear understanding of the role and rules.

Planning mechanisms should be formalized to the extent that they can facilitate an organization's internal communications. It would be incorrect to conclude that all planning processes in any agency should be, or need be, documented, especially if planning roles and rules are clear to all involved and directly affected.

Regardless of the organizational form, the degree of centralization, and the presence or absence of specialized staff in any formalized planning process, there are certain common guidelines for developing and maintaining formal planning. It is most advantageous that police executives keep them in mind when considering formal planning in their agency. They are:

1. Planning is the primary responsibility of management at all levels in the agency.

2. The way in which the planning process is designed depends very much on the scope of agency missions, its size, how it is structured, and the personality of the chief executive.

3. An effective, comprehensive agency planning process can be developed only if there is a clear understanding of the nature of the comprehensive plans to be produced.

4. Management must understand that a comprehensive planning program cannot be introduced into the agency overnight and be expected to produce immediate miraculous results.

5. There must be a very clear understanding of the planning process, including distribution of authority, procedures, and planning nomenclature.

6. If a staff director for planning is appointed, he should report to an appropriate executive at the top levels of the agency.

7. The formal planning system should encompass adequate machinery for implementing plans, reviewing progress, and evaluating results.

8. Once a comprehensive planning program is begun, it should not be allowed to fail, for the result will be worse than if it was not started in the first place.

9. Some three or four years may be required for a formal planning staff to reach a fully working system and to establish satisfactory interactions with managers and planners at other levels within the agency.

10. A major problem in getting started is that of clarifying the duties of managers and staff in providing services to management, and in coordinating the activities of planning groups that already exist within the various headquarters offices and major divisions of the agency.

11. The task of the staff director for planning is a demanding one because of the endless interrelationships between the centralized planning staff, the major subdivisions of headquarters, and the operating units. The many opportunities for potential conflict should be recognized and anticipated. Much care and thought are required in establishing lines of authority.

12. It is very important that the planning director and his staff understand that they do not make decisions; their mission is to help top managers meet *their* planning responsibilities.

The information presented is not the total project, however it does delineate the expectations of the project as it is currently being developed in the second year.

DALLAS

The Dallas, Texas, Police Department has instituted a five-year-plan which reveals an understanding of the planning-change relationship and the need to carefully and continually evaluate change.

> In the 1969 Eisenhower Commissioner's Report, cities of the future were described as consisting of numerous cellular fortresses with "sterilized" arteries linking them. These corridors, under heavy police supervision, were the only safe means of traversing the frightening inner ghetto where street crimes ran unrestrained.
>
> To avoid that situation, we are faced with achieving the necessary change in a manner that permits change without organization or community problems.
>
> It is important for management guidance to develop information in the likely consequence of actions that modify the current system. One way to collect data about such changes is to make the changes on a limited basis and weigh the results. According to the Task Force Report on Science and Technology to the President's Commission on Law Enforcement and Administration of Justice, "Wherever practiced, this kind of controlled experimentation is clearly to be preferred.[6]

CHANGE STRATEGY

In the management by objective approach to patrol administration, it will be necessary to innovate, due to the fact that additional resources, particularly manpower, cannot be counted on. Additionally, the hard-earned tax dollar should be spent efficiently and economically; therefore, all needs for additional resources should be justified in depth. This will cause broad exploration about what procedures are presently used and what alternate procedures may be used to accomplish the same goals with existing resources. Most police departments have some form of research and development unit. (The author recommends this unit to include the formal change agent of the department.) *Research* is the detailed process by which new knowledge may be gained and precipitate change. *Development* is the next stage of implementation. *Innovation* is a part of development in which a new device or idea is introduced to a number of people. It is only at the stage of development and innovation that most operating managers become involved with changing situations.[7]

In developing a change strategy, the patrol administrator first must consider the personnel of the patrol force. The degree of sophistication, status of recruit and in-service training, extent of formal education, executive development programs, existing atmosphere regarding participatory management concepts, and conditions of the personnel after completion, will affect this aspect of the strategy.

Second, the police agency as a whole and the change itself must be evaluated before the strategy may be implemented.

Third, begin the change at the point where a problem has been identified so that positive results will be obvious concerning the change. For example, if you wish to change the method of officer reporting—that is, change the officer's procedure of driving to the police facility to write his report to writing his report in the field so that the officer does not leave his patrol area—then identify a situation where a potential apprehension may have been made if the officer were not in the building but on his patrol beat. Additionally, emphasize the fact that the procedure is obviously more economical, routine contact with the supervisor will enhance the training concept and errors in report writing will be corrected immediately, decreasing the potential for staying behind after shift change to correct the report.

Fourth, include the formal and informal organization and the personnel who will be affected by the change in the diagnosis, data collecting, formulating, goal setting and total planning of the change.

Using the example above, the better approach to change would be to use a pilot district, shift, or sector so that an evaluation of the change could be made. Making a total change rather than a limited one may cause confusion and result in a negative attitude about the change. Potential for success of the selected area is important. If success is attained in the pilot area, then the results can be used to show the potential for total change. Subsequently, each stage of implementation can be refined, making it easier to conclude each subsequent stage successfully.

CHANGE MODELS

Numerous specific change models are pertinent to law enforcement. Each model deals with some aspect of the process of change.

The following review will help the patrol administrator in analyzing the approaches to change.

1. *Modification model for dealing with changes in knowledge and information*

   For managers of organizations to become professional, they must learn to use and modify the knowledge of others. But the knowledge has to be applied in the manager's world rather than in the scientific or academic world.[8]

   The orientation of the manager is toward action and his payoff comes in results and problem-solving. This model views knowledge and the scientific world in a way that does not require polarization. The manager is not forced to have his head in the clouds or his hands in the grease. He modifies the one world to fit the other.[9]

2. *Planned Change Models*

   a. Concentration on the deliberate and collaborative idea of planned change.[10] For change to be deliberate, there must be an effort by some party or parties called change agents to affect the client system. The client system is usually the person or unit in need of and desiring the change.[11]

   b. Lippitt-Watson-Wesby model focuses on the relationships between a change agent and client system and postulates the following stages:

1. The development of a need for change
2. The establishment of a change relationship
3. The clarification or diagnosis of the client system's problems
4. The examination of alternative routes and goals; establishing goals and intentions of action
5. The transformation of intentions into actual change efforts
6. The generalization and stabilization of change
7. Achieving a terminal relationship [12]

   c. Similarly, the National Training Laboratories postulates a model of planned change that has eight phases:

1. Diagnosis of the problem of the client system
2. Assessment of the motivation and capacity of the client system to change itself
3. Assessment of the motivation and resources of the change agent
4. Establishing and maintaining a working relationship with the client system
5. Choosing the appropriate role
6. Selecting appropriate change objectives and targets
7. Provide support and encouragement for change behavior
8. Termination (or new continuity) of helping relationships [13]

d. Buchanan puts forth a nine-step process model of planned change:

1. Clarify or develop the client's motivation to change
2. Assess the change agent's potential helpfulness
3. Establish effective relations between the change agent and the client system
4. Clarify or diagnose the client system's problems
5. Establish instrumental objectives for change
6. Formulate plans for change
7. Carry out plans for change
8. Generalize and stabilize changes
9. Institutionalize planned development or self-renewal [14]

No matter how it is expressed, the first step in planning is the recognition of need for change. For example, if the housing authority of a community can be shown that architectural design can help reduce crime, the need for change will be obvious. In *Defensible Space,* Oscar Newman states that "an architect, armed with some understanding of the structure of criminal encounter, can simply avoid providing the space which supports it."[15]

e. Arnold Judson in *A Manager's Guide to Making Changes*[16] discusses another planned change model: how people are affected and respond to changes and why their resistance is primarily based upon attitudes.

Judson's approach is very close to the formal planning process, except for the inclusion of a communication stage that is a key aspect in change. The innovator or change agent must understand the value of the ability to communicate and that attitudes are directly affected by the communicative ability.

Niehoff emphasized this communication by the innovator (change agent) and response to change by people with a diagram (see Figure 13.1).

COMMUNICATION BY THE INNOVATOR

Formal. The transmission of information by means of formal group meetings, usually neighborhood councils and sometimes in classroom situations.

Personal. The transmission of information by means of face-to-face interaction between the change agent and the recipients, usually in paired or small-group situations.

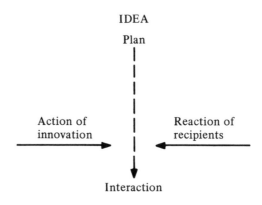

FIGURE 13.1

Audio-Visual. Methods of transmitting information regarding innovations by means of audio-visual devices such as printed materials, pictures, charts, loudspeakers, radio, television, and other mechanical aids that have been developed for influencing public opinion.

Demonstration. The techniques of showing in a pragmatic fashion the advantage of a new idea or technique as a means of convincing the recipient to adopt it.

Feedback. The response to the innovator regarding the proposed new practice.[17]

A study of these models will prepare the patrol administrator, no matter which model or combination of models he chooses. Simplistic attitudes toward change, assumptions that the problem of crime is due to police inefficiency, or one type of police deployment is best for all departments, are all unsupportable. The management of change, coupled with flexibility of action and evaluations of change, will determine future ideas in patrol concepts and operations.

IMPLEMENTING CHANGE/THE CHANGE AGENT

The time has arrived for the patrol administrator to take his place in law enforcement. Opportunities abound for enlightened patrol leaders to experiment with new patrol approaches to achieve the objective. In order to implement change, the change agent must understand the meaning of power and be able to identify the decision-makers of government and his department. In other words, identify those individuals who have the authority to make things happen internally and externally. It is difficult to induce change without some person taking the situation in hand, confronting it, and then acting as a catalyst to initiate the change. It is proposed that the patrol administrators of our country seriously consider being change agents. The willingness to change with the new demands of the position of patrol administrator will enhance the individual departments.

The patrol administrator cannot be alone in his role of change agent. He should select enlightened patrol leaders of his command to participate in being change agents. He should ask leaders of other units of the department to join him in forming a task force to come together as a group to solve complex problems and generate cooperative ideas in developing procedures that enhance the total ability of the department to achieve goals. This group could pave the way for participatory management-concepts that would permeate the entire department.

In some cases the patrol administrator and his contemporaries may be too busy, and an alternate course of action could well be to allow middle management to form the task force. The assignment of one middle manager from each unit to act as change agents for the respective units could produce a task force of change agents with a goal of total development of the department. This type of approach would direct change at three levels: (1) the individual, (2) the group, and (3) the department or system, whichever is appropriate.

Another approach at implementing change would involve the research and planning unit of a department. With the emphasis on participatory management and the evolvement of the personnel of a department being looked upon as individuals, the humanistic view, career development, and career-path concepts are primary considerations. Change agents and career-development officers should be identified as a part of the research and planning units of police departments (see Figure 13.2).

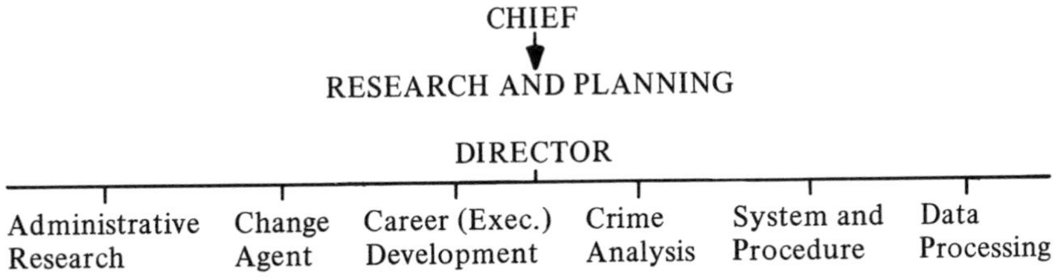

CHIEF

RESEARCH AND PLANNING

DIRECTOR

Administrative Research	Change Agent	Career (Exec.) Development	Crime Analysis	System and Procedure	Data Processing

FIGURE 13.2 Research and Development Organization (including change agent and career development sections).

One of the primary responsibilities of the change-agent unit would be to determine the capability of the department to change. This is a prerequisite to initiating change. Most police departments' awareness of the need for change and capability to plan and manage change is limited. Considerations involved in determining a department's capability to change are: need for change, individual conditions, and resolution of conflict over proposed change and its implementation. Premature, prompt, or unnecessarily delayed acceptance of change does not preclude consideration of other changes.

The change agents must also determine where change is desirable and necessary and accurately define problems, assess and utilize resources within and without the department; innovate, adopt, or adapt solutions in an effective, efficient, and further change-inducing manner. One method that could help improve the change agents' impact on change in the department would be to have them act as an animate suggestion box. The usual procedure for offering suggestions and new ideas is to write the suggestion and put it in a suggestion box. The proposed method would identify the personnel who are acting as change agents to the department and replace the suggestion box procedure with a telephone call. This simplified procedure would of itself stimulate participation and elicit freedom of expression at all levels.

Change decision will cause conflict between competing interests, and this conflict should be resolved before the final decision or change is made. Personnel should have a voice in change decisions before they are made. Therefore, it is imperative that consultation with the people who will be affected by the change take place. The change agent, when implementing change, thus should first and foremost communicate to the recipients of the change. The goal of this communication is to bring about a willingness to accept the intended change. The five methods proposed by Niehoff (formal, personal, audiovisual, demonstration, and feedback) should be used in combination to suit the need. Voluntary compliance can be accomplished if the change is understood and improvement of the organization and its members are the goals.

If the patrol administrator is to implement change successfully, he must be aware of the many obstacles that will confront him. These will come from a variety of areas. Consideration should be given to the following:

1. *Political obstacles.* Conflict over goals and methodology. Factors influencing change: dependence authority, power, city manager, city council, legislature, employee organizations.

2. *Rate of change.* The rate of change must be controlled. Change may be good or it may be bad; it is wrong to assume that all change is good. Change just for the sake of change is wasteful. The suggested change may have to be slowed, if for no other reason but to think out the situation more clearly. In some cases, change has to take place to a point where its merits are clear enough so that a decision to continue or not can be made.

3. *The criminal justice system.* Change can be hindered simply because the intended change may be good for police, but bad for prosecution or corrections. Each change must be reflected upon with the total system in mind.

4. *Community organization.* The patrol administrator as well as the chief of police knows full well the power that can be wielded by community organizations. Texts on police administration instruct the potential chief how to use community power to initiate change. By the same token, a failure on the part of the patrol leader to include the community in planning and implementing change can result in a negative response and a failure of the intended change. For example, a patrol administrator may wish to patrol an area of high incidence purse snatch with a K-9 team on foot. If the residents of the community are not considered and informed, an unfortunate biting incident may cause a negative reaction from the community, which may in turn organize and force the discontinuance of the patrol. The patrol technique may be resulting in a decrease in purse-snatching, but the issue has changed and all potential improvement is lost.

5. *Crisis factor.* Patrol administration may be intimately involved with implementing a change that primary evaluations indicate has the potential of excellent success. However, resources must be diverted because of riots, legal ramifications, athletic contests, etc. Maintaining a constant application of resources to the change becomes difficult and consequently planning for these obstacles is most important.

6. *Financial support.* Even though the power may lie in different points depending on the situation, money is always necessary in implementing change and without it there is no change to any extent. This obstacle may be overcome, but it takes the highest administrative ability and personal diplomacy.

7. *Credibility.* Mutual trust must be developed between the line and staff members of the change team. Whenever implementing change, a sincere reciprocal projection of support from both line and staff is necessary. Understanding the role of line and staff and the

potential for conflict is important. Ways of alleviating the conflict can be developed so change implementation can be achieved.

8. *Acceptance of failure.* Every attempt at change has a certain amount of risk involved. Change agents should not delude themselves or others into thinking every change will result in success or in a "can't miss." Awareness of potential failure allows for realistic approaches, reexamination of methods and self-renewal. Also, failure accepted will not preclude attempts at future changes.

9. *Decisiveness.* Risk is inherent in change. If effective change is to take place, the faint of heart or insecure should not be in an important position of change implementation. Indecisions may well be considered negativism by many and cause the intended change to fail.

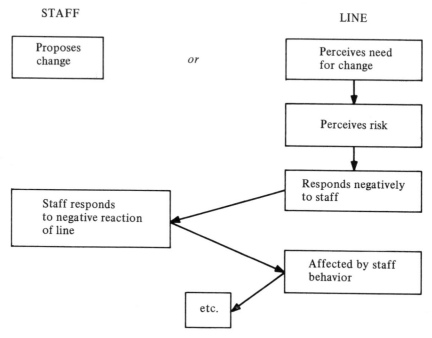

FIGURE 13.3 Change Encounter[18]

The effective change agent cannot forget that important trait of leadership, setting examples. If the patrol administrator is to be a change agent, he will have to be willing to change and take steps to demonstrate his ability to do so. His ability to change should be shown to all internally and externally. The initiation of participatory management programs would be an excellent method of demonstrating his ability to change (see Chapter 2, Patrol Planning Council). This team method of participatory management has byproducts for the patrol administrator as a change agent and for the implementation of change itself, in that the following will occur:

1. Personnel affected by change have a voice in the process.
2. Chance of success will be enhanced by broad input.
3. Improved validity and accuracy of information.
4. Improved communication process.
5. Expeditious feedback necessary for change in objectives.
   (This self-renewal may or may not be necessary; however, the feedback is imperative.)
6. Improved efficiency of the patrol force and the total police department. Relationships with other units are more compatible because of increased confidence and self-actualization of the members of patrol.
7. A better understanding of the goals of the patrol force, and expected performance by each member.

DOZEN CHANGE ISSUES

It would be naive to believe that any police leader has the power or the resources to control the rate and direction of change completely. However, by understanding the processes of change and its components, it is possible to "not let change control the leader." In order to do this, it is suggested the leader learn about the dozen change issues:

1. Realistic approaches to change through knowledge about restrictions on himself and his organization and methods to remove those restrictions as necessary.

2. Goals and priorities that have been set for his department through equal partnership between himself, the chief executive, and the community. These goals and priorities must also be realistic.

3. Reaction to failure and criticism.

4. The process of lateral entry and the consequences this process may bring.

5. Pressure groups within the department and the community (goals, tactics, and techniques).

6. Presenting an open police agency. Allow for citizens to participate in policy and procedures. Disseminate information about

crime and its effect in totality. Cause citizens to come to the department and view patrol allocation, deployment, and distribution. These honest and open methods should stimulate community support and cause the patrol force and the department to become an extension of the community. This extension can be very positive if the patrol leader communicates the goals and strategy of the force effectively. For example, "Let us show you how we are using our patrol force to protect you. We use a priority approach, and with help from the citizens we can do a more effective job." A high-crime area could be pointed out and an explanation given on how it was reduced: citizens agreed to report for work within a given hour and police were specifically assigned to the area for that hour. Result: citizen participation in crime prevention. Change? It sure is, and a good one. There will be no great impact on crime without citizen participation.

7. Career paths. The identification of individuals who have the potential to be leaders and the design of a plan to develop known human resources. This change can make possible in the future police departments in which the total command structure would be qualified as administrators. There will be a collegiality of command. Each command officer of future police agencies will have enough responsibility, authority, and accountability to self-actualize. Additionally, the interchange of department heads and deputies of governmental agencies can produce total effort against crime. Does the sanitation department have an effect on crime? Does the health department? Does public works? Do the officials of each ever converse with one another? If so, has crime and the impact each agency can have upon it ever been the topic of discussion? Efficiency and economy in government can be improved if middle and upper management are allowed to exchange positions along with the knowledge they possess.

8. The fact that it is the nature of law enforcement to be involved in change and crises. Society changes. People are society. People are the clients of police. Therefore, change is the client of police. This fact should cry out to police departments asking for change from: the rigid structure to the fluid-flexible organization that cuts red tape; allows for freedom of expression and thought; teaches that some issues cannot be answered by yes or no, right or wrong, good or bad; provides information to all personnel in direct proportion to their decision-making needs (if patrolmen are going to use discretion and alternatives, they need the information that will make the decisions effective and efficient); and accentuates the individuality of members of the department.

9. Other departments throughout the country and their approach to change and organizational development. New concepts are emerging with regard to structure and personnel. Equipment is not the only thing that needs to be changed in the police agencies of our country. The Kansas City, Missouri, Police Department is experimenting with proactive, reactive patrol, peer-group management, and change in organizational form to provide the necessary services. One form is called ARGUS (Area Responsibility Giving Unified Service). The Dayton, Ohio, Police Department has been experimenting with a centralized-decentralized organization mode.

10. Ways of improving communications. One has been mentioned (Patrol Planning Council). Other methods of improving the communication process are the team-policing concept; hiring communications experts to formulate programs to increase open communication; better equipment (closed-circuit television, audio-visual tape); shorten the chain of command; career development; and well-defined and planned departmental conferences.

11. The amount of personal attention he must commit to the implementation of change and its follow-up evaluation in order to make the change meaningful.

12. The climate of the organization with regard to change. What are the attitudes of the men about change? Do they like the status quo? Are they proud of the department, or do they think the department is not progressive and rates lower than others of the same size and population? Has change come easy in the past, or has resistance been large and organized? Can participation of the persons involved in the change improve chances of success? Many questions need to be answered by the patrol administrator/change agent before he implements change if success is to be achieved.

All of the dozen are important, but number 12 should be done first. The diagnosis of the personnel attitude toward change is essential, because the results will determine the approach and procedure for the change. Second, those persons selected to be change agents must be aware of the existing conditions and attitudes toward change. For example, if the department was found to have a negative attitude toward change, the change agents would have to be leaders who were respected, had credibility, and an ability to communicate. There would have to be a selling job done in order to create an atmosphere in which the change takes place. If the wrong person is selected for change agent, the program is doomed to failure before it even starts.

RESISTANCE TO CHANGE

Resistance to change in patrol stems from three general reasons. First, the patrol force has received lip service regarding its position in police departments. Statements indicating that patrol is the backbone of the department have been just that. Patrol has been the first step in the career of an officer who has traditionally used it as a stepping-stone to a specialized position, usually in the criminal investigation or detective unit. Laymen look upon the plainclothes police officer as having more capability. The news and electronic media have displayed the patrol officer as someone merely used to handle the routine police service who steps aside for the detective when he arrives upon the scene of an incident. In some cities the business community would not even give a preliminary report of a burglary to a patrol officer, but wanted the detective to respond. It matters not why or who is to blame for this view of the patrol officer; what really matters in today's American society is that it change.

Even though there are situations where patrol officers will, out of necessity, continue to direct traffic, guard prisoners or witnesses, etc., enlightened patrol leaders must insure the presentation of an accurate picture of the patrol officer. The concern of citizens over increasing crime, the riots, civil and campus disorders, and the involvement of citizens in crime prevention and community relations show that the process has begun to change the image and importance of the present-day patrol officer. Team-policing concepts are just the beginning of patrol experiments that hopefully will result in concrete facts concerning the impact patrol has on the administration of criminal justice. Enlightened police leaders are using manpower-distribution studies to deploy patrol personnel in a manner that solicits creativity and innovation in patrol strategies.

Second, there has been a lack of initiative on the part of young police officers, rising through the ranks, to accept the very real challenge of the patrol function. Thus, lack of initiative has been assisted by neglect on the part of police chiefs to assign the appropriate personnel to patrol positions. Consequently, the change agents in the police field have not been the patrol leaders. However, this is also changing.

Many progressive law-enforcement agencies require field command as a prerequisite for promotion to a higher echelon of the police department. This is as it should be. The increase in the number of innovative commanders will produce an organizational climate conducive to developing change agents. Concurrent with this will be the ascension of the importance of the training effort within police departments. In-house executive development programs will increase with upper level courses being taught, such as the process of innovation and the management of change. Limited resources in manpower and support services will make the innovator the most important manager because of the ability to produce an improved police agency with existing resources.

The third basic reason for resistance to change in patrol has been the lack of any real research in the patrol function. Questions such as: How do we measure preventive patrol? What effect does saturation patrol have on a specific crime in a specific area? Is it better to have officers work permanent shifts or rotating shifts? What is the crime displacement factor? and What effect, if any, will employee organizations have on a department's ability to affect crime rates? need to be answered.

Additionally, the influence of health, sanitation, employment, type of population, and economic factors on crime should be included in any research if realistic solutions to the total problem are to be reached. The symposiums on Law Enforcement Science and Technology have had a profound effect in the area of research for police. LEAA and the Police Foundation are welcome participants in our country's battle for a safe and secure society.

Patrol commanders everywhere are being cast as important figures in police departments. Seminars and workshops on patrol are being presented in many parts of the country in which leaders in patrol exchange ideas and techniques. A revolution is taking place in patrol, which will hopefully lead to improved strategies for management by objective and achievement of goals. The untapped talent of the emerging patrol commander will be used, not to the detriment of anyone, but for the betterment of everyone in our country.

ATTITUDE AND BEHAVIOR

There is no such thing as an inherent quality in man to resist change. People resist change for several reasons. If a patrolman views a sergeant with respect and credibility, that sergeant will have very little difficulty presenting new ideas and concepts to the patrolman.

This pattern usually occurs throughout the several levels of authority. Patrol leaders who have this attitude usually are aware of mutual confidence, respect, trust, loyalty, empathy, and people-oriented management. The needs and desires of the recipients of change are considered. This results in a lessening of resistance to innovation. The feeling of belonging and that someone cares for the officer and his opinion integrates a positive attitude on the part of the change agent. This attitude permeates the department, and the involvement of subordinates in the planning and the decision-making processes confirms it.

Participation in the change process takes time, but confrontation will result if orders for change are given as they have been in the past. The confrontation may not be face-to-face or physical, but in the mental attitude of the recipient officers. Rules, regulations, manuals of procedure, and general orders are all necessary in a police department, but "Obey the order or suffer the consequences" may not be the best approach. Selection of alternate approaches designed to implement change in specific situations will reduce attitude and behavior resistance. The prime example of this activity is the difference in departments that have developed grievance procedures in anticipation of employee organization and those departments that didn't and now have conflict. Sharing power and participation in decision-making will result in police leaders being successful in achieving the goals of law enforcement, whereas the unwillingness to accept change (or to change on the part of police leaders) will result in having the power taken away, which will affect the opportunity for success in achieving goals.

A change in attitude and behavior on the part of management is necessary if change in attitude and behavior on the part of the recipients of change (subordinates) is to take place. If management in the patrol force projects an attitude of "I only have five years until I retire so don't make any waves," or, "I don't need any education and training. I've been doing it this way for twenty years and it works, so why should I change? I've been around for twenty years and you young men who have been around only five or ten think you have it all," mediocrity will continue.

In order to be objective, two viewpoints of these comments need to be taken. First, and this statement clearly explains the view, "You may have twenty years experience, but more than likely it is one year, twenty times." Second, there are young men who do not plan their strategy for change and attack the power instead of trying to persuade in an objective approach. Naturally, when the attack on the position of power is made, the power is threatened and resistance and confrontation result. Young patrol leaders should strive to have some patience in this approach to change: i.e., take half a loaf instead of a whole loaf, or get a foot in the door and use it as a base from which to work. Remember, patrol administrators, do not be afraid to innovate and create, but do not burn your bridges behind you. Once you have projected an attitude of scorn or looking down on, you may have produced an opponent who will resist any change you suggest or attempt to implement. The statement, "If I can take one step forward even though I may have to back up three, it is still progress" is not without validity. If a patrol administrator can develop an attitude of "reducing the crime of robbery by one each month on each beat," the result at the end of the year will be surprising. This approach is also very realistic, easily grasped, and officers can relate to it rather well. Sometimes change must become very basic and pragmatic for it to work. The basic change of attitude is essential for reducing resistance to change. An example of "turning men off with a bad attitude" is to imply by attitude that they work *for* you instead of *with* you. Contemporary patrol leadership requires that officers be led as individuals, not machines or beats or numbers.

VOLUNTARY ACCEPTANCE

The willingness to change can only be developed if effective communication, interpersonal relationships, and integration of theory and practice are introduced and totally assimilated by the recipients. The patrol leader must not be afraid to face any subordinate or group of subordinates and allow open and honest discussion of the particular change. The cliché, "If two people always agree, one is unnecessary" should be carried to the level of execution throughout the patrol force. Whenever a presentation of change is communicated by a patrol commander, he should have all levels of authority present between himself and those to whom he is making the presentation. For example, if a captain were communicating an intended change, asking for participation in planning, to patrol officers, he should have the lieutenants and sergeants present (if this is the rank structure).

This concept is almost a problem-solving or brainstorming session with everyone participating. In many cases the time it takes to complete this approach is minimal and the dividends are tremendous. However, a reminder to patrol leaders before they use this approach: do your homework. Plan for anticipated questions and appropriate responses. Do not make the presentation unless it is as complete as possible under existing conditions. Select the proper time, since timing can make the difference between successful change and failure. After the presentation, stimulate reaction and project the relationship between change and failure. Be objective and honest by stating both advantages and disadvantages. Maintain a position of flexibility (if voluntary acceptance is attainable by modifying your position, be prepared to make the decision weighing alternatives). Explain incidents and intermediate and long-range expectations, and offer as much support as you may possess for your position of leadership.

Many times, the response may be to give it a try. The patrol leader finds himself in an advantageous position because he can now win the battle. He must pay personal attention to the trial, and follow-up and evaluation become necessary. Additional presentations of status, success and failure, are required and self-renewal should cause increased positive response to the change. The resistance to change caused by involuntary acceptance has been overcome. Voluntary acceptance becomes synonymous with broad support for the change. Once that has been accomplished, there should be smooth sailing. There is an art to the process of change, implementing change, and overcoming resistance to change, and patrol administrators should study that art.

CHANGE AND CONFLICT

More and more it has been recognized that conflict is a central part of police work, especially patrol, because of the voluminous contacts between citizens and police. However, for the patrol leader conflict takes on new meanings. He must self-analyze, diagnose, and understand the difference in his own value systems, and be aware of his different modes of behavior and leadership styles in order to determine which style to use for a given set of circumstances. The diagnosis should consider the factors of difference: i.e., proper identification of problems and accuracy of information. Second, there can be some very real conflicts over methodology. Usually, the goals of the organization can be agreed upon quite easily. However, the method used to reach these goals involves sensitive issues. The patrol leader has to know (after self-analysis) where to intervene in the differences of his subordinates so that the differences do not become open disruptions.

The willingness to change on the part of all concerned is an asset regarding the lessening of conflict, and knowledge is directly related to the willingness, especially at the command level. Conflict in this case can be compared to each individual looking out of a box: each sees a different picture—values, experience, intelligence, education, and perception play a part in the respective position. The patrol administrator must know the when, where, how, and why of intervention in order to resolve conflict. One basic point is to always keep conflict eyeball-to-eyeball.

Whatever the conflict, it is not necessary to push an opponent into the corner, so to speak, over an issue. Whatever is valued by the individual, when attained, should end the conflict. Sometimes time can be a very effective tool in resolving conflict. What looks like an impossible issue one evening may diminish into nothing by the next morning. Patrol leaders should realize the value of time. Additionally, the ability to identify issues and the participants in issues may result in preventing conflict. When the patrol leader analyzes the problem and realizes the conflicting parties are outside the police department, noninvolvement may be the best answer. Liberal-educational backgrounds are most helpful in resolving change/conflict situations.

WOMEN IN PATROL

Many police departments have discontinued the use of the terms "policewomen" and "patrolmen" and have replaced them with the contemporary "police officer." The use of women in policing around the world spreads across the full spectrum. In France, for instance, the use of women in policing is almost nonexistent, while in Japan women are used in all capacities throughout police agencies.

Will the attempt at total assimilation of women in policing reveal an untapped resource, or will the results indicate what many police veterans say, "Women in police work will continue to have a limited role"? Experiments conducted thus far in the United States would lead one to believe that expansion of the female role in police work is inevitable, especially in the area of patrol.

First, it is illegal to discriminate against any person applying for a police position on the basis of sex. Second, the Civil Rights Act of 1964 warns of liability for violations of discrimination by sex. Third, the Law Enforcement Assistance Administration (LEAA) prohibits discrimination on the basis of sex.

The National Advisory Commission on Criminal Justice Standards and Goals has this to say about employing women in the police profession:

Standard 13.6 *Employment of Women.*

Every police agency should immediately insure that there exists no agency policy that discourages qualified women from seeking employment as sworn or civilian personnel or prevents them from realizing their full-employment potential. Every police agency should:

1. Institute selection procedures to facilitate the employment of women; no agency, however, should alter selection standards solely to employ female personnel;
2. Insure that recruitment, selection, training, and salary policies neither favor nor discriminate against women;
3. Provide career paths for women allowing each individual to attain a position classification commensurate with her particular degree of experience, skill, and ability; and
4. Immediately abolish all separate organizational entities composed solely of policewomen except those which are identified by function or objective, such as a female jail facility within a multi-unit police organization.[19]

The obvious conclusion is that patrol administration should take a positive approach in integrating women in patrol in order to achieve objectives.

A Review of Women in Police

The first use of women in a capacity related to policing was in 1845 when six matrons were hired in New York City to care for female prisoners. In the late nineteenth century, women were granted the opportunity to expand their roles to the areas of juvenile work, social problems, minor gambling violations, and some investigative work. In 1906, the first woman was appointed in Germany; in 1910, the United States (Los Angeles Police Department); and in 1914, the Metropolitan Police of London. The duties of these women remained the same in most of the police departments when appointments were made; that is, women were used as supplemental to men

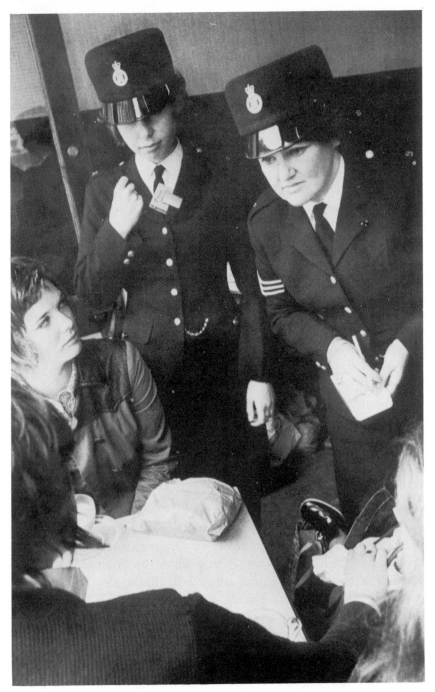

FIGURE 13.4 British Constable and Sergeant questioning youngsters about whom there's been a complaint. Photo Crown Copyright. Reproduced by kind permission of the Controller, Her Majesty's Stationery Office.

in most cases, except for the areas where their sex provided a special ability. In 1960, there were 5,617 female officers in North America. Of these, all but 400 served in urban areas.[20] At the time, women in policing equaled approximately 1% of the total police population; however this percentage is increasing each year.

The 1950s saw policewomen assigned to such tasks as pickpocket details, missing persons, juvenile, vice, narcotics, fraud, crime lab, and training. These assignments were in areas of little danger or as members of decoy squads where danger exists, but male officers are always present. The British team-policing concept of 1966 included a uniformed female police officer and was concluded to give the team more flexibility. In 1969, the Liverpool, England, police experimented with women police using the task force approach. The task force was composed of 68 officers (6 sections, 1 Sergeant, 8 constables, and 1 female constable). The task force arrested more than 5,000 persons during its first year of operation, and the female constable was treated the same as the male constables. The female constable patrolled on foot, in vehicles, and plainclothes and performed well enough to receive commendation.

Presently, several experiments are being conducted regarding women in patrol, New York City and Washington, D.C., being two departments with extensive programs.

Washington, D.C.

In April 1972, the Washington, D.C., Police Department under the leadership of Chief Jerry Wilson became actively engaged in integrating women in the patrol force. Approximately 100 women were to be added to the patrol force when the program was completed. The originating circular entitled "Utilization of Policewomen in Patrol" (Appendix G) became effective on April 17, 1972. The Police Foundation funded persons to achieve evaluation of the programs. Data were determined by reports, questionnaires, interviews, and observations.

Problems and Considerations

Women in patrol in any large number is different, a change, and there are always some who are unwilling to accept changes. Usually, experience and knowledge enhance understanding and the barriers of today become the normally acceptable of tomorrow. At the national meeting of the International Association of Policewomen there was a reported silence regarding women in patrol. However, in 1973 the mood at the meeting apparently changed and patrol was a requested assignment.

Problems facing any implementation plan of women in patrol include: assignment limitations, if any; types of uniform (skirts, pants, shoes, etc.); weapons (type and where carried); attitude of personnel regarding change; and physical requirements. Determining the change capability of the department is also necessary. The use of a pilot program, as done in Washington, D.C., is an effective way to introduce change and to evaluate and determine the status of new programs.

Some Findings

The report by the Police Foundation, "Policewomen on Patrol (Major Findings: First Report, Volume I)" has revealed some findings that stand out. Keep in mind, however, at the conclusion of data collection for the report, the newly hired policewomen had only four-months average experience on patrol. Some of the findings are:

> Police service given by policewomen and policemen is equally acceptable to citizens. Regardless of sex, police officers are highly rated for their attitudes, respect for citizens, and their ability to handle a variety of situations. Citizens tend to believe policewomen should be given an equal opportunity to become patrol officers; hiring policewomen will not affect crime rates or arrest rates; policewomen would be advantageous in handling domestic disputes but disadvantageous in handling street fights or riots.
>
> Policemen, policewomen, and officials agree that fewer women than men can handle violent or potentially violent situations satisfactorily. The women think there is less difference between women and men than do the men. Policemen and officials have negative opinions about policewomen. They think that men are more likely to be "calm and cool," "courageous," "persuasive," "strong," "decisive," "aggressive," "observant," and "emotionally stable." Women are thought more likely to be "understanding," "compassionate," and "intelligent." Policewomen have a more positive opinion about themselves. They think women are more likely to be "persuasive," "decisive," "observant," "emotionally stable," "intelligent," "understanding," and "compassionate." Men are thought more likely to be "strong" and "aggressive."

The study is continuing, and other topics being reviewed include women's performance in violent and potentially violent situations, effect of policewomen on policing in general, and the effect additional patrol experience will have on female performance and on both female and male attitudes.[21]

I predict that the success of women in patrol will be based on individual performance.

DIRECTION FOR PATROL

The National Commission on Criminal Justice Standards and Goals has submitted its final reports to the attorney general of the United States, "A National Strategy to Reduce Crime." The Commission's recommendations are directed at police, courts, corrections, community crime prevention, and the criminal justice system. Many recommendations are directed toward increasing the effectiveness of the police in reducing crime and recognize the patrolman as the primary force in reducing and preventing crime. They are stated here so that educators, police officers, and students can develop effective discussion regarding the future of policing generally and the patrol function specifically.

— Active crime-prevention efforts by the police working with the community
— Diversion of juveniles, drunks, and mental patients from the criminal justice system
— Use of the patrolman as the primary investigator for crimes which come to his attention
— Consolidation or elimination of police departments with fewer than 10 full-time police officers
— Increased use of civilian personnel
— College education entrance requirements for employment of police officers
— Legislation authorizing police officers to obtain search warrants by telephone
— Continuing analysis of crime trends and deployment of special units to react to developing crime trends
— Establishment of different classifications and pay levels within the basic patrolman category
— Development of units within police departments to work with prosecutors, courts, and corrections officials and to follow specific cases and individuals through the criminal justice system.

The Police Role

Maintenance of order and enforcement of law are the two traditional missions of the police. As society has become more complex, many and varied demands have been put upon the police because of their unique authority. In developing its recommendations, the Commission recognized the many functions that police agencies perform, including:

— Prevention of criminal activity
— Detection of criminal activity
— Apprehension of criminal offenders
— Participation in court proceeding
— Protection of constitutional guarantees
— Assistance to those who cannot care for themselves or who are in danger of physical harm
— Control of traffic
— Resolution of day-to-day conflicts among family, friends, and neighbors
— Creation and maintenance of a feeling of security in the community
— Promotion and preservation of civil order

These functions represent the core elements in the contemporary role of police. However, controversy exists as to the emphasis that should be placed on each of these functions. The Commission has recognized that local governments and citizens are in the best position to determine their needs, and the ultimate definition of the police role and the degree of emphasis to be placed on each function should be consistent with the laws and needs of the community that is being served.

It also is crucial that the police role be defined within the legal limits of authority. There are numerous laws that set out the authority under which the police must operate. In addition to, and in accord with the pertinent law, guidelines should be developed for handling such problems as the resolution of family disputes and neighborhood altercations; the taking into custody of adults and juveniles, alcoholics, drug offenders, and the mentally ill; and the control of civil disorders.

Every police agency should write out a detailed statement of its role. The statement should be consistent with the United States Constitution, the laws of the state or city, and the policies of the government the agency serves. The statement should identify the absolute limitations on the use of force by police and should establish guidelines for the use of discretion in making arrests and maintaining order.

— The Commission recommends that police agencies in major metropolitan areas establish a specialized unit responsible for maintaining communication with the community. In smaller agencies, the police chief executive should assume direct responsibility for maintaining communications.

— Every police agency should establish programs that assist and encourage members of the public to take an active role in preventing crime. Police agencies should assist actively in the establishment of volunteer neighborhood security programs, and police agencies in major metropolitan areas should establish crime-prevention units to work with the community in reducing criminal opportunities.

— Every police agency should acknowledge the important role of the news media in reporting on police activities and the need for the police agency to be open in its relations with the media.

— The Commission recommends that every police agency that has racial or minority groups of significant size in its jurisdiction insure that the needs of minorities are actively considered in the establishment of police policy and the delivery of police service. Affirmative action should be taken to achieve a proportion of minority group employees in an agency that is an approximate proportion of their numbers in the population.

— The Commission recommends that every police agency establish procedures to facilitate full and fair processing of complaints about general police services and about individual officers' conduct. Every person making a complaint should receive written verification that his complaint is being processed by the police agency. Every person who files a complaint should be notified of its disposition and personal discussion regarding this disposition should be encouraged.

— Every police chief should insure that all elements within the agency provide maximum assistance and cooperation to the patrol officer and patrol officers should be relieved of minor tasks in order to increase their capability to reduce crime.

— Patrolmen should receive training in conducting investigations and in gathering evidence. Patrol officers should be utilized to conduct the complete investigation of crimes which do not require extensive follow-up investigation and patrol officers should be utilized to follow up and close out investigations of these crimes.

— The Commission recommends that every police agency adopt policing programs that insure stability of assignment in a given geographic area for individual patrol officers who are operationally deployed. Every police agency should insure that officers assigned to geographic policing programs meet regularly with persons who live or work in their area.

— The Commission recommends that every police agency examine and test the team-policing concept to determine its value in improving the agency's efforts to reduce crime, improve the quality of police service, and enhance police-community cooperation.

— Every police department should consider employment of police reserve officers to supplement the regular force of officers and increase community involvement in local police service. These reserve officers should have training equivalent to that given regular sworn personnel.

— Every police agency should establish formal criteria for diverting from the criminal and juvenile justice system all individuals coming to their attention for whom processing into the justice system would be inappropriate or for whom the use of resources outside the criminal and juvenile justice system would be more appropriate.

— Every police agency should conduct workload studies on a regular basis; information obtained from the workload studies should form the basis for establishing patrol and investigation operational objectives and priorities.

— The Commission recommends that police departments in major cities establish tactical squads for flexible, highly mobile, and rapid deployment against special crime problems. The tactical squad should be deployed on the basis of current crime-pattern analysis and projected criminal activity. A full-time force should include an analytical staff element.

— Local governments should analyze the various methods of combining police services, compare the cost effectiveness of each to that of its own operations, and develop applications to its own operations.

— The Commission recommends that any police agency employing fewer than 10 sworn officers combine with one or more agencies to improve efficiency in delivering police services. In remote areas where there is no nearby local agency, combined or contract programs with county or State agencies should be established.

— Police recruitment efforts should concentrate on college-educated applicants. Recruitment resources should be applied according to the agency's needs for personnel with varied ethnic and minority characteristics. Residency should be eliminated as a prerequisite for employment and decentralized application procedures should be utilized.

— The Commission recommends that every police agency require immediately, as a condition of initial employment, completion of at least 1 year of education at an accredited college or university and that by 1983, every police agency require, as a condition of initial employment, completion of at least 4 years of college-level education or a baccalaureate degree at an accredited college or university.

— The Commission recommends that every police agency implement programs designed to aid employees' professional growth and increase their capacity for their present and future roles within the agency.

— Personnel should be recruited for lateral entry at any level from outside police agencies when it is necessary to do so in order to obtain the services of individuals who are qualified for a position or assignment.

— The Commission recommends that every State and local government establish and maintain salaries that attract and retain qualified personnel capable of performing the police function.

— Every State should set minimum entry-level salaries for all State and local police officers and should reimburse the employing agency for a portion of the guaranteed salary.

— Every local government should expand its classification and pay system to provide greater advancement within the basic patrol rank.

— The Commission recommends that every police agency immediately insure that there exists no agency policy that discourages qualified women from seeking employment as sworn or civilian personnel or that prevents them from realizing their full employment potential. Agencies should institute selection procedures to facilitate employment of women and should insure that recruitment, selection, training, and salary policies do not discriminate against women.

— Police agencies should explore all possible uses of civilians and should be innovative in determining the functions they could perform.

— Every police chief executive should develop methods to obtain information from police employees who have daily contact with operational problems in order to assist him in reaching decisions on personnel and operational matters.

— Legislation should be enacted to authorize every police agency and all police employees to engage in collective negotiations in arriving at terms and conditions of employment, police service effectiveness, and equitable representation for police employees and management. Such legislation should specifically prohibit strikes, work stoppages, and concerted job actions, and should provide for the retention of management rights including the setting of management policies, the direction of employees' work, and the setting of hiring, firing, and promotion policies.

— The Commission recommends that every police agency immediately establish command and control centers for the operation of their communications systems and provide a 24-hour, two-way radio capability for continuous communications between the command and control communications center and the field units.

— The Commission recommends that every police agency provide all incoming police personnel with a formalized basic training course in forensic science and evidence-gathering techniques, and that every police agency also develop and deploy specially trained personnel to gather physical evidence 24 hours a day.

— The Commission recommends that every State enact legislation that provides for the issuance of search warrants pursuant to telephone petitions and affidavits from police officers.

— Information from the police regarding such matters as the effect of crimes upon the victims and the likelihood of future crimes by an arrested individual or convicted offender should be made available to and utilized by other criminal justice agencies for reference in making screening, diversion, plea negotiation, sentencing, and parole recommendations. Uniform standards and procedures should be established for making such recommendations.

— The Commission recommends that every police agency issue, where legal and practical, written summons and citations in lieu of physical arrest. Police should establish procedures to seek out expeditiously and take into custody individuals participating in these programs who fail to appear in court.[22]

NOTES

1. Alvin Toffler, *Future Shock* (New York, N.Y.: Bantam Books, 1972).
2. Paul Whisenand and Fred Ferguson, *The Managing of Police Organizations* (Englewood Cliffs, N.J.: Prentice Hall, 1973).

3. Sherman C. Blumenthal, *Management Information System: A Framework for Planning and Developing* (Englewood Cliffs, N.J.: Prentice Hall, 1969).

4. Whisenand and Ferguson, op. cit., p. 95.

5. Printed through courtesy and permission of Los Angeles County Sheriff's Department, Los Angeles, California, 1974.

6. Printed through courtesy of Dallas Police Department, "Five Year Plan" 1973, pp. III, 51–52.

7. Joseph T. Massie, *Essentials of Management* (Englewood Cliffs, N.J.: Prentice Hall, 1971), p. 232.

8. Charles E. Summer, Jr., "The Managerial Mind," *Harvard Business Review* (Jan.–Feb. 1959), pp. 69–78.

9. Joseph T. Massie, op. cit., p. 237.

10. Warren G. Bennis, Kenneth D. Benne, and Robert Chin, eds., *The Planning of Change* (New York: Holt, Rinehart and Winston, 1961).

11. Joseph T. Massie, op. cit., p. 239.

12. Ronald Lippitt, Jeanne Watson, and Bruce Westley, *The Dynamics of Planned Change* (New York: Harcourt, Brace and World, 1958), pp. 131–43.

13. Twentieth Annual Laboratories in Human Relations Training, *Reading Book* (Washington, D.C.: National Training Laboratories, 1966).

14. Paul C. Buchanan, "Crucial Issues in Organizational Development," *Change in School Systems*, Goodwin Watson, ed. (Washington, D.C.: Cooperative Project for Educational Development, National Training Laboratories, National Education Association, 1967).

15. Oscar Newman, *Defensible Space* (New York: Macmillan, 1972).

16. Arnold Judson, *A Manager's Guide to Making Changes* (New York: John Wiley, 1966).

17. Arthur H. Niehoff, "The Process of Innovation," *A Casebook of Social Change*, Arthur H. Niehoff, ed. (Chicago, Ill.: Aldine Publishing Co., 1966).

18. Chauncey F. Bell and Donald B. Manson, "Mythology and the Management of Change," monograph presented at 4th symposium on Law Enforcement, Science and Technology, 1972.

19. National Advisory Commission on Criminal Justice Standards and Goals, "Report on Police Standard 13.6," Washington, D.C., 1973, p. 342.

20. The President's Commission on Law Enforcement and Administration of Justice, Task Force Report, "The Police," Washington, D.C., 1967.

21. "Policewomen on Patrol (Major Findings: First Report, Volume I)," Police Foundation, Washington, D.C., 1973.

22. The National Commission on Criminal Justice Standards and Goals, "A National Strategy to Reduce Crime," Washington, D.C., 1973.

department special order:
effective beat patrol
and its evaluation

Chicago police department
training bulletin:
beat patrol/personal radio

Chicago police department
training bulletin:
vertical patrol

DEPARTMENT SPECIAL ORDER	DATE OF ISSUE 21 October 1970	EFFECTIVE DATE 22 October 1970	NO. 70-53
SUBJECT EFFECTIVE BEAT PATROL AND ITS EVALUATION	DISTRI-BUTION B	AMENDS	
REFERENCE General Order 70-1 Chicago Police Department Rules and Regulations	RESCINDS		

I. PURPOSE

This order:

A. stresses the importance of neat appearance of and proper conduct by beat patrolmen.

B. emphasizes that the patrol function is the basis of successful police operations.

C. defines effective beat patrol.

D. outlines the means by which a beat officer can perform effectively as a member of the patrol team..

E. provides a method for continuous evaluation of the effectiveness of individual and total beat patrol.

II. FUNCTION

The patrol beat is the basic geographical and organizational unit of the Department. Personnel assigned to a patrol beat will:

A. provide continuous, conspicuous, alert and aggressive beat patrol which will translate the Department objectives into action.

B. furnish basic police services by providing assistance to the public to ensure peace.

C. conduct preliminary investigations of incidents to provide information to the specialized units who will complete the follow-up investigation of such incidents.

III. CONDUCT AND APPEARANCE

The cooperation of the people living in the beat area is essential to effective beat patrol. To obtain this cooperation, the beat patrolman will enhance his image by his conduct and by his neat appearance while performing his duties. Strict adherence to the Department's rules, regulations, orders, and procedures which are written as the guideline to proper conduct and neat attire provide the police officer with the manner in which community cooperation may be obtained.

IV. EFFECTIVE BEAT PATROL

The purpose of effective beat patrol is to eliminate the opportunities for committing crime.

A. Effective beat patrol depends on the beat officer's service being:

1. continuous - conscientious attention will be given to everything that occurs within sight or hearing at all times.

2. conspicuous - be seen; crimes are not committed except when persons have the opportunity to do so unobserved. The beat officer will be available to rectify hazardous conditions or to aid persons seeking police assistance.

3. alert - take every opportunity to make contact with the people on the beat. Inspect the out-of-place, the incongruous and the variation from the normal. Play hunches - cautiously.

4. aggressive - seek out those activities, persons, places, and things on the beat which may result in criminal or anti-social action or give rise to dangerous conditions. Enforce traffic laws and report abandoned vehicles. Identify and take corrective action against those conditions on the beat which endanger the peace and safety of the community. Enforce the ordinances of the city which contribute to maintaining city beauty: i.e., illegal advertisements on parkways and city posts; improper parking of new or used vehicles on city streets and parkways by automobile dealers.

B. Mobility

The patrol car serves as a base from which the beat officer operates. The beat officer can conduct his services properly by using the beat car to seek out conditions requiring attention. However, to properly render his services, the beat officer will set out on foot to perform his investigation or inspection after following good communication procedures. The patrol car allows the beat officer mobility by providing:

1. transportation from one police task to another.

2. protection from adverse weather conditions.

3. a means for pursuit.

      4.   conspicuous beat patrol.

C.   Requirements

Effective beat patrol results from meeting certain requirements; these are:

      1.   knowledge of the beat; know its streets, alleys, buildings, hazards, and most important of all, its people.

      2.   use of irregular, and continuous patrol; to see and be seen are the principles of prevention.

      3.   initiate action; whenever an incident or a condition exists which may result in a crime or a hazardous situation, beat officers will:

          a.   inspect the surrounding area and public buildings (including licensed premises).

          b.   inquire of persons whose activities the policeman's training and experience identify as possible offenders or violators.

          c.   inform by reporting those occurrences or conditions as prescribed by Department orders which require action by other units of the Department or agencies of the city, such as abandoned vehicles or hazardous situations.

V.   TEAM WORK

The officer who performs effective beat patrol will be a welcome member of the beat patrol team. But team work also has its requirements symbolized by the ten R's below:

A.   <u>Roll Call</u> Be on time fully equipped for duty. The beat team requires the presence and ability of every member.

B.   <u>Respond</u> to radio assignments as quickly and safely as possible.

C.   <u>Return</u> to "in-service" status as soon as you have completed an assignment. Your team mates depend upon you for assistance.

D.   <u>Request</u> the assistance of specialists such as Criminal Investigation Division personnel and evidence technicians when they are required to complete an investigation.

E.   <u>Report</u> on every police service you render. The report is the basis for follow-up investigations and prosecutions: it should be on the appropriate form and should be complete, accurate and clear. The other members of the Department team depend upon it. A police report becomes a record of the Department and may prove invaluable many years after it has been completed.

F.   <u>Read</u> and remember the orders which affect your team and which require action by you for good police service.

G.   <u>Render</u> assistance to other officers and return to patrol your beat when your presence is no longer needed.

H.   <u>Rely</u> upon courtesy, training, and abilities as a police officer to win the confidence and respect of your team members and the public alike.

I.   <u>Regard</u> department property as you would your own. Your patrol car and every other article of equipment furnished by the Department should be cared for and conserved as if you had purchased it yourself. As a taxpayer you, like every citizen, have a right to expect that this equipment is clean, serviceable and properly used.

J.   <u>Respect</u> the rights of the public. When a police officer has reasonably and properly enforced the law in a lawful manner, the Department and the City will protect and defend him against legal action.

VI.   EVALUATION OF BEAT PATROL EFFECTIVENESS

A.   The number and nature of criminal offenses, accidents and other incidents which the beat officer can prevent or take action to correct determine the degree of effective patrol. If his patrol has been effective, he has:

      1.   probably had fewer offenses reported on the beat during his tour of duty than were previously reported on that watch for that beat over a period of time.

      2.   located and reported all hazardous conditions such as inoperative traffic signals, unlit street lights, holes in the street, broken curbstones lying in the street, etc.

      3.   given particular attention to those locations where traffic accidents have occurred and cited drivers he observes committing moving violations.

      4.   obtained and reported information on criminal or juvenile gang activities by making information reports.

      5.   paid particular attention to the activities of juveniles and arrested curfew violators.

      6.   effected the arrest of offenders who have not been deterred by his patrol.

      7.   diminished vice activity by inspecting and reporting on suspect locations and effected the arrest of vice operators.

8. interrogated and reported suspects.

9. frequently inspected license premises and taken action against any violation that is discovered.

10. made and recorded regular visits to "special attention" and "keep watch" locations posted in the beat book.

B. To evaluate beat patrol requires a knowledge of those conditions which indicate that it is not being effectively performed. Any of the following conditions indicate a deficiency in beat patrol:

1. A high incidence of street crime.

2. Complaints that:

   a. juveniles are damagaing property or are annoying residents.

   b. licensed businesses are not conducted properly; taverns are noisy; restaurants, bowling alleys, etc., hangouts for undesirables.

   c. the police are seldom seen in a neighborhood.

   d. abandoned vehicles or hazardous conditions are not removed or reported upon.

3. District vice officers or other officers make arrests for offenses which could have been effected by the beat officer. Some examples are: street prositutes, juveniles drinking in taverns and taverns open after closing hours.

4. An increasing number of traffic accidents without an increase of enforcement against moving violators.

5. Burglaries or other crimes are not discovered promptly though readily visible from a street or alley.

6. A series of crimes or one crime which required a long period to accomplish goes undetected.

7. Conditions previously reported to the police for patrol attention become the subject of repeated complaints.

C. The importance of beat patrol requires that it be constantly evaluated by both the individual beat officer and his supervisors.

1. A beat patrol officer who applies good patrol techniques and who improves his performance through constant evaluation is an effective member of the Department team.

2. A supervisor who constantly evaluates the performance of his team and who takes immediate action to correct his deficiencies, ensures effective beat patrol and the total success of the Department. Supervisors will:

   a. uphold a member who is properly performing his duty; deal fairly and equitably with all members.

   b. recommend remedial or disciplinary action for inefficient, incompetent or unsuitable members.

Authenticated by:

James B. Conlisk, Jr.
Superintendent of Police

198-68

THE CHICAGO POLICE DEPARTMENT

Training Bulletin

James B. Conlisk Jr.
Superintendent

VOLUME XIV, NUMBER 2
8 January 1973

BEAT   PATROL/PERSONAL   RADIO

The primary function of every police department is patrol, whether it be on foot, motorcycle, car, boat, helicopter, or other type of vehicle. As it became necessary to expand the area that an individual police officer had to cover during his patrol on foot, various modes of transportation were adopted, including bicycles and horses. This Training Bulletin deals specifically with the type of patrol necessitated by the growth of an urban area, including the City of Chicago. Special emphasis is placed on population increases, the construction of numerous large, multiple dwelling units, and other factors which require an increase in calls for police service.

In the past, vehicles were provided to patrol officers, to enable them to move quickly from location to location, maintain radio communications between officers and headquarters, and to transport persons, including prisoners, in emergencies. On 25 June 1969, however, a pilot program utilizing the personal radio was instituted. This program proved so successful, that the program became operational throughout the city. On 10 June 1972, the last radio zone was converted to the use of these personal radios, thus eliminating the use of vehicle radios for normal communications by district beat vehicles. With the advent of this sophisticated method of communications patrol techniques again are being changed to enable the Chicago Police Department to provide more and better service, and to enhance its effectiveness in protecting persons and property, preventing crime, and apprehending criminals.

Foot patrol, probably the oldest and most original of all types of police patrol, has in most cases, been replaced by mobile patrol to provide a more effective and speedier blanket of coverage and to allow two-way communications between the field officer, headquarters, and command. Since it is impractical to assign a foot patrolman to every corner in the city, officers were assigned to vehicles in order that they could traverse numerous corners and other areas. Many people thought that the foot patrolman was archaic, but the recent technological developments in the communications field, namely, the portable radios, have changed this point of view.

The uniformed foot patrolman is the person that the average citizen wants to see. He should be part of the familiar scene and not a total stranger. He can stop and listen to people, and frequently can take or prescribe the necessary immediate action desired or needed by the citizen. The mere presence of the officer provides direct personal contact with the public, inspires a sense of security, and arouses a feeling of protection within the citizen. This feeling should eventually lead to the development of a spirit of public support and helpfulness from the average citizen.

Problems peculiar to a locality or region, are also the immediate concern of the foot patrol officer. His purpose in this and other instances is to act as a counsellor and a mediator, primarily with one objective in mind:

1. To minimize crime and hazards, and maximize good will and community support.

Because he can devote his time while on foot patrol to careful observation, he can identify with persons within his area, locate potential problem areas, and generally, be cognizant of everything within his area of responsibility.

Because of the nature of police work itself, it is practically impossible to establish a set pattern as to when an officer equipped with personal radio and operating a vehicle should park the vehicle and patrol on foot. During different hours of the day, days of the week and seasons of the year, conditions vary in each area of the city. Weather conditions, calls for service, and many other factors effect the times that the motorized officer can patrol on foot. Logically, however, certain areas will warrant foot patrol at various times, and officers assigned to these areas should park and lock their vehicles and spend a reasonable portion of their tour of duty within their beat on foot.

It must be remembered that personal radios are normally assigned to units, such as beats, routes, posts, etc., and not to individual officers. While men assigned to one-man assignments will have their own radios, one radio will be assigned to a two-man team, such as a beat car, squadrol, etc. Factors, based upon experiences, work load, crimes, arrests, etc., used in determining whether one or two men will be assigned to a vehicle also dictate the policy that, when two men are assigned to a vehicle with one radio both men will leave the vehicle and patrol together on foot.

The concept of foot/motorized patrol compliments the beat system. Its a variation and a combination of motorized foot patrol. Actually it can be described as a flexible mobile system of policing based on the coordination and utilization of manpower and mechanical devices.

Rigid requirements concerning a set amount of time to be spent on foot patrol during each tour of duty cannot be established. As stated before, situations requiring extra attention or action are inherent in police work and materialized at anytime. The following guidelines, however, are designed to point out the philosophy behind this patrol technique.

1. Generally, beat officers should attempt to spend half of their tours of duty out of their vehicles on foot patrol.

2. The areas that should be patrolled on foot should be limited to a reasonable distance from the vehicle.

3. The areas to be patrolled on foot should be those most susceptible and receptive to this type of patrol. Manpower is wasted when foot patrol is effected in open areas, or at locations where there is little problem potential, few people or where crimes do not or are not likely to occur.

4. Officers patrolling on foot, as when patrolling in a motor vehicle, must be properly attired and present a neat, clean, and professional appearance at all times.

5. Although not restricted to foot patrol alone, the officer on foot can recognize conditions and situations within his assigned area, on the streets, in the alleys, public places, and in the neighborhood generally more readily.

6. The officer on foot has a better opportunity of becoming familiar with new residents in a changing neighborhood, as well as enhancing his rapport with older residents. He should continue to develop an understanding of various ethnic groups and the social and economic problems within the community so that he is better equipped to handle many of the various problems that arise in changing neighborhoods, (impoverished neighborhoods, etc.).

7. The foot patrolman should achieve positive community support through frequent public contacts, such as visiting with residents and business people alike, treating all citizens equally with firmness, honesty, impartiality and fairness.

8. When confronted with a situation the foot patrolman, (just as when in his vehicle) must immediately determine the type of police action to take, the type and amount of assistance (if any) needed, and take necessary positive action immediately, bearing in mind the best interests of all.

9. The officer on foot must recognize that different techniques for patrol must be employed in different locations at different times of the day, and on different days of the week. He must always remember to be alert to prevent injury to himself. If he is injured he cannot be of help to anyone, including his family and loved ones. There are certain locations which present transmitting problems with the personal radios, and he should be alert for these. (Example, being in an area which poses electronic interference, etc.). He must be wary of conditions and situations that present hazards to himself and others, and take necessary steps for his own safety.

10. The foot patrolman must be capable of detecting crime conditions, such as vice, and conditions that may be conducive to fomenting crime. The unique position that the police officer occupies generally affords him access to information, or sources of information, relative to criminal activities over which he may have no direct control. (Example: Known hoods conducting meetings in some location on his beat). In this case, it is his responsibility and duty to relay such information,

through his supervisor, to the appropriate unit of the Department.

Specific policy concerning foot/motorized patrol, as established by the Chief of the Patrol Division, requires that:

1. Two man units patrol together on foot (as stated previously).

2. Location to be patrolled on foot by beat officers be determined and assigned by supervisors at the beginning of each tour of duty. Beat officers should be encouraged to submit recommendations to their supervisors, based upon their knowledge of their assigned beat, but the final decision must be made by the supervisor.

3. Officers assigned to vehicles will limit the area that they patrol on foot to within a one block radius from their parked and locked vehicle.

Although an officer assigned to a vehicle who is equipped with a personal radio walks within his beat, he may fail to perform adequately if he does not take the time to critically and accurately observe everything about him, and take the time to talk to people within his area with whom he comes in contact. The foot/motorized patrol concept can be extremely rewarding in terms of crime reduction and community relations. It is the responsibility of supervisory and command officers, however, to instill within their members the understanding of the importance of this advanced technique, and assure that they conform to the philosophy involved which will, over a period of time, greatly aid in the accomplishment of the goals of the Chicago Police Department.

OBSERVATION REMINDERS

In the process of patrol, be especially observant of the following:

PERSONS

1. Doorbell ringers and itinerant peddlers.

2. Anyone who attempts to avoid your glance.

3. Paroled convicts and persons known to have been involved in criminal activity before (get to know these individuals if they frequent your beat or adjacent area).

4. Any person running or who seems to be in an unusual hurry (especially during late hours).

5. Anyone loitering in dark corners, doorways, or areaways at unusual hours.

6. Those individuals loitering around disreputable places.

7. Persons who seem to be walking aimlessly without any particular destination.

8. Strangers who become overly "chummy".

9. Persons you observe approaching pedestrians or walking along the curb viewing the interior of vehicles or windows of homes.

10. Shabbily dressed persons carrying bundles in a commercial area after closing hours, or in a residential area where their shabby clothing does not blend with those living in the area.

11. Persons sitting in parked vehicles in commercial areas with the motor running.

12. Persons sitting in parked vehicles or loitering around schools, parks, playgrounds, etc., where children are playing.

13. Inquisitive persons who do not seek specific information or directions.

PLACES

1. Places of questionable business enterprises.

2. Places frequented by persons acting in an unusual manner that would indicate possible criminal intent, or those of a disreputable character.

3. Loosely-operated businesses (also those places that are open 24 hours a day, and are known to be underworld hangouts).

4. Places where gambling or other crimes are known to have previously taken place.

5. The homes of ex-convicts or frequent law violators and their associates.

6. Suspect places where there is an unusual amount of people coming and going.

7. Youth hangouts, (drive-ins, etc.).

8. Known places of ill-repute such as taverns, poolrooms, clubs, etc., that are poorly managed.

9. Places where lights are burning all hours of the night, especially places that are frequented by persons at unusual hours.

HOT CAR HINTS

The "HOT CAR HINTS" given, is provided so that personnel can again be reminded of some of the things which should alert an officer to the fact that the vehicle observed could have been stolen.

The "Hot Sheet" of the Daily Bulletin is an excel- lent tool for the recovery of abandoned stolen autos. **NOTE:** Almost 88% of the cars stolen in Chicago will be recovered by the Chicago Police Department yearly.

In addition to spotting a license number listed as "wanted" by radio, teletype or "Hot Sheet," the following are some of the things which the alert and observant officer should notice which could indicate that an auto is stolen. Any of these factors could warrant a "STOP" and or further investigation:

1. Vehicles driven at high speeds and recklessly.

2. Vehicle being operated without license plate light or without any lights at all.

3. Vehicles parked in an unusual manner on the street.

4. Operator appears unfamiliar with the operation of the auto, or does not appear to belong to that type of vehicle.

5. Commercial vehicles containing valuable merchandise parked unattended and/or unlocked.

6. License plates illegible (bent, dirty, obstructed, obscured, etc.) or do not appear to match the car (dirty plates on a shinny car, new bolts on old plates, other indications of a recent license plate switch).

7. Vehicles overloaded with persons known to belong to a neighborhood gang.

8. License plate/plates missing or not properly affixed.

9. Broken or cracked vent window or other signs of break-in around windows (tool marks or chipped glass, evidence that the frame has been sprung so that the window or vent doesn't properly close, glass replaced that does not match the other glass, such as tinted glass on all areas of the auto except one piece of clear glass where suspect entry could have been made etc.).

10. Missing or scotch taped door lock assembly.

11. Operator commits a traffic violation (most auto thieves apprehended in a stolen vehicle were originally detected because of a traffic violation they committed).

Once the vehicle has been stopped you now have an opportunity to more closely observe the exterior appearance, the occupants, and the interior of the vehicle, BE ALERT FOR THE FOLLOWING:

1. No key in the ignition.

2. Single key in the ignition (most people keep their car key on a key ring or holder with other keys).

3. "Dummy" ignition or ignition key, or ignition pulled.

4. Questionable items on the floor or seats of the vehicle (a screw driver is one of the favorite tools of the auto thief for both entering and starting the vehicle). A "slam puller" or key cutting machine is used in late model vehicles equipped with steering wheel locks. The "slam puller" is used to pull the door or ignition locks so that the key number can be obtained. The steering wheel lock is installed on all G.M. cars since 1969, all American made cars since 1970, and most imported cars starting in 1971.

5. Duplicate keys (a thief is not likely to have the original set), or keys that do not work properly in the various locks.

6. Unsatisfactory responses to questions relating to vehicle ownership or possession of questionable items (verify responses).

7. Driver lacks operator's license (many auto thieves are too young to obtain an operators license).

8. Vehicle identification number plate (serial plate) missing or loosely affixed to vehicle (test by prying with penknife or fingernail. If the plate pops off, it was probably glued or "tacked" on and warrants further investigation. Late model vehicles having the serial number plate in a slot on top of the dashboard should be checked to insure that a different plate has not been placed over the proper plate).

Many stolen vehicles are stopped before the owner has an opportunity to report the theft to the police. Statistics show that 40% of all arrests for auto theft occur before the owner has reported the theft. The alert observant officer could be aware of this and effect arrests even though the Dispatcher might report that the license number checks "Cold". "Cold" plates may also be used on a "Hot" car.

Since the stolen vehicle is a basic tool of the crim-inal, increased "street stops" coupled with a careful investigation on the officer's part will greatly increase the number and variety of criminal arrests he makes.

Portions of this Training Bulletin were prepared with the assistance of Lt. S. Bloome, Patrol Division Admin.

SPECIAL ATTENTION TO DELIVERY TRUCKS

During the shorter periods of daylight, delivery trucks are especially susceptible to crimes, including both thefts and robberies. All personnel should be alert and pay special attention to all delivery trucks they observe with particular notice given to trucks parked when drivers enter apartment and high-rise buildings to make deliveries and leave their trucks unattended.

THE
CHICAGO
POLICE DEPARTMENT

VOLUME VII, NUMBER 51

19 December 1966

Training Bulletin

O. W WILSON
SUPERINTENDENT

VERTICAL PATROL

A new dimension has been added to law enforcement - the concept of vertical policing. In large urban areas where ground space is unavailable for the construction of one - two-story dwellings, more and more vertical building is providing housing for the expanding population. The very nature of vertical building renders policing difficult when conventional methods of motorized patrol are employed.

The Chicago Police Department is charged with the responsibility of enforcing the law and providing police service within the Chicago Housing Authority's high-rise buildings. The Department, the Chicago Housing Authority and the tenants of the high rise buildings all recognized the need for on-the-spot policing to combat the increasing number of crimes unique to high rise complexes. Effectively reducing and preventing these crimes requires interior vertical patrol of the high rise buildings by foot patrolmen, in addition to the routine motorized patrol provided throughout the City.

The Chicago Housing Authority presently maintains 1,112 residential buildings, which occupy 873 acres throughout the City and accomodate a population of approximately 140,500 persons. Building sizes range from one-story single dwelling cottages to 22-story sky-scrapers which each contain 452 dwelling units. Minors make up 66 per cent of the CHA population. Of the total project buildings 179 are seven stories or higher. Such buildings are referred to as "high rise" buildings. They are the buildings within which vertical patrol is conducted.

Definite crime problems including juvenile offenses, vandalism, thefts, robberies, rapes, and assaults, can be identified in the housing projects. Crime occurrence is significantly affected by the type of building architecture. Row houses (2-4 stories), town houses, and walkups show little difference in crime rate from adjacent private residential areas. Available data indicate that housing project policing problems are clearly "high rise" police problems.

The type of crime occurring within the high rise projects closely parallels that of the surrounding community. However, due to building structure and the large concentration of population, certain types of crime occur more frequently and are of a greater problem in high rise complexes. A major problem involves crowds collecting due to either incidents or consequent police action and the interference with the police in the performance of their duties by members of these crowds. All types of youth offenses occur because of the large number of minors living in the projects. A considerable amount of vandalism, rapes, and robberies occurs within elevators. The jamming of elevator doors by children greatly hampers police response to calls within the buildings. Stairwells afford opportune locations for criminal concealment. Objects thrown from balconies are a source of major concern relative to patrol coverage. Still another problem involves mailbox thieves who are active during those times when welfare checks are known to be delivered.

Policing of Chicago Housing Authority high rise

This Training Bulletin is issued weekly to all members of the Chicago Police Dept. Address all communications to Publication Section, Training Division, 720 W. O'Brien Street, Chicago 7, Illinois.
O. W. Wilson, *Superintendent*

Robert E. McCann, *Director of Training*

STAFF
Sergeant George C. Coughlin, *Editor*
Sergeant Martin Joyce, *Associate Editor*
John Switalski, *Contributing Editor*

projects is a district responsibility. The 24-hour manning of vertical patrol posts and vertical patrol sergeants' beats is by district personnel. All vertical patrol posts on every watch are manned by two patrolmen working as a team. All sergeants' beats are one-man operations. High rise foot-posts do not eliminate any of the existing motor patrol beats.

Reporting times for all vertical patrol personnel are the same as for other district watch personnel. Men assigned to odd-numbered posts report for the first roll call at 0700, 1500, or 2300. Men assigned to even-numbered posts report for the second roll call at 0800, 1600, or 2400.

District watch commanders, with the assistance of vertical patrol sergeants, assign patrol teams to the designated vertical patrol posts. Specially localized vertical patrol can be used at the discretion of the watch commander or the vertical patrol supervisor. If in their opinion a building, group of buildings, or an area requires heavier than normal patrol saturation, the watch commander reassigns teams from other vertical patrol posts to the affected areas. Such specially localized patrol, however, is maintained only for periods of short duration.

Transportation to and from vertical patrol posts is provided by district squadrols. Transportation schedules are drawn up by each district concerned to accomodate both early and late roll calls. When ordered by their supervising sergeant, officers on posts who begin their watch on the early roll call proceed to their district station in sufficient time to turn in their communications equipment to designated desk or relieving personnel. Patrolmen who begin their watch on the late roll

call proceed to the station when ordered by the relieving supervising sergeant. In order to insure continuous police coverage, this relief is not accomplished until early roll call relieving personnel are at their vertical patrol posts.

Patrolmen assigned to vertical patrol posts are re- sponsible for patrol of all high rise buildings assigned to their posts and the immediate surroundings of these buildings, including parking lots, playlots, community rooms, laundry facilities, etc.

Vertical patrol sergeants are responsible for per- forming normal supervisory functions as they pertain to high rise policing. Because of the large areas involved and dispersion of vertical patrol posts, each vertical patrol sergeant will be assigned a squad car. Through the use of communications equipment supervising sergeants are constantly in touch with their subordinates. They also make frequent contacts on foot to each post during their tour of duty. A supervisor's field log is maintained in the same manner as in routine beat supervision. In cases where no vertical patrol sergeant's beat has been established during a given watch, a designated district field sergeant assumes the responsibilities of a vertical patrol sergeant in addition to his normally assigned duties.

Inasmuch as the high rise buildings closely approxi- mate one another in general architectural design, standard patrol techniques and procedures can be developed. Vertical patrol procedures are based on teams rather than one-man patrol. All vertical patrol sergeants and patrolmen are equipped with personal two-way (Handi-Talkie) radios. Officers working as teams separate when inspection or observation necessitates such a maneuver. Their radios are their link to each other and to the Communications Center.

Officers engaged in high rise policing familiarize themselves with their assigned vertical patrol post and other posts within their district in the event of post rotation. This familiarization includes:

1. knowing the physical structure of the post, including the location of laundry facilities, community rooms, incinerator rooms, mail rooms, and electrical and maintenance facilities within the buildings.

2. knowing Chicago Housing Authority administrative and maintenance staff who are responsible for the buildings on the post.

3. becoming acquainted with as many persons on the post as possible.

4. keeping informed as to location of frequent crimes areas conducive to potential crimes.

5. learning the identity of subjects known to the police who live in and frequent the post.

6. knowing the location of alarm and call boxes.

Vertical foot patrol is conducted in a completely random manner. In one technique the patrol team rides different elevators to the top floor of the building, where members separate and walk down different stairways to the ground floor, checking hallways, balconies, electrical rooms, laundry facilities, and community rooms on various floors. For safety purposes each officer checks with his partner via his radio. Patrol of exterior areas adjacent to the buildings, such as playlots and parking areas, are a part of the officers' duties. As in motorized patrol, doubling and even tripling back is recommended in addition to application of the officers' intuitive capacities.

During the course of this patrol, officers observe damage to buildings, possible physical hazards to tenants, and other police oriented problems which need correction. Such conditions are brought to the attention of appropriate resident custodial personnel.

Personal (Handi-Talkie) radios are issued to each vertical patrol sergeant and patrolman during roll call at the beginning of each watch. Radios are equipped with rechargeable nickel cadmium batteries, which have a basic 8-hour transmission capability with a reserve safety factor. Officers must assure that prior to going on duty their radios are equipped with the proper color-coded (recharged) battery for their watch.

Officers observe the following operating instructions and procedures for receiving and transmitting:

1. Turn on set with the on-off volume control located at top right.

2. If radio has more than one frequency, select the appropriate frequency.

3. Wait five seconds and then adjust squelch control at top left by turning clockwise until rushing

noise is eliminated.

4. Receiving can usually be accomplished with the aerial retracted. This, however, must be determined by the using officer. Transmission requires full extension of the aerial.

5. Radio transmission is prefaced with the word "Victor," representing vertical patrol. In addition to this code word, each vertical patrolman utilizes the call number corresponding to the post that was assigned to him by his watch commander at the beginning of his tour of duty. Vertical patrol sergeants utilize normal sergeants' beat call numbers beginning with the number 88. District field sergeants who are required to assume the responsibilities of vertical patrol sergeants in addition to their normally assigned duties will utilize their normal beat call signs.

6. Conversation is held to the bare necessity required for safe and effective patrol.

7. The officer who needs transmission priority prefaces his call sign with the word "emergency." All other transmissions are deferred and other stations stand by. Determining the need for beat car response to an emergency is the responsibility of the Communications Center dispatcher or the supervisor who is present at the scene of the emergency. Timely "disregard" instructions also are necessary to keep officers from responding to an emergency which is under control.

The Headquarters Communications Center controls all vertical patrol personnel through a base set console. Vertical patrol posts are assigned investigations by the Communications Center when feasible.

The primary duties of vertical patrol officers include protecting high rise tenants and those lawfully on the premises from violence and criminal actions of others; protecting the buildings and grounds from vandalism, malicious mischief, and willful destruction of property; and detecting crime. To the tenants the police officer represents the Chicago Police Department. His conspicuous presence acts as a deterrent to young and old offenders alike. He can become a respected friend, advisor, arbitrator, and protector of the community he serves. Because he is constantly in the public eye as a representative of the department, the vertical patrol officer must remember that public relations is an important part of his job. Good police work plus common sense and courtesy result in good public relations.

Prepared by M. J. Schneider, Senior Methods Analyst Planning Division.

goal-oriented statistical
data forms

Table B.1 Goal-Oriented Statistical Data Form

First Week of Month

Crime		District I				District II				District III				Summary				
		This Wk.	This Mo. to Date	This Mo. Last Yr.	Projection*	This Wk.	This Mo. to Date	This Mo. Last Yr.	Projection*	This Wk.	This Mo. to Date	This Mo. Last Yr.	Projection*	This Wk.	This Mo. to Date	This Mo. Last Yr.	Projection	%
Murder	S-1	1		3	4	1		0		0		0						
	S-2	1		5		2		1		1		7						
	S-3	0		4		1		7		0		5						
	T	2		12		4		8	17	1		12		7		32	Projection 31	
Rape	S-1	0		4		1		3	4	0		3						
	S-2	1		4		0		8		1		5						
	S-3	3		4	13	0		7		0		4						
	T	4		12	17	1		18		1		12		6		42	Projection 26	
Robbery	S-1	17		99		9		67		11		32	48					
	S-2	6		56		23		109		25		81	110					
	S-3	13		60		31		160		17		60	75					
	T	36		215		63		336		53		173	234	152		724	Projection 673	−7.0%
Aggravated Assault	S-1	9		84		6		26		4		26						
	S-2	4		36		12		54		25		111						
	S-3	12		66		27		101	119	14		65						
	T	25		186		45		181	199	43		202		113		569	Projection 500	−12.1%
Burglary	S-1	49		141	217	34		157		22		87	97					
	S-2	23		118		51		152	225	27		199						
	S-3	40		188		34		173		28		109	124					
	T	112		447	496	119		482	527	77		395		308		1324	Projection 1364	+3.0%
Larceny Over $50	S-1	45		149	199	21		63	93	25		74	110					
	S-2	8		57		34		80	150	8		38						
	S-3	16		67	70	19		70	84	14		83						
	T	69		273	305	74		213	327	47		195	208	190		681	Projection 841	+23.5%
Auto Theft	S-1	20		100		16		90		16		101						
	S-2	22		76	97	24		147		10		42	44					
	S-3	18		92		12		102		12		73						
	T	60		268		52		339		38		216		150		823	Projection 664	−19.3%
Totals		I 308		1413		II 358		1577	1585	III 260		1205		926		4195		

*Indicates increased projection only

TOTAL PROJECTION 4100 or −2.3%

Table B.2 Goal-Oriented Statistical Data Form
Second Week of Month

Crime		District I This Wk.	I This Mo. to Date	I This Mo. Last Yr.	I Projection*	District II This Wk.	II This Mo. to Date	II This Mo. Last Yr.	II Projection*	District III This Wk.	III This Mo. to Date	III This Mo. Last Yr.	III Projection*	Total This Wk.	Total This Mo. to Date	Total This Month Last Yr.	Projection / %
Murder	S-1	0	1	3		0	1	0		0	0	0					Projection 17
	S-2	0	1	5		0	2	1		0	1	7					
	S-3	1	1	4		0	1	7		0	0	5					
	T	1	3	12		0	4	8		0	1	12		1	8	32	
Rape	S-1	1	1	4		0	1	3		0	0	3					Projection 35
	S-2	1	2	4		4	4	8		0	1	5					
	S-3	2	5	4	11	2	2	7		0	0	4					
	T	4	8	12	17	6	7	18		0	1	12		10	16	42	
Robbery	S-1	21	38	99		13	22	67		10	21	32	46				Projection 721
	S-2	13	19	56		14	37	109		25	50	81	110				−0.4%
	S-3	13	26	60		44	75	160		21	38	60	84				
	T	47	83	215		71	134	336	166	56	109	173	241	174	326	724	
Aggravated Assault	S-1	14	23	84		5	11	26		5	9	26	143				Projection 558
	S-2	7	11	36		10	22	54		40	65	111					−1.9%
	S-3	12	24	66		27	54	101	119	19	33	65	73				
	T	33	58	186		42	87	181	192	64	107	202	236	139	252	569	
Burglary	S-1	52	101	141		53	87	157	192	25	47	87	104				Projection 1541
	S-2	27	50	118		59	110	152	243	41	68	199					+16.4%
	S-3	44	84	188	223	57	91	173	201	30	58	109					
	T	123	235	447	520	169	288	482	637	96	173	395	128	388	696	1324	
Larceny Over $50	S-1	52	97	149	214	14	35	63	77	24	49	74	108				Projection 850
	S-2	6	14	57		28	62	80	137	12	20	38	44				+24.8%
	S-3	13	29	67		23	42	70	93	22	36	83					
	T	71	140	273	310	65	139	213	307	58	105	195	232	194	384	681	
Auto Theft	S-1	20	40	100		23	39	90		17	33	101					Projection 693
	S-2	19	41	76	90	26	50	147		8	18	42					−15.8%
	S-3	23	41	92		13	25	102		14	26	73					
	T	62	122	268	270	62	114	339		39	77	216		163	313	823	
Totals	I / II / III	341	649	1413	1437	415	773	1577	1711	313	573	1205	1268	1069	1995	4195	

TOTAL PROJECTION 4417 or 5.3%

*Indicates increased projection only

Table B.3 Goal-Oriented Statistical Data Form

Third Week of Month

		District I				District II				District III						
		This Wk.	This Month to Date	This Month Last Yr.	Projection*	This Wk.	This Month to Date	This Month Last Yr.	Projection*	This Wk.	This Month to Date	This Month Last Yr.	Projection*	Projection	This Wk.	This Mo. to Date	This Month Last Yr.
Murder	S-1	0	1	3		1	2	0	2	0	0	0		Projection 19			
	S-2	0	1	5		0	2	1	2	1	2	7					
	S-3	1	2	4		0	1	7		2	2	5					
	T	1	4	12		1	5	8		3	4	12			5/	13/	32
Rape	S-1	3	4	4	5	1	2	3		1	1	3		Projection 38			
	S-2	1	3	4		1	5	8		1	2	5					
	S-3	0	5	4	7	0	2	7		2	2	4					
	T	4	12	12	17	2	9	18		4	5	12			10/	26/	42
Robbery	S-1	26	64	99		11	33	67		14	35	32	51	Projection 711			
	S-2	3	22	56		24	61	109		14	64	81	94	−1.7%			
	S-3	12	38	60		34	109	160		18	56	60	82				
	T	41	124	215		69	203	336		46	155	173	228		156/	482/	724
Aggravated Assault	S-1	12	35	84		8	19	26	28	5	14	26		Projection 540			
	S-2	8	19	36		8	30	54		27	92	111	135	−5.0%			
	S-3	10	34	66		25	79	101	116	11	44	65					
	T	30	88	186		41	128	181	188	43	150	202	221		114/	366/	569
Burglary	S-1	57	158	141		41	128	157	188	27	74	87	109	Projection 1555			
	S-2	27	77	118		46	156	152	230	42	110	199		+17.4%			
	S-3	39	123	188	233	50	141	173	208	29	87	109	128				
	T	123	358	447	528	137	425	482	627	98	271	395	400		358/	1054/	1324
Larceny Over $50	S-1	49	146	149	215	14	49	63	72	27	76	74	112	Projection 850			
	S-2	10	24	57		14	76	80	112	12	32	38	47	+24.8%			
	S-3	19	48	67	70	18	60	70	88	29	65	83	95				
	T	78	218	273	321	46	185	213	273	68	173	195	255		192/	576/	681
Auto Theft	S-1	17	57	100		18	57	90		14	47	101		Projection 724			
	S-2	25	66	76	97	39	89	147		13	31	42		−12.0%			
	S-3	21	62	92		10	35	102		21	47	73					
	T	63	185	268	273	67	181	339		48	125	216	45		178/	491/	823
Totals	I	340	989	1413	1459												
	II					363	1136	1577	1676								
	III									310	883	1205	1303		1013/	3008/	4195

*Indicates increased projection only   TOTAL PROJECTION 4440 or +5.8%

Table B.4 Goal-Oriented Statistical Data Form
Fourth Week of Month

Crime		District I				District II				District III				Summary			
		This Wk.	This Month to Date	This Month Last Yr.	Projection*	This Wk.	This Month to Date	This Month Last Yr.	Projec-tion*	This Wk.	This Month to Date	This Month Last Yr.	Projec-tion*	This Wk.	This Mo. to Date	This Month Last Yr.	Projection
Murder	S-1	0	1	3		0	2	0	2	0	0	0					
	S-2	0	1	5		1	3	1	3	2	4	7					
	S-3	2	4	4		0	1	7		1	3	5					
	T	2	6	12		1	6	8		3	7	12		6	19	32	Projection 21
Rape	S-1	1	5	4	5	1	3	3		1	2	3					
	S-2	0	3	4		2	7	8		2	4	5					
	S-3	3	8	4	8	4	6	7		1	3	4					
	T	4	16	12	17	7	16	18		4	9	12		15	41	42	Projection 45
Robbery	S-1	26	90	99		22	55	67		10	45	32	49				
	S-2	14	36	56		17	78	109		34	98	81	108				
	S-3	24	62	60	68	53	163	160		10	75	60	83				
	T	64	188	215		93	296	336	180	63	218	173	241	220	702	724	Projection 777 +7.3%
Aggravated Assault	S-1	20	55	84		13	32	26	35	8	22	26					
	S-2	14	33	36		18	48	54		20	112	111	124				
	S-3	19	53	66		31	110	101	121	20	64	65	70				
	T	53	141	186		62	190	181	210	48	198	202	219	163	529	569	Projection 585 +2.8%
Burglary	S-1	40	198	141	219	66	194	157	214	36	110	87	121				
	S-2	48	125	118	138	77	233	152	257	51	161	199					
	S-3	56	179	188	198	60	201	173	222	28	115	109	127				
	T	144	502	447	555	203	628	482	695	115	386	395	427	462	1516	1324	Projection 1678 +26.7%
Larceny Over $50	S-1	52	198	149	219	22	71	63	78	12	88	74	97				
	S-2	13	37	57		26	102	80	112	18	50	38	55				
	S-3	23	71	67	78	17	77	70	85	27	92	83	101				
	T	88	306	273	338	65	250	213	276	57	230	195	254	210	786	681	Projection 870 +27.8%
Auto Theft	S-1	21	78	100		16	73	90		15	62	101					
	S-2	19	85	76	94	30	119	147		19	50	42	55				
	S-3	19	81	92		14	49	102		25	72	73	79				
	T	59	244	268	270	60	241	339		59	184	216		178	669	823	Projection 740 −10.1%
Totals	I	414	1403	1413	1553												
	II					491	1627	1577	1801								
	III									349	1232	1205	1364	1254	4262	4195	

*Indicates increased projection only   TOTAL PROJECTION 4718 or +12.5%

patrol personnel board

The sample shown in Table C.1 is for one sector of Watch I. If the department's watch consists of only eight beats, then there is no need for sectors. However, if the department has more than one sector, then Sector II would be placed below Sector I. Additionally, each watch would have the same personnel information placed directly below the preceding watch.

In the centralized department, the information for the whole department would be on one personnel board. In the decentralized department, the information will be in the district or precinct station. The patrol personnel board is primarily an operational information system. Some of the same information and other information necessary to be maintained on each officer would be centralized in the personnel unit.

When the sample as shown in Table C.1 is extended for the full year, the district and watch commander and any other command officer interested would find a clear picture regarding the following information:

1. Number of officers available for duty by day with projections for the future.
2. Number of officers on leave by day.
3. Number of officers on vacation at any given time. If seniority is used to allow choice of vacation, review will insure that proper procedures are followed and decrease possibility of personnel problems.
4. Using assignment availability factor and crime workload, the sector sergeant can plan ahead in his scheduling of the officers

in his section. This allows the sergeant the necessary authority commensurate with his responsibility.

5. Shows primary officers for permanent beat assignment and car number.
6. Allows sergeant to identify easily any inequity in certain officers' obtaining an unfair share of available days off (Saturdays, Sundays, Holidays).
7. Indicates disciplinary action, thereby giving expeditious review of the sector for the entire year, which would emphasize any officer needing assistance or special counseling.
8. Gives the commander a review of the total medical picture for the district, watch, and sector. Identifies individuals who might be malingering and also identifies those officers not using medical. (In police work, the author believes, because of its unusual working conditions, it is almost impossible not to be feeling bad enough sometime during the year to justify staying home. Many police officers report to work even though they aren't feeling well. It seems that self-respect and attention to duty emerge in many officers regarding medical, and these officers should be commended.)

The chart indicates sickness on the part of three officers on days immediately following their regular days off. Special note should be made when this occurs and also if officers report medical after payday. An inquiry in the beginning may keep potential problems to a minimum.

Key:

X X X   : Regular Days Off

■ ■ ■   : Medical Days Off

√ √ √   : Vacation

H H H   : Holidays

⊗ ⊗ ⊗   : Days Lost Due to Disciplinary Action

Table C.1 Patrol Personnel Board

Watch I

FEBRUARY 1973

Watch Commander	Car #	T 1	F 2	S 3	S 4	M 5	T 6	W 7	T 8	F 9	S 10	S 11	M 12 (H)	T 13	W 14	T 15	F 16	S 17	S 18	M 19	T 20	W 21	T 22 (H)	F 23	S 24	S 25	M 26	T 27	W 28
Lt. J. Jones	101	X	X	X							X	X							X	X			H				X	X	X
Sector I																													
Sgt. A. Adams	110						X	X					H		X	X							X	X					
Off. B. Baker	111	X	X							X	X	X	H					X	X	X	√	√	√	√	X	X	X		
Off. C. Charles	111			X	⊗	⊗						X	X	■						X	X	■	H			X	X	X	X
Off. D. David	112			X	X						X	X	X	X						X	X	X	H						XX
Off. E. Edward	113						X	X	√	√	√	√		X	X						X	X							
Off. F. Frank	114							X	X				H			X	X						H	X	X	X			
Off. G. George	115								X	X			H				X	X					H	X	X	X	X		
Off. H. Henry	116									X	X	X	H				X	X	X	X			H			X	X		

Table C.1 (cont.)

Watch I

FEBRUARY 1973

Watch Commander	Car #	T 1	F 2	S 3	S 4	M 5	T 6	W 7	T 8	F 9	S 10	S 11	H M 12	T 13	W 14	T 15	F 16	S 17	S 18	M 19	T 20	W 21	H T 22	F 23	S 24	S 25	M 26	T 27	W 28
Off. I. Item	117										X	X	X						X	X			H			X	X	X	X
Off. J. James	118	X	X	X						X	X	X	■					X	X	X	■		H			X	X		
Off. K. King					X	X	X				X	X	X							X	X		H					X	X
Off. L. Louis				X	X	X							X	X							X	X	H						XX
Off. M. Martin							X	X					H		X	X							X	X					
Off. N. Nora				■				⊗	⊗				H		X	X	X						H	X	X	X			
Off. P. Paul									X	X			H				X	X	X				H		X	X	X		

departmental general order #72— Greensboro police department

Index as.   Prevention Unit
            Loss Prevention Unit
            Coordinator, Crime and Loss Prevention Unit

Subject: Crime and Loss Prevention Unit

The purpose of this order is to establish a new unit within the departmental organization designated as the Crime and Loss Prevention Unit to define the unit's purposes, objectives, goals and to establish authority, responsibilities as well as program scope of the unit.

This order contains the following numbered sections:

- I. General objectives, policy, and goals
- II. Staffing and organizational placement
- III. Procedures and programs
- IV. Growth and development
- V. Effective date

I. General Objectives, Policy, and Goals

A. General Objectives

To establish a Crime and Loss Prevention Unit within the Patrol Division of the Greensboro Police Department.

B. General Policy

It shall be the policy of the entire Police Department and specifically of the Crime and Loss Prevention Unit to develop and implement comprehensive procedures and programs designed to anticipate, recognize and appraise crime risks and to initiate action to reduce or remove such risk.

C. General Goals

1. To coordinate the activities of the Department in the field of crime and loss prevention.
2. To educate all personnel of the Department in the merits of participation in crime and loss prevention efforts.
3. To prepare and implement long and short term programs dealing with prevention of crime and loss of property.
4. To educate the general public, home and business owners in the advantages of planned programs designed to reduce risk and provide optimum protection for dollars spent or systems changes.
5. To coordinate such programs with civic, business, private groups, city organizations, and individuals toward a common goal of preventative action.
6. To provide a broad base for citizen participation in self-involvement in loss prevention.

II. *Staffing and Organizational Placement*

A. The Crime and Loss Prevention Unit shall be assigned to the Patrol Division under the direct supervision of the Patrol Commander.

B. One supervisor shall be assigned to the unit and will be responsible for programs, personnel and implementation.

1. The supervisor will be designated as the 'Coordinator' of Crime and Loss Prevention programs.

C. Additional personnel assigned to the unit will be responsible to the coordinator for duty assignment and functions.

III. Procedures and Programs

    A.   Procedures

        1. The unit will request and study crime trends of crimes and losses that are generally considered preventable.

           a. Emphasis will be placed on, but not limited to, street crimes, crimes against persons, vandalism, security, auto theft, business losses, property identification and related preventative areas.

        2. Evaluate, when possible, crime scenes in order to formulate preventative plans for future use.

        3. Consult with line Patrolmen, line supervisors, Detectives and Unit Commanders in order to determine what courses of preventative action may best be taken to meet changing trends.

        4. Develop expertise with security hardware, internal systems, protective systems, glazing, locks, safes, intrusion devices, screening and related protective hardware.

        5. Establish and maintain working relations with Building Inspectors, architects, insurance firms, building contractors, wholesale building material companies and other persons wherein updating merchandise in security work can be implemented.

        6. Establish working relationship with news media for crime and loss prevention advertising and coverage.

        7. Prepare and submit proposed ordinances of a security nature that deal with minimum standards for building, security, anti-theft and entry provisions.

           a. Ordinances to cover homes, buildings, automobiles, residential lighting and general security.

        8. Coordinate security efforts with that of the Fire Prevention Bureau to insure exchange of information gained by individual inspections.

    B.   Programs

        The Crime and Loss Prevention Unit shall prepare and submit for approval programs in crime and loss prevention geared to the changing community and community crime trends. General programs shall include but not be limited to:

1. Training of Police personnel in preventative programs and how all units and personnel may assist.
2. Residence and business protection programs.
3. Worthless check prevention programs.
4. Auto theft prevention.
5. "Mark it" programs, marking of all major theft items in homes and businesses.
6. Street lighting programs.
7. Building permit review for security.
8. Neighborhood Watch Programs.
9. Women's Court Watch Programs.
10. "Safe Haven Home" Program.
11. Architectural consulting.
12. Preparation of preventative ordinances.

As programs are planned, approved and implemented, all members of all Police units will be updated in the program prior to public release. Programs will be implemented on a need basis after priorities are established. Program hand-out material prepared to educate in a crime problem will also be prepared under the auspices of the Crime and Loss Prevention Unit and will be distributed to all Police Personnel.

IV. Growth, Development and Reporting

A. Since this is a new field as well as a new venture for the Department, growth will depend on the unit's successful endeavors as well as need to increase in size and scope.
   1. Anticipated growth will be to maintain one to two per cent of police strength assigned to the unit.
   2. Federal funding will be requested to provide for expansion, if justified.
   3. Annual evaluations of goal attainment; programs will be reviewed in order to determine needs.

B. Development
   1. The Crime and Loss Prevention Unit will begin on single, long term base programs and as each program is developed and implemented, additional programs will be added. In addition to programs being added, the base

of operation will be expanded to cover business internal security, ordinance preparation, participation in broad planning activities with city and private agencies.

2. Follow-up systems will be included to enhance compliance after voluntary assistance is sought.
3. Ineffective programs will be modified or if found unsuitable, will be recommended for abandonment.

C. Reporting
   1. General Reporting:
      a. The Coordinator of the Crime and Loss Prevention Unit will prepare daily and monthly reports that shall present, on approved formats or forms, the efforts, surveys and accomplishments of the unit.
      b. Reports will be processed through channels to the Chief of Police.
      c. Carbon copies will be forwarded to the Operations Bureau and all Division and Unit Commanders.
   2. Survey Reports:
      Any survey conducted by the Crime and Loss Prevention Unit of any home or business location will be classified confidential and will be prepared in an original and one copy with the following distribution:
      a. The original report will be presented to the owner of the business or home.
      b. The carbon copy will be retained by the Crime and Loss Prevention Unit under security.
      c. No name of company, address or identifying information shall be included on the confidential report other than an identifying number assigned by the Crime and Loss Prevention Unit.
      d. Officers concerned with the supervision of the unit may review survey forms on a need-to-know basis.

V. *Effective Date*

   A. The effective date of this order shall be

Paul B. Calhoun
Chief of Police

implementation plan for community crime prevention

I. Obtain the Crime Facts for Your Community

The crime-prevention officer must become an expert on the crime facts of his community and be able to relate the local situation to crime facts nationally. Many times a "high sounding" program will fail because the goal is lost in the rush to do something. Crime-prevention programs will be judged by your ability to reduce crime and therefore, you must be knowledgeable about crime statistics.

II. Pick a Base Month to Start a Crime-Cut Campaign

Dramatic results can be shown by focusing on crime prevention during an entire month. The long-range idea, of course, is to keep the pressure on over a long period of time, but a KICK-OFF campaign can do much to give the momentum needed to gain complete community support.

    A.   Select a month far enough in advance to give plenty of time for planning.

    B.   Avoid months that contain built-in obstacles such as:
        (1) Major Holidays
        (2) General Vacation Periods
        (3) Fire Prevention Week
        (4) Elks Convention (and the like)
        (5) LEAA Grant Process

III. *Appoint Crime-Cut Campaign Committee*

Develop a broad-based committee of business and citizen leaders that bring together the entire resources of the community.

A. If a crime-prevention program is to work, it must have the complete and active support of the chief and, therefore, the chief of police should be an active member of the committee and should agree to attend all meetings in person. As crime-prevention officers, you should assume the duties of general secretary and prepare the material for each committee meeting. Other community leaders to be invited on the committee could include the following:

Mayor and City Manager
President of Local A.S.I.S.
Insurance Agents Representative
Representative from the Chamber of Commerce
Representative from the Jaycees
Representative from the P.T.A.
Representative from the Local School Administration
President of Police Union
President of Fraternal Order of Police
President of Teachers Union
President of Banking Association
President of Local Locksmith Association
President of Local Burglar Alarm Association
President of Local Architectural or Builders Hardware Association
Director of Regional Crime Commission (LEAA)
President of Retail Merchants Association
President of Local Service Clubs
President of Ministerial Association
Representatives of Local Press, Radio and TV
Criminal Justice State Planning Agency Representative

B. Develop Subcommittees

The most effective committee work will result from small groups working on specific tasks; therefore, the following subcommittees are suggested:

(1) Finance

        (2) Advertising and Publicity

        (3) Program Committee with sections for

            (a) Home

            (b) School

            (c) Business

IV. Prepare Material for Committees

    A.   Gather pictures of security problems in your community.

    B.   Present crime facts and visual material to full committee at least 30 days before start of crime cut campaign.

    C.   Work with subcommittees on program details.

V. Caution—Keep Publicity at Low Level
During Planning Phase

    A.   Remember—you will want to get the most benefit from your "Campaign Month" because everyone (taxpayers, businessmen, LEAA, your department) will be evaluating your program.

    B.   Anticipate methods by which you can evaluate your program.

        (1) Did sales of security devices change?

        (2) Did you get your crime prevention message out?

        (3) Did crime drop?

        (4) Did apprehensions increase?

        (5) Did public opinion change?

        (6) Did your program increase public interest in crime prevention?

VI. Plan a Kick-Off Breakfast

Invite full crime-cut committee to kick-off breakfast on the first day of your campaign month. "Start early—get the jump on crime."

    A.   Release complete details of plan to the press, radio and TV.

    Posters

    Engravers (Operation Identification)

    Court watchers

    Spot announcements

    Open security product exhibit

    B.   Announce plans for a daily news conference to cover:

        (1) Yesterday's crime reports

        (2) Apprehensions resulting from citizen calls

        (3) Number of crimes preventable with simple security

        (4) Suggestion of the day (you will need 30)

        (5) Number of suspicious person calls

        (6) Number of security violations found by police (Example: Have x number of officers check 5 parked cars each day for keys left or unlocked and valuables left in vehicle.

VII.   *Hold a Committee or Subcommittee Breakfast Each Monday of Campaign Month*

Use this to keep committees enthused with program. Committee members can assist as speakers or you can show crime prevention films.

VIII.   *Hold Summary Breakfast One Week after Close of Campaign Month*

    A.   Review campaign

    B.   Announce plans for long-range program and offer security survey services to the business community.

IX.   *Hold Regular Meetings with Full Crime-Cut Committee*

    A.   Set meeting at regular intervals. Twice a year or every month—frequency is not as important as getting the commitment to meet and do some important community work.

    B.   Make valuable use of committee.

        (1) Keep them up-to-date

        (2) Solicit feedback on community feeling

        (3) Use as a sounding board for new projects

        (4) Present problems for their solution

X.   *Remember Your Own Department*

    A.   Follow the same track as your citizens program, but keep your fellow officers one step ahead on information. They should not learn about a new idea put out by you from a citizen.

B. Keep your department up-to-date by making use of
    (1) Regular in-service training
    (2) Daily bulletins
    (3) Full disclosure to every man on the state of program development at any time.

San Diego, Cal. police department instruction

POLICE DEPARTMENT INSTRUCTION	DATE:	NO:
	January 25, 1973	1.5–Administration
TO:	**SUBJECT:**	
COMMANDING OFFICERS	CARRYING FIREARMS ON DUTY	
ORIGIN:	**PAGE OF**	
CHIEF OF POLICE	1 1	
DISSEMINATION:	**RETAIN:**	
ALL SWORN PERSONNEL	UNTIL FURTHER NOTICE	

N — Section 8.04 of the Rules and Regulations states that on duty officers shall
E — carry a revolver and ammunition that is issued or approved by the Depart-
W — ment. No provision is made for carrying automatic pistols while on duty.

An exception to this rule concerning automatic pistols may be made by a Commanding Officer when the Officer concerned is engaged in undercover work or other activities that require complete concealment of the weapon.

Some officers prefer to carry weapons other than the issued revolver such as the 357 magnum or combat masterpiece. Such weapons are acceptable for carrying on duty *provided they will fire the standard issued ammunition.* All such weapons must first be tested and approved by the rangemaster.

No ammunition is to be carried on duty that is not issued by the Department. This includes extra ammunition carried in the gun belt or in equipment cases.

No issued ammunition is to be cut off at the end, flattened, scored, or changed in any way to make it mushroom on impact.

Hideout Weapons

Some Officers have deemed it expedient to carry a second "hideout" weapon and a variety of weapons, some of them unsafe, have been carried for this purpose. The rules and regulations make no provision for a second weapon.

Effective with the publication of this bulletin, any Officer desiring to carry a second weapon must carry either a Colt or Smith and Wesson revolver, 38 special caliber, and short barreled so that it can be carried concealed. Such weapons must be tested and approved by the rangemaster.

Second weapons must be carried completely concealed and not merely carried in the belt with the butt protruding.

Only Department issued ammunition will be carried with such a second weapon.

These guidelines are reprinted by permission of the San Diego, California Police Department.

POLICE DEPARTMENT INSTRUCTION	DATE: February 26, 1971	NO: 1.6—Administration
TO: COMMANDING OFFICERS	**SUBJECT:** USE OF FIREARMS	

ORIGIN:
    CHIEF OF POLICE
	PAGE OF
	   1 1	

DISSEMINATION: ALL SWORN PERSONNEL	RETAIN: UNTIL FURTHER NOTICE	

Only the most vicious criminal offenses result in death sentences and the appellate courts have effectively blocked the execution of those sentenced to death. Our society, our courts, and our law-making bodies place a greater value on the preservation of life than the value placed on the solution of criminal offenses or the punishment for their commission. Enforcement officers must be equally selective in using firearms considering that their use may result in death.

The Department considers that firearms are *defensive weapons* and are to be used *only:*

1. To protect the life of an officer or another person or to prevent serious injury when there is no other alternative.

2. To apprehend a violent person who is *known to be armed and dangerous* and who cannot be apprehended without risking loss of life or serious injury.

Unless one of the above conditions is present, the use of a firearm is *not permissible.*

Following are some commonly recurring situations in which firearms are *not to be used:*

1. To fire at any person fleeing to evade arrest whether or not he has been identified.

2. To fire at a person running from the scene of a crime, or at any person described as a possible suspect by a radio broadcast or other communication.

3. To fire warning shots, to fire at a stolen automobile, or to fire at any moving automobile in an effort to disable it or to deflate the tires.

Shooting under some of the above conditions would be legally permissible, but the Department takes the position that they do not warrant the use of deadly force unless the element of self-defense or protection of life is present.

Any officer firing a gun on duty, accidentally or otherwise, is required to immediately submit a detailed report of the incident on Form PD-153. All such incidents will be reviewed by supervisory personnel.

POLICE DEPARTMENT INSTRUCTION	DATE: June 12, 1973	NO: Administration 1.7
TO: COMMANDING OFFICERS	**SUBJECT:** REPORTING AND INVESTIGATING SHOOTING INCIDENTS	
ORIGIN: CHIEF OF POLICE	**PAGE** OF 1 2	
DISSEMINATION: ALL SWORN PERSONNEL	**RETAIN:** UNTIL FURTHER NOTICE	

To insure that shooting incidents are investigated and to insure that safe practices are followed in handling firearms, the following regulations are adopted and will become effective with the publication of this instruction.

1. *Shooting While on Duty*

    A. Any officer firing a gun while on duty will immediately make a report to the duty Captain and before concluding his tour of duty will submit a report of the incident on PD-153. This includes any shots fired accidentally in a locker room or elsewhere.

    B. On receipt of information that a shot has been fired, the Watch Commander will dispatch a supervisor to investigate and submit a report of the incident.

    C. All reports will be submitted to the commanding officer of the officer concerned or in his absence to the Watch Commander who will review them and forward them to the appropriate Inspector.

    D. After review by the Inspector, all reports will be forwarded to the appropriate Assistant Chief. If no further action is indicated, the reports will be filed in the personnel office.

2. *Wounding or Death of a Person by Gunshot*

    A. If an officer is wounded or wounds or kills anyone by gunshot, the Watch Commander will immediately notify:

        1. The Assistant Chief of Operations.
        2. The Inspector of Investigations. (If not available, notify the Captain of Investigations Section I or the Homicide Unit Lieutenant.)
        3. A representative of the City Claims Office.

    B. Reports prepared by detectives will be submitted to the Inspector of Investigations and by him to the appropriate Assistant Chief.

    C. If after review no further action is taken, the reports will be filed in the personnel office.

    D. In any shooting incident that is assigned a case number, the personnel office will forward copies to the Records Division.

3. *Security and Handling of Firearms in Police Stations*

    A. Lockers in a police station that contain firearms must be kept securely locked.

    B. Except as part of an inspection or a sanctioned practice, firearms will not be aimed or dry fired in or around any police facility.

C. Except as part of an inspection or a sanctioned practice, firearms will not be cleaned, repaired, loaded, or unloaded in any police facility. This does not include shotguns or other weapons removed from the armory for a special purpose.

4. *Displaying Firearms*

A. Officers shall not display their firearms, or draw them in any public place except for necessary inspection or use, nor shall a firearm be carelessly left anywhere unattended. All loaded firearms coming into the possession of any member of the Department shall, immediately upon receipt, be unloaded, unless required in such loaded condition as evidence.

B. Officers shall not intentionally fire their guns except as authorized by law or at a target range. Officers firing a gun *on* or *off duty*, accidentally or intentionally, except on a target range, shall report same *immediately* to the Patrol Captain either by radio or telephone, and as soon as practicable by submitting a written report.

5. *Other Firearms Regulations*

A. Regulations regarding carrying firearms and ammunition may be found in Administrative Rules Section 8.04, which covers all the equipment an officer is required to carry.

B. Regulations pertaining to the use of firearms by police officers may be found in Department Instruction 1.6.

circular 57 utilization of policewomen on patrol

SUBJECT:	DISTRIBUTION
UTILIZATION OF POLICEWOMEN ON PATROL	A
	ORIGINATING UNIT
	ASO
	EXPIRATION DATE
	April 15, 1973

This department is now actively engaged in a program of integrating significant numbers of policewomen into the patrol force. Some experienced policewomen are being reassigned to patrol duties to assist in the initial phase of the program. Approximately 100 new policewomen will be added when they complete recruit training. The majority of the patrolwomen will be assigned to the 1st and 7th Districts.

During the balance of the calendar year the procedures regarding policewomen will be closely evaluated. Outside consultants funded by the Police Foundation will be assisting by collecting data from reports, questionnaires, interviews, and observations.

In keeping with the goal of the program to achieve complete interchangeability of policemen and policewomen in as many areas as possible, the following guidelines are established:

1. During this experimental year, unit commanders shall assign patrol police-women in the same manner as patrolmen.

2. Patrolwomen shall be assigned interchangeably with patrolmen of like experience.

3. No special beats or special cars shall be created for female patrol officers.

4. During their learning period, patrolwomen shall be assigned to a variety of beats in the same manner as patrolmen in their learning period.

5. Patrolwomen, like patrolmen, shall be assigned to scout cars, station duty, foot beats, and traffic duty so that they may learn all aspects of patrol work.

6. Patrolwomen shall not be preferred to patrolmen for station duty. This shall not preclude women being assigned to the station in the same manner as men.

7. The new policewomen shall be assigned to work in scout cars just as often as new policemen are.

8. Scout cars with one male and one female officer shall answer radio runs as 10-4 units. (Not as 10-99 or as 10-4W)

9. 10-4 units with inexperienced patrolwomen shall be treated no differently than 10-4 units with inexperienced patrolmen.

10. Patrolwomen shall not be assigned as a third officer in a scout car desig-nated as a 10-4 unit.

11. Scout cars to which patrolwomen are assigned shall patrol an assigned beat and shall *not* be used merely as an extra unit for taking minor calls and reports.

12. Once a patrolwoman gains patrol experience she should be considered for possible assignment alone or as the experienced partner of a 10-4 unit based on her individual capabilities and knowledge.

13. A patrolwoman who has demonstrated sufficient skill and knowledge in patrol work shall be certified for patrol by her officials in the same manner as male officers.

14. Policewomen may be considered for motor scooter training and be employed as motor scooter officers after completion of proper training.

15. New policewomen shall be assigned initially to the uniformed patrol sections of the districts. Later on they may be considered for reassignment to tactical, community relations, and investigative units of the districts in the same manner as men of like experience. Policewomen shall not be given priority in those assignments.

16. Although experienced policewomen who are reassigned to patrol duty to help the initial phase of the patrol project are to be encouraged to remain in patrol at least through August, they may apply for special assignments advertised throughout the department and be selected as manpower needs allow and they may be reassigned within the Patrol Division upon approval of the Chief of Police.

17. Policewomen who have completed their probationary year and six months of patrol duty shall be given preference in special assignments over policewomen or policemen without patrol experience.

18. If during this evaluation period problems should arise in carrying out any aspect of the patrolwoman project, commanders shall provide the Chief of Police in writing with sufficient information to enable him to properly appraise the situation.

19. As of the effective date of this circular, wherever there appears to be a conflict between these guidelines and earlier communications, these guidelines shall control.

Jerry V. Wilson
Chief of Police

JVW:COC:fsp